INSIDERS' GUIDE® to Nashville

INSIDERS' GUIDE® to Nashville

TENTH EDITION

JACKIE SHECKLER FINCH

Globe Pequot
GUILFORD, CONNECTICUT

All the information in this guidebook is subject to change. We recommend that you call ahead to obtain current information before traveling.

Globe Pequot

An imprint of The Rowman & Littlefield Publishing Group, Inc.
4501 Forbes Blvd., Ste. 200
Lanham, MD 20706
www.rowman.com

Distributed by NATIONAL BOOK NETWORK

This Globe Pequot edition 2019

Maps by XNR Productions, Inc.

British Library Cataloguing in Publication Information available

Library of Congress Cataloging-in-Publication Data available

ISBN 978-1-4930-4344-6 (paperback)
ISBN 978-1-4930-4345-3 (e-book)

∞™ The paper used in this publication meets the minimum requirements of American National Standard for Information Sciences—Permanence of Paper for Printed Library Materials, ANSI/NISO Z39.48-1992.

Printed in the United States of America

Contents

Appendix: Living Here

Directory of Maps

About the Author

An award-winning journalist, **Jackie Sheckler Finch** has covered a wide array of topics—from birth to death with all the joy and sorrow in between. She has written for many publications and has been named the Mark Twain Travel Writer of the Year by Midwest Travel Writers a record five times—in 1998, 2001, 2003, 2007, and 2011. She shares her home with her resident entertainer and watchdog, Pepper. One of her greatest joys is taking to the road to find the fascinating people and places that wait over the hill and around the next bend.

Acknowledgments

Many thanks to Nashville residents, public-relations officials, and business owners who took the time to help me update this book. Thanks especially to Heather Middleton of the Nashville Convention & Visitors Bureau for her patience and answers to my endless questions and to Dan Rogers for sharing his awesome knowledge.

My gratitude to my Globe Pequot editor, Sarah Parke, and to my project editor, Emily Chiarelli, for their encouragement and keen attention to detail.

This book is dedicated to my family: Kelly Rose; Mike Peters; Sean and Emma Rose; Stefanie, Will, Trey, and Arianna Scott; and Logan and Grayson Peters.

A special remembrance to my husband, Bill Finch, whose spirit goes with me every mile and step of the way through life's journey.

—Jackie Sheckler Finch

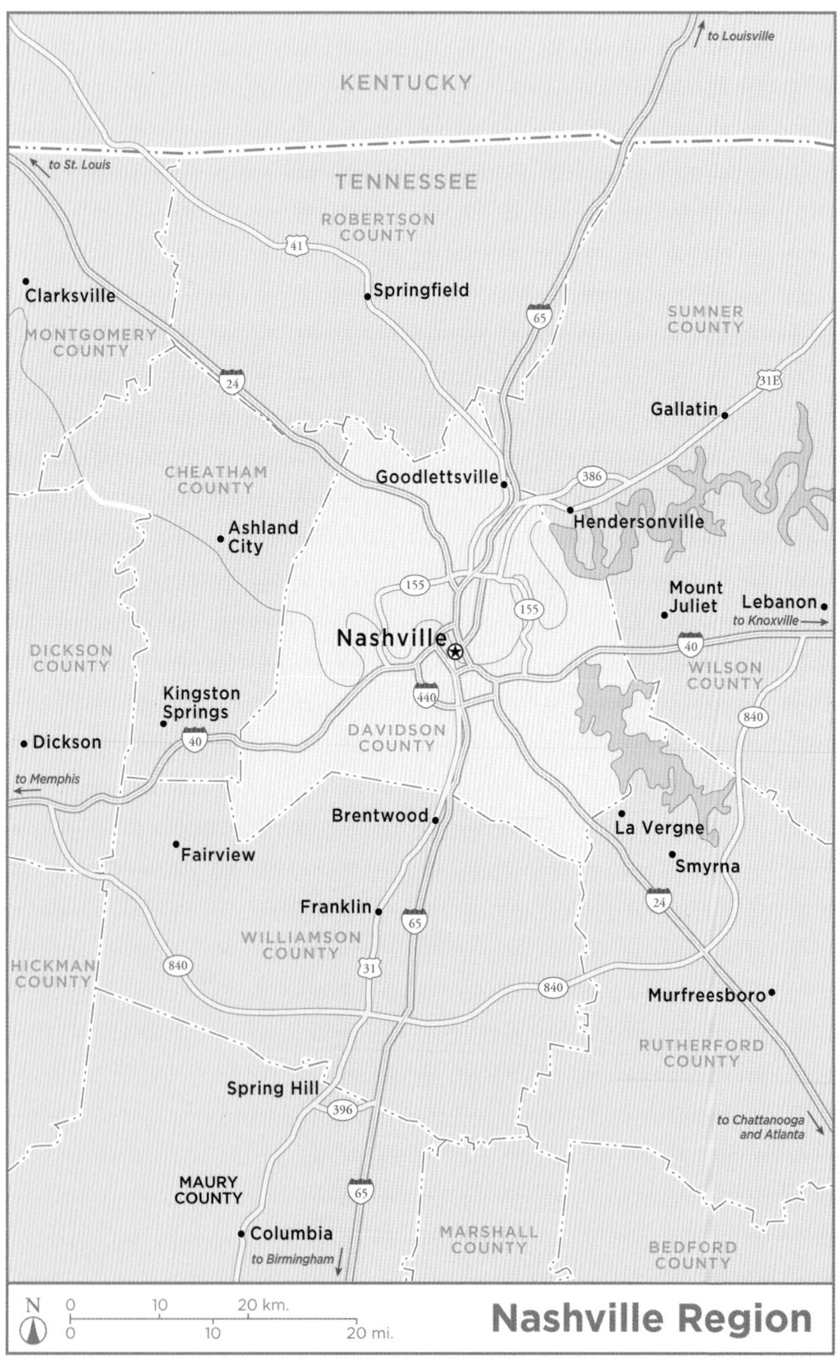

to Louisville
KENTUCKY
TENNESSEE
to St. Louis
ROBERTSON COUNTY
41
Springfield
Clarksville
MONTGOMERY COUNTY
65
SUMNER COUNTY
24
31E
Gallatin
CHEATHAM COUNTY
Goodlettsville
386
Hendersonville
Ashland City
155
Mount Juliet
Lebanon
to Knoxville
155
Nashville
40
DICKSON COUNTY
WILSON COUNTY
440
Kingston Springs
840
Dickson
40
DAVIDSON COUNTY
to Memphis
Brentwood
La Vergne
Fairview
Smyrna
Franklin
24
65
WILLIAMSON COUNTY
HICKMAN COUNTY
840
31
840
Murfreesboro
RUTHERFORD COUNTY
Spring Hill
396
to Chattanooga and Atlanta
MAURY COUNTY
65
Columbia
to Birmingham
MARSHALL COUNTY
BEDFORD COUNTY
N
0 10 20 km.
0 10 20 mi.
Nashville Region

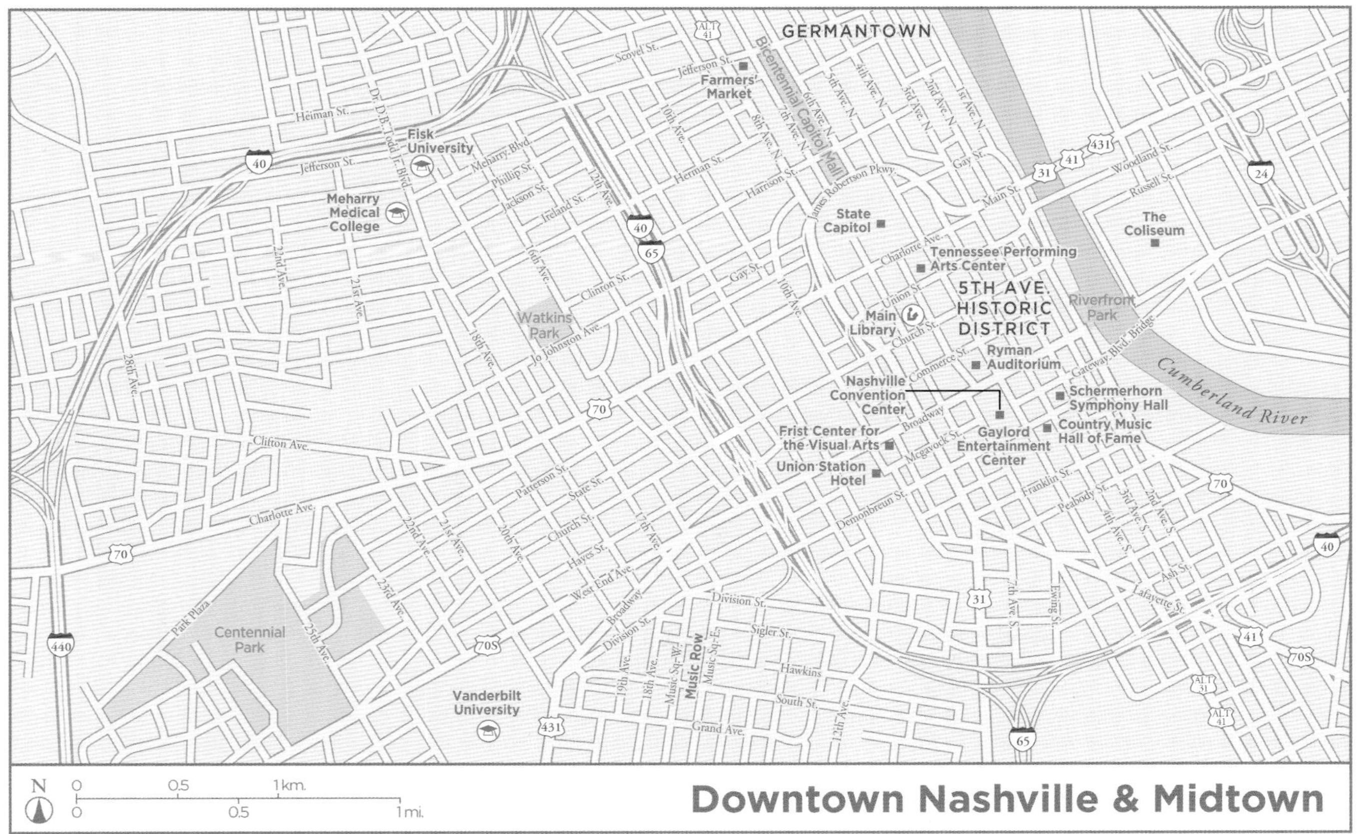
GERMANTOWN
Farmers' Market
Bicentennial Capitol Mall
State Capitol
Tennessee Performing Arts Center
5TH AVE. HISTORIC DISTRICT
Main Library
Ryman Auditorium
Riverfront Park
Cumberland River
The Coliseum
Nashville Convention Center
Schermerhorn Symphony Hall
Country Music Hall of Fame
Gaylord Entertainment Center
Frist Center for the Visual Arts
Union Station Hotel
Fisk University
Meharry Medical College
Watkins Park
Centennial Park
Vanderbilt University
Music Row
N
0
0.5
1 km.
0
0.5
1 mi.
Downtown Nashville & Midtown

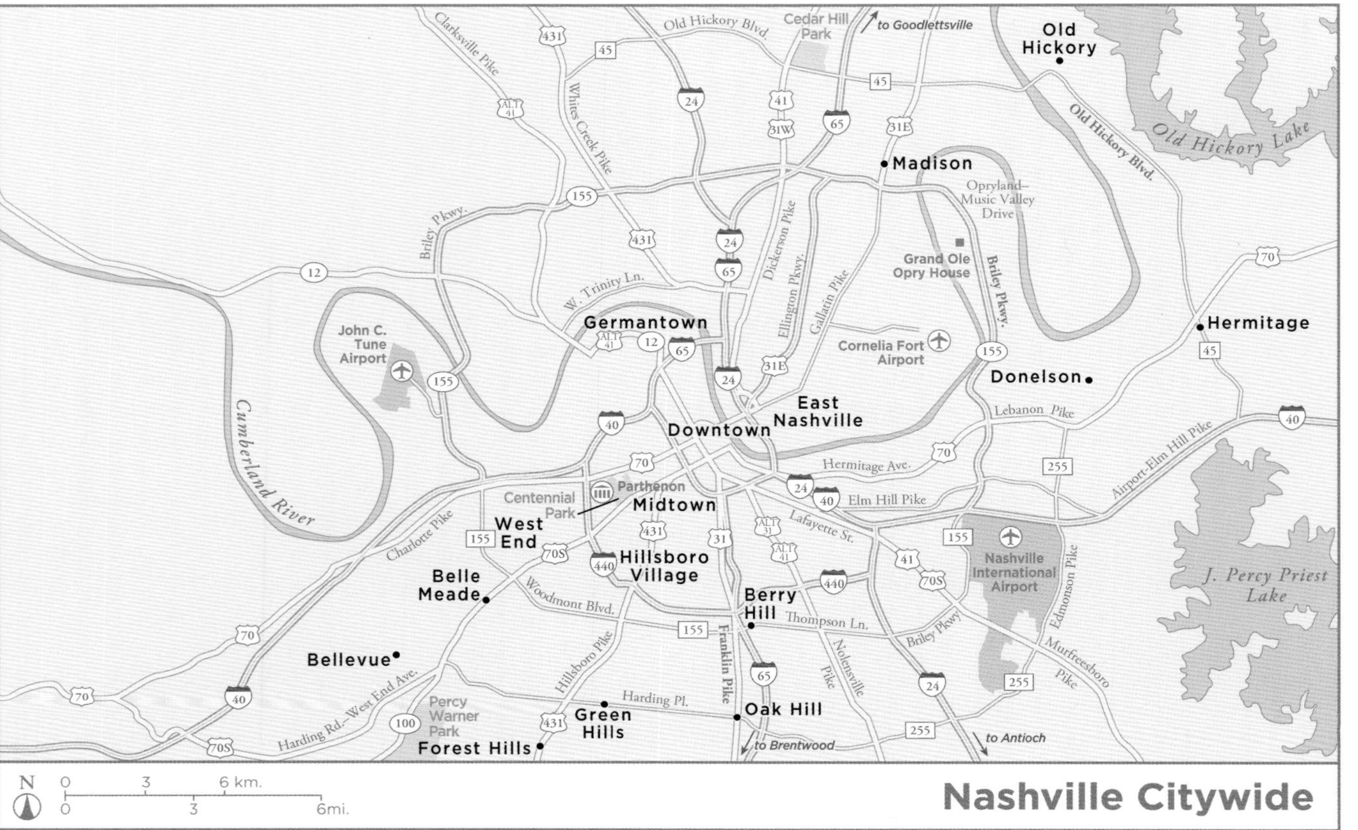
Nashville Citywide
Old Hickory
Madison
Hermitage
Donelson
Germantown
Downtown
East Nashville
Midtown
West End
Hillsboro Village
Belle Meade
Berry Hill
Bellevue
Green Hills
Oak Hill
Forest Hills
Old Hickory Lake
J. Percy Priest Lake
Cumberland River
Cedar Hill Park
to Goodlettsville
to Brentwood
to Antioch
John C. Tune Airport
Cornelia Fort Airport
Nashville International Airport
Grand Ole Opry House
Opryland–Music Valley Drive
Parthenon
Centennial Park
Percy Warner Park
Old Hickory Blvd.
Clarksville Pike
Whites Creek Pike
Briley Pkwy.
W. Trinity Ln.
Dickerson Pike
Ellington Pkwy.
Gallatin Pike
Lebanon Pike
Hermitage Ave.
Elm Hill Pike
Airport-Elm Hill Pike
Edmonson Pike
Murfreesboro Pike
Lafayette St.
Nolensville Pike
Thompson Ln.
Franklin Pike
Harding Pl.
Hillsboro Pike
Woodmont Blvd.
Charlotte Pike
Harding Rd.–West End Ave.
0 3 6 km.
0 3 6mi.
N

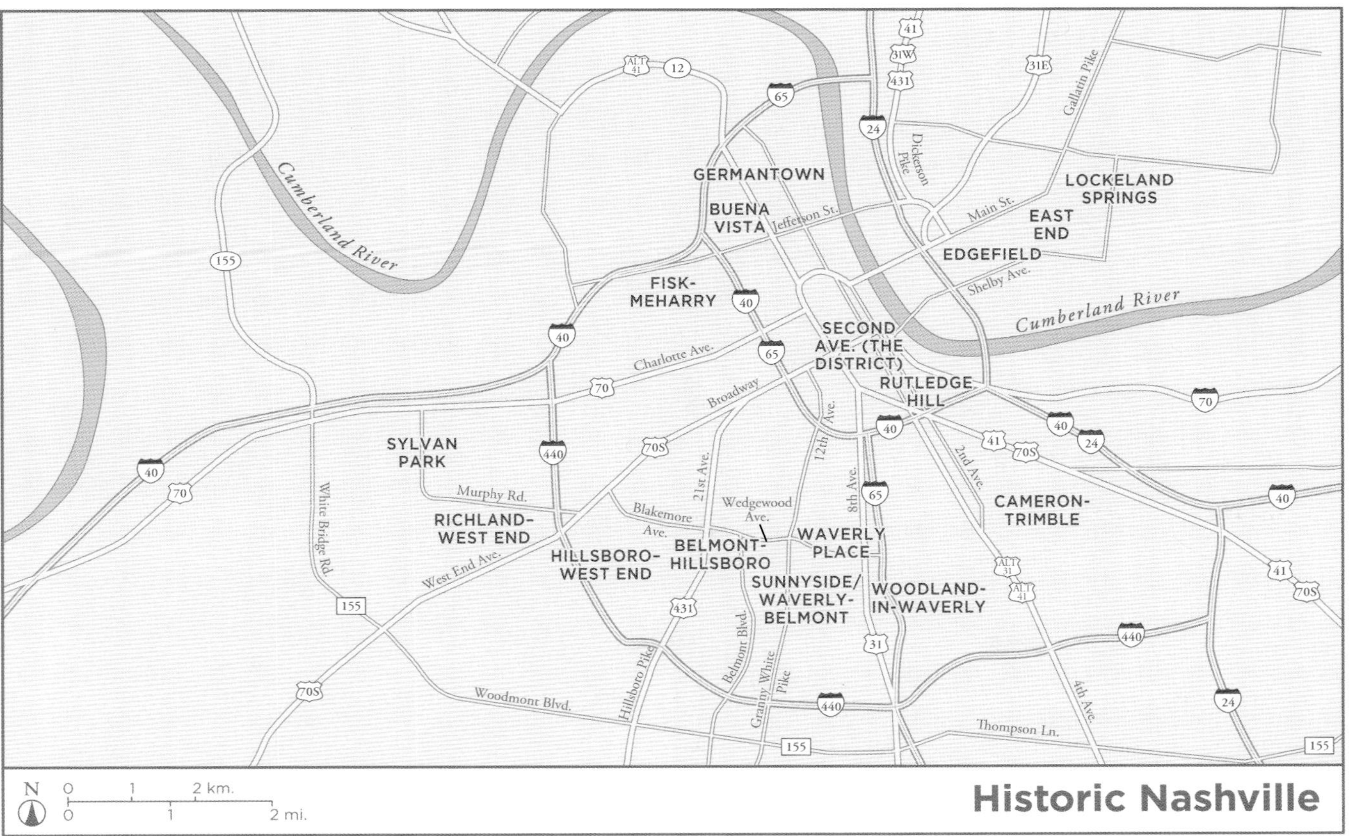
Historic Nashville
GERMANTOWN
BUENA VISTA
FISK-MEHARRY
SECOND AVE. (THE DISTRICT)
RUTLEDGE HILL
EDGEFIELD
EAST END
LOCKELAND SPRINGS
CAMERON-TRIMBLE
SYLVAN PARK
RICHLAND-WEST END
HILLSBORO-WEST END
BELMONT-HILLSBORO
WAVERLY PLACE
SUNNYSIDE/WAVERLY-BELMONT
WOODLAND-IN-WAVERLY
Cumberland River
Cumberland River
Jefferson St.
Main St.
Shelby Ave.
Gallatin Pike
Dickerson Pike
Charlotte Ave.
Broadway
12th Ave.
8th Ave.
2nd Ave.
4th Ave.
21st Ave.
Wedgewood Ave.
Blakemore Ave.
Murphy Rd.
West End Ave.
White Bridge Rd.
Woodmont Blvd.
Hillsboro Pike
Belmont Blvd.
Granny White Pike
Thompson Ln.
N
0 1 2 km.
0 1 2 mi.

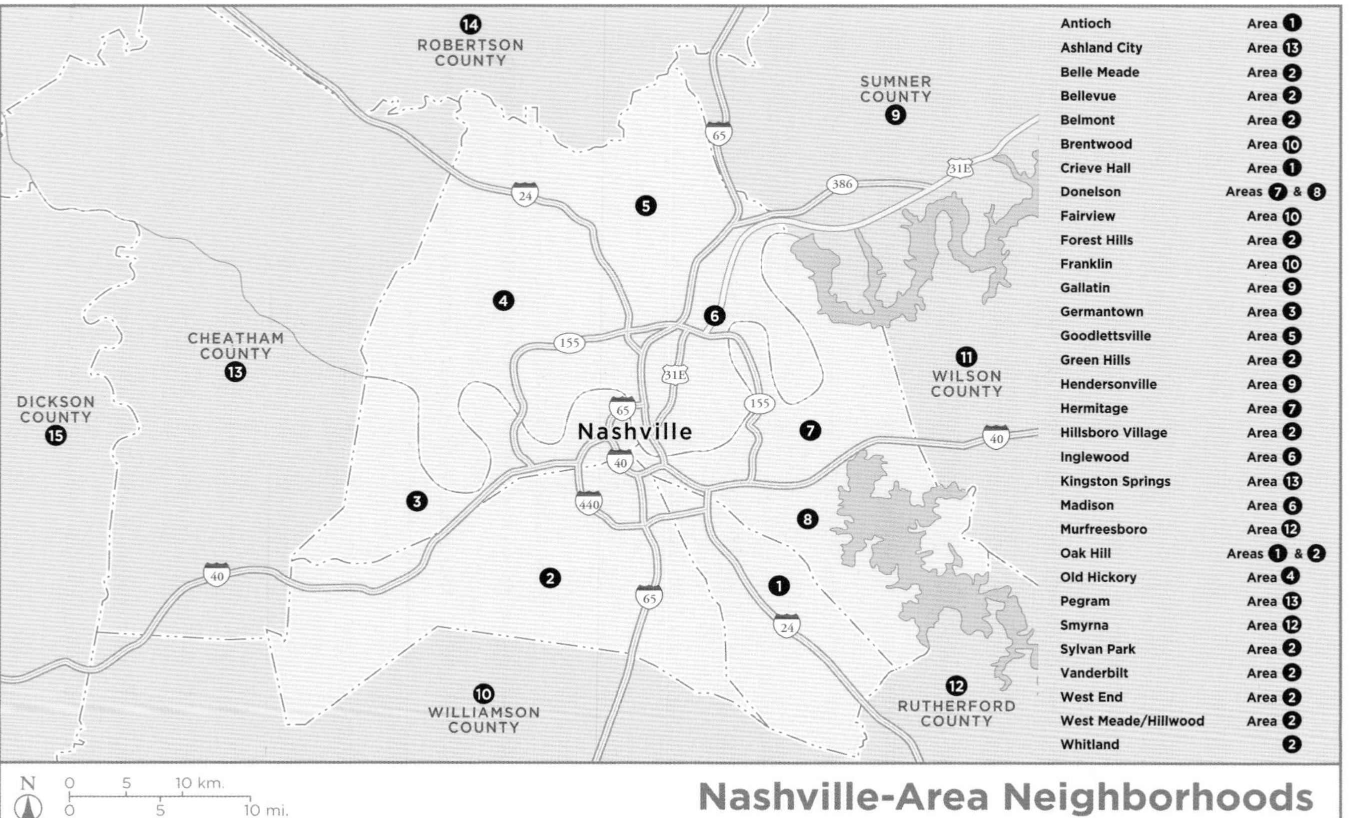
Nashville-Area Neighborhoods
Nashville
14 ROBERTSON COUNTY
SUMNER COUNTY 9
CHEATHAM COUNTY 13
DICKSON COUNTY 15
11 WILSON COUNTY
10 WILLIAMSON COUNTY
12 RUTHERFORD COUNTY
1
2
3
4
5
6
7
8
24
65
386
31E
155
40
440
N
0 5 10 km.
0 5 10 mi.
Antioch Area 1
Ashland City Area 13
Belle Meade Area 2
Bellevue Area 2
Belmont Area 2
Brentwood Area 10
Crieve Hall Area 1
Donelson Areas 7 & 8
Fairview Area 10
Forest Hills Area 2
Franklin Area 10
Gallatin Area 9
Germantown Area 3
Goodlettsville Area 5
Green Hills Area 2
Hendersonville Area 9
Hermitage Area 7
Hillsboro Village Area 2
Inglewood Area 6
Kingston Springs Area 13
Madison Area 6
Murfreesboro Area 12
Oak Hill Areas 1 & 2
Old Hickory Area 4
Pegram Area 13
Smyrna Area 12
Sylvan Park Area 2
Vanderbilt Area 2
West End Area 2
West Meade/Hillwood Area 2
Whitland 2

How to Use This Book

Insiders' Guide to Nashville is meant to be used, and used often. It is not a coffee-table book (even though we believe it will add a certain grace and elegance to your table—and when friends ask about it, you can tell them where to get one of their own). Just be sure to take it with you whenever you go out, so you can avoid potentially unpleasant conversations like this:

"Honey, what was the name of that little barbecue place that sounded so appetizing?"

"It's in our *Insiders' Guide.* Didn't you bring it?"

"I thought *you* had it."

"Aarrgghh!"

Obviously, how you use the book is not nearly as important as that you use it. That said, we'd like to make a few suggestions that will help you make the most of this book, so you soon will feel like an Insider yourself.

First of all, feel free to experience the book on your own terms. Obviously, if you and the family are hungry right now, you'll want to go immediately to the **Dining** chapter. If you're looking for something exciting to do, turn to **Attractions, Kidstuff, Recreation,** or **Entertainment**. In the mood to discover why Nashville is known worldwide as "Music City"? We've devoted a hefty chapter to that subject, too, and you may be surprised at the diversity of sounds you can find here. Need a way to get from point A to point B? Then you may want to go first to the **Welcome to Nashville** chapter. Or you might choose to take the casual approach and simply flip through the book, skimming the pages to see what catches your eye. We've designed *Insiders' Guide to Nashville* to be self-contained. That means each chapter essentially stands on its own, so wherever you start reading, you'll find the information you need to enjoy that aspect of Nashville life. And there are lots of cross-references.

While our primary focus is Nashville and Davidson County, we'll also take you through parts of the 14-county Metropolitan Statistical Area—including Cannon, Cheatham, Dickson, Hickman, Macon, Robertson, Rutherford, Smith, Sumner, Trousdale, Williamson, Maury, and Wilson Counties. You'll visit towns and communities such as Hermitage, Old Hickory, Brentwood, Franklin, Hendersonville, Goodlettsville, Murfreesboro, Lebanon, Springfield, Smyrna, and Madison, to name a few. And our **Itineraries** chapter will give you tips on how to enjoy specific aspects of Music City. Moving to the Nashville area or already live here? Be sure to check out the pages at the back of the book, where you will find the **Living Here** appendix that offers sections on relocation, education and child care, retirement, and media.

Within all chapters, you will find frequent cross-references and even, for the sake of convenience, some cross-listings.

Throughout this book you'll find **Insider's Tips** (indicated by an i), which offer quick insights, and **Close-ups,** which provide in-depth information on topics that are particularly interesting, unusual, or distinctly Nashville.

You'll also find listings accompanied by the ★ symbol—these are our top picks for attractions, restaurants, accommodations, and everything in between that you shouldn't miss while you're in the area. You want the best this region has to offer? Go with our **Insiders' Choice.**

Don't hesitate to personalize this book—make it your own! Scribble notes in the margins, circle places you have visited, underline points of interest. You might also discover some diner or nightclub that has escaped our notice. Make a note of it and, if you would be so kind, share it with us so we can include it in our next edition.

Please remember that, in a rapidly growing metropolitan area such as Nashville, things are bound to change. By the time you read this book, there will be new places to visit and experiences to savor—and, unfortunately, some old favorites that might have bid us farewell. Menus will be revised and schedules altered. It's always a good idea to call before visiting an attraction or restaurant.

We're pleased that, whether you're a visitor, a newcomer, or perhaps even a longtime resident wanting to see whether you've been missing anything, you have chosen us to be your companion here in Nashville. We sincerely hope we're able to make your experience a memorable one.

WELCOME TO **Nashville**

In the more than 200 years since its founding in 1779, the community now known worldwide as Nashville, Tennessee, has earned fame and prestige in many areas and, in the process, gained a proportionate number of nicknames. "Music City" . . . "Athens of the South" . . . "Wall Street of the South" . . . "The Buckle of the Bible Belt" . . . "City of Parks"—those are just a few of the names Nashville has been given throughout its history.

The problem we have with such nicknames is that each is severely limited, generally paying tribute to only one facet of what is truly a multifaceted metropolitan area. At the same time, we appreciate that each of these names, in its own way, serves as a tribute to some of the accomplishments that have made our city great. In other words, it is significant that Nashville has inspired so many terms of endearment, and so we'll look at these nicknames in greater detail later in this chapter. But first, we'd like to take time to point out something that, although you probably already know it, can occasionally get obscured by all the hype. And that is: Nashville is a *wonderful* place to live or to visit.

The "Batman Building" rises over Broadway. Jackie Sheckler Finch

i With its two pointy peaks and dark facade, the tallest building in Nashville quickly got a nickname—the Batman Building. Actually, the Commerce Street skyscraper is the AT&T Tower, but hardly anyone calls it that because it resembles the shape of the comic book hero's mask. Built in 1994, the eye-catching $94 million structure is 632 feet tall and was originally designed for BellSouth by architects at Earl Swensson Associates. The architects have said the Batman resemblance wasn't intentional, and they did not even notice it on the small models prepared for the project.

You might say that Nashville is the embodiment of Southern hospitality. Waitresses call you "honey" while serving you down-home delicacies such as fried chicken, made-from-scratch biscuits, grits, and country ham. People smile and speak to you on the street and are generally willing to give you the time of day or directions if you need them. Adding to the laid-back hospitable atmosphere are a few antebellum mansions, some of which could have been used as sets for *Gone With the Wind;* elegant Victorian homes; and lush flowering gardens. Nashville is a casual place, and many businesspeople wear cowboy boots with their suits. If you're thinking now that we're merely catering to stereotypes, rest assured that these scenes are all very real, although they're only a part of the big picture. There are, of course, plenty of Nashvillians who wouldn't be caught dead in cowboy boots, for example, and many who prefer to dine on continental cuisine and live in modern condominiums. Such is the diversity that characterizes this town.

This is a place where, fortunately, quality of life and cost of living don't go hand in hand. According to the ACCRA Cost of Living Index, for midyear 2018 Nashville's cost of living was 68.48 percent of the national average. In Tennessee you pay no state income tax—although this may someday change.

Of course, with attractions like the *Grand Ole Opry,* the Country Music Hall of Fame & Museum, the Ryman Auditorium, historic Belle Meade Plantation, the Hermitage estate of Andrew Jackson, and countless museums, art galleries, and outdoor recreational activities, Nashville remains a top tourist destination among Americans as well as visitors from other countries.

SOME BASIC FACTS

Nashville, the capital of Tennessee, is the center of a 14-county metropolitan statistical area (MSA) with a population of more than 1.9 million, which makes it the most populated MSA in the state. The Nashville-Davidson-Murfreesboro MSA covers the counties of Davidson, Cheatham, Dickson, Maury, Robertson, Rutherford, Sumner, Wilson, and Williamson, as well as five counties that were added when the area's MSA was expanded in 2003: Cannon, Hickman, Macon, Smith, and Trousdale.

In addition, Montgomery, with its county seat of Clarksville, is considered part of the "Nashville Economic Market."

Nashville–Davidson County has a combined metropolitan government. According to the US Census Bureau, the 2017 population of Nashville–Davidson County was 659,042. That population makes Nashville the largest city in Tennessee. In 2016, Nashville gained the population crown from Memphis with its population of 652,717. Nashville's 533 square miles make it one of the United States' largest cities in area.

i Close to 40 historical markers decorate the roadsides and neighborhoods of west Nashville. They commemorate significant sites in the Battle of Nashville, the last major battle of the Civil War.

i Tennessee ties Missouri as the most neighborly state in the nation. Eight states border Tennessee: Arkansas, Alabama, Georgia, Kentucky, Mississippi, Missouri, North Carolina, and Virginia.

Nashville is one of the fastest-growing large cities in the nation, with vigorous population growth that has continued for more than three decades. What brings so many people here is a strong economy that even in times of economic slowdown has bucked national trends, maintaining below-average unemployment rates and luring big corporate employers.

A PROGRESSIVE & SOPHISTICATED CITY

When Nashville and Davidson County formed their combined city-county metropolitan government in 1962, it was one of the first of its kind. The act served a dual purpose: increasing a tax base that had been dwindling because of numbers of people moving from the city to the suburbs and eliminating much duplication of services, thus resulting in a more efficient form of government. Still, several cities located within the boundaries of Metro Nashville opted to remain separate from the new metropolitan government. These include Belle Meade, Berry Hill, Goodlettsville, and Forest Hills. While located within the Nashville city limits, they maintain their own city governments and provide different levels of service to their residents.

Downtown Nashville today is a vibrant, thriving area that is a blend of old and new. While many of the old buildings that line Broadway have changed little since the turn of the 20th century, steel-and-glass skyscrapers loom nearby. Just down the street from the legendary honky-tonks where many of yesterday's country singers and songwriters first plied their trade, you'll also find newer attractions such as the Hard Rock Café, Jason Aldean's Kitchen + Rooftop Bar, John Rich's Redneck Riviera, Luke's (Bryan) 32 Bridge, Dierks Bentley's Whiskey Row, FGL (Florida Georgia Line) House, Blake Shelton's Ole Red

Nashville skyline Courtesy of Tennessee Department of Tourist Development

Nashville and A.J.'s (Alan Jackson) Good Time Bar.

The Ryman Auditorium, a true landmark since its completion in 1892, has served as a tabernacle, assembly hall, and theater as well as onetime home of the *Grand Ole Opry.* The beautifully restored building still plays host to a variety of entertainers, including modern-day legends such as Bruce Springsteen and Bob Dylan.

i Nashville is one of the largest cities in the United States in terms of area. It occupies 533 square miles. In comparison, Los Angeles covers 468 square miles.

Nashville Vital Statistics

- **Founded:** 1779 as Fort Nashborough; established as town of Nashville by North Carolina Legislature in 1784
- **Mayor/governor:** Mayor David Briley and Governor Bill Lee
- **Population:**
  Nashville–Davidson County: 659,042
  Nashville-Davidson-Murfreesboro Metropolitan Statistical Area: 1.9 million
  Tennessee: 6.7 million
- **Area:**
  Nashville: 533 square miles
  Nashville Economic Market: 5,225 square miles
- **Counties in the Nashville area (with major cities and county seats):**
  Davidson County (Nashville is the capital)
  Cannon County (county seat Woodbury)
  Cheatham County (county seat Ashland City)
  Dickson County (Dickson, county seat Charlotte)
  Hickman County (county seat Centerville)
  Macon County (county seat Lafayette)
  Maury County (county seat Columbia)
  Montgomery County (county seat Clarksville)
  Robertson County (county seat Springfield)

Rutherford County (Smyrna, county seat Murfreesboro)
Smith County (county seat Carthage)
Sumner County (Hendersonville, Portland, county seat Gallatin)
Trousdale County (county seat Hartsville)
Williamson County (Brentwood, county seat Franklin)
Wilson County (county seat Lebanon)

- **Major airport/major interstates:** Nashville International Airport; I-24, I-40, and I-65 converge in Nashville
- **Nickname:** "Music City"
- **Average temperatures:**
  Winter: High 39°F, low 30°F, mean 39°F
  Summer: High 88°F, low 67°F, mean 78°F
  Annual: High 70°F, low 48°F, mean 59°F
- **Average annual precipitation:** Rainfall: 47.3 inches; snowfall: 11.0 inches
- **Major colleges and universities:**
  Nashville: Vanderbilt University, Belmont University, Fisk University, David Lipscomb University, Meharry Medical College, Tennessee State University, Trevecca Nazarene University
  Nashville area: Austin Peay State University, Cumberland University, Middle Tennessee State University
- **Major area employers:** Vanderbilt University and Medical Center, HCA Holdings Inc., Nissan North America, Kroger Company, Saint Thomas Health Services, Randstad Staffing, Shoney's Inc., Electrolux Home Products
- **Famous sons and daughters:** Andrew Jackson, Wilma Rudolph, Kitty Wells, Pat Boone, Miley Cyrus, Gregg Allman, Shooter Jennings, Bill Belichick, Edwin Starr, Kitty Wells, Julian Bond, Reese Witherspoon
- **Public transportation:** WEGo Public Transit operates intercity bus lines, downtown trolleys, and 2 downtown land ports
- **Military base:** Fort Campbell, on the Tennessee-Kentucky state line at Clarksville, Tennessee, and Fort Campbell, Kentucky

- **Driving laws:**
  General speed limits: 70 mph on interstates in rural areas, 55 mph in urban areas, 20–45 mph in residential and business areas
  When it's raining or snowing, the law requires use of headlights as well as windshield wipers.
  HOV lanes (marked with a diamond): Two or more people must be in your vehicle for use from 7 to 9 a.m. Mon through Fri (inbound), and 4 to 6 p.m. Mon through Fri (outbound).
- **Alcohol laws:**
  You must be 21 to legally purchase or consume alcoholic beverages.
  The blood alcohol level at which one is legally presumed to be intoxicated is 0.08.
  Beer can be purchased in grocery and convenience markets on Sun, but liquor stores are closed.
  Liquor-by-the-drink is available in restaurants on Sun after 10 a.m.
  Bars can remain open until 3 a.m.
- **Daily newspapers:** *The Tennessean*
- **Weekly newspaper:** *The Nashville Scene*
- **Taxes:** State sales tax is 7 percent. With a local option tax of 2.25 percent, combined 9.25 percent tax applies in most counties to almost all purchases. Hotel-motel occupancy tax is 14.25 percent, plus $2 city tax in Nashville–Davidson County.
- **Chamber of commerce:** Nashville Area Chamber of Commerce, 211 Commerce St., Suite 100, Nashville, TN 37201; (615) 743-3000; nashvillechamber.com
- **Visitor center:** Nashville Convention and Visitors Corporation, One Nashville Place, 150 Fourth Ave. N., Suite G250, Nashville, TN 37219; (800) 657-6910; visitmusiccity.com
- **Time/weather:** National Weather Service: weather.gov; Central Standard Time

A large street mural honors Nashville. Jackie Sheckler Finch

"MUSIC CITY"

From Roy Acuff, Minnie Pearl, Ernest Tubb, and Hank Williams to Garth Brooks, Faith Hill, Alan Jackson, and Shania Twain, Nashville has long been known as the world's capital of country music. But while country music remains Nashville's signature sound, other styles of music call Nashville home as well. Music City is headquarters for the growing contemporary Christian and gospel music industry, and stars of the genre—such as Amy Grant, Michael W. Smith,

i Union soldiers brought baseball to Nashville during the Civil War, playing in the area where the Bicentennial Capitol Mall State Park now stands. In the early 1900s Nashville had a Southern Association team that played at Sulphur Dell Park, in the same area, and won championships in 1901, 1902, and 1908.

Jars of Clay, and dc Talk—all live or spend large amounts of time here. Premier jazz and classical label Naxos USA moved its US headquarters from New Jersey to the Nashville area in 1998.

Record labels, recording studios, music publishers, video production firms, booking agencies, management companies, and more support all this activity; in turn, these industries increase the city's appeal to artists, musicians, songwriters, and executives from around the world.

Nashville is a great place to make music, learn, work, worship, play, or be yourself. At the risk of sounding like a broken record (which we suppose is appropriate), we'll again state that Nashville is a wonderful place to live or to visit. Whatever your reason for being here (or planning to be here), for however long, enjoy your stay. This city has a lot to offer. Welcome!

Getting Here, Getting Around

Question: How do you get to the *Grand Ole Opry?* Answer: Practice, practice, practice!

Okay, it's an old joke, slightly paraphrased. But we use it to make the point that, with just a little practice and some practical knowledge, you'll soon find your way without problem to the Opryland area, the downtown/Music Row area, or anywhere else you want to go in metropolitan Nashville.

If you do happen to lose your bearings, don't lose your cool. Stop and ask directions—remember, you're in the land of Southern hospitality! It's reassuring to note that, in Nashville, it seems almost everyone is originally from somewhere else, which means that, like you, they've been lost before and will surely get lost again. Once you understand a few of the ground rules, such as the names and directions of the interstates and primary crosstown routes, you'll discover that getting around in Nashville is a bit like life itself: You're bound to make a few wrong turns along the way, but you'll be wiser for the experience. (Hey, do you think there might be a song in that?)

Of course, if you prefer, you can leave the driving to somebody else. Nashville has a number of transportation alternatives. We'll tell you about them later in this chapter.

ARRIVING BY AIR

NASHVILLE INTERNATIONAL AIRPORT (BNA), 1-40 and Donelson Pike, 8 miles southeast of downtown, 1 Terminal Dr., Nashville, TN 37214; (615) 275-1675; flynashville.com. Nashville International Airport has 15 airlines serving more than 50 North American cities and several overseas with 380 daily arrivals and departures. The airport, which prides itself on efficiency and customer service, is generally known for on-time performance. In addition to visual arts, Nashville International Airport hosts some of the best local talent that Music City has to offer. On four stages located in the terminal, the airport features live musical entertainment ranging from jazz to country—this is Music City, after all. Free Wi-Fi is available throughout the terminal.

The Nashville airport pays homage to its Music City roots. Jackie Sheckler Finch

Airlines serving Nashville International Airport include the following:

Air Canada, (888) 247-2262, aircanada.com

American Airlines, (800) 433-7300, aa.com

Delta, (800) 221-1212, delta.com

Frontier Airlines, (801) 401-9000, flyfrontier.com

Southwest, (800) 435-9792, southwest.com

United, (800) 241-6522, united.com

Getting to & Leaving from the Airport

Nashville International is about 8 miles southeast of downtown Nashville at I-40 and Donelson Pike. It's also near the intersection of two other major interstates: I-65 and I-24.

Once you've driven onto the airport grounds, simply follow the signs to short-term, long-term, or satellite parking; arrivals; or departures. If you're waiting to pick up someone from an arriving flight, look for the blue and white signs leading you to the free "Waiting Area," a parking pull-off where you can watch the arrival boards. There are a number of parking spaces in front of baggage claim on 10-minute timers. You must stay with your vehicle when parking in these spaces. When your 10 minutes are up, you will immediately be asked to leave.

Parking at the Airport

You'll pay up to a maximum of $28 a day in the valet area, up to $18 a day in the long-term area, or up to $9 a day in the satellite "economy" lot about a mile from the terminal. If you park in the long-term or satellite lots, you can catch a complimentary shuttle to and from the terminal.

Ground Transportation

Various taxi services are available at the ground level; just get out by the curb and wait. Please note, however, that the ground transportation area is one level below the baggage claim area, so you'll have to take the escalator or elevator after picking up your luggage.

Taxi meters start at $7 and are $2.10 a mile afterward. There is a flat rate of $25 to the downtown area and Opryland Hotel area, plus an additional passenger charge of $1 when accompanying one original passenger proceeding to same destination. Most hotels in the Briley Parkway/airport area offer free shuttle service to their guests. Jarmon Transportation is the official shuttle service for the airport. Shuttles depart every 15 minutes. The Downtown-West End Express is $25 for a round-trip or $14 for one way.

If you'd prefer to captain your own ship, on-site rental car agencies include:

Alamo (800-331-1212; alamo.com)
Avis (800-331-1212; avis.com)
Budget (800-527-0700; budget.com)
Dollar (800-800-4000; dollar.com)
Enterprise (800-736-8222; enterprise.com)
Hertz (800-654-3131; hertz.com)
National (888-826-6890; nationalcar.com)
Payless (800-729-5377; paylesscar.com)
Thrifty (800-367-2277; thrifty.com).

All of these rental agencies have convenient locations at the airport.

GETTING AROUND

Knowing the Laws

A night in jail, or even a ticket from a police officer, might be fodder for a great country song, but you'd still probably rather avoid these situations if possible. Therefore, it pays to know the following laws pertaining to getting around in the fine state of Tennessee.

Driving under the influence. Driving under the influence of alcohol or drugs in Tennessee is a serious no-no. The minimum penalty for a first conviction is 48 hours to 11 months and 29 days in jail, a $350 to $1,500 fine, court-ordered DUI school, and the loss of your license for a year. In addition, there can also be considerable court costs, increased insurance premiums, and other expenses. So just don't do it.

Buckling up. State law requires the driver and all front-seat passengers to wear a seat belt. Under Tennessee's child restraint law, children under 1 year old or those weighing 20 pounds or less must be placed in a rear-facing child passenger restraint system; children 1 through 3 and weighing more than 20 pounds must be placed in a forward-facing child passenger restraint system. Children 4 through 8 and those less than 5 feet tall must use a belt-positioning booster system. Additionally, children through age 12 should be placed in a rear seat if available. Older children and those taller than 5 feet must be sure to buckle up.

Turning right on red. Tennessee law permits right turns at a red light after coming to a complete stop, unless otherwise posted.

> i As you make your way around town, look for the Wayfinding signs. Placed in strategic locations, the markers will help you to locate attractions and places of interest.

Highways

Nashville's location at the confluence of three major interstates means that getting into or out of town by ground is generally convenient. That's not to say that you won't run into congestion during peak hours—you will, although state and federal highway officials are always working on ways to make area traffic flow more smoothly. (We're giving the Tennessee Department of Transportation, commonly known as TDOT, the benefit of the doubt here; in the interest of full disclosure, however, you'll often hear TDOT described in less-than-flattering terms when road construction projects—like the ongoing work on Interstates 24, 40, and 65—result in major gridlock.)

I-65, which runs north–south, connects Nashville with Bowling Green, Kentucky, and, ultimately, the Chicago area to the north. Going south, it leads to Huntsville before winding up in Mobile, Alabama. Nashville-area exits, from north to south, include Old Hickory Boulevard/Madison (exit 92), Briley Parkway/Dickerson Pike (exit 89), Trinity Lane (exit 87), James Robertson Parkway/State Capitol (exit 85), Shelby Street (exit 84), Wedgewood Avenue (exit 81), Armory Avenue (exit 79), Harding Place (exit 78), and Old Hickory Boulevard/Brentwood (exit 74).

i In 1978, Tennessee became the first state in the nation to require the use of safety seats for children who are passengers in motor vehicles. Within a decade, all 50 states passed laws mandating some form of child restraint in automobiles.

I-40, a major east–west connector, links Nashville with Knoxville and, eventually, Wilmington, North Carolina, to the east; and with Memphis and—if you're in the mood for a *long* drive—Barstow, California, to the west. Nashville-area exits, from east to west, include Old Hickory Boulevard (exit 221), Stewarts Ferry Pike (exit 219), Nashville International Airport/Donelson (exit 216), Briley Parkway (exit 215), Spence Lane (exit 213), Fessler's Lane/Hermitage (exit 212), Second Avenue/Fourth Avenue (exit 210), Demonbreun Street (Music Row)/Broadway/Charlotte Avenue/Church Street (exit 209), 28th Avenue (exit 207), 46th Avenue/West Nashville (exit 205), Briley Parkway/White Bridge Road/Robertson Avenue (exit 204), Charlotte Pike (exit 201), Old Hickory Boulevard (exit 199), and Bellevue/Newsoms Station (exit 196).

I-24 is a diagonal route running northwest–southeast. It will take you from Chattanooga in the southeast to Clarksville or, going farther northwest, to near St. Louis. Nashville-area exits include, from northwest to southeast, Briley Parkway (exit 43), Murfreesboro Road (exit 52), Briley Parkway/Airport (exit 54), Harding Place (exit 56), Antioch/Haywood Lane (exit 57), Bell Road (exit 59), and Hickory Hollow Parkway (exit 60).

I-440 is a major bypass connecting I-40 in west Nashville to I-65 in south Nashville and I-24 in the southeastern part of the city. Its exits are at West End Avenue (exit 1), Hillsboro Pike/21st Avenue (exit 3), and Nolensville Road (exit 6).

Opened in 2012, the Highway 840 loop about 30 miles outside Nashville runs from an I-40 interchange near Lebanon to an I-40 interchange near

Dickson, along the way connecting I-40, I-24, and I-65. Extending from TN 46 to TN 246, the $753 million Tennessee National Guard Parkway took 26 years to complete.

Other major highways running through Nashville include US 31, 41, and 70.

> Nashville's famous skyline can help you get oriented if you momentarily lose your way. Or you can always stop and ask someone for directions—remember, you're in the land of Southern hospitality.

Briley Parkway, also known as Highway 155, encircles Nashville and bisects all three of its major interstates. Beginning in the east at its juncture with Charlotte Avenue, it runs northeast to meet I-65; heads southeast, briefly following the Cumberland River through the Opryland area and meeting I-40 near Nashville International Airport; then continues south before turning back east, crossing I-24 and becoming one with Thompson Lane. Thompson Lane becomes Woodmont Boulevard, which becomes White Bridge Road northeast of West End Avenue and runs to Charlotte Pike, completing the Highway 155 loop.

Harding Place begins in the southwestern part of the city as Harding Pike (US 70 S.), then branches east from US 70 S. and becomes Harding Place. After crossing Granny White Pike (12th Avenue) in south Nashville, it inexplicably becomes Battery Lane for a brief stretch before resuming the name of Harding Place when it crosses Franklin Road, which is known as both Eighth Avenue and US 31. Harding continues east, then veers northward and becomes Donelson Pike.

Old Hickory Boulevard is even more perplexing. Beginning in the southwest, at Highway 100 on the west side of Percy Warner Park (see our **Recreation** chapter), it runs east until it crosses Nolensville Road (also known as Fourth Avenue or US 31 Alternate) and changes its name to Bell Road. But wait . . . it's far from through. Back near where we started, Old Hickory also heads north

> Don't make the mistake of using one of those gigantic broadcast towers you see to get your bearings—Nashville is ringed by several, each identical and prominently placed atop a conspicuous hillside. Plenty of newcomers have gotten lost at night by using a broadcast tower as an orientation point.

from Highway 100 at Edwin Warner Park (see Recreation) before turning into River Road. It also seemingly materializes just east of Charlotte Avenue's juncture with I-40, then heads north. Up north, *way* north, Old Hickory masquerades as Highway 45. It passes, from west to east, across Dickerson Pike (known variously as US 31 W., US 41, and Highway 11), I-65, and Gallatin Pike (aka US 31 E. and Highway 6), through the Madison and Old Hickory areas of metropolitan Nashville. It then heads southeast, crossing Lebanon Pike (US 70, Highway 24) in the Hermitage area, and, still acting as Highway 45, crosses I-40 near J. Percy Priest Lake on its way out of town. (Finally!)

A word to the wise: Just because you've been on Old Hickory once before and are now on it again doesn't necessarily mean that you're anywhere near where you were the first time. In other words, you probably shouldn't use this boulevard as an orientation point.

Local Streets

The Cumberland River, which played such an important role in the founding of Nashville, remains an important orientation point for residents and visitors. If you're trying to figure out how the streets are laid out, start at the river, which runs north–south through the center of town. West of the river, or on the downtown side, numbered avenues run parallel to the river. East of the Cumberland, however, it is streets and not avenues that are numbered, though they still run parallel to the river.

Five bridges cross the Cumberland in the downtown area. From north to south, they are Jefferson Street, Victory Memorial, Woodland Street, Shelby Avenue (for pedestrians and bicyclists only), and the Gateway Boulevard Bridge. Additionally, a railroad bridge crosses the river between the Jefferson and Victory Memorial Bridges.

Primary downtown streets running perpendicular to the numbered avenues include James Robertson Parkway, which circles the State Capitol; Union Street; Church Street; and Commerce Street. Broadway serves as the north–south dividing line.

You'll notice that in the downtown area many of the numbered avenues are one-way, so pay attention to make sure you're not turning the wrong way.

The numbered avenues generally change names as they head out of town. For example, First Avenue becomes Hermitage Avenue and then Lebanon Road; Second Avenue actually merges with Fourth Avenue before changing into Nolensville Road; Eighth Avenue becomes Franklin Road. This phenomenon is not limited to numbered avenues downtown, either. It's a simple fact of Nashville that many roads change names, some several times. After a while, you'll get used to it. You'll also notice that many a road is referred to as both a "pike" and a "road" or an "avenue," depending on which sign or map you're looking at. For example, Charlotte Avenue is also Charlotte Pike, Hillsboro Pike is also Hillsboro Road, and Murfreesboro and Nolensville Roads are also known as pikes. There are many other examples of this. In some cases the "pike" designation is more common; in other cases "road" or "avenue" is favored. The "pike" references are holdovers from older days when roads were often known as turnpikes. Don't worry too much about which word you use.

Buses

If your group would like its own bus for travel inside or outside Nashville, you can find dozens of companies listed in the yellow pages under "Buses—Charter & Rental." Many of these offer guided tours of the Nashville area. For more information see our **Music City** chapter.

GREYHOUND BUS TERMINAL, 709 Fifth Ave. S., Nashville, TN 37203, (615) 255-3556, greyhound.com. From its Nashville terminal, Greyhound offers service to more than 2,000 destinations in the continental United States, including Memphis, site of the closest Amtrak station.

PUBLIC TRANSPORTATION

Regional Transportation

REGIONAL TRANSPORTATION AUTHORITY OF MIDDLE TENNESSEE, 430 Myatt Dr., Nashville, TN 37115, (615) 862-8833, musiccity star.org. The RTA serves Cheatham, Davidson, Dickson, Maury, Montgomery, Robertson, Rutherford, Sumner, Williamson, and Wilson Counties. The RTA organizes carpools and vanpools throughout those counties and operates regional bus routes between downtown Nashville, Hendersonville, and Mt. Juliet. Commuters can park for free at one of the many park-and-ride lots located throughout the area, then connect with their carpool, vanpool, or bus. Fares are $5.25, except Donelson which is $2. Students, senior citizens, and

i The Nashville Convention & Visitors Bureau partners with several area hotels to offer visitors discounts on hotel rates. You can also get discounted attraction tickets through the CVB. For details check out the CVB's website, visitmusiccity.com, or call (800) 657-6910.

people with disabilities pay reduced rates. Special 10-trip ticket packages are available. For other rates, contact the RTA or visit the website.

Taxis

Taxi fares in Nashville are regulated by law. The meter starts at $7 when you get in the cab, and you'll pay $2.10 a mile to your destination. A $1 charge per additional passenger is added to the total. A fare from the Opryland area or the airport to a downtown location will run about $25.

It's best to reserve your cab at least 30 minutes in advance. You'll often find taxis waiting at the curb near popular downtown restaurants, however, so you might not have to call. By law, taxis are not supposed to "cruise" for customers, but visitors from big cities generally don't know this, and the law is not regularly enforced.

Many companies take credit cards, but others do not; sometimes that decision is left to the discretion of the individual driver, so it's a wise idea to specify that you plan to use a credit card when you call or before climbing into a cab.

Some Nashville cab companies include **Taxi Taxi of Nashville**, (615) 333-3333, nashvillecab.com; **American Music City Taxi**, (615) 865-4100, musiccitycab.com; **Checker Cab**, (615) 256-7000, nashvillecheckercab.com; and **Yellow Cab Inc.**, (615) 256-0101, yellowcab-nashville.com.

Limousines

Nashville is a town of stars and special occasions, which means it's a limousine kind of town. The yellow pages list dozens of limousine services, most of which are available 24 hours a day, 7 days a week. All accept major credit cards. As with any other service, you get what you pay for, and prices cover a wide range. Expect to pay more during peak times such as prom and graduation season, the December holiday season, and during big events—don't even try getting a last-minute limo for the Country Music Association Awards, for example. For such times, reservations have to be made as much as 4 months in advance.

Prices range from about $85 an hour for a 6-person model to $130 or more an hour for a 10-person stretch with all the amenities. Also plan to add a driver gratuity of 15 to 20 percent; some companies will automatically add this to your bill. Most companies have a 3-hour minimum on weekends and a 2-hour minimum during the week. Weeknights during nonpeak seasons are generally a little cheaper; if you can, plan your special night during the week to increase your chances of getting what you want.

Here are a few of Nashville's limo companies: **Allstars Limousine**, (615) 516-5701, allstarslimousine.com; **Grand Avenue**, (615) 714-5466, grandavenueworldwide.com; and **Signature Limousine Service**, (615) 244-5466, nashvillelimo.com.

History

The history of Nashville is a tale of drama and adventure as rich as any to be found in a theater or on television. Filled with fascinating characters, the Nashville tale has spellbinding plots with action, battles, victories, defeats, mysteries, political intrigue, and romance. In this chapter we tell you about Nashville's past and highlight some of the people and events that made Nashville the interesting, dynamic city it is today. Pull up an easy chair, sit back, and learn about this fascinating city.

THE SETTLEMENT

The first settlers arrived here in 1779, but they weren't the first to inhabit the area. The land was first a home, hunting ground, and burial ground for prehistoric Indians. In the late 1600s and early 1700s, French traders from Canada and what would become Louisiana established a trading post next to a high bluff along the Cumberland River near a salt lick (where animals came for a necessary supply of salt) and a sulphur spring. The spot, later known as French Lick, was just north of where the downtown area is today.

Around 1769, while the area was still being shared by various tribes, another French-Canadian fur trader arrived. Jacques-Timothe De Montbrun, a tall, athletic, dark-skinned man, came to French Lick from Kaskaskia, Illinois. He built a hut at French Lick and spent many winters buying furs from the Indians, which he would then sell in New Orleans. He finally settled in the area in the late 1780s and later operated a store and tavern at the square, where Second Avenue N. is today. De Montbrun, later known as Timothy Demonbreun (pronounced de-MUN-bree-un), is often referred to as the "first citizen" of Nashville.

As Demonbreun and the other traders bartered with the Indians at French Lick, others ventured into the area in search of food and furs. Between 1769 and 1779, "long hunters"—explorers from the colonies of North Carolina and Virginia who lived and hunted in the wilderness for months or even years at a time—could be found here. Some of the long hunters, including Uriah Stone, for whom the Stones River is named, are legendary. Local lore has it that Thomas Sharpe Spencer, a large man known as "Big Foot," lived for months in a hollow sycamore tree. Spencer, who planted corn at Bledsoe's Lick, where

Sumner County is today, is credited with being the first settler to plant in Middle Tennessee.

During the 1770s the colonies along the East Coast in Virginia and North Carolina were becoming crowded. Settlers began hearing the call of the West. In those days, the area we now know as east Tennessee was "the West," and some people settled there in the early 1770s. In 1783 the American Revolution came to an end. The colonies had won their freedom. Also that year the North Carolina Legislature created Davidson County. A year later the legislature established the town of Nashville; the population was 600. In the years that followed, Nashville grew rapidly, evolving from a frontier crossroads into an influential western town.

> **i** In 1784 Nashborough became Nashville. The English "borough" was replaced with the French "ville," most likely as a sign of appreciation for France's assistance during the American Revolution against Great Britain.

The new Fort Nashborough opened in 2017 on the site of the original Nashville settlers' fort on the Cumberland River. Jackie Sheckler Finch

THE JACKSON ERA

In 1796 Tennessee became the 16th state in the Union. Nashville's first church—a Methodist church near the courthouse, jail, and stocks—was built that year, too. Three years later, the town's first newspaper was printed. Between 1796 and 1800, Davidson County's population grew nearly 170 percent, from 3,600 to 9,600. Andrew Jackson is credited for much of the city's growth and influence during the first half of the 19th century. After arriving as a 21-year-old public prosecutor, he achieved success quickly and, in part because he often accepted land grants as payment for his services, became very wealthy. Upon his arrival in town, he boarded at the home of John Donelson's widow (Donelson was mysteriously killed in 1786 while en route from Kentucky to

> **i** Tennessee got its nickname as the Volunteer State during the War of 1812 when volunteer soldiers from Tennessee displayed uncommon valor fighting under General Andrew Jackson to defeat the British at the Battle of New Orleans.

HISTORY

Music City Center hosts conventions and events. Courtesy Nashville Convention & Visitors Corporation

Notable Events in Nashville History

December 25, 1779: Fort Nashborough is founded.

1784: North Carolina Legislature establishes town of Nashville, population 600.

June 1, 1796: Tennessee becomes the 16th state in the Union. Also, Nashville's first church is built.

1806: Nashville is incorporated as a city.

1850: Nashville's population tops 10,000. The Adelphi Theater opens.

1854: Nashville & Chattanooga Railroad is completed.

June 8, 1861: Tennessee becomes 11th and final state to join the Confederacy.

February 24, 1862: Nashville is captured by Union troops.

April 15, 1865: President Lincoln dies; Andrew Johnson becomes the 17th US president.

December 2, 1865: Battle of Nashville, the last major conflict of the Civil War, is fought.

July 24, 1866: Tennessee is first state to be readmitted into the Union.

1866: Fisk School (now known as Fisk University), a free school for African Americans, opens.

1873: Vanderbilt University is founded, opening its doors in 1875.

1876: Meharry Medical College, now the country's largest private medical school for African Americans, opens.

1892: Union Gospel Tabernacle, later renamed Ryman Auditorium, opens.

November 28, 1925: The *WSM Barn Dance* (later named the *Grand Ole Opry)* makes its radio premiere.

1943: Roy Acuff and Fred Rose establish Acuff-Rose Publishing, a leader in the publishing of country songs.

1952: Owen Bradley opens a studio on 16th Avenue S., the beginning of Music Row.

1957: Chet Atkins and Owen Bradley begin developing the "Nashville Sound."

1957: Nashville public schools are desegregated.

1958: The Country Music Association is founded.

May 10, 1960: Nashville becomes Tennessee's first major city to desegregate public facilities.

1962: Voters approve the merger of Nashville and Davidson County governments.

1972: Opryland USA theme park, the start of the Opryland complex, opens.

March 16, 1974: *Grand Ole Opry* leaves the historic Ryman Auditorium and moves into the *Grand Ole Opry* House at Opryland. President Richard Nixon participates.

1993: The renovated Ryman Auditorium reopens.

1996: Nashville Arena opens (it is renamed Gaylord Entertainment Center in August 1999) and became Bridgestone Arena in 2010.

1997: Opryland theme park closes. NFL's Houston Oilers (later the Tennessee Titans) relocate to Nashville, becoming Tennessee's first NFL team.

April 16, 1998: Tornadoes strike downtown and east Nashville.

May 11, 2000: Opry Mills opens on the site of the former Opryland theme park.

2000: Native son Al Gore becomes the Democratic nominee for president and loses to George W. Bush in the closest presidential race in US history.

May 17, 2001: The new Country Music Hall of Fame Museum opens downtown.

June 9, 2001: The new downtown library opens.

June 2006: The Musicians Hall of Fame & Museum opens.

October 2006: The Schermerhorn Symphony Center opens.

September 2007: The Barbershop Harmony Society opens it headquarters.

May 1 & 2, 2010: Powerful thunderstorms produced record rainfall, flooding hundreds of businesses and forcing the evacuation and rescue of hundreds of people from their homes.

May 2013: Music City Center convention complex opens.

Andrew Jackson and his wife Rachel are buried at the Hermitage.
Jackie Sheckler Finch

Nashville), where he met and fell in love with the Donelsons' daughter Rachel, who had separated from her husband, Lewis Robards. Jackson and Rachel Donelson Robards were married in 1791 and repeated their vows in 1794 after discovering—amid something of a social scandal—that Rachel's divorce from her first husband had never been made official. The Jackson marriage remained a topic of gossip for quite some time.

Meanwhile, Jackson, who had served in the US Senate and as a justice of the state supreme court, was preparing for battle. In 1812 Congress declared war on Great Britain, and the War of 1812 began. Jackson, a colorful figure described as both a "roughneck" and a "gentleman," became a national hero for his role in the war. He led American troops to victories over the Creek Indians (British allies) and over the British themselves in New Orleans in 1815. News of a peace treaty signed two weeks before the New Orleans battle didn't reach the combatants in time, so Jackson's last and greatest military victory was actually won after the war had ended.

Jackson had a reputation among his troops as a tough-as-nails military man, and, after one of his soldiers said he was as tough as hickory wood, Jackson's nickname became "Old Hickory." Numerous reminders of the nickname remain throughout Nashville today.

In 1824, despite winning the popular vote, Jackson lost his bid for the presidency of the United States to John Quincy Adams. But he returned victorious in 1828, becoming the first man from west of the Appalachian Mountains to be elected president. More significant, however, was his role in the founding of a new Democratic party characterized by a spirit of reform and interest in the welfare of the common man. The roots of today's Democratic Party date from this time. Jackson was elected to a second term as president, serving through 1837. His wife, Rachel, died of a heart attack in December 1828, before his first inauguration.

Having a hometown hero in the White House did much to boost Nashville's reputation. While president, Jackson made several trips to his plantation, the Hermitage, 12 miles northeast of Nashville, often entertaining renowned guests there. When his term was up, he returned to the Hermitage. Jackson died at his home June 8, 1845, and is buried next to his wife in the Hermitage's garden.

Nashville saw much progress during the Jackson era. By 1840 the city had a population of 6,929—a 25 percent increase from the 1830 census. In 1843 Nashville was named the permanent capital of Tennessee. There was much to enjoy about life in Nashville in the mid-1800s. The city was thriving. In 1860, it was the eighth largest city in the South and had two publishing houses, five daily newspapers, five banks, and numerous mills, factories, breweries, and wholesale houses. But the city's growth and prosperity were about to come to a four-year halt.

Capitol Houses Legislators and Dead People

Children have a favorite bit of trivia about the **Tennessee State Capitol**. "A man is buried in the wall," a boy visiting the landmark said to no one in particular. He is right. But there is more than one person entombed in the stately building. Our tour guide quickly let us know what the children were chattering about.

"There are two people buried in the building and two buried in the lawn," our tour guide said.

But the building is an impressive place for reasons other than that. Construction on the Greek Revival-style building began in 1845 and was completed in 1859. Its architect, **William Strickland** of Philadelphia, began his career as an apprentice to Benjamin Latrobe, architect of the US Capitol in Washington, DC

They chose the highest hill in downtown Nashville. Legend says that the property's owner, Judge George Washington Campbell, acquired it in 1811 as part payment of a debt for a cow. The capitol is one of only a few in the nation still in use today. Tours are free during the week.

The building houses the governor's offices, the Chambers of the State Senate, House of Representatives, and Constitutional Officers. On legislature meeting days, visitors can view the Senate and House from their galleries, accessed by the second-floor stairwells.

When Strickland died in 1854 before the capitol was finished, he was buried in the northeast wall of the building near the north entrance—as he had requested.

The structure was made of hewn stone quarried nearby. It was modeled after a Greek Ionic temple and stands 236 feet long, 109 feet wide, and 206 feet from the ground to the tower top. The porticoes at each end resemble the Erechteum in Athens, and the tower is patterned after the monument of Lysicrates in Athens. When it was completed, it was one of the most magnificent public buildings of its time.

Then the **Civil War** broke out. During the Union occupation of Nashville (1862-1865), the capitol was transformed into Fortress Andrew Johnson.

The artillery located there never had to be fired in battle but was used for drills and celebrations. Early photographs from that period show a large number of soldiers perched on the roof.

Another reminder of the War Between the States is located halfway up the first flight of stairs on the right. A chip in the handrail is a scar from a bullet fired from the stairs above during a particularly bitter fight in the legislature over the ratification of the 14th Amendment in 1866. The amendment, which granted citizenship to African Americans, was opposed by many in the General Assembly. The opposition didn't have enough votes to block passage of the amendment, so they tried to run from armed guards so there wouldn't be a quorum. The guards' willingness to shoot made them abandon that strategy and the amendment passed. Therefore, Tennessee became the first Confederate state to be readmitted to the Union.

The capitol is also filled with historic portraits, murals, ceiling frescoes, and original gasoliers, chandeliers which were converted from gas to electricity around 1895. First-floor offices have period carpeting, draperies, some antique furniture, and accent pieces. One office also contains photos of Memphis resident Elvis Presley when he was honored by the legislature.

On the east side of the building is a large statue of Andrew Jackson on horseback. If it looks familiar, it is because it's the same as one in Jackson Square in New Orleans. The one in Nashville is the first of three casts of "Old Hickory," the original designed by sculptor Clark Mills and erected in 1880.

On the north side of the lawn is the tomb of **President James K. Polk** and **his wife Sarah**. It was designed by William Strickland and was originally erected on the grounds of their home, near the corner of Seventh Avenue North and Union Street. The tomb was moved to its current location after Sarah's death in the 1890s.

And the fourth grave? **Samuel Morgan** is buried there.

If the name isn't familiar, Morgan was a Nashville businessman who served as chairman of the Capitol Building Commission when the building was being constructed. When legislators, worried about the rising cost tried to cut back on expenses, such as substituting wood for the marble in the hallways, Morgan led the fight to keep the grand and enduring materials.

He died June 10, 1880, and is buried in a corner wall of the State Capitol. "He worked pro bono (for free) here for 14 years," our guide said. "He deserved to be buried here."

The Tennessee State Capitol is the seat of state government. Jackie Sheckler Finch

THE CIVIL WAR YEARS

Nashvillians had long discussed the issue of slavery, and they watched as the nation became divided over it. Though slavery was allowed in this Southern city, slave owners made up a minority of its total population of 16,988 in 1860. Included in that number were 3,211 slaves (nearly 19 percent of the population) and 719 free African Americans.

Tennessee was the last state to secede from the Union and the first to rejoin after the war ended. As its young men signed up for battle, Nashville mobilized quickly and became a key center for the manufacture and storage of weapons and other supplies to support the Southern army. But Nashville didn't remain a Confederate city for long. When Union troops captured nearby Fort Henry and Fort Donelson, gaining control of the Cumberland River to Nashville, they had a clear shot at the city. The Army of Tennessee could not defend the capital, so the Confederate commander ordered his troops to exit. When the troops abandoned Nashville, the city panicked. Some citizens boarded the first trains out of town; others packed what belongings they could onto wagons and carriages and fled.

> i Demonbreun Street is named for French-Canadian fur trader Jacques-Timothe De Montbrun, who is often referred to as the "first citizen" of Nashville. The street is on the area that was once his farm.

On February 24, 1862, after federal troops had closed in, Nashville mayor Richard B. Cheatham surrendered the city.

Serving as a Union base took a toll on Nashville. Buildings and homes were destroyed to make room for forts. Churches and other buildings were taken over to serve the military's needs. More than half of the city's trees were cut down. Some of the citizens managed to make a living by providing residents and the military with supplies and services or working for federal operations.

On November 30, General John B. Hood's Confederate soldiers met with a Union force at the Battle of Franklin. Hood attacked, and in less than 6 hours, the Confederate army suffered about 7,000 casualties (including those killed, wounded, or captured); the Union casualty count was 2,500. The Battle of Franklin was known as one of the bloodiest hours of the Civil War.

The Union force withdrew to Nashville. Hood advanced. By December 2 the Confederates had settled into a position in the hills just south of town. They waited. Thomas waited, too, unwilling to attack until the time was right. On December 8, Nashville was hit by a severe ice storm. Both armies were immobilized but remained ready. On December 15, after the ice thawed, Thomas and his Union soldiers attacked the Confederates. Moving from the river toward the south and the east, the federal forces pushed Hood's troops back. One day later, Thomas wiped out three Confederate positions, and the rest of the Southern forces retreated to the south. The Battle of Nashville resulted in 6,000 Confederate casualties, many of whom were captured on the battlefield, and about 3,100 Union casualties.

The Battle of Nashville was the last major conflict of the war. On April 9, 1865, Gen. Robert E. Lee, leader of the main Confederate army, surrendered to Gen. Ulysses S. Grant at Appomattox Court House, Virginia.

Close-up

The Maxwell House: Much More than Coffee

When **John Overton Jr.** began construction on his downtown luxury hotel in 1859, many locals derisively referred to the project as "Overton's Folly." After all, Nashville at that time had a population of fewer than 17,000 and little apparent need for such a showplace. Time would prove these naysayers wrong, however, as the **Maxwell House Hotel** would develop a national reputation—and a name that today lives on, most notably in a popular-brand beverage.

But we're getting ahead of the story. The completion of Overton's hotel, designed by Isaiah Rogers of Cincinnati, was significantly delayed by the outbreak of the Civil War. The first residents of the unfinished building were Confederate troops, who dubbed it **Zollicoffer Barracks** in honor of Gen. Felix K. Zollicoffer, a former Nashville newspaperman who had joined the rebel army as a volunteer. By 1862 the building, like the rest of Nashville, had fallen into the hands of Union troops, who used it first as a barracks, then a hospital, and, finally, a prison. It was in this last configuration that tragedy struck the building, as several Confederate prisoners reportedly were killed when a stair collapsed in September 1863.

After the war, construction resumed, and in September 1869 the Maxwell House Hotel officially opened at the corner of Cherry (now Fourth) and Church Streets. It didn't take long for the new hotel to establish itself as a place for the elite to meet. The dining room became famous not only for its menu's quality but also for its quantity, with sumptuous spreads of rich foods, especially during holidays and other special occasions. "Christmas menus might offer a choice of as many as 22 meats, including roast quail, Minnesota venison, Cumberland Mountain black bear and broiled pheasants," according to a history of the hotel prepared by today's hotel (more on that later).

Several US presidents stayed at the Maxwell House, including Tennessee's own Andrew Johnson, Hayes, Cleveland, Benjamin Harrison, McKinley, Theodore Roosevelt, Taft, and Wilson. The wide range of other prominent politicians, civic and business leaders, socialites, and entertainers who sampled the hotel's hospitality includes social reformer Jane Addams, actress Sarah Bernhardt, orator William Jennings Bryan, Wild West star Buffalo Bill, opera star Enrico Caruso, inventor Thomas Edison, automaker Henry Ford, and the famous midget Tom Thumb.

As you've probably guessed by now, the hotel also became noted for its coffee, provided by local entrepreneur **Joel Cheek.** That Cheek-Neal brand of coffee was served to **President Theodore Roosevelt** when he visited Nashville on October 22, 1907. This was a major event to Nashvillians, and crowds lined the streets to watch the popular president arrive. After speaking briefly at the Ryman Auditorium, Roosevelt traveled on to the Hermitage, Andrew Jackson's former home, where he had breakfast. Asked for his opinion of the Cheek-Neal coffee he had been served, the president pronounced it "good to the last drop." Advertising copywriters have been known to kill for phrases like that, of course, and those words have served as a slogan for the Maxwell House brand ever since.

On August 1, 1928, the giant **General Foods Corporation** bought the Cheek-Neal Company for a price—in cash and General Foods stock—that was reported to be around $45 million, at the time the largest financial transaction in Nashville history. The fortune generated by this sale, incidentally, lives on in **Cheekwood Botanical Garden & Museum of Art.** Cheekwood is the former estate of entrepreneur Leslie Cheek, who earlier had the foresight to invest in his cousin Joel's coffee company. (For more information about Cheekwood, see our **Attractions** chapter.)

As for "Overton's Folly," the original Maxwell House Hotel lived on for many more years, being converted into a residential hotel in its later years. The Maxwell House literally went out in a blaze of glory on Christmas night 1961, when it was destroyed by fire. The corner of Fourth and Church Streets is now occupied by a bank and office building commonly referred to as the SunTrust building. But the Maxwell House name lives on, not only in a best-selling coffee brand but also in another Nashville hotel. In 1979 the **Clarion Maxwell House Hotel** opened at 2025 MetroCenter Blvd.; in 1991, under new ownership, it became the **Regal Maxwell House.** In 2002 the hotel was renovated and underwent another name change, becoming the **Millennium Maxwell House,** which advertises "the Southern traditions of gracious hospitality." Enjoy a meal in Praline's, the hotel restaurant, and be sure to try the coffee, which remains "good to the last drop."

ATHENS OF THE SOUTH

Fisk Memorial Chapel was erected in 1892.
Jackie Sheckler Finch

After the Civil War ended, Nashville began its restoration. It had fared better than some other Southern cities during the war, but there was damage to repair. The next two decades would produce a truly revitalized Nashville, a city that would be a leading commercial center and a growing center of higher education for blacks and whites.

Nashville would soon become known as the Athens of the South for its abundance of colleges and universities. The postwar period marked the opening of such institutions as Fisk University, Vanderbilt University, Meharry Medical College, and Peabody College.

The year 1892 marked the premiere of one of Nashville's most famous landmarks—the Union Gospel Tabernacle, later renamed Ryman Auditorium. Riverboat captain Thomas G. Ryman built the facility after being inspired by Georgia evangelist Sam Jones, a traveling Southern Methodist minister. Ryman wanted a permanent site for Jones's revivals and other religious gatherings. Jones preached there on a few occasions, but by 1900 the building was gaining a reputation as a premier theater in the South. It hosted theatrical and musical productions and political rallies. After Ryman died in 1904, the venue was

> i To learn more about Nashville's role in the civil rights movement, visit the Civil Rights Room at the Nashville Public Library. The downtown library, at 615 Church St., is located at the site of several downtown restaurants where African Americans were once refused service and mistreated before the historic sit-ins of 1960.

> **i** Native son Andrew Johnson, who never attended school but became president after Abraham Lincoln was shot, held virtually every local, state, and federal office. He was an alderman, mayor, state representative, state senator, governor, congressman, senator, and vice president before becoming president of the United States.

renamed for him. It was home to the *Grand Ole Opry* from 1943 to 1974 and, in recent years, has begun serving as host to special engagements of the *Opry*. Today it is on the National Register of Historic Places, and since reopening in 1993 after a renovation, it is one of Nashville's most popular entertainment venues. (See our **Music City** and **Attractions** chapters for details.)

GRAND OLE OPRY

During the 1920s a new type of music was beginning to develop: old-time music, later called hillbilly music and eventually known as country music. A Nashville-based radio program would have a lot to do with the development of this emerging genre.

Ryman Auditorium Courtesy of Nashville Convention & Visitors Corporation

Nashville's famed *Grand Ole Opry* premiered in 1925. Interested in radio as an advertising medium, the prosperous National Life and Accident Insurance Company launched radio station WSM on October 5, 1925. The station's call letters came from the insurance company's slogan: "We Shield Millions." The station played a mixture of classical, jazz, and other pop music, with a few banjo players, fiddlers, and other performers of the newly popular "old-time tunes" thrown in here and there. Soon after WSM hit the airwaves, popular Chicago radio announcer George D. Hay came to Nashville's fledgling station and started a show similar to the *WLS National Barn Dance* he had hosted in Chicago.

On November 28, the station showcased the talents of 78-year-old fiddler Uncle Jimmy Thompson and his niece/piano accompanist, Eva Thompson Jones. With 1,000 watts, WSM had one of the strongest signals of any station in America, and that night, listeners from around the country called and sent telegrams with their enthusiastic praise of the program. The *Grand Ole Opry* was born.

The *WSM Barn Dance,* as it was called for a time, began airing its old-time music program every Saturday night, mainly featuring local amateur acts. Among the early stars the show produced were Thompson and Uncle Dave Macon. The *Barn Dance* became the *Grand Ole Opry* in December 1927. The name change came about when, one evening, after an NBC classical music program from Chicago had aired, Hay introduced a short program of music from *Barn Dance* regulars by saying, "For the past hour, we have been listening to the music taken largely from Grand Opera, but from now on we will present the *Grand Ole Opry!*" Soon after that the program expanded to a 4-hour broadcast, and WSM became a 5,000-watt station reaching 50 percent of America.

After relocating a few times, including a stint at the War Memorial Auditorium, the *Grand Ole Opry* moved to the 3,000-seat Ryman Auditorium in 1943. The Ryman became known as "the Mother Church of Country Music." In 1974, the *Opry* moved to a specially built, state-of-the-art production facility at what was then the Opryland theme park, where it continues to entertain country music fans old and new and remains the longest-running radio program in America. (See our **Music City** chapter for details.)

WORLD WAR II

When Japan bombed Pearl Harbor on December 7, 1941, igniting World War II, Nashville was on its way toward recovery from the Depression. The war gave the city the push it needed to get back on its feet. While thousands of residents headed off to war, area manufacturers went into wartime production.

Erected in 2003 in the center of the Music Row Roundabout, nine larger-than-life nude figures cavort and prance 40 feet in the air. Named "*Musica*," the sculpture features a naked woman at the top holding aloft a tambourine. *Musica* is said to be the largest bronze figure group in America. Created by Nashville artist Alan LeQuire, *Musica* celebrates the history and diversity of music in Nashville. *Musica* in Latin means "arts of the muses." Since Nashville is often called "the Buckle of the Bible Belt," the nude figures will sometimes have a scarf or other piece of clothing tossed over their naked parts by some concerned person.

The Middle Tennessee area, with its varied terrain, was chosen as the site of the world's largest military training efforts, which brought in hundreds of thousands of army personnel. Thousands more, stationed at nearby military camps, descended on Nashville on the weekends for entertainment. More than 1 million came through the city during the first year of war.

By the early 1960s the city was home to eight insurance companies that had more than $2 billion in assets.

The postwar period also saw Nashville's growth as a religious center. A number of missionary-training colleges were opened, religious publishing houses flourished, and denominational headquarters were established in the city. Nashville had a huge number of churches. The "Protestant Vatican" and "Buckle on the Bible Belt" were added to the city's list of nicknames.

The 1950s brought the interstate highway system, which would greatly influence the lives of Nashvillians as well as Americans everywhere. In 1950 WSM radio announcer David Cobb referred to Nashville as "Music City USA" for the first time. In other music news, country music fans mourned the death of 29-year-old Hank Williams, who was found dead in the backseat of his car January 1, 1953.

Tennessee marked its 100th anniversary as a state in 1896 but had to wait until 1897 for the party. From May 1 to October 31, 1897, Nashville hosted the Tennessee Centennial Exposition in West Side Park, now Centennial Park. Officials had begun planning the event in 1893, but a lack of funds forced them to delay the festivities for a year. Support from the railroad companies helped ensure the exposition would be a success.

The six-month celebration, produced at a cost of more than $1.1 million, featured numerous exhibits, amusement rides, dancers, and a dazzling display of lights. The centerpiece of the exposition was a replica of the Parthenon, the temple of Athena, goddess of wisdom, that stands on the Acropolis in Athens, Greece. Nashville's replica, built following plans provided by the king of Greece, was intended to be a temporary structure, like the exposition's exhibit buildings that were constructed of wood and plaster. During the Centennial Exposition, the Parthenon housed works of art.

The Tennessee Centennial Exposition was hailed as a success. It welcomed more than 1.7 million visitors from around the world and was the first such event in America to earn a profit.

After the exposition, the exhibit buildings were torn down, but Nashvillians were fond of their Parthenon, a symbol of the city's reputation as the Athens of the South, and let it stand. The City Parks Board rebuilt the facility out of concrete after it began to deteriorate in the early 1920s. A wide selection of art can be found in the Parthenon's art gallery. In 2001 a $13-million-plus renovation of the Parthenon was completed. (See our **Attractions** chapter for more information.)

MUSIC CAPITAL

By the 1960s, Nashville had already become a music city. The *Grand Ole Opry* had been introducing the nation to new country performers for years, and other industry-related businesses had begun operating. Acuff-Rose Publishing, a leader in country-song publishing, was established by Roy Acuff and Fred Rose in 1943. In the late 1940s and early 1950s, RCA Victor, Decca Records, Capital Records, and Mercury Records had set up shop in Nashville.

In 1957 Chet Atkins, a versatile musician who could play country, jazz, classical, or pop, was producing records and beginning to develop what would become known as the "Nashville Sound," a new style of country music. Atkins and Owen Bradley used new recording techniques and blended pop elements such as background vocalists and horns into their country recordings to produce a more modern sound that became popular with music fans.

As the recording business grew, other music businesses began operating in Nashville. Song publishers, performing-rights organizations, and booking agencies came to town. The Country Music Association was founded in 1958 to promote the growing industry. Country stars also began recording television shows. Jimmie Rodgers, Fred Rose, and Hank Williams were the first inductees into the Country Music Hall of Fame. Pop, rock, and folk music artists could

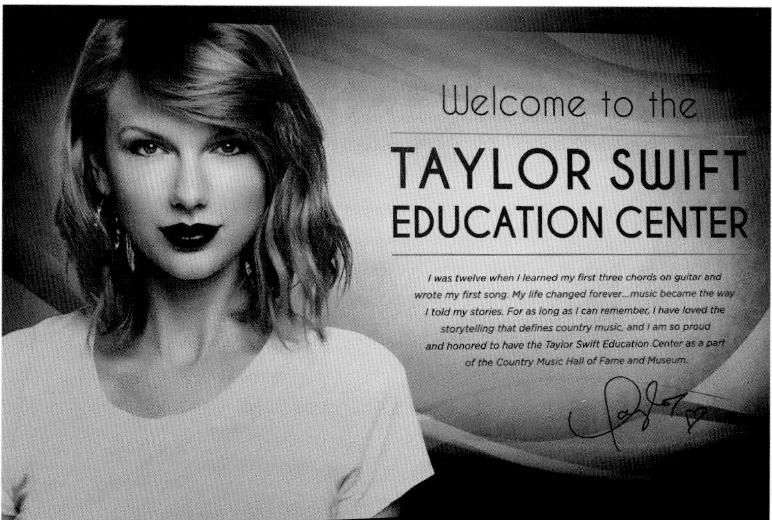

Taylor Swift funded the interactive Taylor Swift Education Center at the Country Music Hall of Fame & Museum. Jackie Sheckler Finch

be found in Nashville studios, too. Bob Dylan, for example, recorded an album here in the mid-1960s.

While it is undoubtedly the country music capital of the world, Nashville also boasts a strong tradition of gospel and pop music. Today Nashville is the center of the growing contemporary Christian and gospel music industry, and each spring the city hosts the Gospel Music Association's Dove Awards show. You can find every genre of gospel here, from traditional black gospel to Christian rock, pop, country, folk, and rap to Southern gospel.

A number of pop and rock artists come here to record, and some call Music City home. Don't be surprised if you find rockers such as Kid Rock, Bon Jovi, or John Mellencamp sitting beside Amy Grant or Vince Gill at a music club or restaurant.

Accommodations

Accommodations are in demand year-round, but with just a bit of planning, you shouldn't have any trouble finding a place to stay in Music City. Most likely your biggest problem will be choosing from among our numerous and varied lodging options. The Nashville area has about 350 hotels and motels with more than 42,000 rooms combined. We have everything from the spectacular Gaylord Opryland Resort & Convention Center to elegant luxury hotels in historic buildings to budget motels and long-term corporate lodging.

When choosing your accommodations, keep in mind that Nashville covers a wide area. For convenience, you might want a hotel that's closest to your primary interests. Properties are concentrated in three areas: Opryland/Music Valley, near the airport, and downtown. In addition, as you travel away from downtown in any direction, you'll find a number of motels and a few hotels, most of which are near interstate exits. Do you want to stay near the *Grand Ole Opry* and Music Valley? Or would you prefer the Midtown (West End/Vanderbilt) area, close to the heart of Nashville's music industry and Music City's top restaurants and nightspots? Maybe you're here on business and would like to room somewhere near the airport or in the downtown business district. Downtown Nashville is also a good choice if you plan to do lots of sightseeing—you'll be within walking distance of historic Second Avenue, the Country Music Hall of Fame & Museum, the State Capitol, and other attractions.

HOTELS & MOTELS

Nashville-area hotels and motels serve more than 14 million visitors annually, including tourists and convention delegates. Since it is the country music capital of the world, Nashville welcomes thousands of country music fans each year. There are so many hotels and motels in Nashville; we have chosen just a small, representative portion of the properties in various areas of town. If you have a favorite trustworthy chain and don't see one of its properties listed here, check the chain's central hub to find out if there is a location in Nashville.

Unlike most chapters in this book, this chapter is divided into six geographic categories—Downtown, Midtown (West End/Music Row), East (Opryland/Airport), North, South and Southeast, and West; that's to help you quickly locate a suitable property in your preferred area. We have listed a variety of properties in all price ranges.

Price Code

The following price code table represents the average cost of a double-occupancy room during peak season. Prices do not include accommodations tax in Nashville–Davidson County. The hotel/motel occupancy tax is 5 percent of the gross room rate, and that's in addition to the state sales tax of 9.25 percent, plus a $2 city tax.

$	**Less than $100**
$$	**$100 to $175**
$$$	**$175 to $250**
$$$$	**More than $250**

Downtown

BOBBY HOTEL, 230 Fourth Ave. N., Nashville, TN 37219; (615) 782-7100; bobbyhotel.com; $$$$. Opened in April 2018, the boutique hotel in downtown Nashville offers 144 guest rooms and reportedly honors a supposed world traveler named "Bobby" who has equipped the new hotel with the best of what he has found on his travels. The hotel's pet ambassador Sasha welcomes guests as they enter the pet-friendly hotel which offers a pet room-service menu and dog treats in the guest room minibars. Guest rooms also have an embroidered towel with Sasha's friendly face on it. For $25, guests can take the towel

Bobby Hotel guest room Courtesy of Bobby Hotel

ACCOMMODATIONS

home with them and the proceeds go to County Road Animal Shelter where Sasha was a rescue dog. The hotel has 4 bars/restaurants. The Tavern at Bobby is the main restaurant serving breakfast, lunch, and dinner. Bobby's Café has garage doors that open to a 36-seat outdoor patio. Bobby's Garage Bar has a garage-inspired decor that includes lamps made from gas pumps and chairs converted from oilcans. Bobby's rooftop lounge features a dipping pool and cabanas. But it is the renovated 1956 Sceniccruiser bus hoisted onto the hotel's roof near the edge that draws gasps. Climb aboard and sit in the driver's seat for even bigger gasps.

CAMBRIA NASHVILLE DOWNTOWN, 118 Eighth Ave. S., Nashville, TN 37203; (615) 515-5800; cambrianashville.com; $$$$. The 255-room Cambria Nashville Downtown is in the popular SoBro (South of Broadway) neighborhood, close to many of Nashville's top attractions, such as Bridgestone Arena, Music City Center, Nissan Stadium, Country Music Hall of Fame, Broadway honky-tonks, and more. The decor is a salute to Music City with elements such as an art installation that mimics sound waves, wallpaper patterned with vintage amplifiers, and guitar-shaped bedside tables. Guest rooms feature free Wi-Fi and tons of plugs, USB ports, and charging stations. The hotel also has a rooftop pool deck with an indoor-outdoor bar, meeting space, outdoor pool, Cetera Grab & Go Market, fitness center, and valet parking for $39 plus tax per night. TRUE is the hotel eatery with a 130-seat dining room and poolside bar, but it is also a live concert venue. Check the website to see what local and national acts will be taking the TRUE stage.

DOUBLETREE HOTEL–NASHVILLE, 315 Fourth Ave. N. Nashville, TN 37219; (615) 244-8200; doubletree3.hilton.com; $$$. This full-service downtown hotel offers 338 nicely furnished guest rooms, including 10 suites. The Doubletree Hotel, a contemporary-style, 9-story angular building, sits at the corners of Fifth Avenue and Deaderick and Fourth Avenue and Union. It's in the heart of downtown Nashville, a short walk from both the State Capitol and Second Avenue entertainment. The hotel's spacious corner rooms feature large wraparound windows and have a sitting area with sofa. All rooms have coffeemakers, hair dryers, 2 dataport phone lines, and TV with free in-room movies. Guests are greeted with a signature chocolate chip cookie. Extra amenities for guests on the ninth-floor executive level include terry-cloth bathrobes and free breakfast. All guests have access to the indoor pool and exercise room on the second floor. Laundry services are available, and there is a business center with high-speed Internet access in the lobby. Patio 315 is open seasonably for lunch, happy hour, dinner, and special events. Patio 315 offers fire pits, large lawn games, and TVs including a movie-screen-sized projection screen to watch sports and events. Fourth & U Restaurant and Bar emphasizes urban dining using local and regional products. Local musicians entertain at Fourth & U on weeknights and until late on Thurs, Fri, and Sat nights. There's also a Starbucks cafe in the lobby.

FAIRLANE HOTEL, 401 Union St., Nashville, TN 37219; (615) 988-8511; fairlanehotel.com; $$$$. The name of this 81-room boutique hotel gives a hint to its decor and vibe. Pure 1960s and 1970s. The building was originally the home of Fidelity Federal Savings & Loan and many of its mid-century architecture have been preserved. Ellington's on the hotel's fourth floor is open daily for lunch and dinner and brunch on the weekends. Ellington's menu features Scottish salmon, Gulf shrimp and grits, diver scallops, pork chops, lamb chops, steaks, oysters, shrimp, chicken, pasta, and much more. Union Teller Coffee Counter offers coffee and handmade pastries. Or try deli sandwiches, hand-rolled bagels, pickled vegetables, and the popular Wilensky sandwich with its seared beef salami, mustard, fried egg, and Swiss cheese on an onion roll. Hotel parking is $36 plus tax per night. Every day at 5 p.m. (which used to signal the end of the workday), the resident "Governor" cruises through the lobby with a vintage bar cart serving local spirits and bottled Coca-Cola.

404 HOTEL, 404 12th Ave. S., Nashville, TN 37203; (615) 242-7404; the404nashville.com; $$$$. How easy is this to remember? The 404 Hotel is named after the street address where it can be found in the Gulch area. The small, chic hotel offers modern comfort plus a James Beard–nominated restaurant named, appropriately, the 404 Restaurant. Opened in 2014, the 404 Hotel certainly doesn't try to hide that the building was once a mechanic's garage. Instead, the rooms pay homage to the building's industrial roots. Vintage and custom furniture along with king-size beds complement the decor of exposed timber and steel trusses. Marble countertops blend with concrete floors. A rotating gallery of work by local artists adds colorful touches. The restaurant itself is across the street at 507 Twelfth Ave. S., (615) 251-1404, and seats about 200. The hotel offers 4 rooms with keyless entry. The restaurant seats 40. Both are artsy, stylish places to stay and to eat just a few blocks from downtown Nashville.

★ **THE HERMITAGE HOTEL,** 231 Sixth Ave. N., Nashville, TN 37219; (615) 244-3121; thehermitagehotel.com; $$$$. Downtown Nashville's Hermitage Hotel has earned AAA's prestigious five-diamond rating. It's the only five-diamond hotel in Tennessee. First opened in 1910, the hotel is listed on

> i The unique men's restroom at the Hermitage Hotel is a landmark that may get as many female visitors as male. The room, decorated in art deco black and green glass, has been the site of photo shoots and music videos.

the National Register of Historic Places and is said to be the only remaining commercial Beaux Arts structure in the state. Over the years it has welcomed such luminaries as Franklin and Eleanor Roosevelt, John F. Kennedy, Richard Nixon, Al Jolson, Greta Garbo, and Bette Davis. Cowboy star Gene Autry once showed up with his horse Champion. Others who have called the hotel home include Jack Dempsey, Minnesota Fats, Al Capone, and Mickey Spillane.

Today, the Hermitage Hotel features 123 spacious and luxurious guest rooms and suites, some of which have a view of the State Capitol. Each room includes a marble bath with double vanities, soaking tub, and separate shower; down-filled duvet; complimentary high-speed Wi-Fi; three 2-line telephones; DVD/CD player; 65-inch flat-panel television, and in-mirror bathroom televisions. The hotel offers concierge service, 24-hour room service, business center, laundry and dry-cleaning service, a fitness room, and many other amenities. Afternoon tea and evening cocktails are served in the grand lobby. Rachel's Boutique offers artisan goods from more than 35 local designers and other items. The hotel's Capitol Grille is the oldest and longest-running Southern restaurant in the state, featuring fresh vegetables grown and harvested on the hotel's historic Glen Leven Farm as well as prime beef and steaks. Those who are traveling with pets will want to know that the hotel has an excellent pet program that includes custom pet beds, dog-walking service, and a room-service pet menu prepared by hotel chefs.

HILTON SUITES NASHVILLE DOWNTOWN, 121 Fourth Ave. S., Nashville, TN 37201; (615) 620-1000; 3.hilton.com/en/hotels/tennessee/hilton-nashville-downtown-BNANSHF/index.html; $$$$. Hilton Suites is one of downtown Nashville's most popular hotels. The location can't be beat: It's just off Broadway next to Bridgestone Arena, between the Country Music Hall of Fame & Museum and the Nashville Music City Center, just a short walk from all sorts of dining, shopping, and entertainment options.

Each of the hotel's 330 suites features a large living room with sofa bed, a separate bedroom with either a king bed or 2 double beds, and a large bathroom. Each suite has a microwave oven, refrigerator, coffeemaker, iron and

Hilton Suites Nashville Downtown is in the heart of "Music City."
Jackie Sheckler Finch

ironing board, and large work desk. Other amenities include room service, an indoor pool, a workout room, free *USA Today* delivery, a 24-hour business center, and a concierge/transportation desk. Four restaurants are on-site.

HOLSTON HOUSE, 118 Seventh Ave. N., Nashville, TN 37203; (615) 392-1234; hyatt.com; $$$. Opened in January 2018, this 191-room Hyatt hotel occupies the historic 1920s-era James Robertson Hotel building, which has been listed on the National Register of Historic Places since 1984. The site is across the street from Bridgestone Arena, near some of Music City's hottest venues. Many of the building's old art deco touches have been preserved. The hotel has meeting space, 2 top-floor penthouse suites with terraces, fitness center, business center, pet-friendly rooms, rooftop pool, and bar, plus 3 dining and cocktail places. The hotel's signature restaurant TENN features American cooking with a Southern twist. TENN serves breakfast, brunch, lunch, and dinner. Check the website for hours.

HOTEL INDIGO, 301 Union St., Nashville, TN 37201; (615) 891-6000; ihg.com; $$$. Opened in 2009, the Hotel Indigo in downtown Nashville is within walking distance to restaurants, nightlife, and attractions. Located in Printers Alley, the boutique hotel is housed in the renovated American Trust

Building at Third Avenue North and Union Street. The hotel features 96 rooms, vibrant colors, hardwood floors, plush bedding, spa-inspired showers, and complimentary Wi-Fi throughout the hotel. Enjoy breakfast on-site at the District Bar & Kitchen, which also serves lunch and dinner.

★ **JW MARRIOTT NASHVILLE, 201 Eighth Ave. S., Nashville, TN 37203; (615) 291-8600; marriott.com; $$$$.** Opened in July 2018, the JW Marriott Nashville is directly across from Music City Center and 2 blocks from the city's famous "Honky Tonk Highway" on Lower Broadway. The sparkling 33-story glass tower has 533 guest rooms and suites with stunning views. The hotel offers a spa, 16 meeting rooms, 2 ballrooms, gym, outdoor event lawn, and rooftop pool at the Cabana Club. Atop the hotel, Bourbon Steak features creative cuisine with 360-degree views of Nashville's skyline. On the hotel's main level, Stompin Grounds Restaurant & Market is a casual takeout market along with a modern sit-down restaurant. For an out-of-this-world Music City experience, guests can book the hotel's coveted Presidential Suite for "The Reserve"–a 7-course dining experience at Bourbon Steak, reserved poolside cabana, VIP boot fitting at Lucchese Bootmaker, couple's full-day spa pampering, and—hold on for it—a private songwriting session in-suite with Nashville's top hitmakers.

The JW Marriott Nashville opened in 2018.
Jackie Sheckler Finch

NOELLE, 200 Fourth Ave. N., Nashville, TN 37219; (615) 649-5000; noelle-nashville.com; $$$$. Noelle opened its doors in December 2017 to begin the next stage of its life. The 224-room boutique hotel was originally built in 1930 at the height of Nashville's cultural boom. Today, Noelle pays homage to the building's first life as the classic art deco Noel Place, one of Nashville's first luxury properties, named after the Noel family who owned the land upon which it was built. Listed on the National Register of Historic Places since 1984, the structure later housed offices until it was converted back to a hotel with a slightly differently spelled name. Labeling itself as "an experiential hotel, designed for the adventurous," Noelle is in historic Printers Alley with easy access to Broadway and popular Music City attractions. The 13-story hotel offers a sleek decor with local art and such unusual amenities as a water station in the corridor of each guest floor where guests can fill glass bottles with still or sparkling water. The hotel features a gym with Peleton bikes, the Keep Shop with Nashville designer items, a vintage printing press shop called Little Prints, and a lobby bar named Trade Room. Dining spots include Drug Store Coffee on a street level of the hotel, Makeready Libations and Liberations restaurant with a tavern-inspired menu, and the open-air Rare Bird on the roof. Valet parking is $42 per night.

RENAISSANCE NASHVILLE HOTEL, 611 Commerce St., Nashville, TN 37203; (615) 255-8400; marriott.com; $$$$. This 31-story hotel is a top pick for convention-goers. After a day of meetings and walking the trade-show floor, you can unwind at one of the many nearby restaurants and nightspots. The Renaissance boasts 649 deluxe rooms, including 24 suites. Extra amenities include laundry and valet service, complimentary shoeshine, covered parking in the adjacent multilevel garage (there is a parking fee), a gift shop/newsstand, concierge service, and free newspapers. In-hotel dining options include Little Fib, featuring sophisticated Southern cuisine. Spanning Commerce Street, high-energy The Bridge on the third floor features 8 massive 60-inch TVs and a 42-foot bar. The Bridge offers live music and serves lunch and dinner. The lobby also houses the Coffee Camper coffee shop.

i The geographic center of Tennessee is located 1 mile from downtown Murfreesboro. The site is marked by an obelisk.

SHERATON GRAND NASHVILLE DOWNTOWN, 623 Union St., Nashville, TN 37219; (615) 259-2000; marriott.com; $$$$. A tasteful choice in downtown Nashville accommodations, this elegant, 28-floor hotel is within walking distance of numerous attractions. Sheraton Nashville Downtown has 482 rooms and 7 suites, Rooms on the upper floors offer splendid views of the State Capitol and other Nashville sites. The hotel offers an exercise room, indoor pool, 2,300 square feet of meeting space, and a business center. Valet service is available in the adjacent 8-story garage; there is a fee to park. The hotel's Broadway Kitchen is a popular gathering spot for breakfast. The Library Bar Sessions lounge, on the first floor, serves cocktails, lunch, and dinner and features locally sourced cuisine and more than 50 varieties of bourbon.

THOMPSON NASHVILLE, 401 11th Ave. S., Nashville, TN 37203; (615) 262-6000; thompsonhotels.com; $$$$. Opened in 2016, this luxury boutique hotel in the Gulch area of downtown Nashville offers 224 rooms with an emphasis on a Music City decor. Work by local artists is displayed throughout the 12-story hotel and guest room minibars feature drinks from WithCO, a company created by Nashville entrepreneurs. A library of vinyl records from Jack White's Third Man Records and a vintage turntable provide music in the lobby. Guests can follow a Third Man designed map of the neighborhood to stroll from the hotel to Third Man Records. Third Man records are also available for sale in the hotel's minibar. Disc jockeys from Third Man host vinyl night on Mondays at the 12th-floor L.A. Jackson rooftop bar. For a special treat, Thompson Nashville guests can book a one-on-one consultation, in-room fitting, and styling session with a denim specialist from Nashville-based Imogene + Willie. The hotel has 3 dining experiences created by James Beard Award–winning chef John Besh. The Marsh House features "Gulf to Gulch" seafood dishes. The rooftop bar L.A. Jackson offers cocktails and Southern snacks. Killebrew has a coffeehouse breakfast and lunch.

ACCOMMODATIONS

★ **21C MUSEUM HOTEL NASHVILLE,** 221 Second Ave. N., Nashville, TN 37201; (615) 610-6400; 21cmuseumhotels.com; $$$$. Opened in 2017, this fashionable boutique hotel is about a 10-minute walk from the Ryman Auditorium, about 15-minute walk from Nissan Stadium and Broadway entertainment. But it seems a world away. Located in the historic 1900 redbrick Gray & Dudley Hardware Building, 21c offers 124 guest rooms and suites, plus a restaurant/bar, fitness center, business center, lobby, gift shop, ballroom, meeting facilities, spa, pet-friendly rooms, and contemporary art gallery. Rooms have free Wi-Fi, flat-screen TVs, contemporary art, and iPod docks, plus minibars and Nespresso machines. Decor is wood floors, high ceilings, custom vintage furniture, and tall windows. Seven rooftop suites have outdoor terraces. Teal-colored penguin sculptures seem to magically appear around the hotel and are favorite selfie photo spots. The penguins' teal color is said to "reflect the spirit of openness, innovation, and engagement," which is what transformed the old building in the heart of downtown Nashville "into a center for contemporary culture and hospitality."

UNION STATION HOTEL, 1001 Broadway, Nashville, TN 37203; (615) 726-1001; unionstationhotelnashville.com; $$$$. The Union Station train shed opened in October 1900 and pushed Nashville into the 20th century, linking the city by rail to the country's important railroad cities. The Romanesque Revival–style building took more than 2 years to complete, and its opening was a grand occasion. When the building reopened as the Union Station Hotel in 1986 after a 2-year renovation, it was another grand affair. What had become something of an eyesore was saved by historic preservationists in the 1970s, and today it is a magnificently restored National Historic Landmark. The Union Station Hotel offers some of the most elegant and luxurious accommodations in town.

Beautiful stained-glass panels adorn the spacious, 3-story lobby's 65-foot-high vaulted ceiling, while an abundance of decorative gilded accents lend to the room's classic elegance. Here and there you'll notice reminders of the hotel's

Bobby Hotel lobby Courtesy of Bobby Hotel

past, such as the ornate clock in the lobby, which years ago was used to time incoming trains.

The 7-story hotel has 125 unique guest rooms, including 11 suites, plus 12,000 square feet of meeting space. Some rooms have vaulted ceilings and open toward the lobby. All rooms have exterior views. High-speed Wi-Fi access is available. Union Station's location near downtown puts you just blocks away from some of Nashville's trendiest restaurants and clubs in the District, West End, and Music Row areas.

Midtown: West End/Music Row

HAYES STREET HOTEL & BAR, 1909 Hayes St., Nashville, TN 37203; (615) 320-0110; hayesstreethotel.com; $$$$. This comfortable boutique hotel is 1 block off West End, near Baptist Hospital, Vanderbilt, and Centennial Park. It is a good choice for medical guests (relatives of local hospital patients receive special rates), but it is just as popular with tourists, business travelers, and visiting families of Vanderbilt students. The hotel has 105 rooms, all with a kitchen sink, microwave, refrigerator, coffeemaker, and hair dryer. There are 6 larger suites that have living rooms with sleeper sofas. A free continental breakfast with locally roasted Bongo coffee is served each morning in the lobby's dining area. The Hayes Street Bar offers custom cocktails, brews, and bites along with live music.

HUTTON HOTEL, 1808 West End Ave., Nashville, TN 37203; (615) 340-9333; huttonhotel.com; $$$$. The Hutton Hotel offers 250 guest rooms and 3 luxury suites. The style is modern and contemporary with a soft and elegant twist. Two private spa treatment rooms offer a wide range of services, including in-room treatments. A state-of-the-art fitness center and complimentary business center are available. The Hutton offers fully-equipped Writers Studios, creative spaces for music professionals. Priding itself on being a "green" business, the Hutton features a recycling program, LED or fluorescent lighting, and an ecofriendly hybrid courtesy vehicle, plus much more. With a menu of contemporary American cuisine, the WestEnd Kitchen & Bar offers breakfast, lunch, and dinner. Analog features live music, comedy shows, dance acts, and poetry readings.

KIMPTON AERTSON HOTEL, 2021 Broadway, Nashville, TN 37203; (615) 340-6376; aertsonhotel.com; $$$$. Opened in June 2017, the boutique hotel offers 180 guest rooms including 12 suites. Decor features leather-stitched headboards, 50-inch TVs, Cararra marble bathrooms, hooded bathrobes, original Hatch Show Print art, views of Vanderbilt University, and a quote from Cornelius Vanderbilt himself. The hotel name is a salute to Jan Aertson, a Dutch immigrant whose descendant Cornelius Vanderbilt became a railroad tycoon and donated $1 million to establish Vanderbilt University. The hotel's restaurant Henley proclaims it has "a Southern soul and French technique." Menu items include duck and dumplings (Magret duck breast, pumpkin dumplings, and candied citrus), Bear Creek Farms skirt steak (with sweet onion potato pave, arugula, and pickled shallot), and Bear Creek Farm pork chop (with charred radicchio and applesauce). The hotel features a rooftop pool, spa, fitness, center, and complimentary hosted wine hour and morning coffee and tea. Look for the one-of-a-kind rope desk in the lobby. A neat touch is Kimpton's custom-designed bikes for a ride around town.

LOEWS VANDERBILT PLAZA HOTEL, 2100 West End Ave., Nashville, TN 37203; (615) 320-1700; loewshotels.com/Vanderbilt-hotel; $$$$. Tasteful, sophisticated, and luxurious, Loews Vanderbilt Plaza Hotel welcomes many business guests and VIPs. The 11-story hotel features 340 guest rooms, including 14 suites. The complex is conveniently located on West End, close to Vanderbilt University, Centennial Park, several good restaurants, downtown Nashville, and Music Row.

Loews will accommodate virtually any request if you give a little notice. Loews Vanderbilt Plaza has a business center, exercise facility, gift shop, salon and day spa, room service, dry-cleaning service, 24,000 square feet of meeting space, and more. Ruth's Chris Steak House at the hotel is a steak lover's dream. For relaxing after a long day of meetings, try the hotel's restaurant, Mason's, featuring modern Southern dishes. Located on the lobby level, the POD Organic Market offers organic snacks and drinks, plus fresh pastries, salads, and flatbreads. The POD also carries local favorites such as Frothy Monkey Coffee and Yazoo Beer. The hotel's complimentary courtesy vehicle—a new Mercedes GL450 SUV—is available from 7:30 a.m. to 10 p.m. to take guests within a 3-mile radius of the hotel.

East: Opryland/Airport

FIDDLER'S INN OPRYLAND, 2410 Music Valley Dr., Nashville, TN 37214; (615) 885-1440; fiddlersinnopryland.com; $. This 204-room motel has been in business since 1975. It's one of the more affordable choices in the Music Valley area, appealing to families, bus groups, and budget-minded business travelers. Extras are an outdoor pool, complimentary continental breakfast, free Wi-Fi, exercise room, business center, and a gift shop. The Opryland resort is just across the street, offering lots of restaurants, shops, and sightseeing.

Music Valley attractions are within walking distance. Free parking for hotel guests, motor homes, and motor coach groups.

GAYLORD OPRYLAND RESORT & CONVENTION CENTER, 2800 Opryland Dr., Nashville, TN 37214; (615) 889-1000; marriott.com; $$$–$$$$. The Gaylord Opryland Resort is the star of Nashville accommodations. Even if you don't stay at this awe-inspiring property, it's worth stopping by to visit. Thousands of locals, tourists, and business travelers drop by every day to walk through and marvel at the 3 enormous themed atriums. And it's a tradition for Nashvillians to visit during the holidays when the hotel property turns into a Christmas fantasyland aglow with more than 3 million lights.

The Opryland resort is one of the largest convention and resort properties in the nation and is the world's largest combined hotel–convention center under one roof. The hotel opened in 1977 and has 2,711 guest rooms (including 171 suites); 600,000 square feet of meeting and exhibit space; 152 meeting rooms; 5 ballrooms; 3 indoor gardens spanning 9 acres; dozens of shops, restaurants, and lounges; 3 swimming pools; and a fitness center. You can get a workout just walking from one end to the other. The 3 indoor gardens are the Conservatory, the Cascades, and the largest, the 4.5-acre Delta, which has a 150-foot-high roof composed of more than 650 tons of glass. The Delta even has its own river—big enough to carry passengers on flatboats on a guided tour of the area.

Breakfast, lunch, and dinner options at the Opryland hotel are plentiful. Numerous restaurants and lounges offer something for every taste, including

Gaylord Opryland Resort Courtesy of Nashville Convention & Visitors Corporation

Cascades American Café, Fuse Sports Bar, Delta Marketplace, Conservatory Café, Jack Daniel's, Solario Cantina, Wasabi's Sushi, American Craft Tavern, Old Hickory Steakhouse, Ravello, Findley's Irish Pub, Stax (a build-your-own-burger restaurant), and Paisano's Pizzaria & Vino, a casual pizzeria and wine bar. There are also more than 30 specialty shops selling everything from Jack Daniel's gift baskets to fine bath products.

> **i** March, with an average precipitation of 5.6 inches, is the rainiest month in Nashville.

New in 2018, SoundWaves offers 4 acres of indoor/outdoor water attractions. Billed as a first-of-its-kind water and music attraction, SoundWaves has fun for adults, young children, and families, with an adult-only area available. The 111,000-square-foot indoor water park maintains an 84-degree tropical temperature year-round with a unique roof that gives natural light. The 3-level water park includes an indoor slide tower with slides ranging from 32 to 46 feet tall, a double flow rider, rapid and lazy rivers, and an activity pool with rock climbing. Seasonal outdoor features include a 315,000-gallon wave pool with a giant LED movie screen and a 45.5-foot slide.

The resort also offers golf at Gaylord Springs Golf Links, carved from the banks of the Cumberland River. The Scottish-links-style, par 72 layout has an 18-hole course bordered by limestone bluffs and beautiful federally protected wetlands. The resort offers shuttle service to the airport, *Grand Ole Opry*, Ryman Auditorium, Gaylord Springs Golf Links, Wildhorse Downtown Nashville, Opry Mills mall, and *General Jackson* Showboat.

HOTEL PRESTON, 733 Briley Pkwy., Nashville, TN 37217; (615) 361-5900; hotelpreston.com; $$$. Located 2 miles from the Nashville airport, Hotel Preston has 12 floors with 196 guest rooms and suites. Opening its doors in 2004, Hotel Preston is upscale and personalized. The hotel features a "You Want It—You Got It" program, which offers guests special amenities and comforts such as pet fish companions, lava lamps, CDs, books, rubber duckies, milk and cookies, and more. Amenities include organic coffee and tea, pillow-top mattresses, designer toiletries, and ergonomic swivel chairs. Quirky extras include Primp Kits for him, her, and Spot. The hotel includes a 24-hour fitness center, outdoor pool, meeting space for 8 to 800, in-room business work space, same-day dry cleaning and laundry services, and premium channels plus movies on demand. Café Isabella restaurant and bar serves Italian comfort food with Southern roots. The hotel also offers complimentary 24-hour shuttle service to the airport.

North & Northwest

INN AT FONTANEL, 4133 Whites Creek Pike, Nashville, TN 37190; (615) 876-2537; fontanelmansion.attractions/inn-at-fontanel; $$$. A Southern Living Idea House built on the Fontanel property in 2013 was converted into a luxury 6-suite boutique hotel in 2014. The spacious suites are connected by 2,700 square feet of deck, plus share the two-story-high Great Room, which contains a dining room, kitchen, and living room. Just think of sleeping on the property once owned by country music legend Barbara Mandrell. In fact, it was Mandrell who chose the unusual name for what was considered the largest log cabin in the world. Mandrell and her family lived in the mansion from 1988 to 2002. Today, you can tour the mansion—it looks as though the family has just stepped out—and enjoy other activities on the property: zip lines, concerts at the Woods Amphitheater, hiking trails, shops, and dining at Cafe Fontanella's Italian Kitchen. The inn offers a nifty breakfast for guests to start the day. A common gathering area for guests, the Great Room includes a dining room, living room, and kitchen. Complimentary amenities include newspapers, Wi-Fi, parking, golf cart usage, and pillow candy by Goo Goo.

MILLENNIUM MAXWELL HOUSE NASHVILLE, 2025 Rosa L. Parks Blvd., Nashville, TN 37228; (615) 259-4343; millenniumhotels.com; $$$. The Millennium Maxwell House is the namesake of the famous Maxwell House Hotel (see the related Close-up in our **History** chapter) that opened in downtown Nashville in 1869. The hotel was the site for many important business and social events, and it enjoyed a national reputation. And yes, the hotel is connected to the famous brand of coffee, although the hotel had the Maxwell House name first. President Theodore Roosevelt, on a visit to Nashville in the early 1900s, commented that the coffee was "good to the last drop." The original Maxwell House was destroyed by fire in 1961. The current hotel opened in 1979; it sits just off I-65, 1.5 miles from downtown.

Atop a knoll overlooking downtown Nashville, this 10-story hotel has 287 spacious and well-appointed rooms. Amenities include an outdoor pool and fitness center. The hotel's free shuttle will take you to the airport or any location within a 5-mile radius. On-site Praline's offers breakfast, lunch, and dinner. The sports-bar-themed Maxwell's Lounge is open nightly.

> i In Nashville nearly 55,000 jobs are related to hospitality.

B&BS

The following is a selection of B&Bs in and around Nashville. We haven't listed all the available properties, but we have chosen a sample that represents several locations, accommodations, and price ranges.

Associations & Reservation Services

BED AND BREAKFAST ASSOCIATION OF TENNESSEE, 1200 Paint Rock Rd., Kingston, TN 37763; (865) 376-0113; tennessee-inns.com. This state association is a nonprofit organization established to market Tennessee bed-and-breakfast inns. Its member inns are fully licensed by the state and have passed the association's biennial inspection program. Call the listed number for a free brochure that describes each inn, or visit the website.

NATCHEZ TRACE BED & BREAKFAST RESERVATION SERVICE, P.O. Box 826, Madison, TN 37116; (800) 377-2770; natcheztracetravel.com. This service has a directory of a few dozen inns in Tennessee, Alabama, and Mississippi. All are along the Natchez Trace, a historic route that runs from Nashville to Natchez, Mississippi. Call or visit the website for reservations, details on homes, and a free map of the Trace.

B&Bs in & Around Nashville

BIG BUNGALOW, 618 Fatherland St., Nashville, TN 37206; (615) 256-8375; thebigbungalow.com; $$$. Built in the early 1900s, this lovely home sits in historic Edgefield, just east of the Cumberland River and downtown Nashville. The Big Bungalow offers 3 rooms, each with its own private bath, plus cable television in every room and free Wi-Fi. A computer is available for guest use, as are a refrigerator and microwave. Guests are invited to relax on the large, screened-in back porch. Breakfast features specialties of the house. Check on the events schedule at the Big Bungalow for music right in the living room. Four or five songwriters sit in a circle and perform their original songs. It's a good chance to hear the next big country hit or maybe meet the next big country star. As a licensed massage therapist for many years, innkeeper Ellen

i Your bed-and-breakfast hosts can recommend good restaurants, attractions, and shopping spots in the area. Be sure to ask about their favorites—there's nothing like a real Insiders' view.

Warshaw offers massages as a great way to end the day or to start a new morning. Children 10 and over are welcome. No pets are permitted.

DAISY HILL BED AND BREAKFAST, 2816 Blair Blvd., Nashville, TN 37212; (615) 297-9795; daisyhillbedandbreakfast.com; $$$. Housed in a classic 1925 Tudor Revival home, Daisy Hill is about half a mile from Vanderbilt University and a little more than a mile from Nashville's Music Row. Located in historic Hillsboro Village, Daisy Hill offers 3 European-themed rooms with antique furnishings and private bathrooms. A maximum of two people to a room. Common areas are a garden, screened porch, living room with fireplace, library, and dining room where drinks and snacks are always available. Greet the day with a full hot breakfast served by innkeepers.

1501 LINDEN MANOR, 1501 Linden Ave., Nashville, TN 37212; (615) 298-2701; nashville-bed-and-breakfast.com; $$$. The inn has 3 large guest rooms, each with a private bathroom. The Vanderbilt Room has a queen-size 4-poster bed covered in romantic, floral-print linens. This room has a fireplace, which makes it especially cozy. The Belmont Room, also with a queen-size bed, has a soothing blue color scheme and a Victorian garden theme. The Linden Room has a king-size bed and a private, outside entrance. The room's private bath has a shower and a hot tub. The Vanderbilt and Belmont baths have showers but no tubs. Guests are welcome in the sitting room, formal dining room, large wraparound porch, and back deck. Afternoon refreshments are served on the porch when the weather is nice, and there's always a bottomless cookie jar, popcorn, and plenty of beverages available. The inn has the first electric charging station at any Tennessee bed-and-breakfast. A blink charging station is free for guest use. For pianists, the inn offers a more-than-century-old piano which guests can play.

HANCOCK HOUSE, 2144 Nashville Pike, Gallatin, TN 37066; (615) 452-8431; bbonline.com; $$$. Hancock House is a 15-room colonial revival log inn. In the late 1800s it was a stagecoach stop and toll gatehouse known as Avondale Station. Over the years 2 small cabins were attached to the back of the original building. Between the 3 structures is a courtyard, just off the dining room. The main house has 5 bedrooms, each with a private bath and

> i If the name of the bed-and-breakfast contains the word *barn*, it usually means the inn has accommodations for guests' horses.

fireplace. The Chamber room, located on the ground floor, has an antique Murphy bed and a whirlpool tub. The Nannie Dunn room, half a flight of stairs up and off the dining room, has an antique bed. Upstairs are the Bridal Suite, with an antique canopy 4-poster bed and a romantic whirlpool for two, and the Felice Ferrell room, named for the home's previous owner, which has an antique elevated bed. All accommodations include a full country breakfast, served in your room, in the dining room, or outdoors in the courtyard. The Hancocks also serve afternoon tea and other beverages and plenty of fresh fruit.

★ **TIMOTHY DEMONBREUN HOUSE,** 746 Benton Ave., Nashville, TN 37204; (615) 383-0426; tdhouse.com; $$$$. The Timothy Demonbreun House may be Nashville's most luxurious bed-and-breakfast. The 22-room mansion is owned by Richard Demonbreun, the great-great-great-great-grandson of Frenchman Timothy Demonbreun, who is considered Nashville's first citizen (see the **History** chapter). The home is named in Timothy's honor, although he never lived on the property (the home was built long after his death). The 10,000-square-foot 1906 mansion, located in the Woodland-in-Waverly historic district, is listed on the National Register of Historic Places. The B&B offers 4 guest rooms—Cabernet Room, Chardonnay Room, Game Room, Merlot Room—each with a queen-size bed, fireplace, private bath, and access to the heated pool and spa. The home has a wine cellar where guests can select from an assortment of wines. A full, made-to-order breakfast is served each morning. The B&B has several chefs and a full waitstaff. Private dining is available by reservation.

URBAN COWBOY, 1603 Woodland St., Nashville, TN 37206; (347) 840-0525; urbancowboy.com; $$$. Eight suites are housed in a historic Victorian mansion. The suites have soaring ceilings and clawfoot tubs. But each suite also has its own distinct decor—The Midnight Rider, The Victorian, The Captain, The Tower, The Lion's Den, The Muse, and the Rose Room. At the back of the property, The Cabin can sleep up to 4. The Stable House out back is home to the Public House Bar and Kitchen which features wood-fired food and craft cocktails.

CAMPGROUNDS

Nashville and its immediate area offer more than a dozen campgrounds, most of which have sites for both recreational vehicles and tent campers. Some camping opportunities are also available at nearby state parks.

Although most area campgrounds will be happy, when possible, to accommodate campers who just show up looking for a site, you are strongly encouraged to make reservations. Sites tend to fill up, especially during nice weather. You wouldn't want to load up the family and all your camping gear and head for Nashville only to find nowhere to stay.

We list state park camping opportunities under a separate heading. For more information about recreational and other opportunities in Tennessee state parks, see our **Recreation** chapter.

All campgrounds are open year-round unless otherwise indicated. Please note that prices are subject to change; off-season rates may be a little cheaper.

Private Campgrounds

NASHVILLE EAST/LEBANON KOA, 2100 Safari Camp Rd., Lebanon, TN 37090; (615) 449-5527; koa.com/campgrounds/nashville-east. Though adjacent to I-40, Lebanon KOA features 35 acres of rolling hills that leave all hint of the highway behind. Approximately 100 RV and tent sites are available for overnight use, including RV sites with full hookups, water and electrical sites, and shaded tent sites with water and electricity. Other sites are available on long-term leases.

Lebanon KOA has all the basic amenities—showers, fire rings, laundry—plus many extras: pet walk station, swimming pool, tennis court, playground, volleyball courts, target green golf course, horseshoe pit, ping-pong table, convenience store, and 30 acres of mowed fields. A new addition is custom-built cabins to rent.

NASHVILLE I-24 CAMPGROUND, 1130 Rocky Ford Rd., Smyrna, TN 37167; (615) 459-5818; nashvillei24kampground.com. This wooded campground, open since 1971, is affiliated with the Good Sam family of campgrounds. It has more than 100 sites for tent camping and recreational vehicles plus 3 cabins. Amenities include a swimming pool, grocery store, game room, Wi-Fi, half basketball court, laundry, recreation room, and 2 playgrounds.

NASHVILLE KOA RESORT, 2626 Music Valley Dr., Nashville, TN 37214; (615) 889-0282; koa.com/campgrounds/nashville. This year-round KOA features 430 sites for various uses, from tent camping through different types of RV hookups. Thirty cabins are also available, and there are 4 lodges that feature bathrooms and kitchenettes. There's a grocery store and laundry on-site; recreational opportunities include a swimming pool, miniature golf, game room, basketball court, bicycle rentals, bocce ball, dog park, and 2 playgrounds. Notes Café offers breakfast, lunch, or snack. The campground has a public computer and shuttles to local attractions, as well as a concierge to help arrange tickets.

NASHVILLE NORTH KOA, 1200 Louisville Hwy., Goodlettsville, TN 37072; (615) 859-0348; koa.com/campgrounds/nashville-north. This year-round campground has 100 sites, ranging from tent camping to full RV hookups to cabins offering full-size beds and bunk beds. Cable TV hookups are available. There is also a swimming pool, creek side pet trail, pet park, free Wi-Fi, and outdoor pavilion. On Thurs nights from May through Oct, the campground offers a catered dinner and live country music in the outdoor pavilion. Shuttle tours pick up people here for trips to nearby attractions.

TWO RIVERS CAMPGROUNDS, 2616 Music Valley Dr., Nashville, TN 37214; (615) 883-8559; towriverscampground. A Good Sam Club, Two Rivers has 104 RV sites but does not allow tent camping. A pool, game room, swimming pool, and playground area are also on the campground. There's a full concierge staff plus showers, laundry, a convenience store, free Wi-Fi, free coffee, and free live entertainment in season. Shuttles are available to downtown.

YOGI BEAR'S JELLYSTONE PARK, 2572 Music Valley Dr., Nashville, TN 37214; nashvillejellystone.com; (615) 889-4225. This campground offers a variety of options for travelers. In addition to 233 pull-through sites for recreational vehicles and a tent-camping area, the park has 8 rental cabins. Amenities include miniature golf, mining sluice, 9-hole golf course, jump pad, archery, sand volleyball, outdoor laser tag, basketball, planned activities for kids, canine corral and pet walk, and summertime concerts. The park also has a laundry, convenience store, and Hot Rod Ice Cream Shoppe.

US Army Corps of Engineers Campgrounds

Corps of Engineers campgrounds must be reserved through the National Recreation Reservation Service, which bills itself as North America's largest camping reservation service. You can make your reservations by calling the NRRS—which offers more than 45,000 reservable facilities at 1,700 locations managed by the Corps and the USDA Forest Service—toll-free at (877) 444-6777 or by visiting reserveamerica.com, a website with detailed maps, directions, prices, regulations, and anything else you'd need to know.

Most of these sites offer ample opportunity for fishing, boating, skiing, and swimming, as well as for viewing such wildlife as white-tailed deer, rabbits, raccoons, skunks, wild turkeys, and squirrels.

Please note that most Corps campgrounds require a 2-night minimum on weekends and a 3-night minimum on holiday weekends. Operating season varies by campground and by year. It's best to check the website for current details.

J. Percy Priest Lake Area

ANDERSON ROAD CAMPGROUND, 4010 Anderson Rd., Nashville, TN 37217; (615) 361-1980; recreation.gov/camping/campgrounds/232515. A lovely lakeside campground, Anderson Road offers 37 shaded electric and nonelectric sites, along with hot showers, dump station, picnic shelter, boat launch, laundry, beach, and public telephones.

POOLE KNOBS CAMPGROUND, 493 Jones Mill Rd., La Vergne, TN 37086; (615) 459-6948; recreation.gov/camping/campgrounds/232677. Poole Knobs, near Smyrna, has 87 campsites and a group camping area as well as hot showers, dump station, boat launch, picnic shelter, and electric hookups.

SEVEN POINTS CAMPGROUND, 1810 Stewarts Ferry Pike, Hermitage, TN 37076; (615) 889-5198; recreation.gov/camping/campgrounds/232702. Seven Points has 59 sites with water and electricity for RV or tent camping. A dump station is available. Prices are $20 to $26. Amenities include hot showers, laundry facilities, a swimming area, and boat ramp.

This is one of the Corps's busiest campgrounds in the country; draws include the day-use area, which offers a beach and group picnic shelter, plus nearby attractions such as the Hermitage and the *Grand Ole Opry*.

Old Hickory Lake Area

CAGES BEND CAMPGROUND, 1125 Benders Ferry Rd., Gallatin, TN 37066; (615) 824-4989; recreation.gov/camping/campgrounds/232539. Located on the shores of Old Hickory Lake, Cages Bend has 42 sites with electrical and water hookups for $30 to $35 a night. Hot showers, an accessible restroom, a dump station, a boat launch, and laundry facilities are also available. Shopping, grocery stores, gas stations, and a marina are all within about 10 miles. Waterskiing and fishing are popular here; you're also located near religious theme park Trinity City and not too far from Opry Mills shopping mall. The campground generally is open from Apr through Oct.

CEDAR CREEK CAMPGROUND, 9264 Saundersville Rd., Mt. Juliet, TN 37122; (615) 754-4947; recreation.gov/camping/campgrounds/232545. Cedar Creek has 61 sites with electricity and water, as well as hot showers, an accessible restroom, dump station, laundry facilities, picnic shelter, and boat launch. Area attractions include the Hermitage and the *Grand Ole Opry*. The campground generally is open from Apr through Oct. Fees are $30 to $35 a night.

Nearby State Parks

Tennessee state park campsites are available on a first-come, first-served basis. While the following state parks are open year-round, many of them have reduced capacity during the winter, with portions of the campgrounds closed. In general, this is from early November through early April, but it really depends on the weather.

For more information about state parks, see our **Recreation** chapter. You can also call the individual park or, if you'd especially like to know about other state parks, call the department at (800) 421-6683. A reservation service is available by calling (866) TENN-PKS. Current information can also be found online at tnstateparks.com.

CEDARS OF LEBANON STATE PARK, 328 Cedar Forest Rd., Lebanon, TN 37090; (615) 443-2769; tnstateparks.com/parks/cedars-of-lebanon. Named for the cedar trees found throughout the area, Cedars of Lebanon has 117 campsites, plus 30 tent and pop-up sites, as well as an 80-person group lodge and 9 two-bedroom cabins. Campsites with water and electrical hookups are $35 a night; tent sites are $25. Amenities include hot showers and flush toilets, laundry, dump station, and a camp store that's open in-season. Cabins have a fully equipped kitchen, woodstove, and television; pay phones are nearby. Cabin rates are $210 to $225. Linens and towels are provided.

MONTGOMERY BELL STATE PARK, 1020 Jackson Hill Rd., Burns, TN 37029; (615) 797-9052; tnstateparks.com/parks/montgomery-bell. This almost 4,000-acre park, north of US 70 and 7 miles east of Dickson, offers 94 RV campsites with electrical and water hookup. Fees are $15 to $35. There are 3 backcountry campsites. Montgomery Bell State Park also has 8 fully equipped 2-bedroom cabins (one of which is wheelchair accessible) that sleep 5 to 9 people apiece. The inn offers 120 rooms and 5 suites. A conference center can host up to 500 people and an on-site restaurant is open every day. Group camping is available in 47 rustic cabins that sleep 120 people in all. Campers are required to bring their own linens, foodstuffs, and campfire supplies such as wood or charcoal.

Dining

Hungry? If you're not right now, you will be by the time you read through a few pages of this chapter. We're going to stimulate your appetite by telling you about some of the Southern-style comfort food, hearty pastas, thick and juicy steaks and burgers, freshly baked breads, tasty vegetarian meals, delectable desserts, and spicy international dishes you can find in Nashville. We list ethnic eateries, fine dining spots, barbecue joints, catfish houses, romantic bistros, and much more. Nashville is probably best known, though, for "meat-and-threes." For those of you who aren't familiar with the term, a meat-and-three is a place where you can get a down-home Southern entree—like fried chicken, meat loaf, turkey and gravy, or country-fried steak—accompanied by three vegetables. And when we say vegetables, we mean anything from mashed potatoes, corn, and green beans to deviled eggs, macaroni, and Jell-O. Corn bread, rolls, or biscuits come with the meal, too. We have an abundance of these beloved meat-and-threes, places like Swett's and Elliston Place Soda Shop. They are longtime favorites, and we highly recommend them for their good home cooking and Southern hospitality. Some of our restaurants are nationally known (places like the Loveless Cafe and the Pancake Pantry), and other establishments that started here have gone on to become national or regional chains—places such as O'Charley's, J. Alexander's, and Whitt's Barbecue.

OVERVIEW

In this chapter we're primarily highlighting places that are unique to Nashville. We have lots of fast-food restaurants, bars, pizza franchises, and family-style eateries (including the always-popular Cracker Barrel and P.F. Chang's China Bistro), but you already know what to expect from those places. We want to steer you to some of our local favorites. We've arranged this chapter alphabetically by category of cuisine—American, Asian, barbecue, Italian, steak, and so on.

Most major restaurants take credit cards and debit cards. Some of the smaller establishments, like a few of the meat-and-threes, take cash and personal checks only. Finally, keep in mind that Nashville's restaurant scene seems to be constantly growing and changing. Operating hours shift, businesses change hands, chefs play musical chairs, eateries close and reemerge with new names and menus, and new restaurants open up regularly. If you're planning a special meal out, it's a good idea to call first, at least to make sure of the operating hours.

Along with Southern cuisine, Acme Feed & Seed also has a sushi bar.
Jackie Sheckler Finch

Price Code

Use the following price code as a general guide for the cost of dinner entrees for one, excluding appetizers, alcoholic beverages, desserts, and tip. Keep in mind that drinks, desserts, and extras for two can significantly add to the bill and will often put you in a new price category. Your tab for breakfast and lunch will most likely be less expensive.

$	**Less than $20**
$$	**$20 to $30**
$$$	**$30 to $45**
$$$$	**$45 to $65**
$$$$$	**More than $65**

AMERICAN/CONTEMPORARY AMERICAN

BEACON LIGHT TEA ROOM, 6276 Hwy. 11, Bon Aqua, TN 37025; (931) 670-3880; beaconlighttearoom.com; $$. The Beacon Light restaurant has dished up Southern food along with spiritual succor since 1936. Beacon Light is known for its delicious country ham, biscuits, and homemade preserves, but it's become notorious for the decor, which can only be described

> A recipe for Chicken Florentine Panini won a tasty $1 million for Denise Yennie, a Nashville accountant, in a Pillsbury Bake-off Contest.

as Christian kitsch. Jesus tchotchkes, Jesus paintings, porcelain lions and lambs, and religious knickknacks of all types crowd every nook and cranny of the place. There are even plastic "our daily bread" boxes on each table; toaster shaped, they dispense scripture passages instead of bread. The Southern-fried menu is excellent, by the way. Beacon Light is open for lunch and dinner Tues through Fri and breakfast, lunch, and dinner Sat and Sun. Reservations are accepted. Beacon Light got its name from the 1931 government-built beacon light which used to direct old prop planes flying the mail between Memphis and Nashville. The light is gone but the restaurant stands close to where the light once stood.

CAPITOL GRILLE, Hermitage Hotel, 231 Sixth Ave. N., Nashville, TN 37291; capitolgrillenashville.com; $$$$. More than a few restaurant critics consider the Capitol Grille to be Nashville's premier dining establishment. The elegant restaurant is under the lobby of the historic and luxurious Hermitage Hotel. The Capitol Grille is pure luxury—think truffles, foie gras, caviar, and lobster, all of which are, naturally, on the menu. Creative Southern cuisine is the specialty. While the menu changes from time to time, expect to find such standout dinner entrees as grilled Tennessee Black Angus beef tenderloin with foie gras hollandaise. Fabulous side dishes include fried green tomatoes with spicy pepper relish and white truffle mac and cheese. Desserts don't disappoint. For breakfast there are the traditional eggs and bacon, pancakes, and cereals, as well as Maine lobster and shirred eggs, and eggs Benedict with beef tenderloin medallions. The lunch menu might include Vidalia onion bisque with a miniature brie sandwich and smoked Virginia bacon; grilled salmon BLT; or Maine lobster raviolis. A spectacular brunch is served weekends from 11 a.m. to 2 p.m. Reservations are recommended.

DEMOS' STEAK & SPAGHETTI HOUSE, 300 Commerce St., Nashville, TN 37203; (615) 256-4655; demosrestaurants.com; $$. While its name is frequently mispronounced, Demos' (DE-mo-SEZ) menu never leaves you guessing. This American-Italian-Greek restaurant has lots of pastas with a variety of sauces and 4 or 5 steaks that are good for the price. Demos' has a nice, semi-casual/semi-upscale, family-friendly environment. The blackened chicken pasta and Greek-style chicken salad are good choices. Demos' has a weekday lunch special, but be prepared to wait about 20 minutes for a seat, and it's always first-come, first-served. Demos' is open daily for lunch and dinner. Other locations are at 1115 Northwest Broad St., Murfreesboro (615-895-3701); 161 Indian Lake Blvd., Hendersonville (615-824-9097); and 130 Legends Dr., Lebanon (615-443-4600).

EASTLAND CAFE, 97 Chapel Ave., Nashville, TN 37206; (615) 627-1088; eastlandcafe.com; $$$. Like its name says, the Eastland Cafe is in East Nashville and has quickly become a neighborhood favorite. No wonder. The Eastland has a welcoming atmosphere, comfortable surroundings, and ever-changing good food. Casually elegant, the restaurant features dark mahogany wood panels and warmly lit tables. Small plate favorites include fried green tomato Napoleon with jalapeño candied bacon, pimento cheese, and pepper jelly or potato gnocchi with mushrooms, asparagus, parmesan cream sauce, pernod, and herbs. Popular entrees include diver sea scallops with vanilla-scented parsnips, smoked leek hearts, and white Russian puree or grilled pork chop with green chile mac and cheese, collard greens, and orange chile vinaigrette. For dessert, blueberry beignets with warm white chocolate sauce and powdered sugar are tops.

ELLISTON PLACE SODA SHOP, 2111 Elliston Place, Nashville, TN 37203; (615) 327-1090; ellistonplacesodashop.com; $$. Plate lunches and milkshakes are the claims to fame of this 1950s-style diner. One of Nashville's oldest restaurants, Elliston Place Soda Shop first opened in 1939, and little has changed here over the years. The restaurant has had only 3 owners, and it still has some of its original chairs and booths. Old miniature jukeboxes sit on each table; they don't work anymore, but the big jukebox still spins hits from the '50s and '60s. Mon through Sat, diners can choose from 2 entrees, including daily specials like turkey and dressing, fried chicken, and catfish. For the "three" part of your meat-and-three, choose from among 10 vegetables and side dishes, including fresh turnip greens, fried corn, baked squash, cucumber and onions, lima beans, potato salad, and macaroni and cheese. Your meal comes with corn bread or a biscuit. If you want to indulge further, have one of the soda shop's celebrated shakes.

ETCH, Encore Tower, 303 Demonbreun St., Nashville, TN 37201; (615) 522-0685; etchrestaurant.com; $$$$. For a hint at how special this restaurant is look no farther than some of the first items on the appetizer list—butter and cauliflower. Really? But this is no ordinary stuff. The "Bread and Butter" offers unusual butters to savor—prosciutto truffle, smoked parmesan black pepper, ginger cashew, and malt vinegar. Although cauliflower is not at the top of many people's favorite veggies, the Etch's roasted cauliflower with truffled pea pesto, salted almonds, red bell sauce, and feta cream is glorious. And you haven't even gotten to the entrees yet. Just imagine those. Opened in 2010 by Nashville favorite chef Deb Paquette, Etch is located on the ground floor of the Encore Tower in the SoBro district. The restaurant features 2 private dining rooms, a full bar, and an open kitchen with bar-style seating. Lunch and dinner are served. Etch offers local and regional craft beers, classic and couture cocktails, and an extensive wine list.

THE FARM HOUSE, 210 Almond St., Nashville, TN 37201; (615) 522-0688; thefarmhousetn.com; $$$$. Opened in 2013, the Farm House serves food exactly as its name describes—straight from the farm. The menu offers traditional Southern cuisine with a contemporary twist. House-cured meat and local ingredients are featured. An example is the popular Springer hot chicken with pickled garlic, potato, and biscuit. Another creative offering is the octopus with seafood sausage, fingerlings, dill, serrano, and beurre blanc. A favorite is the rhubarb and strawberry compote with sweet ricotta and cinnamon crostini. Located in Nashville's SoBro neighborhood, the restaurant decor uses furniture made from repurposed barnwood, barn doors, barn-like ceiling, handcrafted woodwork, handmade accents, and Tennessee heirlooms. Tennessee and regional craft beers are featured, as is a special blend Tennessee wine made specifically for the Farm House, plus high-quality bourbons and a house-flavored moonshine. The Farm House is open Mon through Sat for dinner and Tues through Fri for lunch. Brunch is served on Sun from 10 a.m. to 2 p.m.

GRAY & DUDLEY, 221 Second Ave. N., Nashville, TN 37201; (615) 610-6460; grayanddudley.com; $$$. Opened in 2017, Gray & Dudley is inside the new 21c Museum Hotel Nashville so you know it must be hip. Both its menu and its decor definitely are. The name comes from the building's past life as Gray & Dudley Hardware Company. Among the restaurant's art is a series of ceramic sculptures by Beth Cavener Stichter that combine human and animal traits. Folks usually have to look twice at the unusual sculptures which are certainly conversation starters. The restaurant offers breakfast, brunch, lunch, and dinner. The menu by Executive Chef Rob Newton has choices such as Sunburst Trout with green onions, dill, turmeric, and peanuts; pan-roasted duck breast with apple puree, lemon vinaigrette, and spicy chili crisp; and chicken liver tart with parsley, gooseberries, and almonds. Dessert might require some debating. Cheesecake in a jar with ginger streusel and vanilla-chai gooseberries or Vietnamese coffee cream beignets with dulce de leche crema and powdered sugar? The restaurant serves beer, wine, and cocktails. For creative cocktails, sidle up to the bar and order a specialty such as Damn the Man (Old Forester Signature 100, Montenegro, apple, cinnamon, and bitters) or The Fat Man Walks Alone (Del Maguey Vida, Cocchi di Torino, clove, and rosemary).

GRAY'S ON MAIN, 322 Main St., Franklin, TN 37064; (615) 435-3603; graysonmain.com; $$$. Set in a ca. 1876 Victorian building in Historic Downtown Franklin, Gray's on Main serves Southern cooking with a twist. The restaurant takes its name from the Gray Drug Co., a landmark pharmacy housed in the building for nearly 100 years. Gray's on Main opened in 2013 with a focus on locally and regionally sourced ingredients. On the second floor, a bar and music hall celebrates the brandy culture of the late 19th century. Gray's is a great place to hear some of the area's finest musicians. Diners' favorites include fried pimento cheese balls with moonshine pepper jelly; fried green tomatoes with roasted creamy corn and goat cheese; and bacon-wrapped figs with Benton's bacon, goat cheese, and balsamic reduction. Gray's is open for lunch, dinner, late night, and Sunday brunch.

HARDING HOUSE AT BELLE MEADE PLANTATION, 5025 Harding Rd., Nashville, TN 37205; (615) 356-0096; hardinghousebellemeade.com; $$. A charming restaurant at a historic landmark, Harding House features Southern cooking for lunch and brunch. Fried catfish, meat loaf, shrimp and grits, molasses baked beans, and pimento cheese and green tomato egg rolls are house favorites.

HUSK, 37 Rutledge St., Nashville, TN 37210; (615) 256-6565; husknashville.com; $$$$. The food fairly sings, "farm fresh." A big sign brings that message home even more clearly, showing the various farmers and produce origins. With its simple farm-friendly name, Husk serves Southern food gone modern. Nestled in a charming brick house that was built into the side of a hill in the late 1800s and is much bigger than it looks, Husk concentrates on heirloom grains and vegetables, and they grow much of their own produce in the restaurant's garden. The menu incorporates wood-fired and outdoor cooking. A menu that is updated daily offers such delicious specialties as Bear Creek Farm pork prime rib with Farmer Dave's butternut squash, kale, and spiced peanut. A sweet ending to the meal might include hibiscus and lime pavlova with vanilla wafer and peppermint.

J. ALEXANDER'S, 73 White Bridge Rd., #130, Nashville, TN 37205; (615) 352-0981; jalexanders.com; $$$. J. Alexander's is another local restaurant success story. Since the first J. Alexander's opened on White Bridge Road in 1991, more have popped up all over the country, from San Antonio to Jacksonville, Florida. The publicly traded company has more than 25 locations. J. Alexander's is known for its casual but nice atmosphere, good service, and contemporary American menu. The restaurant has great prime rib, a variety of salads and homemade dressings, flavorful pasta dishes, homemade soups, and made-from-scratch desserts. One of the first restaurants in the area to open its kitchen to the view of diners, it cooks all the grilled products over a hardwood, open grill.

JOHN A'S RESTAURANT, 2421 Music Valley Dr., Nashville, TN 37214; (615) 885-1540; johnasrestaurant.com; $$. Live music and good food make a winning combination at John A's. Started by John Anthony Hobbs, John A's features Southern comfort food like fried chicken livers, fried green tomatoes, fried pickles, catfish, beans and corn bread, and Tennessee pork chops. If those are not what you are craving, the menu also offers steak, prime rib, grilled tuna, salmon filet, and shrimp. A popular item is St. Louis Ribs, named in honor of John A's friend, famed St. Louis baseball great Stan Musial.

MARGOT CAFE & BAR, 1017 Woodland St., Nashville, TN 37206; (615) 227-4668; margotcafe.com; $$$$. If your epicurean fantasies are set in Provence or Tuscany, you'll enjoy dining at Margot, which specializes in rustic French and Italian cuisine. Chef Margot McCormack opened this restaurant in June 2001. It quickly became a hot spot for east Nashville residents, and the buzz spread around town. It's now one of Nashville's *in* places to dine. Housed in a renovated 1930s gas station building in east Nashville's Five Points area, Margot is cozy and vibrant, with brick walls, antique mirrors, and simple, colorful furnishings setting the tone for either a dress-down or dress-up occasion. Margot also has a nice patio for outdoor dining in the summer. The menu changes daily, and there are usually 6 or 7 entree choices. Recent menu samples include buttermilk fried quail with braised Covey Run red mustards, apple, pickled red onion, hot water corn bread, and maple sherry vinaigrette. Dessert includes persimmon pudding, banana Nutella bread pudding, or apple cider sorbet with pecan lace cookie. The restaurant has a nice wine list, with many selections from France and Italy, and about 30 varieties available by the glass. Margot is open for dinner Tues through Sun. Reservations are suggested, especially on weekends.

THE MELTING POT, 166 Second Ave. N., Nashville, TN 37201; (615) 742-4970; meltingpot.com/nashville; $$$$. Voted Best Restaurant in Nashville and Best Place for a Romantic Dinner in a *Nashville Scene* readers' poll, this fondue restaurant is a fun spot when you're in the mood for something a little different for dinner. The atmosphere is relaxed and intimate. Allow

2 hours for the complete Melting Pot experience. The menu is based on courses. Your meal starts with a cheese fondue course, prepared by the server; the cheese course is followed by a salad. For the entree course, you cook your choice of meats or vegetables in the melting pot in the center of the table. Lobster-tails, center-cut fillet, Cajun-rubbed meats, and sausages are just a few of the choices. The final course is the dessert fondue—a variety of chocolate fondues in which you dip pound cake, cheesecake, bananas, strawberries, pineapple, and nutty marshmallows. It's a good idea to have reservations, especially on the very busy Fri and Sat nights. The Melting Pot is open daily for dinner.

THE MERCHANTS, 401 Broadway, Nashville, TN 37203; (615) 254-1892; merchantsrestaurant.com; $$$$. Downtown Nashville's Merchants is a casual fine-dining restaurant that serves American food with a Southern flair. The romantic atmosphere and excellent food make this a good choice for a special dinner. The restaurant occupies 3 floors of a historic building that once housed a pharmacy and hotel. The second floor is the main dining room—it has a more upscale atmosphere and menu than the first floor; the third floor is a banquet space. If you're dining on the second floor, try the pan-seared salmon fillet with caper dill beurre blanc atop a bed of linguine with shrimp and scallops, all enclosed in a pastry net. Lamb chops are a favorite, too. Your tab will be about 50 percent less in the first-floor Casual Bar & Grill, where a popular entree is Johnny Cash's Chili with hot buttered corn bread, cheddar cheese, buttermilk cream, and scallion. Merchants does a brisk weekday lunch business and opens both floors for the lunchtime crowd. The restaurant has a good wine selection. Reservations are recommended for second-floor dining, especially on busy Fri and Sat nights. Merchants is open daily for lunch and dinner.

MIDTOWN CAFÉ, 102 19th Ave. S., Nashville, TN 37203; (615) 320-7176; midtowncafe.com; $$$. This small restaurant just off West End has a devoted following of Insiders who like the eclectic American cuisine and casually elegant atmosphere. At lunch it's a prime spot for high-ranking business lunches, while the dinner crowd ranges from business types to romantic couples, mostly 40-somethings and up. Midtown's crab cakes are great as an appetizer, entree, or sandwich. The fresh catch of the day is always in demand, and the Caesar salad is a lunch favorite. Veal, pasta, steaks, and lamb dishes round out the menu. Midtown has a fantastic wine list, too. The restaurant is open for breakfast and lunch Mon through Fri and for dinner Mon through Sat. Reservations are recommended. Midtown Café offers a free shuttle service for travelers staying in downtown hotels and for locals looking to enjoy dinner and transportation to downtown performances.

MONELL'S, 1235 Sixth Ave., Nashville, TN 37208; (615) 248-4747; monellstn.com; $$. At Monell's on Sixth Avenue you sit at a big table with other guests and enjoy an all-you-can-eat family-style meal. Guests pass bowls and platters of food around the table and serve themselves. The food is Southern, with entrees like meat loaf, fried chicken, and country-fried steak; plenty of fresh vegetables; home-cooked side dishes; biscuits; and corn muffins. The menu changes daily. Monell's original location on Sixth Avenue N. is in Germantown in a renovated Victorian house. Monell's is open for breakfast and lunch daily, for dinner Tues through Sat. A Midnight Country Breakfast is offered on Sat from midnight to 3 a.m. Monell's doesn't serve alcohol, but you can bring your own wine. Seating is first-come, first-served. Cafe Monell's at 2826 Bransford Dr. (615-298-2254) features the same menu, but it's served cafeteria-style. Another location is Monell's at the Manor, 1400 Murfreesboro Pike (615-365-1414).

THE MOCKINGBIRD, 121 12th Ave. N., Nashville, TN 37203; (615) 741-9900; mockingbirdnashville.com; $$$. Described as "a modern diner serving up global fare and delicious fun," The Mockingbird was opened in 2017 by partners Brian Riggenbach and Mikey Corona. If Brian's name sounds familiar, it may be because he was Season 24 winner of the Food Network's show *Chopped*. Located in the Gulch, The Mockingbird boasts a whimsical decor combining an American diner vibe with Mexican and art deco touches. A fun menu features creative small plates, large plates, and sides—all with fun names. For example, the Don't Worry, Be Happy small plate features grilled cheese, whipped brie, jalapeño jam, and chimichurri, while the Tray Chic small plate offers house-cured meat, chicken liver mousse, pastrami, seasonal pickles, and beer mustard. For large plates, try I Eat, Therefore I Ham, a combo of pork porchetta, butternut squash caponata, apple cider demi, and radicchio. Or choose the Poultry in Motion large plate with caramel chicken breast and leg, spicy umami sauce, and Korean fried rice. Cocktails, beer, and wine are available.

PANCAKE PANTRY, 1796 21st Ave. S., Nashville, TN 37212; (615) 383-9333; thepancakepantry.com; $$. While famous as a breakfast place, Pancake Pantry packs 'em in at lunch, too. Southern plate lunches and meat-and-three dishes join more traditional fare like patty melts and BLTs. The pancake list is long and offers such specialties as banana bread pancakes, chocolate pancakes, Smoky Mountain buckwheat pancakes, Caribbean pancakes, apricot-lemon delight pancakes, and much more.

PARK CAFÉ, 4403 Murphy Rd. Nashville, TN 37209; (615) 383-4409; parkcafenashville.com; $$$$. Delicious food, low-key sophistication, and a creative environment have made this restaurant in west Nashville's Sylvan Park neighborhood a favorite. Colorful art and funky accessories adorn the maze of cozy, dimly lit dining rooms. The frequently Asian-inspired menu is equally interesting. It isn't too lengthy, which simplifies the selection process. Favorites include the pan-seared trout with roasted cauliflower, cauliflower puree, pine nut and golden raisin gremolata, and balsamic reduction; salmon with coconut jasmine rice, Szechuan green beans, chile plum sauce, and grilled lime; and the grilled tenderloin with bearnaise sauce, sauteed asparagus, and pommes frites; Park Café's desserts are really too good to share with your dining partner, so if you have a sweet tooth, you'll want to order your own. The crème brûlée Napoleon and warm molten chocolate cakes are always popular. Park Café is open for dinner Mon through Sat. Reservations are suggested but not a must.

THE PIE WAGON NASHVILLE, 1302 Division St., Nashville, TN 37203; (615) 888-4943; $$. This diner has been a favorite among locals for decades. It's been around at least since the early 1920s. It's open for breakfast and lunch only—hours are 7 a.m. to 5 p.m. Mon through Fri.; 11 a.m. to 3 p.m. on weekends. The inexpensive, cafeteria-style cuisine is simple home cookin', or comfort food as some people call it. Lunch entrees might include fried chicken, meat loaf, or grilled catfish, with vegetables and side dishes like real mashed potatoes, green beans, stewed tomatoes, turnip greens, and macaroni and cheese. There's also corn bread and homemade desserts. The friendly counter workers will treat you like family. Nashville's second-oldest restaurant, The Pie Wagon closed its doors in April 2018 but reopened in September 2018 under new owners Nikechia and Rodney Anderson.

PUCKETT'S GROCERY & RESTAURANT, 500 Church St., Nashville, TN 37219; (615) 770-2772; puckettsgro.com; $$. Puckett's is where real people go for real food. Sometimes with a mix of real music thrown in. Puckett's roots go back to the '50s when the Puckett family had a grocery store that just happened to serve food. Or maybe it was the other way around. Anyway, Puckett's found a good thing and doesn't mess with its recipe for success. In 2004, Puckett's opened a place in Franklin (120 Fourth Ave., 615-794-5527). Puckett's has won numerous awards, including Best BBQ in Nashville in the People's Choice Annual BBQ competition. Yep, the menu has barbecue and so much more—fried green beans for appetizer; Whiskey Platter for entrée: grilled Atlantic salmon or chicken breast, brushed with Puckett's signature Tennessee whiskey glaze and served with smashed sweet potatoes and steamed veggies.

Puckett's Grocery & Restaurant in Leiper's Fork has served folks since 1953.
Jackie Sheckler Finch

For dessert, the skillet pecan cobbler topped with Hattie's vanilla ice cream and caramel drizzle is a sweet ending. For breakfast, try Bubba's Eggs Benedict, a split biscuit topped with bacon or sausage, two fried eggs, and white pepper gravy on a bed of home fries. The original Puckett's opened in 1953 in Leiper's Fork and is still going strong (4142 Old Hillsboro Rd., 615-794-1308).

ROLF AND DAUGHTERS, 700 Taylor St., Nashville, TN 37208; (615) 866-9897; rolfanddaughters.com; $$. Opened by Chef Philip Krajeck, this Germantown area restaurant got its name from Philip's middle name Rolf and his daughters. The lofty space features exposed brick, reclaimed wood, and hanging Edison bulbs. In warm weather, the front patio is a popular place to be. Rolf and Daughters offers beer, cocktails, and a nice wine list. The changing menu has featured such goodies as pastured chicken, octopus, beef short rib, heritage pork, beef tongue, and octopus. The homemade pasta draws raves.

SKULL'S RAINBOW ROOM, 222 Printers Alley, Nashville, TN 37201; (615) 810-9631; skullsrainbowroom.com; $$$$. David "Skull" Schulman opened his popular establishment in 1948 and lovingly tended it for five decades. Skull got his nickname after he suffered a fractured skull in an automobile accident. If the walls and performance stage could talk, they have heard and seen legends perform here—Etta James, Elvis Presley, Patsy Cline, Paul McCartney, Bob Dylan, Waylon Jennings, Jerry Lewis, and actor Andy Griffith. In 1998, however, Skull was murdered during a robbery in his beloved club. The Rainbow Room closed and stayed shuttered for almost 17 years. After a three-year major renovation, Skull's Rainbow Club reopened in 2015 under a new ownership group led by Nashville businessman Phil Martin. The room now offers top-rated French American Coastal cuisine, cocktails, jazz music, and classic burlesque. Popular menu items include Boeuf En Croute (rib eye braised in red wine, shallots, and mushrooms, wrapped in brie and puff pastry) and Maple Leaf Farms duck breast pan seared and finished with a wild berry demi-glace. A $20 cover charge is for guests who would just like to see the burlesque show and not purchase dinner. The burlesque shows are offered once a night at 10 p.m. on Wed and Thurs and at 11 p.m. on Fri and Sat.

THE SOUTHERN STEAK & OYSTER, 150 Third Ave. S., Nashville, TN 37201; (615) 724-1762; thesouthernnashville.com; $$$. Located on the first floor of the 29-story Pinnacle tower at Symphony Place, the Southern offers breakfast, lunch, and dinner daily, as well as a bustling bar. The menu features a combination of indigenous flavors and exotic ingredients served in an inviting homelike atmosphere. Get ready for a culinary adventure with a Southern twist. Take time to read the menu for such unusual treats as Bahn Mi Tacos—slow-braised pork belly, pickled daikon, carrot, cucumber, cilantro sprigs, and spicy hoisin served with kimchi. Or try the fish 'n' grits—sea-to-fork catch with stone-ground sweet potato grits, bacon-braised cabbage, and spicy tasso vinaigrette. The Southern has a New Orleans–style shuck-to-order oyster bar and real wood-fired grill powered by salvaged hickory wood. Nestled in Nashville's first LEED-certified high-rise, The Southern follows that green philosophy by using locally grown produce when possible, sustainable seafood, and local beef.

THE STANDARD AT THE SMITH HOUSE, 167 Rosa L. Parks Blvd., Nashville, TN 37203; (615) 254-1277; smithhousenashville.com; $$$$. This 3-story 19th-century brick home features a refined Southern-themed menu. Once a boardinghouse and society club that hosted Nashville's elite, the Standard is a treasure from the past. Magnificently renovated, it offers a cantilevered walnut spiral staircase, chandeliers, Victorian furniture, and a New Orleans–style boardwalk on the side of the house with working gas lamps. The menu offers such treats as bacon-wrapped bacon—White Marble Farms pork, with speckled bean and sweet corn succotash. The Standard is well known for its truffle hash cakes and lump crab bisque. If the Smith House looks familiar, it may be because it starred in a 2004 music video for Alison Krauss and Brad

Paisley's "Whiskey Lullaby." The video won the CMA's Music Video of the Year award.

SUN DINER, 105 Third Ave. S., Nashville, TN 37201; (615) 742-9099; sundinernashville.com; $$. Opened in 2016, Nashville's first 24-hour diner features the history of Sun Records and serves a wide variety of food for those who want breakfast for dinner or dinner for breakfast. The diner spotlights some of the biggest music stars who got their start with Sam Phillips at Sun Records in Memphis. The diner decor and the dishes honor such Sun legends as Elvis Presley, Johnny Cash, Jerry Lee Lewis, Carl Perkins, and Conway Twitty. The Million Dollar Quartet dish salutes Presley, Cash, Lewis, and Perkins with crispy bacon, sausage, hash browns, eggs, fruit, and a choice of toast, pancake, or waffle. The Love Me Tenders are hand-breaded chicken tenders served with fries and a side of ranch dressing. The Cry, Cry, Cry Hot Wings—named for the first major hit record from "The Man in Black"—features one pound of jumbo chicken wings tossed in Sun Diner's signature hot sauce.

SWETT'S RESTAURANT, 2725 Clifton Ave., Nashville, TN 37209; (615) 329-4418; swettsrestaurant.com; $$. Swett's is legendary for its meat-and-three meals. This family-owned restaurant has been serving up Southern food—soul food, if you prefer—since 1954. Diners choose their meat-and-three in a cafeteria line. Entrees, like fried chicken, beef tips, and ham, and a variety of vegetables, including potatoes, corn, and beans, fill the plates. A meat-and-three meal wouldn't be complete without corn bread, and Swett's has some of the best. Dessert choices are many—peach cobbler, pecan pie, chess pie, cheesecake, carrot cake, fudge pie, sweet potato pie, and much more. Swett's is open daily for lunch and dinner.

360 BISTRO, Harper Hills Plaza Shopping Center, 600 Hwy. 100, Nashville, TN 37205; (615) 353-5604; 360bistro.com; $$$$. Chef Joe Townsend is developing a loyal following with his creative flair, unusual ingredients, and glorious creations. An elegant array of entrees ranges from seafood and elk to boar and duck. The menu might change every day, dictated by the freshest seafood, meat, game, and produce. The entire menu is farm driven and made from scratch. A favorite is Alan Bros. beef tenderloin, chive potato puree, brussels sprouts, and mustard demi-glace. Desserts are decadent and excellent. Try the buttermilk pie with grape jam and whipped cream or the sticky toffee pudding with vanilla gelato, fig cheesecake, or cappuccino panna cotta. In addition to an excellent menu, 360 offers more than 100 wines by the glass and was honored with *Wine Spectator's* 2018 Best of Award of Excellence. Try the interesting wine-tasting flights, weekly selections of wine served in 3-ounce tasting portions. The flights are available in light-body reds, full-body reds, light-body whites, and full-body whites.

TIN ANGEL, 3201 West End Ave., Nashville, TN 37203; (615) 298-3444; tinangel.com; $$$. Tin Angel is a casual, cozy bistro-style restaurant that serves contemporary American cuisine with an occasional international twist. One of the few historical landmark buildings left on West End Avenue, the Tin Angel home has lovely brick walls and floors, plus a freestanding fireplace built of brick salvaged from old Church Street. It also has, of course, period tin ceilings. If the place looks familiar it was the setting for Jennifer Nettles's 2016 video of "Unlove You." Favorite dishes include warm goat cheese salad and lobster and shrimp risotto, sauteed with roma tomatoes and basil on lemon herb risotto and fresh spinach. Tin Angel is one of our reliable standbys—good food, good atmosphere, good wine list, and rarely a wait. For dessert, try the apple blackberry crisp, hot from the oven with crumb topping, served with housemade cinnamon ice cream. The dessert is baked to order so allow 15 minutes for preparation. Well worth the wait. Tin Angel serves dinner 7 nights a week.

URBAN GRUB, 2506 Twelfth Ave. S., Nashville, TN 37204; (615) 679-9342; urbangrub.net; $$$. Urban Grub has been drawing happy diners ever since it opened in 2012. With its unusual moniker, Urban Grub is a casual restaurant offering an upscale dining experience. The menu is a combination of Southern traditions with a "flavored-up tweak." Standouts include fresh-shucked oysters, smoked and grilled meat, and a charcuterie that's a meal in itself. Specialties include bacon-wrapped trout with cranberry beans, parmesan, sage, and Meyer lemon; Kentucky lamb chops, and a 24-hour braised andouille pork shank. Dessert choices include vanilla bean donuts with bacon toffee cream cheese ice cream, Whisper Creek caramel, and chocolate-covered bacon or banana pudding pie with shortbread crust, roasted banana cream, vanilla wafer

Urban Grub offers regional specialties.
Jackie Sheckler Finch

crumble, sliced bananas, and toasted vanilla meringue. Urban Grub also offers a good wine list and interesting cocktails. Hard to believe this star on the Music City dining scene was once a car-wash site. The wonderfully designed indoor-outdoor space is a comfy setting for the popular 12 South restaurant.

VARALLO'S CHILE PARLOR & RESTAURANT, 264 Fourth Ave. N., Nashville, TN 37219; (615) 256-1907; varallosnashville.com; $$. Varallo's is run by Todd Varallo, grandson of the legendary Frank Varallo Jr., who for years operated Varallo's on Church Street. Known as Nashville's oldest restaurant, the original location opened in 1907 and was operated by the Varallo family until Frank retired in December 1998. Though Frank and his wife, Eva, are missed, Varallo's Too is still serving up the tasty food that helped make the family famous. The signature item here is "three-way chili," which is a combination of chili, spaghetti, and a tamale originated by Frank Sr. back in the '20s. The daily plate lunch specials feature your choice of meats and vegetables. Favorites like country-fried steak, meatballs, meat loaf, and turkey and dressing are accompanied by fresh "creamed" potatoes, turnip greens, broccoli casserole, and squash casserole. Homemade peach or blackberry cobbler and banana pudding are among the great ways to end a meal here. If you come for breakfast, you can order what Eva Varallo describes as the best hotcakes in town (made from her own recipe, of course), along with the usual bacon, eggs, and biscuits. Varallo's serves breakfast and lunch daily; closed weekends.

WOOLWORTH ON FIFTH, 221 Fifth Ave. N., Nashville, TN 38219; (615) 891-1361; woolworthonfifth.com; $. Part of the Fifth Avenue Historic District, Woolworth was built in the 1890s, became a Woolworth Five and Dime store in 1913, and has been an eyewitness and participant in Nashville's dramatic history. The Jim Crow laws of the 1890s prohibited African Americans from eating at these public lunch counters. But change began on February 13, 1960, when a group of mainly college students from local black universities walked into Woolworth, Kress, and McClellan downtown lunch counters, sat down, and asked to be served. It didn't work. But the students and activists

Woolworth on Fifth is known for its fried chicken and veggies. Jackie Sheckler Finch

didn't stop. Instead they kept walking in, sitting down, and ordering food. In fact, US Congressman John Lewis's first arrest—in a long career of being arrested almost 50 times for nonviolent protest—took place while sitting in at this Woolworth lunch counter. Today, after a major renovation and restoration, a new Woolworth on Fifth opened in February 2018 to honor its history "by serving as a welcome table for all." Civil rights photos and memorabilia add to the historic feeling. A continuous loop of old song and dance plays on a big movie screen while the restaurant serves breakfast, lunch, and dinner. Menu items include such standard Southern favorites as sweet potato pancakes with sweet bourbon butter and Vermont maple syrup; crispy pork belly; hot fried chicken skin with heirloom carrots, dill pickle, shaved celery salad, crumbled blue cheese, and ranch dressing; shrimp and grits; and pot roast. Folks often come for the history and keep returning for the comforting cuisine.

YELLOW PORCH, 734 Thompson Ln., Nashville, TN 37204; (615) 386-0260; theyellowporch.com; $$$$. More than one potential diner has zoomed past this tiny yellow cottage, which is tucked between a gas station and a row of strip malls on a busy thoroughfare across from 100 Oaks Mall. That's their loss: Yellow Porch offers exquisite continental/fusion cuisine and an excellent wine list, all served in a subdued, dimly lit room that invites friendly conversation and romance. The menu is versatile and creative, often blending disparate elements into a unique signature dish. While the menu often leans toward Asian or Mediterranean inspirations, classic entrees like pork chops and chicken are given their due as well. The menu changes often as seasonal ingredients become available—all the more reason to keep coming back. Yellow Porch is open Mon through Sat for lunch and dinner.

ASIAN

ASAHI JAPANESE SUSHI BAR, 5133 Harding Pike, Nashville, TN 37205; (615) 352-8877; $$. Asahi serves some of the freshest and most delicious sushi and Japanese dishes in town. If you're not a sushi eater, try one of the teriyaki bento boxes. The tempura is great, too. Beer, wine, and several types of sake are available. This relaxed and friendly restaurant is in the Belle Meade area, at the corner of Harding Road and Harding Place. Asahi is open daily for dinner, and Mon through Sat for lunch.

INTERNATIONAL MARKET & RESTAURANT, 2010 Belmont Blvd., Nashville, TN 37212; (615) 297-4453; internationalnashville.com; $. International Market is one of those real "Insider" places that's really off the beaten path for most tourists. Popular with students at nearby Belmont University, as well as with Music Row workers and residents from the Hillsboro-Belmont-Vandy areas, this cafeteria-style restaurant has been serving Thai and other Asian food since 1975. It's fresh and affordable—you can get a satisfying meal for $10 or less. The buffet features more than two dozen items, including mild to extra-spicy beef, chicken, and pork dishes; rice; egg rolls; and soup. Beverages include bottled beers and juices from the cooler, jasmine tea, and sodas. Next to the seating area are shelves stocked with mostly Asian cooking items—bottles of soy, hoisin, and chile sauces; cans of curry paste and coconut milk; packages of noodles; and boxes of tea—as well as ceramic teapots and bowls and a few gift items. International Market is open daily for lunch and dinner.

TANSUO, 121B 12th Ave. N., Nashville, TN 37203; (615) 782-6786; tansuonashville.com; $$$. Meaning "to explore" in Cantonese, Tansuo invites guests to explore contemporary Chinese cuisine served for lunch and dinner. Menu specialties include dim sum choices of lamb dumplings (ground lamb, cumin, scallions, and seasoned soy sauce), Toishan Sui Mai (open-face pork dumplings, salted fish, crab paste, and seasoned soy sauce), and Sesame Golden Eggs (soft rice dough, shiitake mushrooms, silken tofu, sesame seeds, and chile oil). Main entrees are Peking Duck, General Tso's Chicken, Hong Kong Style Cumin Short Ribs, Shanghai Red Pork Shank, and much more. Tansuo is located in the Gulch.

BAKERY/CAFE

BONGO JAVA CAFE, 119 Third St. S., Nashville, TN 37201; (615) 256-1777; johnnycashmuseum.com; $. When visiting this new museum honoring the "Man in Black," stop by the Bongo Java Café in the museum to taste Johnny Cash's Iron Pot Chili made from a recipe created by the man himself. The cafe also offers a delicious assortment of pastries and baked goods as well as sandwiches, salads, and, of course, Bongo Java coffee. Unusual menu items include a fried bologna and pimento cheese sandwich and The Elvis, which features The King's favorite peanut butter, honey, bananas, and bacon served on honey wheat bread. The museum and cafe are open daily from 9 a.m. to 6 p.m.

BREAD & COMPANY, 2525 West End Ave., Nashville, TN 37204; (615) 292-7323; breadandcompany.com; $$. Nashville traditionally has been associated more with biscuits than with baguettes, but when Anne Clay and her son, John Clay III, opened the European-style Bread & Company bakery in November 1992, they were welcomed enthusiastically. The bakery introduced many Nashvillians to hearth-baked, crusty breads. Now we're positively addicted. Bread & Company bakes about 18 different breads, including the always-popular light sourdough farm bread; pane paisano, a round loaf perfect for tearing apart and dipping into olive oil; and the dense and chewy raisin-pecan. The stores also sell outstanding gourmet sandwiches. A rotating trio of daily soup offerings always includes the popular tomato-basil. The busy cafe also has a daily breakfast bar, where you can get made-to-order omelets, pancakes, waffles, and other morning meals. Bread & Company has gourmet packaged foods and takeout, which can come in very handy for last-minute dinner parties (no one needs to know that you didn't make that Waldorf salad yourself) or for those evenings when you just don't want to cook. Bread & Company is open daily for breakfast, lunch, and dinner; on Sun for breakfast and lunch. Breakfast is served all day for those late risers or folks who just love breakfast no matter the time.

CAFÉ LULA AT THE RYMAN, 116 Fifth Ave. N., Nashville, TN 37219; (615) 458-8760; cafelula.net; $. Named in honor of Lula C. Naff, the long-time manager of the Ryman, Café Lula offers a nice menu for a quick snack or a leisurely entree. Choices include Nashville hot chicken, chipotle seared salmon, coffee-crusted pork chop, pulled pork, fish of the day, and much more. The 1892 Burger honors the year the Ryman was built and is a tasty combo of 1/3 pound lean Angus beef with coriander mustard, cheddar, lettuce greens, tomato, and pickles. A full bar features local brews, wine, and cocktails, along with a daily happy hour from 3 to 5 p.m. Located in the heart of the Music Center universe, Café Lula is a great people-watching site. Situated right outside the front doors of the Ryman Auditorium, Café Lula has floor-to-ceiling windows to see the action on Broadway. Or choose a seat on the covered porch. Café Lula is open daily 9 a.m. to 5 p.m. with extended hours when there are events at the Ryman.

CITY LIMITS BAKERY & CAFE, 361 Clofton Dr., Nashville, TN 37221; (615) 646-0062; citylimitsbakerycafe.com; $$. If you can get past the beautiful, tempting pastries, sweet rolls, cookies, and brownies lined up under the glass case at this cozy, upbeat cafe, you'll find that there are quite a few good sandwiches and salads on the menu. By now that's no secret to Bellevue residents, who have been packing in ever since the restaurant opened in early 2002. Located in a strip shopping center at Old Harding and Clofton, next to the railroad tracks, the colorful and comfortable cafe has about 20 tables indoors and a few outside on the sidewalk. There's also a tiny sitting area with sofas and chairs—just the spot for an afternoon cappuccino. Place your order at the

> Nashville-based Tomkats Catering has come a long way since it started more than 20 years ago with one truck labeled Ricky Ricardo's Chili Express. The company has catered more than 500 motion pictures and served diet requests from such stars as Sandra Bullock, Nicole Kidman, Gwyneth Paltrow, Matthew McConaughey, and Colin Farrell.

counter, get a table, and you can pick up your food a few minutes later when your number is called. City Limits Cafe is open daily for breakfast and lunch.

CREMA, 15 Hermitage Ave., Nashville, TN 37204; (615) 255-8311; crema-coffee.com; $. The delicious aromas wafting from this coffeehouse on Rutledge Hill are a great way to wake up or provide a quick pick-me-up at any time of day or night. Crema got its name from the foamy, golden-brown elixir that develops in the filter and encrusts the top of an espresso. Every week Crema features a new coffee along with favorite regulars such as cappuccino, cafe au lait, tea, mate chai, cider (seasonal), and hot cocoa. Cold drinks include iced coffee, juices, and soft drinks. To go with the drinks, sweet choices include mile-high muffins, croissants, cookies, cakes, cheesecakes, and biscotti. Crema also serves bagels, quiche, and sandwiches. Crema at Pinewood Social is also open at 33 Peabody St., pinewoodsocial.com.

BARBECUE

BAR-B-CUTIE, 5221 Nolensville Rd., Nashville, TN 37211; (615) 834-6556; bar-b-cutie.com; $$. Hickory pit barbecue is the specialty at Bar-B-Cutie, a Nashville favorite since 1948. Barbecue and ribs are most in demand here, but the restaurant also serves a good mesquite-grilled chicken sandwich as well as turkey and roast beef. Barbecue plates come with 2 side items and bread. This is a no-alcohol, family-style restaurant. The dining room is busy, and the restaurant does a brisk takeout and drive-through business, too. Bar-B-Cutie is open daily for lunch and dinner. Other locations are at 501 Donelson Pike (615-872-0207); 8456 Hwy. 100 (615-646-1114); 805 Old Fort Pkwy. (615-217-8883); 326 Harding Place, Suite I (615-454-3454); 1203 Murfreesboro Rd. in Franklin (615-784-9454); and 2037 N. Mt. Juliet Rd. in Mt. Juliet (615-733-5995).

CARL'S PERFECT PIG BAR-B-QUE, 4991 US 70E, White Bluff, TN 37187; (615) 797-4020; carlsperfectpig.com. $$. We've been tempted to keep Carl's Perfect Pig under our hats, but now that the unassuming little country restaurant has been featured on an Emeril Lagasse–hosted special on cable TV's Food Network, we might as well just come clean. The truth is, we'd be hard-pressed to find any better barbecue or ribs around these parts than the old-fashioned, open-pit kind that's cooked and served up at the Perfect Pig. Located about 30 minutes west of Nashville in the rural community of White Bluff, the restaurant also is a favorite stop for catfish, fried chicken, and "country vegetables" like pinto beans (served with corn cakes), yellow squash and cheese, baked beans, turnip greens, potato salad, and coleslaw. Carl's Perfect Pig is open Wed through Sat for lunch and early dinners and for lunch on Sun. If you plan to visit on a Sunday, you'll want to get there before the after-church crowd arrives, unless you don't mind waiting in line for a table.

HOG HEAVEN, 115 27th Ave. N., Nashville, TN 37203; (615) 329-1234; hogheavenbbq.com; $$. Hog Heaven doesn't look like much—it's a tiny white cinder-block building tucked in a corner of Centennial Park behind McDonald's—but once you taste their barbecue, you'll understand the name of the place. This is some good eatin'. Hog Heaven's hand-pulled pork, chicken, beef, and turkey barbecue is pretty famous among Nashville's barbecue connoisseurs. The menu is posted on a board beside the walk-up window. After you get your order, you might want to hop on over to Centennial Park and dig in, since the only seating at the restaurant is a couple of picnic tables on a slab of concrete right in front of the window. You can order barbecue sandwiches, barbecue plates that come with 2 side orders, and barbecue by the pound. The white barbecue sauce is just right on top of the chicken, and the regular sauce comes in mild, hot, or extra hot. Quarter-chicken and half-chicken orders are available, and Hog Heaven has spareribs, too. Barbecue beans, potato salad, coleslaw, turnip greens, white beans, green beans, black-eyed peas, and corn on the cob are among the side dishes. The homemade cobbler is a heavenly way to end a meal here. The restaurant is open Mon through Sat for lunch and dinner.

JACK'S BAR-B-QUE, 416 Broadway, Nashville, TN 37203; (615) 254-5715; jacksbarbque.com; $$. Jack Cawthon opened his first barbecue restaurant in 1976 after studying in the barbecue hot spots of Memphis, Atlanta, Texas, Kentucky, and the Carolinas. Today he satisfies Nashville's appetite for barbecue at 3 locations and is also known for his catering (some of Music City's biggest stars have called on Jack's for that). The Broadway location backs up to the historic Ryman Auditorium, and diners there can sit on Jack's Backdoor

Patio, in view of the Ryman's backstage door. Jack's serves Tennessee pork shoulder, ribs cut St. Louis–style, Texas beef brisket, smoked turkey and chicken, and Texas sausage. Side items include baked beans, potato salad, and coleslaw. For dessert, try the chess pie, chocolate fudge pie, and brownies. Beer is available. Jack's is open daily for lunch and dinner. Other locations are at 334 W. Trinity Ln. (615-228-9888) and 1601 Charlotte Ave. (615-341-0157).

WHITT'S BARBECUE, 5211 Alabama Ave., Nashville, TN 37209; (615) 385-1553; whittsbarbecue.com: $$. Whitt's has been serving barbecue to Nashvillians for more than 2 decades. It has been voted the No. 1 barbecue restaurant time after time in local publications' readers' polls. You can count on speedy service and quality barbecue that's been slow-cooked over hickory coals and topped off with a vinegar-based sauce. Whitt's serves pork, turkey, and beef barbecue in sandwiches or on plates. The plate portions are huge and come with 2 side items and rolls or corn bread. Whitt's miniature chess, fudge, and pecan pies are the perfect after-meal treat. Whitt's is open Mon through Sat for lunch and dinner. Whitt's has about a dozen Nashville-area locations, as well as restaurants in Clarksville, Springfield, and other areas of Middle Tennessee. Some locations have dine-in areas; all have drive-through windows. Other locations are at 5310 Harding Rd. (615-356-3435); 3621 Nolensville Rd. (615-831-0309); 4601 Andrew Jackson Pkwy., Hermitage (615-885-4146); 2535 Lebanon Pike, Donelson (615-883-6907); and 105 Sulphur Springs Rd., Murfreesboro (615-890-0235).

BREAKFAST

LOVELESS CAFE, 8400 Hwy. 100, Nashville, TN 37221; (615) 646-9700; lovelesscafe.com; $$. The legendary Loveless Cafe is the real thing: country cookin' just like Grandma's. Take it from a Southerner who spent half her childhood at her grandparents' farm, where there was always a plate full of fluffy white biscuits sitting atop a dish of greasy bacon and sausage in the kitchen. The meals were Southern and country—always plenty of fried food and bowls of hot gravy. The Loveless always brings back memories of Granny's house. The Loveless is open daily for breakfast, lunch, and dinner. We're partial to the Southern-style breakfasts, which are served all day. Choose from eggs, omelets, sausage, bacon, grits, waffles, and pancakes—all served with plates full of biscuits, bowls of gravy, and homemade blackberry and peach preserves. If you don't know the difference in the types of gravy offered (and we've learned there are many of you in this boat), take note: Cream gravy is the creamy white kind made with milk, flour, and bacon or sausage drippings; redeye gravy is made

Loveless Café Courtesy of Tennessee Department of Tourist Development

from ham drippings and black coffee instead of milk. If you're planning to come here on a Saturday or Sunday, you'll want to call a day or two ahead and make reservations. While you're waiting to be seated, check out some of the photos of celebrities who have dined here.

NOSHVILLE DELICATESSEN, 4014 Hillsboro Cir., Nashville, TN 37215; (615) 269-3535; noshville.com; $$. This New York–style deli is famous for its enormous sandwiches, but it also serves a good breakfast. Assorted bagels and cream cheeses, plus eggs, omelets, griddle cakes, assorted toasts, and cereal satisfy just about any morning appetite. Read more about Noshville in the Deli section of this chapter. The deli is open daily but closes early, at 2:30 p.m., on Mon, Tues, and Wed.

PANCAKE PANTRY, 1796 21st Ave. S., Nashville, TN 37212; (615) 383-9333; thepancakepantry.com; $$. The Pancake Pantry has been a Nashville breakfast tradition for decades. Locals are willing to stand in line as long as it takes to get a table and a stack of pancakes at this Hillsboro Village restaurant. The line usually snakes out the door and down the sidewalk. Urns of complimentary hot coffee are a welcome warmer during wintertime waits. Once inside, the longtime waitresses will make you feel right at home. In addition to a variety of pancakes, you'll find all the familiar breakfast foods on the menu.

The busy restaurant is known to draw celebrities regularly, so you'll never know who might occupy the table next to you (try not to stare). The Pancake Pantry is open daily for breakfast and lunch. Parking is free behind the Pancake Pantry but motorists must obtain and place a receipt on the vehicle dashboard. Receipts can be obtained from a machine at the entrance to the lot. Press 1 for 1.5 hours of free parking to dine at Pancake Pantry.

i The Demonbreun Street area adjacent to Music Row, once lined with country music museums and gift shops, has been redeveloped and resurrected into an upscale live music and dining destination.

PFUNKY GRIDDLE, 2800 Bransford Ave., Nashville, TN 37204; (615) 298-2088; thepfunkygriddle.com; $$. Located in a tiny cottage, the Pfunky Griddle lets you create the pancake of your dreams. Custom-made fireproof tables with built-in griddles are ready and waiting for you to mix and stir up a unique pancake. Be aware that this is a cook-your-own place. When you order pancakes, you get a pitcher of batter and choice of toppings—berries, chocolate chips, nuts, M&Ms, and the like. If you want French toast, you get a bowl of eggs and milk sprinkled with cinnamon and a plate of sliced wheat loaf. If you order eggs, that's what you get—ready for you to cook. If the pancakes seem to taste better here, part of it could be the special batter—hand ground from scratch using whole wheat, cornmeal, buckwheat, rye, and brown-rice flours for the 5-grain recipe, and unbalanced, unbromated enriched white flour for the old-time mix. The Pfunky Griddle also serves sandwiches and salads. If the name sounds strange, chalk it up to the owner Penelope Pfuntner. All in all, it's a pfun place. A second location is at 525 N. Thompson Ln. in Murfreesboro (615-410-2980). Open Tues through Sun for breakfast and lunch.

STAR BAGEL CAFE, Sylvan Park, 4504 Murphy Rd., Nashville, TN 37209; (615) 292-7993; starbagelcafe.com; $. Star Bagel has some of the best bagels in town. There are all sorts of yummy ones to choose from here. Plain bagels and multigrain are two of the most ordered varieties, but there are also cinnamon-raisin swirl, sun-dried tomato, wild blueberry, and egg bagels. Star Bagel's cream cheeses include light plain, wild blueberry, light spicy cucumber, herb and garlic, olive pimento, and the ever-popular honey walnut raisin. If a heartier breakfast is in order, you can top your bagel with any combination of eggs, bacon, salami, and cheese. For lunch, order from the menu of deli sandwiches such as hot pastrami and Swiss, roast beef and cheddar, and tuna melt—or create your own sandwich. Star Bagel is open every day from 6 a.m. to 5 p.m.

BURGERS

BROWN'S DINER, 2102 Blair Blvd., Nashville, TN 37212; (615) 269-5509; $. This weathered building, an expanded dining car, is a genuine tavern—what you might call a dive. But it serves what many people consider the best cheeseburger in town. Plenty of seating is available in the dining room, where there's a big-screen TV. But the real atmosphere is in the dark bar (beer only), a popular hangout for songwriters, businesspeople, and regular working folk, with a TV that's generally tuned to a sports event. Chili dogs, fried fish, and a few sandwiches are among the other menu items, but the burger with fries is really your best bet. This is real Nashville at its most unpretentious. Brown's is open daily for lunch and dinner.

FAT MO'S, 2620 Franklin Rd., Nashville, TN 37204; (615) 298-1111; fatmos.com; $$. Insiders may disagree about who has the best burger in Nashville, but there's no argument about who has the biggest. When your ads and signs proclaim "the biggest burgers in town!" you have to deliver, and this popular establishment offers the Fat Mo's Super Deluxe Burger, more than 27 ounces of fresh beef cooked up in 3 patties and topped with grilled mushrooms and onions, barbecue sauce, bacon, and jalapeños—enough to feed the whole family. Those with less hearty appetites (or smaller families) can choose from burgers of only 16 or 8 ounces; even the Little Mo's Burger weighs in at 5 ounces, which is bigger than a Quarter Pounder, and it's cooked fresh. There are several more locations throughout the area where you can indulge. Other sandwiches include fried and grilled chicken, catfish, roast beef, hot dogs, and corn dogs. Fat Mo's also has fries in "plain" and "spicy" varieties, onion rings, cheese sticks, fried mushrooms, and stuffed jalapeños. And be sure to save room for an old-fashioned milkshake, ice cream cone, or sundae. While you'll have to wait several minutes for your order, you'll find the difference between Fat Mo's and fast-food burgers to be well worth it. The restaurants are open daily for lunch and dinner. Check the website for numerous other locations around the Nashville area.

HUGH BABY'S, 4816 Charlotte Ave., Nashville, TN 37209; (615) 610-3340; hughbabys.com; $. Named after founder Pat Martin's uncle "Hugh Baby" Coleman, the fast-food joint opened in August 2017 in West Nashville.

Hugh Baby's features great burgers and nostalgia. With a capacity of 67 guests, Hugh Baby's has a simple bright decor with red, turquoise, and white colors. A smiling pig mascot welcomes guests with a high-five and is already a popular selfie spot. The covered patio has green turf, picnic tables and benches, plus tables and chairs, and a small playground for kids. The menu features burgers, barbecue, hot dogs, milkshakes, and fries. On Fridays only, Hugh Baby's offers a "delicacy" made famous in Corinth, Mississippi—a Slugburger, a combo of ground pork and soy meal deep fried and served with pickles, chopped onions, and mustard. A Depression-era favorite, Slugburgers had soy grits, flour, or another cheap non-meat filler added as an "extender" to take the place of costlier ground pork or beef. Slugburgers were originally sold for a nickel or a "slug" which is where the burgers got their name, although children still like to joke that they are eating real slug worms. Hugh Baby's has proven so popular that there is now another Nashville location, opened in April 2018 at 3001 West End Ave. (615-610-3382).

BOLTON'S SPICY CHICKEN & FISH, 624 Main St.; Nashville, TN 37206; (615) 254-8015; boltonsspicy.com; $$. This east Nashville roadside stand is the only one that offers fish as well as hot chicken. The recipe is reportedly based on Prince's famous concoction—the proprietor's uncle once worked at Prince's and for decades operated a now-shuttered famous rival, Columbo's. Since the food is not quite as spicy as the others, you might dare to up the heat level a notch. It's still plenty hot, though. Bolton's has another stand at 2309-A Franklin Place (615-383-1421).

HATTIE B'S HOT CHICKEN, 112 Nineteenth Ave. S., Nashville, TN 37203; (615) 678-4794; hattieb.com; $$. Opened in 2012, Hattie B's gives you fair warning what to expect: Southern means no heat; mild is a touch of burn; hot makes you feel the heat; damn hot is a fire starter; and Shut the Cluck Up is top-level burn notice. Pickle slices and white bread can help relieve the burn. Southern sides include black-eyed pea salad, greens, pimento mac and cheese, and coleslaw. Banana pudding is a sweet ending to a hot meal. Hattie B's has

Hattie B's serves mild to very spicy Nashville hot chicken. Jackie Sheckler Finch

Close-up

Hot Chicken Comes Home to Roost

Perhaps one of the oddest food trends to hit an American city in recent years has been the, well, explosion of hot chicken restaurants in Nashville. In fact, this particular variety of Southern food is so, er, sizzling, that a new eatery seems to open up every few months or so. It's fair to say that hot chicken has positively burst upon the scene here.

Okay, enough with the bad puns. What is hot chicken, you may wonder? This is a unique brand of fried chicken that's highly seasoned, some would say to incendiary proportions. When we say this stuff is hot, trust us—it's positively flameworthy. The chicken is served Southern-style, on a slice of white bread; the bread soaks up all the spicy chicken juices and is one of the best parts about eating a hot chicken dinner. The usual accompaniment to all this spicy fried deliciousness is a side of dill pickles, baked beans, and potato salad. It's all washed down with sweet tea.

Hattie B's Courtesy of Nashville Convention & Visitors Corporation

Most hot chicken restaurants are little more than shacks with devoted proprietors who passionately guard their hot chicken recipes, and most operate on a takeout–only basis. It's best to call and order ahead at these places to avoid long waits. Here are a couple of our very favorites.

both indoor and outdoor seating. Be prepared for long lines. In 2014, Hattie B's opened another location at 5209 Charlotte Ave. (615-712-7137). Another Hattie B's is at 2222 Eighth Ave. (615-970-3010).

PRINCE'S HOT CHICKEN SHACK, 423 Ewing Dr., #3, Nashville, TN 37207; (615) 226-9442; princeshotchicken.com; $$. The pioneer of Nashville hot chicken, Prince's was started by Thornton J. Prince III. According to legend, back in the 1930s Prince came home from a night of catting around to find his girlfriend fixing him a Sunday dinner of fried chicken. To get revenge on her cheating lover, the gal dumped a hefty helping of hot spices on the chicken. The plot backfired. Prince loved the hot chicken so much that he refined the recipe and opened a restaurant. The hole-in-the-wall joint with about a half dozen tables is located in the middle of a strip mall. Look for the long lines. Prince's offers four degrees of heat—mild, medium, hot, and extra hot. The chicken is cooked when ordered in cast-iron skillets, so the wait is seldom short but loyal diners say it's worth it. Another location, Prince's Hot Chicken Shack South is at 5814 Nolensville Pike (615-810-9388). Closed Sun.

ROTIER'S RESTAURANT, 2413 Elliston Place, Nashville, TN 37203; (615) 327-9892; rotiersrestaurant.com; $$. Rotier's—part old-timey diner, part burger joint, part tavern—has Nashville's most legendary burgers. Their cheeseburger has been voted the city's best in local readers' polls for going on a decade. First-timers here might be surprised to see that the burgers are served on French bread instead of buns, so they look more like sandwiches. For the full Rotier's experience, you must have a chocolate shake with your burger. Rotier's is also known for their old-fashioned plate lunches and dinners. Closed Sun.

CAJUN/CREOLE

BRO'S CAJUN CUISINE, 3214 Charlotte Ave., Nashville, TN 37209; (615) 329-2626; broscajun.com; $$. Bro's location has changed a few times in recent years, but the delicious food is still the same. Gumbo, red beans and rice, crawfish étouffée, fried catfish on Friday—all the favorites are still on the menu. (And the rolls of paper towels are still on the tables.) Bro's is one of those Insiders' favorites that has a devoted following. The affable owner, Darrell Breaux of Lafayette, Louisiana, cooks up authentic Cajun foods with just the right amount of spice. From Oct 15 to Dec 24, the restaurant sells deep-fried turkeys, injected with onions and seasonings. Bro's is open for lunch Mon through Thurs until about 3 p.m.; on Fri, Bro's is open until 8 p.m., and on Sat from 4 to 8. Closed Sun.

CARIBBEAN

CALYPSO CAFE, 3307 Charlotte Ave., Nashville, TN 37209; (615) 356-1678; calypsocafe; $$. Calypso Cafe puts a fresh, flavorful Caribbean spin on Nashville's traditional meat-and-vegetable plates. At Calypso, the meat is rotisserie chicken with spicy, all-natural Caribbean barbecue or mild Jamaican curry sauce, while the vegetable choices include Cuban black beans, flavorful mustard greens with tomatoes and onions, spiced sweet potatoes topped with coconut, and bean and corn salad. Caribbean sweet corn bread–coconut muffins are a delicious alternative to traditional Southern corn bread. Calypso Cafe also serves a variety of sandwiches, salads with homemade dressings, and desserts. Don't forget to get some refreshing fruit tea, which comes with seemingly endless refills. Calypso Cafe has a small kids' menu and is a great place for takeout. The restaurants are open daily for lunch and dinner. Calypso Cafe is also located at 301 Gallatin Ave. (615-227-6133) and at 700 Thompson Ln. (615-297-3888).

CATFISH

COCK OF THE WALK, 2624 Music Valley Dr., Nashville, TN 37214; (615) 889-1930; cockofthewalkrestaurant.com; $$. This catfish restaurant in the Opryland/Music Valley area has been a favorite since it opened in the mid-1980s. Many Nashvillians consider the catfish here some of the best around. The large restaurant is themed to the early-19th-century riverboat days, and the staff dresses in period attire. Meals are served on tin plates and in tin cups. The servers, dressed as keelboatmen, flip corn bread in iron skillets. If you're not in the mood for catfish, try the chicken, shrimp, or steak. The restaurant is open for dinner Mon through Sun and also serves lunch on Sun.

RIVERVIEW RESTAURANT & MARINA, 110 Old River Rd., Ashland City, TN 37015; (615) 792-7358; riverviewrestaurantandmarina.com; $$. The dockside restaurant on the Cumberland River has been serving up catfish since the 1970s. Today, the menu includes shrimp, steak, fish, pork, chicken, crab cakes, and much more. During the summer, the deck is a hot destination. For a sweet treat, try the blackberry wine cake.

DELI/PASTRY

NOSHVILLE DELICATESSEN, 4014 Hillsboro Cir., Nashville, TN 37215; (615) 269-3535; noshville.com; $$. Nashvillians enthusiastically welcomed the arrival of Noshville, an authentic New York deli that became an instant favorite. Noshville serves tasty, high-quality food in a lively atmosphere. It's a fun place, and the sandwiches are huge. Meats are piled high. A bowl of kosher pickles on the table makes everything complete. Noshville also serves a selection of soups, salads, and entrees like homemade meat loaf, corned beef and cabbage, and pot roast served with a vegetable and choice of potato. There are several smoked fish platters available and plenty of juices, specialty coffees, and desserts. Noshville is open for breakfast and lunch on Mon, Tues, and Wed; for breakfast, lunch, and dinner Thur through Sun.

FRENCH

MARCHÉ ARTISAN FOODS, 1000 Main St., Nashville, TN 37206; (615) 262-1111; marcheartisanfoods.com; $$$. Located in East Nashville, this charming cafe is a popular place for breakfast and brunch. Chef Margot McCormack is at the helm, so you know the food is a treat. Initially started as a gourmet food market, Marché soon added dining, and a sit-down cafe was born. The French-inspired menu changes monthly to spotlight seasonal ingredients. The soup and dinner omelets vary nightly. An excellent first course is the market salad with plums, goat cheese, almonds, and white balsamic vinaigrette. A wonderful second course is the pan-seared sockeye salmon with sweet corn–potato hash, shiitake, and grilled green onion. The menu suggests wine or high-gravity beer pairings for every dish. In season, the mussels and littleneck clams in a fennel bacon and cream sauce are rich and tasty. Take time to browse around Marché and enjoy take-home treats such as pastries and prepared foods. The shabby chic atmosphere is casual and comfortable.

MIEL, 343 53rd Ave. N., Nashville, TN 37209; (615) 298-3663; mielrestaurant.com; $$$. "Miel" means "honey" in French, and this is definitely a sweet spot. Opened in 2008 in the historic Johnson's Meat Market building in Sylvan Park, Miel features an open kitchen and a lovely landscaped garden patio. If the heirloom vegetables and salad greens taste unbelievably fresh, they are. Many are grown just 10 minutes from the restaurant on Miel's Farm alongside the Cumberland River. The farm is also the restaurant's compost site for a commitment to organic farming and sustainable agricultural practices. Owner Seema Prasad preserved the market's 1940s character of high ceilings and added benches from the old Franklin Courthouse in the 2 dining rooms. A fantastic French menu offers such favorites as butter-poached squid with cucumber mignonette, preserved horseradish, and Mutsu apples and and foie gras pan seared with apricots and Banyuls-maple gastrique. The bouillabaisse is scrumptious with plenty of prawns, scallops, mussels, and fish in saffron, tomato, and country sausage stew. Many diners go straight for the risotto with country ham, stewed greens, and Parmigiano-Reggiano with a poached farm egg and scallops. The roasted plum cake with brown sugar buttercream or profiteroles with dark chocolate-bourbon ganache are wonderful endings to a special meal.

PENINSULA, 1035 Eastland Ave., Nashville, TN 37206; (615) 679-0377; peninsulanashville.com; $$$. Hard to describe but easy to enjoy, Peninsula offers Spanish and Portuguese fare accented with French techniques. Serving lunch and dinner, Peninsula features a seasonal menu that changes weekly. The meat-heavy menu by Executive Chef Jake Howell (who also offers some vegetarian dishes) has featured such creative treats as pork with clams and cabbage, braised rabbit with garlic broth and calabrese pepper, and lemon pepper chicken gizzards. Peninsula serves beer, wine, and cocktails. Opened October 2017, Peninsula got its name as a nod to the Iberian Peninsula where great food is a long tradition. The restaurant features floor-to-ceiling glass windows, a wrought iron chandelier, carved wooden panels, and a bar top inlaid with lovely painted tiles.

GERMAN

BAVARIAN BIERHAUS, 121 Opry Mills Dr., Nashville, TN 37214; (615) 238-0687; bierhausnashville.com; $$. Opened in 2017 in Opry Mills, the restaurant is the dream of two former Army buddies who were deployed to Germany and enjoyed its culture, food, and beer. The 15,000-square-foot massive bierhall brings a touch of Bavaria to Music City. The bierhall offers 500 seats inside and 120 seats in the biergarten outside as well as a large private dining room for 100 guests. Authentic German bands entertain and encourage

> i The Martha White brand of cooking products isn't a fictitious advertising symbol. There was a real Martha, and she was the daughter of Richard Lindsey, who founded Royal Flour Mill in Nashville in 1899. Lindsey named his finest flour after his little girl.

visitors to dance and to toast with their beer steins. Bavarian Bierhaus offers 12 Bavarian beers on tap as well as other German brews in bottles. Menu favorites are chicken schnitzel, currywurst, Reubens, potato pancakes, Black Forest cake, and apple strudel. A children's menu is also available.

VON ELROD'S, 1004 Fourth Ave. N., Nashville, TN 37219; (615) 866-1620; vonelrods.com; $. Nothing fancy here. Just good beer and sausages in a beer garden setting. Opened in October 2017 in the old Trailblazer Station bus depot in Germantown, Von Elrod's is massive with an open floor plan, covered patio, and beer garden. The name comes from founder Austin Elrod Ray who visited Oktoberfest in Munich and dreamed of opening something like that in Nashville. Guests sit at long community tables and can choose beer from 36 taps served in huge steins or bottles of beer ranging from basic to world class. Cocktails, wine, and shandies are also available. Murals decorate the walls and large chandeliers hang overhead. The menu features housemade sausage, hot dogs, fried cheese curds, pulled pork, fresh-baked German pretzels, burgers, deviled eggs, ribs, and more. Brunch on Sat and Sun has sports on big screen TVs and plenty of food, plus a kids' menu. Guests can enjoy a challenging round of cornhole to try their skills at Hammerschlagen, a competition where participants try to drive nails into a stump with the wedge side of a machinist hammer. Fun to watch and try.

GREEK

ATHENS FAMILY RESTAURANT, 2526 Franklin Rd., Nashville, TN 37204; (615) 383-2848; athensfamilyrestaurant.com; $$. It is fitting that while you are in the "Athens of the South," you should be able to dine at an authentic Greek restaurant. Opened in 2005, Athens Family Restaurant features family recipes from various parts of the Greek islands. The native Greek owners have incorporated the Greek concept into a very broad menu ranging from gyros, souvlaki, moussaka, and spanakopita to the honey-sweet baklava. The food is fresh and tasty, the surroundings reminiscent of Greece, and the cloth-covered tables and comfortable chairs friendly enough to linger over a leisurely meal. Decor includes fishing nets on the walls, Greek paintings, and other island items. The restaurant also serves breakfast, with eggs, omelets, pancakes, French toast, and other early morning treats, as well as heart-healthy choices such as yogurt and fresh fruit, on the menu. The owner is fond of saying that you don't have to spend a fortune to visit Greece. Just stop by his restaurant, and you'll think you are there—if only for a meal. The restaurant has a second location in Berry Hill at 2526 Eighth Ave. S. (615-383-2848).

INDIAN

SHALIMAR, 3711 Hillsboro Pike, Nashville, TN 37215; (615) 269-8577; shalimarfinedining.com; $$$. One of the first Indian restaurants in Nashville, Shalimar's delicious food and fine service have earned it a very good reputation. Chicken tikka masala and chicken curry are favorite entrees, and the restaurant has a nice assortment of traditional Indian naan breads. For dessert, try the rice pudding or the gulab jamun, sweet dough swimming in a rosewater broth. Shalimar doesn't serve alcohol, but you can bring your own; there's no cork fee. The restaurant is open daily for lunch and dinner and has a popular Saturday lunch buffet. Located in a rather nondescript building in Green Hills, the restaurant has an enclosed patio for outdoor dining.

SITAR, 116 21st Ave. N., Nashville, TN 37203; (615) 321-8889; sitarindiannashville.com; $$. This small and casual restaurant is where many folks go when they have a craving for spicy Indian foods. Business execs, the music-business crowd, performers, and students alike frequent Sitar. For dinner, chicken and lamb dishes are favorites, and there are vegetarian meals here, too. Sitar is open for lunch and dinner daily.

IRISH

MCNAMARA'S IRISH PUB & RESTAURANT, 2740 Old Lebanon Rd., Nashville, TN 37214; (615) 885-7262; $$. For a touch of good ole Ireland, visit McNamara's Irish Pub & Restaurant where the hospitality, food, and music of the Green Isle join with warm Southern hospitality for a wonderful experience. Traditional Irish fare includes Caledonia Scotch Eggs, Mourne creamy irish potato soup, ploughman's lunch (imported Irish cheese, cold cuts on a bed of lettuce with homemade brown bread, chutney, and fresh fruit), shepherd's pie, fish-and-chips, Kerry lamb, corned beef and cabbage, and Irish stew. A Leprechaun Menu is for children 12 and under. Founded in 2010 by local musician Sean McNamara, the pub features Irish music, including the pure tenor voice of Sean McNamara himself.

ITALIAN

ANTONIO'S OF NASHVILLE, 7097 Old Harding Rd., Nashville, TN 37221; (615) 646-9166; antoniosofnashville.com; $$. Bellevue residents often lament the lack of good places to eat on their side of town, but they are blessed with this fine Italian restaurant. Antonio's of Nashville serves gourmet Italian cuisine in a casually elegant atmosphere. It's a perfect place for a romantic date, whether you're wearing blue jeans, a tux, or an evening dress. All foods here are fresh and prepared to order. A favorite is the Piccata di Vitello, veal scaloppini lightly sauteed with mushrooms, green onions, garlic, capers, and white wine, served with sauteed spinach and Yukon gold mashed potatoes. Tiramisu is the ideal end to a meal here, but the fresh berries zabaglione (a sauce of sugar, eggs, cream, and Marsala) is a tempting alternative. Antonio's is open nightly. Reservations are recommended, especially on weekends.

CITY HOUSE RESTAURANT, 1222 Fourth Ave. N., Nashville, TN 37210; (615) 736-5838; cityhousenashville.com; $$$. Located in the quaint residential neighborhood of Germantown, City House serves top-notch Italian dishes and memorable desserts. Follow the winding path to a former sculptor's studio that is home to City House with its rustic brick and well-worn wood. House-cured meats, fresh pastas, comforting soups, and simple grated cheese add to the taste and charm. Pizzas are a favorite here, baked in a brick oven behind the counter. Try one with house-cured salami, tomato sauce, and house-made mozzarella. For dessert, it's a hard choice, but you can't go wrong with the almond ricotta skillet cake with lemon marmalade and lemon ricotta gelato. The City House serves dinner only. Closed Tues.

MOTO, 1120 McGavock St., Nashville, TN 37203; (615) 736-5305; mstreetnashville.com; $$$. Opened in 2014, Moto specializes in "rustic-modern" Italian cuisine served in chic comfort. Brick warehouse walls, vibrant colors, dark woods, and frosted hanging lights add to the contemporary atmosphere. Moto is open only for dinner. The menu offers a contemporary approach to authentic Italian cooking. Moto uses products from local farms and artisans as well as products imported from Italy. House-made pasta dishes, steaks, chops, and seafood are abundant. The blueberry lasagna with wild mushrooms and blueberry balsamic is a popular special. Dessert favorites are the chocolate budino with caramel and pistachio pizzelle, and the mixed berry pound cake with vanilla streusel, strawberry gel, and soul cream gelato. Moto has a large bar and lounge area and offers about 250 wines, plus couture cocktails including its own house-made limoncello. The name Moto is a nod to the Italian word for "motion," fitting since this was once a mechanic's shop in the Gulch.

PASTARIA, 8 City Blvd., Nashville, TN 37209; (615) 915-1866; eatpastaria.com/Nashville; $$$. James Beard award–winning chef Gerald Craft heads up this casual Italian restaurant so you know it must be good. Opened in the ONEC1TY development in September 2017, Pastaria lives by the mantra "La Verita" or "the truth" representing Chef Craft's dedication to featuring the simplicity and quality of genuine Italian cuisine. Tall ceilings, natural light, and an open floor plan make Pastaria a pleasant place to dine. The restaurant also features a large dinner bar, cocktail area, and gelato counter. Popular menu items include red wine braised beef with creamy polenta, roasted carrots, and fresh mint or toasted spaghetti with clams. Pizza choices include margherita, marinara, pepperoni, four cheese, or Hawaiian with tomato, mozzarella, jalapeño, pineapple, and house-made Canadian bacon.

i Looking for a late-night meal? An option is Cafe Coco (open 24 hours a day). The Waffle House, which you can find in virtually every corner of town, is a perennial around-the-clock favorite.

MEXICAN

LA HACIENDA TAQUERIA, 2615 Nolensville Pike, Nashville, TN 37211; (615) 256-6142; lahanashville.com; $$. La Hacienda, a Mexican grocery store, tortilla factory, and restaurant, introduced many Music City residents to authentic, freshly prepared Mexican food. La Hacienda is owned by the Yepez family, who sought to create an authentic Mexican restaurant where the area's Hispanic residents could feel at home. They opened the original 60-seat location in 1992 and later expanded it to seat 250. The casual, bustling dining room is packed at lunchtime with workers enjoying a quick Mexican-food fix. The burritos are delicious. They're filled with beans, your choice of meat (chicken, beef, pork, Mexican sausage, tripe, tongue), onions, cilantro, avocado, and salsa. Tacos are just as good. We're partial to the chicken tacos—perfect little soft tortillas topped with flavorful shredded chicken, diced onions, and fresh cilantro and accompanied by an avocado slice, lime wedge, and green and red sauce. There are several combination platters, including the spicy rotisserie chicken served with rice, beans, corn or flour tortillas, and a salad. Desserts include delicious sopapillas, flan, cheesecake, churros, and tres leches cake. After your meal, visit the grocery store, where you can pick up a package of tortillas made at La Hacienda Tortilleria. La Hacienda is open daily for lunch and dinner.

LAS PALETAS, 2905 12th Ave. S., Nashville, TN 37204; (615) 386-2101; laspaletasnashville.com; $. Paletas are to Mexico what gelato is to Italy. The tasty frozen desserts are similar to our Popsicles, but these aren't like any Popsicle the Good Humor man carried. Las Paletas proprietors Irma and Norma Paz, two daughters of Mexico, have brought their native treats to Nashville, where they operate a "Popsicle factory" in a small shop across the street from Sevier Park. You'll find exotic flavors like hibiscus and tamarind—even jalapeño, if you dare—as well as more traditional fruit flavors (with the fruit frozen inside), chocolate, and vanilla. Flavors change, but look for favorites like rose petal, cucumber chili, spicy chocolate with wasabi, hibiscus, and chai tea. Las Paletas really is a factory—the sisters provide paletas to Nashville's growing number of Hispanic grocery stores and restaurants. But they do plenty of walk-in business, too; just don't be surprised by the store's rather industrial appearance. Las Paletas is open 11 a.m. to 5 p.m. Tues through Sun.

ROSEPEPPER CANTINA, 1907 Eastland Ave., Nashville, TN 37206; (615) 227-4777; rosepepper.com; $$. West Nashvillians who typically never think about crossing the Cumberland for dinner are now heading to this lively east Nashville restaurant in droves. Located in a historic neighborhood, Rosepepper Cantina is colorful and fun. It's part bar, part restaurant, with an open, casual, and vibrant feel. When the weather's nice, diners can head to the patio and enjoy a meal alfresco. A diverse menu features steak, seafood, chicken, fish, and plenty of flavorful tamales, enchiladas, tacos, burritos, and much more. Inside, the walls are decked out in everything from Mexican and Southwestern art to posters to corrugated metal.

SAINT AÑEJO, 1120 McGavock St., Nashville, TN 37203; (615) 736-5301; mstreetnashville.com; $$. Saint Añejo bills itself as featuring "inspired Mexican cuisine." Take time to peruse the menu to see what that means. Dishes are creative, using basic Mexican recipes that have been jazzed up for taste treats. Tacos, nachos, guacamole, quesadillas, burritos, enchiladas, and more standards are offered, as are specialties like seared tuna with fresh corn, black bean salad, and poblano rice. For dessert, try the tres leches (three milks) with house-made sponge cake and house-made whipped cream. Craft margaritas are constructed with premium spirits, fresh botanicals, and wonderful combinations of nectars and spices. Sangria, beer, and wine also are available. Enormous convertible windows open the space out to M Street, plus an elevated large patio shares an indoor/outdoor bar with the interior. Located in a private mezzanine that overlooks the first level, the Tequila Library Lounge is a great place for a tequila tasting.

TACO MAMACITA, 1200 Villa Place, Nashville, TN 37212; (615) 730-8552; tacomamacita.com; $$. An eclectic restaurant, the funky fusion Taco Mamacita joined the dining scene in December 2009. As the name implies, the menu has plenty of tacos, including some very creative ones, along with many other choices. The basic and delicious fresh chicken tortilla soup features roasted chicken, diced tomato, freshly sliced avocado, queso fresco, lime, and chopped cilantro served hot pot style with house-made broth topped with tortilla chips. The roasted Peruvian chicken with lime juice and seasonings, plus salad and two side dishes, is a feast. The Oy Vey features slow-cooked chipotle beef brisket topped with Mama's ranchero sauce, crispy lettuce, pico de gallo, Monterey Jack cheese, guacamole, and fresh escabeche. Taco Mamacita also pleases the thirsty with signature cocktails made with premium tequilas and fresh-squeezed juices. Try the seasonal mojitos or margaritas or, if you're brave, the Durty Sanchez, a 12-ounce can of PBR accompanied by a tequila chaser.

MIDDLE EASTERN

ANATOLIA, 48 White Bridge Rd., Nashville, TN 37205; (615) 356-1556; anatolia-restaurant.com; $$. Part of Nashville's ever-growing variety of ethnic eateries, the Turkish restaurant Anatolia is an all-around delight. The elegantly uncluttered dining space, adorned with a few Middle Eastern rugs and eye-catching accessories, is comfortable and inviting, and the friendly and professional staff go the extra mile to make you feel welcome. The menu of entrees is divided into two parts: grilled specialties, which include familiar chicken, lamb, and beef kebabs, and "classic Turkish home cooking," a small selection of special recipes. If you aren't familiar with Middle Eastern food, you might want to try the lamb stew, a combination of lamb cubes and 10 vegetables served piping hot with a scoop of rice and a bowl of cool yogurt sauce. Those with more adventurous tastes might consider the homemade Turkish ravioli: ground beef–stuffed homemade pasta in a garlic-yogurt sauce topped with hot butter, red pepper, and mint. A small wine list includes a couple of Turkish selections. For dessert, try the specialty, kunefe. This heavenly concoction of shredded puff pastry, unsalted cheese, and light syrup, served warm, gets better with every bite. Anatolia is located in the Lion's Head Village shopping center. The restaurant is open daily for lunch and dinner.

KALAMATA'S, 3764 Hillsboro Pike, Nashville, TN 37215; (615) 383-8700; kalamatasnashville.com; $$. Freshness and flavor abound at this casual restaurant located in Green Hills's Glendale Center strip mall. Kalamata's specializes in Middle Eastern and Mediterranean foods. Be sure to check out the daily specials on the chalkboard before placing your order. One of the Lebanese-style savory pies topped with spinach, cheese, or meat makes a fine appetizer, as do the traditional tabbouleh and the stuffed grape leaves. The made-to-order sandwiches are chicken or beef/lamb gyros, served in a warm pita with lettuce, tomato, and cool, creamy yogurt-cucumber sauce; a falafel pocket; and a Mediterranean grilled vegetable wrap. Those with heartier appetites will be pleased with the beef, chicken, or lamb kebab plates that are served with basmati rice or roasted potatoes, Greek salad, and freshly baked pita. Pistachio baklava, cheesecake, and tiramisu are a few of the tempting ways to end a meal here. Open Mon through Sat for lunch and dinner.

> i When Luke Bryan first moved to Nashville, he waited tables at a local restaurant. He lasted only three days. But he has had long-standing success as a country singer.

NIGHTLIFE

THE BEER SELLAR, 107 Church St., Nashville, TN 37201; (615) 254-9464; originalbeersellar.com. This casual beer bar has a huge selection of—you guessed it—beer: 50 draft beers and 100 bottled brands, including many imports. They pour a lot of flavored brews, too, including cider, vanilla, and cherry. The 175-capacity room is frequented by an eclectic bunch, including college students and the over-60 crowd. Some come just for the tasty sandwiches or to watch a game. Darts, a pool table, and foosball also provide amusement. Open daily until 2 a.m.

FLYING SAUCER DRAUGHT EMPORIUM, 111 10th Ave. S., Nashville, TN 37203; (615) 259-3039; beerknurd.com. Nashville's Flying Saucer, behind the Union Station Hotel, is a good choice for beer connoisseurs. If your beer experiences have been limited to the occasional can of Budweiser, or a Corona when you're feeling adventurous, Flying Saucer will wow you with its selection of more than 200 brews from around the globe, 80 of which are on tap. Check the blackboard for the new arrivals. The spacious establishment offers samplers, featuring a selection of 5-ounce servings. The black and gold plates on the wall are tributes to patrons who have tried every beer on the menu at least once. Even if you don't like beer, you can enjoy the casual ambience, tasty bar food, and the covered outdoor patio. Flying Saucer is open daily.

Live music is enjoyed at Acme Feed & Seed. Jackie Sheckler Finch

M.L. ROSE CRAFT BEER & BURGERS, 2535 Eighth Ave. S., Nashville, TN 37204; (615) 712-8160; mlrose.com. Billed as a neighborhood bar, the M. L. Rose offers a laid-back atmosphere with plenty of room to move around and more than 85 beers, some on tap, some in bottles. The casual pub decor features a long L-shaped bar, wood-paneled walls, a punched-tin ceiling, CD jukebox, pool tables, arcade basketball game, and walls full of movie and music posters, as well as other memorabilia. The menu offers burgers, chili, waffle fries, steak sandwiches, and other bar food. M. L. Rose has two other locations at 4408 Charlotte Ave. (615-750-2920) and at 431 Eleventh Ave. N. (615-729-4445).

MERCY LOUNGE, 1 Cannery Row, Nashville, TN 37203; (615) 251-3020; mercylounge.com. Located in the historic 1860s Cannery building off Eighth Avenue S., Mercy Lounge opened in 2003 and quickly became one of the nighttime hot spots with one of the coolest vibes in town. Hardwood floors, comfy padded couches and chairs, and funky old lamps and tables create a fun and welcoming feel. The spacious bar is also known for presenting top-notch musical talent, leaning toward rock. There's lots of room to wander about: In addition to a music room and a bar area, Mercy Lounge has pool tables in the back room and an outdoor deck.

i The tabletops and bar at Sperry's in Belle Meade were built on-site from Liberty ship hatch covers used in World War II. The bar top is hand carved from this wood. The unique finish was achieved by repeated applications of an epoxy resin, then rubbed to a mirror shine.

THE PATTERSON HOUSE, 1711 Division St., Nashville, TN 37203; (615) 636-7724; thepattersonnashville.com. Opened in 2009, the Patterson House is named for the Tennessee governor, Malcolm R. Patterson, who vetoed statewide prohibition in 1909. With its speakeasy decor, the bar showcases well-made drinks and the talented bartenders—clad in vintage vests and Windsor ties—who create them. You know this is a serious drinking place when you hear about the 8 kinds of twice-filtered ice used. Some of the ice is cracked with a small wooden bat, some of it is crushed, or shaved. May sound like overkill, but bartenders say the ice types are made to complement each drink perfectly. Dimly lit with bookcases lining the walls, the Patterson House decor is rich with dark textures and colors and vintage chandeliers. An elaborate roster of cocktails features more than 50 different cocktail recipes. The Patterson House is popular, but folks seem prepared to wait for a seat at the bar or a booth.

THE PALM, 140 Fifth Ave. S., Nashville, TN 37203; (615) 742-7256; thepalm.com; $$$$$. The Nashville edition of this upscale chain, located across the street from the Bridgestone Arena, opened in 2000 amid much star-studded fanfare. Since then it has hosted such entertainment luminaries as Robert Redford, James Gandolfini, Tim McGraw, and Faith Hill. Top-tier politicos and industry titans—as well as Titans of the NFL variety—are also regulars. The Palm is famous for the cartoons of celebrities that decorate its walls, but it has also quickly earned a reputation as the best restaurant in town. Thick, juicy steaks are the main reason to come. A premium wine selection and rich dessert menu that includes 7-layer iced carrot cake ensure that customers walk away satisfied. The Palm is open for lunch and dinner on weekdays and dinner only on weekends. Reservations are recommended for dinner.

SPERRY'S, 5109 Harding Pike, Nashville, TN 37205; (615) 353-0809; sperrys.com; $$$$. This is a neighborhood restaurant, Belle Meade–style. Doctors, lawyers, judges, and well-dressed couples have been dining at Sperry's since 1974. Owned by the Thomas family for more than 25 years, Sperry's is a comfortably upscale restaurant with good food and good service. Deep red carpets and wood tables contribute to the warm and cozy atmosphere. Sperry's is known for its steaks and seafood. Fresh swordfish and tuna, a blue cheese–stuffed fillet, and rack of lamb Dijon are always in demand. There are daily specials. Desserts like bananas Foster and Death by Chocolate cake satisfy tastes beyond the 37205 zip code. Sperry's is open for lunch and dinner Mon through Sat, and brunch and dinner on Sun. Sperry's has a second location in Franklin at 650 Frazier Dr. (615-778-9950).

i *Grand Ole Opry* star Terri Clark sang for tips at Tootsie's on Nashville's famed Lower Broadway before hitting the top of the charts.

PIZZA

MANNY'S HOUSE OF PIZZA, 15 Arcade Alley, Nashville, TN 37219; (615) 242-7144; mannyshouseofpizza.com; $. House of Pizza has been satisfying downtown workers' pizza cravings for almost 3 decades. Located in the historic Arcade mall (see our **Shopping** chapter), between Fourth and Fifth Avenues and Union and Church Streets downtown, the New York–style pizzeria serves pizza by the slice or by the pie. Don't expect to find any goat cheese, sun-dried tomatoes, or other gourmet ingredients; most of the pizza sold here is of the cheese-and-pepperoni variety, though you do have a choice of crusts. Also on the menu are lasagna, spaghetti, calzones, stromboli, salads, and sub sandwiches. Dessert is cannoli, regular or chocolate dipped. The restaurant seats about 50 to 60. Manny's is open Mon through Fri from 11 a.m. to 4 p.m.

PIZZA PERFECT, 357 Clofton Dr., Nashville, TN 37221; (615) 646-7877; pizzaperfectonline.com; $. The appropriately named Pizza Perfect has been a favorite for years. Pizza Perfect makes delicious pizzas with all sorts of yummy toppings. Pizza Perfect also has calzones, sub sandwiches, spaghetti, manicotti, lasagna, and salads. The restaurants are open daily. Pizza Perfect also has a Vanderbilt location at 1602 21st Ave. S. (615-329-2757).

PUB FOOD

ACME FEED & SEED, 101 Broadway, Nashville, TN 37201; (615) 915-0888; theacmenashville.com; $$$. A favorite with tourists, Acme Feed & Seed has one of the most conspicuous locations in Nashville—right in the heart of downtown with views of Broadway and the riverfront. The huge Victorian-era white-painted brick warehouse with red and white checkerboards was once Acme Farm Supply before the popular business closed in 1999. The building sat mostly vacant until 2014, when plans were hatched for Acme Feed & Seed. Each of the three floors is filled with interesting artifacts. The roof offers one of the best views in town. Live music and DJs often add to the party atmosphere. The menu offers creatively named bar food with an emphasis on Southern cooking, such as the Local Yokel—smoked chicken and green chili burrito with rice and beans. The Rule the Roost is hot chicken with green peppercorn aioli, American cheese, and pickles on white bread with hand-cut fries. Redneck Lo Mein is lo mein noodles, smoked chicken, collard greens, corn, black-eyed peas, caramelized onions, and andouille soy glaze. Drinks are abundant.

Acme Feed & Seed was once a farm supply store in downtown Nashville. Jackie Sheckler Finch

BROADWAY BREWHOUSE MIDTOWN, 1900 Broadway, Nashville, TN 37201; (615) 340-0089; broadwaybrewhouse.net; $$. Broadway Brewhouse carries on the tradition of a roadhouse with cold beer and hot food. The menu features spicy foods like chipotle chicken wings, Cuban-Jamaican–style mojo-crusted jerk chicken, and molasses-jalapeño dipping sauce. Brewhouse carries bunches of beer—more than 2 dozen on tap and about 100 in bottles. It's the kind of place where you visit once as a stranger. When you return, the waiters and servers know your name, as do several of the patrons. Other locations include Broadway Brewhouse West at 7108 Charlotte Pike (615-356-5005); Broadway Brewhouse Downtown at 317 Broadway (615-271-2838); Brewhouse 100 at 8098 Tennessee 100 (615-673-2981); and Brewhouse South at 1855 Galleria Blvd. in Franklin (615-778-1860).

MCCABE PUB, 4410 Murphy Rd., Nashville, TN 37209; (615) 269-9406; mccabepub.com; $$. The casual and friendly McCabe Pub is a combination neighborhood pub and sports bar. It's known for great hamburgers, lots of good vegetables (mashed potatoes, green beans, squash casserole, broccoli casserole, sweet potato casserole, and steamed veggies, to name a few), and great desserts. The home-cooked plate lunches and dinners, with entrees like fried catfish, pork chops, fried chicken livers, and meat loaf and your choice of vegetables, satisfy nearby Sylvan Park families, couples, and singles and lure out-of-the-neighborhood regulars as well, including the Music Row set.

★ **THE ORIGINAL CORNER PUB,** 1105 51st Ave. N., Nashville, TN 37209; (615) 298-9698; originalcornerpub.com; $$. This neighborhood bar and restaurant draws a variety of locals, from college students to old-timers. There's a casual, relaxed feel here. That alone has given this haunt a stable of regulars who like to hang out at the bar and watch sports. The Corner Pub serves a variety of beers and ales, plus hot and cold sandwiches, burgers, and the like.

ROCK BOTTOM NASHVILLE, 111 Broadway, Nashville, TN 37201; (615) 251-4677; rockbottom.com; $$. Rock Bottom Nashville offers an expanded menu with plenty of food options, plus beer, wine, and cocktails. The restaurant serves salads, pasta, sandwiches, pizza, and entrees such as salmon, steak, and chicken. For dessert, try the creative Bourbon Pecan Pie Mason Jar, a mason jar filled with salted caramel sauce and rich and buttery Kentucky Bourbon pecan pie topped with vanilla ice cream and more caramel sauce, sprinkled with toasted graham cracker crumbs and fresh mint.

WHISKEY KITCHEN, 118 12th Ave. S., Nashville, TN 37203; (615) 254-3029; mstreetnashville.com; $$. How can you not like a place that calls itself "tavern chic"? One look at the Whiskey Kitchen menu and you'll understand. This is sure a cut above regular pub food. Crocodile-leather wall coverings and reclaimed oak add a comfy vintage vibe. The large convertible windows and a good-size patio are wonderful weather additions. The menu has plenty of solid appetizers, Southern classics, wraps, burgers, hot chicken, and wood-fired pizza. Of course, drinks are a must, and Whiskey Kitchen has a huge selection of world-class whiskeys, bourbons, ryes, and scotches, plus other thirst quenchers.

i *Grand Ole Opry* star Randy Travis worked as a dishwasher, short-order cook, and singer at the Nashville Palace, a mile from the *Opry* House, just 15 months before joining the *Opry*.

SEAFOOD

CANEY FORK RIVER VALLEY GRILLE, 2400 Music Valley Dr., Nashville, TN 37214; (615) 724-1200; caneyforkrestaurant.com; $$$. Modeled after the fish camps along the nearby Caney Fork River, this restaurant has a rustic feel and a menu with a Southern twist. Located near Gaylord Opryland Resort and the huge Opry Mills shopping center, Caney Fork has an outdoorsy theme with an indoor cabin and porch, 2 fireplaces, a 3,000-gallon pond with a waterfall and live fish, and a restored 1939 Dodge flatbed truck cab. Fishing and hunting artifacts abound, including record trophy game mounts, a couple of bears, tons of vintage lures, and a bar top consisting of more than 1,000 hand-cut fishing ads cropped from old magazines. For exciting sports shows, the bar has multiple televisions. Comfort cooking is served here as well as broiled, blackened, grilled, and fried seafood. Old standbys like fried dill pickles and fried green tomatoes are popular appetizers. Barbecued ribs, a bunch of burger choices, meat loaf, fried chicken, fish-and-chips, grilled salmon, blackened ahi tuna, and many more choices are on the menu.

STEAK

FLEMING'S PRIME STEAKHOUSE & WINE BAR, 2525 West End Ave., Nashville, TN 37203; (615) 342-0131; flemingssteakhouse.com; $$$$. Fleming's is one of many upscale steak house chains that have discovered Nashville. Fleming's distinguishes itself from the competition with its easy yet slightly formal atmosphere. The steaks are all cooked to perfection. Other entree options include Australian lamb chops, veal and pork chops, salmon, tuna, swordfish, and lobster-tails. The wine list includes 100 premium wines by the glass. Fleming's is open for lunch and dinner from Mon through Fri and for dinner on Sat and Sun. Valet parking is available.

JIMMY KELLY'S STEAKHOUSE, 217 Louise Ave., Nashville, TN 37203; (615) 329-4349; jimmykellys.com; $$$. Steak lovers have plenty of very good new restaurant choices in Nashville, but generations of Nashvillians continue to return to Jimmy Kelly's, a fixture on Nashville's restaurant scene since 1934. The specialty is aged hand-cut steaks, and the corn cakes are legendary. If you're not in the mood for beef, try the veal chops, lamb chops, or fresh fish. A dessert favorite is the homemade Tennessee blackberry cobbler topped with French vanilla ice cream. Jimmy Kelly's is comfortable, and the service is top-notch. The restaurant is open for dinner Mon through Sat. Reservations are recommended.

KAYNE PRIME, 1103 McGavock St., Nashville, TN 37203; (615) 259-0050; mstreetnashville.com; $$$. Kayne Prime is a steak house and much more. Opened in 2011, Kayne Prime calls itself an "artful fusion of a chef-chic boutique restaurant with a great American steakhouse." The interior features dark woods, rich red leathers, and walls of reclaimed railroad ties to complement views of historic train yards, Union Station, and downtown Nashville. That's where the restaurant got its name—from the historic Kayne train switchyard located directly across Eleventh Ave. Cuisine features local products when possible, and menus change seasonally. The house-made bacon with maple cotton candy is a savory hit. The menu has plenty of seafood, chicken, and, of course, steak, including Wagyu beef. The menu also tells where the beef came from, such as the bone-in tenderloin from Michael's Meats in Columbus, Ohio. Open for dinner only. Dress code for men includes no shorts, hats, jerseys, open-toed shoes, flip-flops, or sleeveless shirts.

VEGETARIAN

THE WILD COW, 1896 Eastland Ave., Nashville, TN 37206; (615) 262-2717; thewildcow.com; $$. The Wild Cow draws diners with a varied menu of creative meatless meals and a commitment to using local, organic produce and dairy. But first that name. Owners John and Melanie Cochran chose the Wild Cow as a symbol of more humane farming before "factory farms" took over, a return to the "wild cow" that would roam free and graze on natural feed. The Wild Cow also offers a gluten-free menu. Everything on the menu is vegan unless diners prefer to add or choose dairy cheese, which is organic, rennet-free, and from free-range cows. There's also a kiddie menu for ages 12 and under. For beverages, a wide variety of fresh-brewed fair-trade teas are available, along with an array of organic quality sodas and soy milk, plus wine made from organic grapes, hard cider from organic apples, and "high alcohol" beer. The Wild Cow also holds events to help raise awareness and funds for organizations that deal with animal welfare, environmental protection, safe and humane farming, and world hunger.

> i Music venues aren't the only places to hear great live music in Nashville. Most restaurants, bars, pubs, coffeehouses, and sometimes even bookstores and shopping malls present songwriters and bands on a regular basis.

Music City

They don't call it Music City for nothing. Nashville is truly the place to be if you are a lover of music, whatever the style. Whether you're an aspiring singer or songwriter, an aficionado of live music in intimate settings, a student of country music history, or a starstruck fan eager to discover more about the lifestyle of your favorite artist, you can find plenty in Nashville to meet your desires. By the way, for insight into Nashville's development as a music capital, check out our **History** chapter. If you're a tourist in Nashville, you've probably been keeping your eyes peeled for a glimpse of a country music star as you stroll down Music Row. You might spot someone ducking into a studio or driving by, but you're probably more likely to bump into your favorite star in an ordinary place like the post office, the mall, or the grocery store. Running into a music star is just about an everyday occurrence here in Music City.

OVERVIEW

The main sections of this chapter are as follows:

- **Attractions.** Country music–related museums include general-interest sites, like the Country Music Hall of Fame & Museum and the *Grand Ole Opry* Museum, plus a shrine or two tailored to particular artists. Tour companies offer packages that will take you to various Nashville attractions and, in some cases, past the current or former homes of an assortment of stars.

- **Record stores.** Yes, we still prefer to call them record stores, even though most of them now deal instead in CDs. But there are actually places in Nashville where you can still find vinyl, especially vintage vinyl.

- **Live music.** Here you'll find a world of choices covering practically every musical style you can think of. You'll find venues large and small, including ones specializing in performances by songwriters—and opportunities for you to perform, if that's one of your dreams.

Courtesy of Nashville Convention & Visitors Corporation

- **Annual events.** It seems that some kind of yearly festival, concert series, jubilee, or other musical event is always going on here, celebrating Nashville's musical heritage, its thriving present, and its promising future.

Of course, as we've said elsewhere in this book—and as we'll continue to emphasize—one of the aspects that many newcomers find surprising about Music City is the sheer diversity of its output. While country music remains by far the most visible (or should we say audible?) style, you can find an eclectic selection that includes about any kind of music you might possibly want to hear. This really isn't a new development, as a quick study of the recording industry will attest. Nashville actually had a thriving rhythm-and-blues scene well before the city became known as the country music capital of the world. From the early days of the city's recording industry on up to today, a stunning array of non-country artists—including Burl Ives, Ray Charles, Bob Dylan, James Brown, R.E.M., Leontyne Price, Neil Young, REO Speedwagon, Johnny Winter, Carol Channing, Paul McCartney, Elvis Costello, the Allman Brothers, B. B. King, Dave Brubeck, Joe Cocker, Dean Martin, and Yo La Tengo—have

Tommy Sims Courtesy of Nashville Convention & Visitors Corporation

recorded albums here. While many of these artists have drawn upon country influences on their Nashville records, others have not, simply recognizing the wealth of talent and facilities available here. More and more people, perhaps, are realizing that, regardless of category, good music is good music, and music is an international language Nashville speaks fluently.

Price Code

Use the following as a guide to the cost of an adult admission to an attraction. Keep in mind that children's admission prices are generally lower (usually about half the cost of adult admission), and very young children are admitted free to most attractions. Discounts for senior citizens, students, and groups are usually available.

$	**Less than $10**
$$	**$10 to $20**
$$$	**$20 to $30**
$$$$	**More than $30**

Barbershop Harmony Society was founded in 1938.
Courtesy of Nashville Convention & Visitors Corporation

ATTRACTIONS

BARBERSHOP HARMONY SOCIETY, 110 Seventh Ave. N., Nashville, TN; (615) 823-3993; barbershop.org; free. Founded in 1938, the society preserves and promotes barbershop quartet singing. Barbershop quartets began in America at the turn of the 20th century, and today the society has about 25,000 members and about 2,000 quartets. It has more than 820 chapters in the United States and Canada, with an increasing number in other countries. The location houses the society's headquarters staff, Harmony Marketplace retail gift shop, and merchandising operations. It is also the home of the Old Songs Library, the world's largest privately held collection of sheet music, containing 750,000 sheets and 125,000 titles from the heyday of Tin Pan Alley.

COUNTRY MUSIC HALL OF FAME & MUSEUM, 222 Fifth Ave. S., Nashville, TN 37203; (615) 416-2001; countrymusichalloffame.org; $$$$. Located at Fifth Avenue S. and Demonbreun Street, Nashville's Country Music Hall of Fame & Museum takes up an entire city block and boasts more than 40,000 square feet of exhibit space devoted to the history of country music. As you walk through the museum, you'll view music memorabilia, hear clips of country recordings past and present, and learn about the music and its stars.

The Country Music Hall of Fame & Museum showcases memorabilia from old and new performers. Jackie Sheckler Finch

Exhibits are arranged in a chronological fashion, beginning with the roots of country music and continuing to the present. You could spend hours observing the museum's amazing collection of memorabilia, which includes Mother Maybelle Carter's 1928 Gibson guitar, a rhinestone-studded stage suit worn by Hank Williams, matching duds worn by the Dixie Chicks, and even San Quentin Penitentiary parolee Merle Haggard's letter of pardon from California governor Ronald Reagan. Also on view are copies of every gold and platinum country record.

After the museum, your final stop will be the round, 4,500-square-foot Hall of Fame, where bronze likenesses of the dozens of Hall of Fame members are on display. Live entertainment at the museum includes songwriter performances and occasional appearances by big-name country acts. Also onsite is a gift shop. Two-day tickets, group discounts, and package tours that include a stop at historic RCA Studio B are available. The museum is open daily except Thanksgiving, Christmas Day, and New Year's Day. (For more about the museum, see the Close-up "Structurally Sound.")

The Country Music Hall of Fame & Museum features outstanding architecture. Courtesy of Nashville Convention & Visitors Corporation

GRUHN GUITARS, INC., 2120 Eighth Ave. S., Nashville, TN 37204; (615) 256-2033; guitars.com; free. A must-stop for guitarists or serious music fans, world-famous Gruhn's is Nashville's largest guitar dealer. The store specializes in high-quality new, used, and vintage guitars, banjos, and mandolins, with prices ranging from a few hundred dollars to as much as $150,000. Gruhn's has a strong celebrity clientele, but owner George Gruhn is quick to note that his store has "plenty of things that mere mortals can afford." Instruments range from new Martin and Gibson guitars to pre–World War II Martin and Gibson acoustics and 1950s and 1960s electric guitars. Gruhn's is open Mon through Sat.

HATCH SHOW PRINT, 224 Fifth Ave. S., Nashville, TN 37203; (615) 577-7710; hatchshowrpint.com; free. In business since 1879, Hatch Show Print is one of the oldest letterpress poster print shops in America (see our **Attractions** chapter for more information). The shop is best known for its posters of early *Grand Ole Opry* stars. Today Hatch is owned and operated by the Country Music Foundation, which operates the Country Music Hall of Fame & Museum (see listing above). The shop still produces its trademark posters

Close-up

Structurally Sound

The home of the **Country Music Hall of Fame & Museum** is not just a building. It is an architectural salute to the history of the beloved form of music. It's no accident that the dark, narrow windows on the sweeping facade resemble piano keys. That's just one of many elements that the Hall of Fame's designers incorporated into the modern building as symbols of country music.

Recognizing that country music is an art form whose roots stretch from farms and factories to churches and prisons to country stores and urban bars, the designers, Tuck Hinton Architects, used a variety of materials and included many symbolic representations throughout the attraction. Some symbols, like the windows, are obvious. Others are subtler. Seen from above, the building's curved facade and drum-shaped segment resemble a bass clef, while the front wall's slanted end is a nod to late-1950s Cadillac tail fins.

A not-so-obvious symbol is the hall's riveted-steel structure and Mississippi yellow pine flooring in the conservatory, which allude to early-20th-century bridges and factories. Suggesting an Appalachian stream, or perhaps the flow of artistic inspiration from the Hall of Fame's legendary members, water from a fountain cascades alongside a long staircase; at the bottom, the stream ends in a "wishing well" pool in the spacious conservatory, a space designed to symbolize the "front-porch" origins of country music.

There are several other symbols, but perhaps the most apparent architectural expression of country music is the building's Hall of Fame drum or rotunda, which acknowledges the beloved anthem "Will the Circle Be Unbroken." Around the exterior circumference of the silo-like space are slabs of Crab Orchard stone, designed to represent notes from the famous Carter Family song. Atop the drum is a tower/steeple/chandelier modeled after the WSM-AM 650 radio tower, a tribute to the station's role in the creation of the *Grand Ole Opry* and the popularization of country music worldwide. Inside the rotunda, which has an almost sacred feel, are additional reminders of the unbroken circle, or continuity, of country music, from its earliest days to the present.

Visitors are invited to make their own print at Hatch Show Print.
Jackie Sheckler Finch

and other designs. Its 14-by-22-inch posters advertising local rock bands and would-be country stars can be seen in window displays around town. Hatch sells samples of its posters in the shop. You can drop by daily and take a tour to learn more about letterpress art. You can even pull the press to create your own keepsake print.

Close-up

Where Elvis & Others Made Music Hits

While most people were settling down for the night, Elvis Presley would slip into the nondescript building and sit at a well-worn piano. For the next couple hours, Elvis would warm up by harmonizing on gospel, often with the Jordanaires. Then he would get down to the serious business of recording songs. About the time the sun came up, Elvis would call it a night. Elvis did most of his work in historic **RCA Studio B.** He recorded 262 songs at the legendary studio, almost 70 percent of his entire list. He once recorded 12 songs in 12 hours.

Known as the "Home of 1,000 hits," **Studio B** is located on the corner of 17th Avenue on Music Row. The studio was built in 4 months for $37,515 at the request of Chet Atkins and Steve Sholes for the RCA Victor record label. In his autobiography, Atkins said the studio plans were drawn up on a napkin.

Opened in November 1957, Studio B is a simple single-story building. The area of the studio and control room has a second story that contains an echo chamber. The place was called Studio B because there was also a Studio A. Not beautiful by any stretch of the imagination, Studio B was known for its distinctive acoustics. The walls were designed in an accordion shape, changing angles every 4 feet in an attempt to make the room as "dead" as possible. The walls are covered in 1-foot-square acoustic tiles all the way to the ceiling beginning 3 feet from the floor. Instead of using carpet as in most recording studios, Studio B had tile so the sound would bounce naturally throughout the room. The result was excellent natural sound.

Elvis's first Studio B session was June 10, 1958, and his last on June 10, 1971. Those sessions yielded a string of top hits including "How Great Thou Art," "A Big Hunk of Love," "It's Now or Never," "Crying in the Chapel," "Little Sister," and "(You're the) Devil in Disguise." He also used Studio B to record the soundtracks for a number of his movies. Because atmosphere was important to Elvis, he had red, green, blue, and white lights installed around the ceiling when he was recording one of his Christmas albums. In order for it to be released in time for the holiday season, it was recorded in July. Not filled with holiday spirit in the middle of summer, the crew strung lights, put up a

The piano played by Elvis Presley is still at Historic Studio B where Elvis recorded many of his hits. Jackie Sheckler Finch

Christmas tree, and turned the air-conditioning as low as it would go to create the festive Yuletide feeling. To this day, the lights remain.

Likewise, when Elvis was taping "Are You Lonesome Tonight," the glaring studio lights weren't conducive to a romantic tune. Elvis had all the lights turned off so it was almost pitch black in the studio. With only six people in the room with him—two guitars and the Jordanaires singing backup—Elvis did the song in one taping.

Initially, Chet Atkins would try to attend Elvis's recording sessions. But Chet couldn't stay up all night like Elvis so he'd usually just come in, say hello, and go home to bed while they recorded all night. Studio B's fame rests not only on the many hits recorded here, but also on its role in creating what came to be known as the **Nashville Sound.** By the time the studio opened, rock 'n' roll's popularity had drawn many young fans away from country music. In response, Atkins and other Nashville producers and engineers experimented with making records in a smooth, pop-oriented style aimed at an adult audience. The sophisticated Nashville Sound lessened the use of steel guitars and fiddles, adding mellow strings and vocal choruses.

The outside of the building contains a souvenir from a newcomer to town, Dolly Parton. A subtle difference in the bricks on the building's exterior is a reminder of Dolly's recording visit. The story goes that she was so excited to be recording at the studio and so thrilled to be driving a new car that she accidentally ran into the building. Dolly always joked that was her first big hit.

In 1977, RCA closed Studio B. A few years later, the studio was donated to the Country Music Hall of Fame & Museum. RCA donated the studio's equipment. In 2002, Studio B became part of a partnership with the Curb Family Foundation, the Country Music Hall of Fame & Museum, and Nashville's Belmont University. Today, Studio B is a tourist attraction, as well as a working studio and learning laboratory for Belmont students. A video shows some of the greats who recorded at the studio. Hitmakers include Eddy Arnold, Waylon Jennings, Bobby Bare, Dolly Parton, Jim Reeves, Floyd Cramer, Charley Pride, Porter Wagoner, Perry Como, the Everly Brothers, Roy Orbison, Rosemary Clooney, and Barbra Streisand.

All the Studio B equipment is original, including what many consider the most important piano in music. A well-worn Steinway Grand once played by Elvis and Floyd Cramer and others still bears the scratches and scuffs from years of use. Today, visitors are asked not to play the piano, but they can sit at it for souvenir photos. More than 35,000 songs were recorded in Studio B and, as tour guides always say, "You are walking on history when you come to Studio B."

For more on Studio B, see the **Attractions** section in this chapter.

HISTORIC RCA STUDIO B, 1611 Roy Acuff Place, Nashville, TN 37246; (615) 416-2001; studiob.org; $$$$. Visitors to the Country Music Hall of Fame & Museum can purchase a pass for $40.95 that that allows them access to RCA Studio B on Music Row and to the Country Music Hall of Fame & Museum. (A ticket to the Hall of Fame is required.) The legendary facility is Nashville's oldest surviving recording studio. More than 1,000 top 10 hits, including tunes by Elvis Presley, Dolly Parton, Willie Nelson, Waylon Jennings, and the Everly Brothers, were recorded at the studio from 1957 to 1977. Tours are offered daily and depart from the Country Music Hall of Fame & Museum (see Hall of Fame listing in this chapter).

i *Grand Ole Opry* star Trace Adkins proposed to his now wife while making his *Opry* debut.

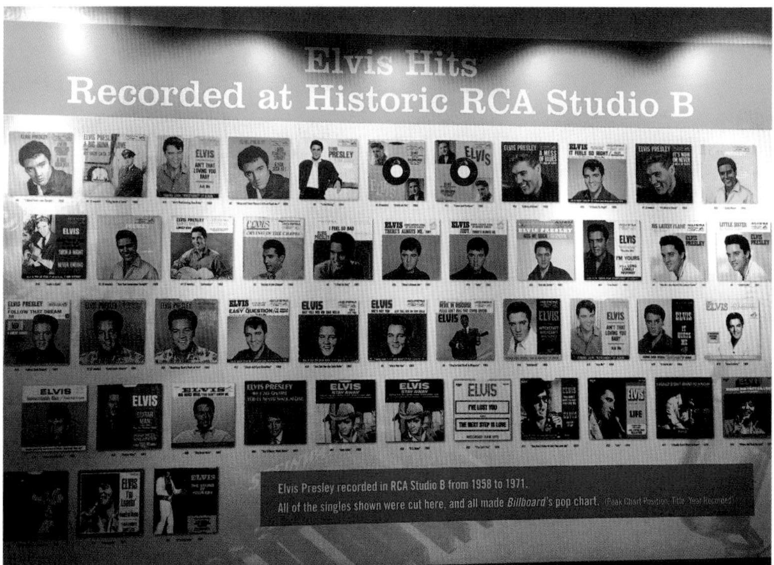

Elvis Presley recorded 262 songs at Historic Studio B. Jackie Sheckler Finch

JOHNNY CASH MUSEUM, 119 Third Ave. S., Nashville, TN 37201; (615) 256-1777; johnnycashmuseum.com; $$$. Walk through the "Man in Black's" fascinating life at the Johnny Cash Museum, which opened in 2013. Located in the heart of downtown Nashville, the museum boasts the world's largest collection of Johnny Cash artifacts and memorabilia, mostly the collection of one man—museum founder Bill Miller. Visitors can listen to Cash music from various decades and see clips of him in movies and TV shows. Exhibits highlight different periods in Cash's life including his hardscrabble childhood days in Dyess, Arkansas; Air Force years; famous prison concert tour; and marriage to June Carter. A wealth of items in the museum range from a young Cash's Future Farmers of America card to

Trace Johnny Cash's career at the Johnny Cash Museum. Jackie Sheckler Finch

the stone wall from Cash's lakeside room in his Hendersonville house. The lakeside room was where Cash filmed his heart-stopping "Hurt" video and where he hosted "guitar pulls" with famous friends like Bob Dylan and Kris Kristofferson. Open daily 9 a.m. to 7 p.m.

MUSIC CITY WALK OF FAME PARK, Nashville's Music Mile on Demonbreun Street between Fourth and Fifth Avenues, Nashville, TN 37203; (800) 657-6910; visitmusiccity.com/walkoffame; free. The Music City Walk of Fame on Nashville's Music Mile is a landmark tribute to those from all genres of music who have made significant contributions to preserving the musical heritage of Nashville and have contributed to the world through song or other industry collaboration. Inductees are announced throughout the year and honored at a special ceremony with a permanent platinum-and-granite, star-and-guitar sidewalk marker. Inductions are held twice a year. Created in 2006, the Music City Walk of Fame got a $2.5 million makeover in 2015 and is located alongside the Nashville Music Garden directly across the street from the County Music Hall of Fame & Museum.

The Music City Walk of Fame honors Nashville music legends. Courtesy of Nashville Convention & Visitors Corporation

A statue of Thomas Ryman stands outside the auditorium he built.
Jackie Sheckler Finch

★ **RYMAN AUDITORIUM AND MUSEUM,** 116 Fifth Ave. N., Nashville, TN 37219; (615) 889-3060; ryman.com; $$. Home of the *Grand Ole Opry* from 1943 to 1974, the Ryman is one of Nashville's most famous historic attractions and, today, is one of the city's most popular concert venues. Exhibits and information on the history of the building and country music are displayed on the main floor. Exhibits include memorabilia and photographs of such *Opry* stars as Kitty Wells, Hank Snow, and Ernest Tubb. Among the other attractions are life-size bronze statues of Minnie Pearl and Roy Acuff, Bill Monroe, and Little Jimmy Dickens and a gift shop with a selection of recordings and souvenir merchandise. (See our **History** and **Attractions** chapters, along with the live-music listings in this chapter, for more on the Ryman.)

Close-up

Players Behind the Music

With a slogan of "Come see what you've heard," the **Musicians Hall of Fame & Museum** reopened in early 2013 after being displaced by the construction of the Music City Center. Originally dedicated in 2006, the Musicians Hall of Fame & Museum honors the players—whether stars, session pickers, or sidemen—from all genres of music. Located on the first floor of the historic Nashville Municipal Auditorium, the museum is within walking distance of Broadway attractions.

The museum is the brainchild of Joe Chambers, a guitar store owner, who said the idea had been brewing for about a decade. When Chambers found out that Jimi Hendrix's apartment from his seminal years in Nashville had been razed, he decided that Nashville should not lose another piece of music history.

"I looked all over the world. There was no musicians' museum anywhere in the world," Chambers said. "I thought it was time there was one."

When another of the Nashville clubs where a young Hendrix performed was being renovated, Chambers tracked down the contractor and asked to salvage the basement stage. The contractor agreed, and Chambers used his memory of a famous photograph of Hendrix playing on that particular stage to guide the way. Now the Musicians Hall of Fame honors the Guitar God with an exhibit featuring the rescued and restored stage, complete with a purple haze and Hendrix music.

Musicians Hall of Fame & Museum founder Joe Chambers said he created the facility to honor the musicians who played on popular songs. Jackie Sheckler Finch

The museum is divided into cities that have a history of recorded music—Nashville, Memphis, Detroit, Muscle Shoals, Atlanta, Los Angeles, and New York. One of the instruments that Chambers is most proud of owning is the cigarette-burned old piano that he bought for $200 from CBS Records. It was on this piano that Billy Sherrill and cowriters worked out arrangements for such legendary hits as "Stand By Your Man," "Almost Persuaded," and "The Most Beautiful Girl."

Chambers's extensive collection includes:

- Lightning Chance's bass, heard on all the early Everly Brothers albums, Conway Twitty's "It's Only Make Believe," and Hank Williams's last recording sessions, which brought "Your Cheating Heart."
- Pete Drake's steel guitar played on Bob Dylan's "Lay Lady Lay" and George Harrison's album "All Things Must Pass."
- Scotty Moore's personal items from his long career in Elvis Presley's band.
- Marshall Grant's basses from Johnny Cash's "Walk the Line" and "Ring of Fire," along with the amp from "Folsom Prison Blues" and "A Boy Named Sue."

"The deal is that the instruments you see are the actual ones that you heard on a record. These are the unsung heroes, the people behind the records, behind the stars. You may not know Lightning Chance, but you will know the record he played on and will get to see his instrument," Chambers said.

"I fell in love with Nashville the first time I came here," said Chambers, who arrived in 1978 and wrote such popular songs as "Somebody Lied" for Ricky Van Shelton, "Old 8X10" for Randy Travis, and "Good Ones and Bad Ones" for George Jones. "The more that I lived here, the more I learned about how many great musicians have been through here and started here. It's really a secret. I hope the museum helps show that it isn't a secret anymore."

Early in his career, Jimi Hendrix played on Nashville's Jolly Roger stage that was saved and moved to the Musicians Hall of Fame & Museum. Jackie Sheckler Finch

For more on the Musicians Hall of Fame & Museum, see the **Attractions** chapter.

Close-up

Reformed Riverboat Captain Builds "Mother Church of Country Music"

In the late 1800s, riverboat captain Thomas Ryman decided to go downtown and heckle a preacher at a Nashville revival. Instead, Ryman got converted.

As part of his newfound faith, Ryman vowed to build a beautiful tabernacle for the minister, the Rev. Samuel Jones, that he had set out to torment. The result is one of Nashville's most popular landmarks, the old Ryman Auditorium. Of course, the thing that made the Ryman so legendary was not the religious revivals that rang through the auditorium. It was the country music that drew legions of people when the Ryman served as the longtime home to the *Grand Ole Opry.*

Although its size doesn't compare to the new *Opry* home at Opryland Park, the Ryman is still hallowed ground as "The Mother Church of Country Music." It served as a mecca drawing visitors from around the world and entertainers of all levels—beginners to top-of-the-field performers.

When it opened in 1892, the Ryman was known as the Union Gospel Tabernacle. The facility took seven years to build and cost $100,000. Famous preachers such as Billy Sunday and Norman Vincent Peale delivered sermons from its stage. In 1904, the name was changed to the Ryman Auditorium in honor of the converted steamboat captain. The hall soon became known as

TRINITY MUSIC CITY U.S.A., 1 Music Village Blvd., Hendersonville, TN 37075; (615) 822-8333; trinitymusiccity.com; free. In mid-1994 California-based Trinity Broadcasting Network purchased the late Conway Twitty's estate, known as Twitty City, and turned it into Trinity Music City U.S.A. Free tours of the Trinity Music Church Auditorium, WPGD Studio, and Twitty mansion are available at designated times throughout the week. The gardens, gift shop, and Solid Rock Bistro are open daily. The state-of-the-art virtual-reality theater features free films shot in the Holy Land. Worship services are held in the auditorium Sun at 10:30 a.m. At Christmas, visit Trinity Christmas City with over a million sparkling lights on 30 acres of beautifully decorated grounds.

a first-rate performance venue for such greats as Enrico Caruso, John Philip Sousa, Isadora Duncan, Mae West, Charlie Chaplin, Martha Graham, Gene Autry, Will Rogers, and Katharine Hepburn.

In 1943, the *Grand Ole Opry* took up residence in the Ryman and remained there until March 16, 1974. During those years, the Ryman was always packed on Saturday nights for such legends as Hank Williams, Marty Robbins, Patsy Cline, and Roy Acuff. Even a young Elvis Presley was thrilled to step on the famed stage to sing "Blue Moon of Kentucky"—until he was booed off by the audience and told he should go back to driving a truck.

After a massive renovation, the Ryman is now attracting a whole new generation of visitors for special musical events or self-guided tours. True to its country roots, the Ryman Auditorium welcomes visitors to take their time, rest in the original 100-year-old oak pews, and snap photographs. In fact, you can even step on the old wooden stage and have your photo taken behind the famous Ryman Auditorium microphone.

Or you can pose in the main lobby with bronze statues of two of the *Opry*'s most loved performers—Roy Acuff and Minnie Pearl. The life-size figures rest on an original 1892 oak pew from the Ryman.

A video does a great job of detailing the history of the Ryman and its importance today. Other tour highlights include a large display illustrating the history of the former Ryman manager Lula C. Naff and the building's early Variety Years, and memorabilia and photographs of some of the biggest stars from the *Opry* years, including Hank Williams, Patsy Cline, and Loretta Lynn.

In its heyday, the Ryman was not air-conditioned. On hot summer nights, especially in the balcony, the temperature often exceeded 100 degrees. But those hard wooden seats were still at a premium as something special and they continue to draw music lovers for a memorable experience.

WILLIE NELSON AND FRIENDS MUSEUM, 2613 McGavock Pike, Nashville, TN 37214; (615) 885-1515; willienelsonmuseum.com; $. This museum and gift shop is in Music Valley across from the Gaylord Opryland hotel. There are lots of exhibits on Willie Nelson, including awards, guitars, clothing, and other personal items. Other displays pay tribute to Patsy Cline, Elvis, and other stars. The gift shop has all sorts of souvenir items, including lots of T-shirts and sports merchandise. The museum is open daily, except Thanksgiving and Christmas, with extended hours during the summer.

Close-up

Tennessee History Honored at Bicentennial Capitol Mall

The little Ohio girl thought she was going to a shopping mall and seemed surprised when our trolley stopped. "Where are the stores?" the 5-year-old asked. That's when trolley driver Mike explained that the beautiful outdoor Bicentennial Capitol Mall we were visiting was not a shopping center.

"It's a mall like the National Mall with all its memorials in Washington D.C.," Mike said. "Before they built this, this area was nothing but a swamp. Now it's a really popular place to come."

With that, the girl and her mother hopped off the trolley to walk among the monuments and read about the state's history.

Opened June 1, 1996, Bicentennial Capitol Mall State Park was created to serve as a lasting monument to Tennessee's 200th birthday celebration.

Our driver guide said that trolley riders are often surprised at the huge state park in the shadow of the State Capitol in downtown Nashville. The 19-acre park was designed to give visitors a taste of Tennessee's history and natural beauty. It also preserves the last unobstructed view of the capitol. A self-guided tour starts at the Tennessee Map Plaza at the entrance to the park on James Robertson Parkway. The 200-foot granite map is inlaid in a large area at the top of the park. On it, you'll find major roads, 95 counties, rivers, geographic formations, and details of each county.

Next, walk under a trestle which serves as a reminder of the importance of railroading in Tennessee's history. Under the west end of the trestle are restrooms; under the east end is a visitor center and gift shop.

The tour passes into the Rivers of Tennessee Fountains, an area containing 31 vertical water fountains, one for each of the predominant waterways in Tennessee. A bowed and arched granite wall has inscriptions with information about the waterways. Along the east side of the park is the Walkway of the Counties with a time capsule for every one of Tennessee's 95 counties. The capsules will be opened in 2096.

The Court of Three Stars is a focal point of the park. Made of red, white, and blue granite, the area represents the three grand regions of the state–East,

Bicentennial Capitol Mall State Park celebrates the history of Nashville and of Tennessee. Jackie Sheckler Finch

Middle, and West Tennessee. This is also the site of the largest carillon in the world, a 95-bell carillon honoring the state's musical heritage. The 95 bells represent the citizens of the 95 counties. A 96th bell, known as the answer bell, is located on the grounds of the State Capitol and rings in answer to the 95 bells symbolizing government answering to the people.

The carillon plays four times an hour and then plays longer on the hour. Among the songs it plays are the "Tennessee Waltz," "Rocky Top," "Love Me Tender," and "Old Man River."

Near the north end of the park, the World War II Memorial features an 18,000-pound-granite globe floating on 1/8 inch of water. The countries on the globe are as they were during the war. Visitors can stop the globe and turn it with their hands.

Along the west side of the park, a 1,400-foot Wall of History is engraved with historic events that have occurred over the past two centuries. Each 10-year period along the wall is marked by a granite pylon. The wall breaks at the time of the Civil War to represent the divisive nature of the war on Tennessee. Then the wall lines back up again after the Civil War, representing the reunification of the state.

TOURS

Several companies provide guided tours around Nashville. Depending on the type of tour selected, tickets generally range from about $40 for a short, basic tour to upward of $105 for a tour that includes dinner on the *General Jackson* showboat. The typical tour, however, costs around $50 and lasts about 3 hours.

GRAY LINE OF TENNESSEE, 186 N. First St., Nashville, TN 37213; (615) 883-5555; graylinetn.com; $$$$. This tour company offers about 15 tours. The most popular is the "Discover Nashville" tour, a sightseeing trip that takes you to the State Capitol, Parthenon, Music Row, and other areas. A good bargain is the $44 Music City tour on the hop-on hop-off trolley with stops at 15 places and an informative guide driver talking about more than 100 points of interest. The "Homes of the Stars" tour includes a drive past the former or current homes of Garth Brooks and Trisha Yearwood, Dolly

The Gray Line bus company offers "hop-on, hop-off" tours. Jackie Sheckler Finch

Parton, Taylor Swift, Dierks Bentley, Jack White, Reese Witherspoon, Martina McBride, and others.

I RIDE NASHVILLE, Commerce St., Nashville TN 37201; (615) 244-0555; iridenashville.com. iRide Nashville offers customized tours, as well as team building, commercial rentals, special events, and Segway service. See Nashville up close and personal on this unique two-wheeled personal transportation device. Riders must be at least 12 years old and minors must be accompanied by a parent or guardian. Riders must sign a liability release, must be able to step on and off the platform and maintain normal balance at all times, must have use of left hand, and must wear comfortable walking-type footwear and dress for the weather. Helmets are required and furnished. Cost is $75 per person for a 2.5-hour tour. Tours offered daily during daylight hours.

NASHTRASH TOURS, 900 Rosa L. Parks Blvd., Nashville, TN 37208; (615) 226-7300, (800) 342-2132; nashtrash.com; $$$$. Combining big hair, gossip, a pink bus, and "fancy cheese hors d'oeuvres," NashTrash Tours offers what is definitely the wackiest tour of Nashville. This nearly 2-hour musical-comedy excursion, hosted by the Jugg Sisters—Sheri Lynn and Brenda Kay—promises "a hilarious, trashy journey through Music City." In addition to dishing out the dirt on country stars, the Juggs make time for makeup and styling tips and casserole recipes. Two other tours also are available—Pip's Music Row Confidential Tour and the Ben & Morey Tour. They take you to lots of local country music "scandal spots," including the Davidson County Jail, the legendary Tootsie's Orchid Lounge, the Ryman Auditorium, Printers Alley, Music Row, and the guitar-shaped pool where Elvis was said to have gone skinny-dipping. Fair warning—"No bachelorette parties are allowed on any tour," the Juggs note. "And if your group behaves like a bachelorette party, you will be charged a $20-per-head penalty fee." Check the website for tours and book ahead of time so you'll have a seat. The Juggs's Big Pink Bus departs from the north end of the Farmers' Market on Eighth Avenue N. next to the Bicentennial Mall.

RECORD STORES

ERNEST TUBB RECORD SHOP, 417 Broadway, Nashville, TN 37203; (615) 255-7503; etrecordshop.com. Ernest Tubb founded his downtown store on Commerce Street in 1947. Today the downtown store is at 417 Broadway. It specializes in early and hard-to-find country recordings but also stocks the latest country hits, so you'll find CDs and cassettes by everyone from Hank Snow, Webb Pierce, and Johnny Bush to George Strait and Alan Jackson. The store also has recordings by small-label artists such as Mike Snider and Johnny Russell. Hours of operation vary. With free admission, the *Midnight Jamboree* at Ernest Tubb Record Shop takes place Sat night at the Texas Troubadour Theatre at the Music Valley Drive location (2416 Music Valley Dr., 615-889-2474). The Texas Troubadour Theatre also hosts Nashville Cowboy Church on Sunday mornings at 10 a.m., led by Harry Yates and Joanne Cash Yates (Johnny Cash's sister).

Ernest Tubb founded his downtown store in 1947. Jackie Sheckler Finch

GREAT ESCAPE SUPERSTORE, 5400 Charlotte Ave. N., Nashville, TN 37209; (615) 385-2116; thegreatescapeonline.com. A bargain hunter's paradise for more than 20 years, Great Escape offers tens of thousands of used CDs, cassettes, albums, comic books, computer games, and other items. Collectors will find some vintage recordings here. Most CDs cost $6 to $9, while most tapes and records range from 99 cents to $3.99. The store pays cash or store credit for used products. Bring a photo ID if you have products to sell. Other shop is located at 111 North Gallatin Pike, Madison (615-865-8052); thegreatescapemadison.com. (See the **Shopping** chapter for more.)

GRIMEY'S NEW & PRELOVED MUSIC, 1060 E. Trinity Ln., Nashville, TN 37216; (615) 226-3811; grimeys.com. This little shop is well known among local rockers for its great collection of indie rock. If you're a vinyl aficionado, you'll want to check out the store's extensive collection, which includes many new releases on vinyl.

> i Upon her induction into the *Grand Ole Opry* in 1999, Trisha Yearwood was presented with a necklace belonging to her idol, Patsy Cline.

> **i** You can listen to several months' worth of performances of the Ernest Tubb Record Shop's famous Midnight Jamboree online at the show's website, etrecordshop.com/mj.htm.

The store also sells a lot of soul, funk, electronica, and hip-hop. You'll find just about everything here but mainstream country. Most used CDs are priced at $8.99. If you have music to sell, the store will pay you up to $5 in cash or $6 in trade; be sure to bring a valid ID if you want to sell your stuff. Grimey's also presents artist in-store appearances, promotes local concerts, and sells tickets to select area shows. The store has a good website that provides music news, CD reviews, audio samples of new releases, and more. The store is open daily.

PHONOLUXE RECORDS, 2609 Nolensville Rd., Nashville, TN 37211; (615) 259-3500. Phonoluxe sells used CDs, cassettes, albums, videos, DVDs, and laser discs. For music lovers on a budget, it's a must-stop. CDs are priced from $2 to about $10, and albums start at $1 and go all the way up to $200 for some of the rare, autographed recordings. Phonoluxe sells current and out-of-print recordings. The store pays cash for your used products (up to $5 per CD); just bring a photo ID. In business since 1987, the store is located between I-440 and Thompson Lane. Call for hours.

THIRD MAN RECORDS, 623 Seventh Ave. S., Nashville, TN 37203; (615) 891-4393; thirdmanrecords.com. Founded by musician Jack White, Third Man Records opened in Nashville in 2009. The facility is a record store, record label offices, photo studio, darkroom, and live venue with analog recording booth. The name "Third Man" refers to White's fondness for the number three. Most of the records are recorded, printed, and pressed in Nashville and produced by Jack White. The Third Man Novelties Lounge in the store contains a collection of vintage novelty machines. Half-hour tours at $20 give visitors an inside look at the direct-to-acetate recording facilities and label offices.

LIVE MUSIC

Places to Hear Live Music

Music is woven into the very fabric of Nashville; it seems to be everywhere here, as befits a town called "Music City." You're likely to find someone singing out on the street at any time of the day or night. While you may expect buskers to congregate along the Second Avenue entertainment district, they'll also entertain you while you wait in line at the Pancake Pantry. You're even likely to be serenaded at the airport. Live music is such an integral part of this town that you'll find it almost everywhere, from bars, restaurants, and coffeehouses to grocery stores and bookshops, street corners, and churches.

Live Music Venue signs around town indicate places where live music can be heard. Jackie Sheckler Finch

The revitalization of the downtown area—especially in "the District," which is the name given to Second Avenue, Printers Alley, and Lower Broadway—has provided a wealth of entertainment opportunities for tourists and locals and given more performers a place to play. In many cases there is no cover charge, which means you can hop around from one establishment to another without spending a fortune. Often these performers are playing for free, so if you like what you hear, drop a bill into the tip jar or in the hat if one is passed around.

The Larger Venues

Tickets for shows at these venues are available by calling Ticketmaster at (615) 242-9631 or by calling the venue box office.

ALLEN ARENA, DAVID LIPSCOMB UNIVERSITY, 1 University Park Dr., Nashville, TN 37204; (615) 966-1000; lipscomb.edu/venues/allen-arena. This 5,500-seat theater opened in October 2001 on the campus of David Lipscomb University. The arena is located on the campus's south end near the tennis courts and softball field. While the arena is used primarily for university sporting events, quite a few concerts have been held here. Lipscomb is a Church of Christ–affiliated school, so most of these shows have been of the Christian music variety—bands like dc Talk, Jars of Clay, and Third Day. However, the occasional up-and-coming country artist plays Allen Arena, too.

i *Grand Ole Opry* star Little Jimmy Dickens's first radio job was to crow like a rooster to open the morning program.

Nissan Stadium is home of the Tennessee Titans football team. Jackie Sheckler Finch

BRIDGESTONE ARENA, 501 Broadway, Nashville, TN 37203; (615) 770-2000; bridgestonearena.com. Although it features ice hockey and other sporting events, the Bridgestone Arena was designed primarily for concerts. Extra care has been devoted to the acoustical systems, and the sound is exceptional. The arena, which contains more than a million square feet of total space, seats as many as 20,000 for an in-the-round concert and 18,500 using its 40-by-60-foot proscenium stage. Since its opening in 1996, this venue formerly known as the Gaylord Entertainment Center has hosted the likes of Tim McGraw and Faith Hill, the Rolling Stones, the Dixie Chicks, Jimmy Buffett, Eric Clapton, and Mary J. Blige. Last-minute ticket buyers can take comfort in the fact that 20 box-office windows are available to speed the process.

CURB EVENT CENTER, 2000 Belmont Blvd., Nashville, TN 37212; (615) 460-8500; belmont.edu/curbeventcenter. Belmont University's 90,000-square-foot state-of-the-art sports and entertainment complex opened in late 2003. The facility includes a 5,000-seat arena, which presents occasional concerts and other entertainment events. Amy Grant and the Chinese Golden Dragon Acrobats were among the first entertainers to perform at the facility. Tickets are available through Ticketmaster. Parking is in the attached garage or along nearby streets.

Grand Ole Opry Features Legendary Performers and Newcomers

In the center stage of the *Grand Ole Opry* is a special piece of wood. It is from the old Ryman Auditorium. "Can you imagine what it has seen?" asked Dan Rogers, marketing manager for the *Opry.* "If it could talk, think about all the legends it could tell about."

Over the years, thousands of performers have stood on this circle—Hank Williams, Jim Reeves, Patsy Cline, Porter Wagoner, Dolly Parton, Loretta Lynn, Garth Brooks, Johnny Cash, June Carter Cash, Little Jimmy Dickens.

Even a skinny truck driver from Memphis named Elvis Presley.

When the *Grand Ole Opry* moved to its present 4,400-seat home at Opryland USA in 1974, the circular section of the old Ryman stage was taken along as a reminder of the place the *Opry* had called home for more than three decades.

From its simple beginnings on November 28, 1925, the *Grand Ole Opry* has never missed a Saturday night broadcast. Its audience, at first only a few hundred with primitive radios and crystal sets, has grown to include millions around the world.

It used to be that the *Opry* was pure country, but that isn't so anymore. When I attended a show back in 2006, one of the performers was a 16-year-old girl making her debut on the *Grand Ole Opry.* Her first disc wouldn't hit the shelves until a month later but, judging from the enthusiastic audience, newcomer Taylor Swift was already beginning her rapid ascent to stardom.

The show has a little bit of everything now. And if you don't like one singer, you can just wait a few minutes and the show will have out someone you do like.

The *Opry* has come a long way since that first radio broadcast in 1925. The featured performer that night was an 88-year-old fiddler, Uncle Jimmy Thompson, who boasted that he could "fiddle the bugs off a 'tater vine." The announcer was George D. Hay, who billed himself as the Solemn Old Judge—although he was only 30 years old.

Before long, solo musicians and groups such as the Gully Jumpers, the Possum Hunters, and the Crook Brothers showed up to volunteer their talents on the WSM Barn Dance, as it was known then. Two years later, Hay opened the show with an ad-lib, which somehow stuck, and the weekly show picked up the nickname by which it has been known ever since—the *Grand Ole Opry.*

According to legend, the show followed an NBC program of classical music and operatic selections. That evening, Hay began his show by announcing that "for the past hour you've been listening to grand opera. Now, we'll present *'Grand Ole Opry.'*"

An exhibit backstage at the Grand Ole Opry honors Roy Acuff. Jackie Sheckler Finch

One of the secrets of the *Opry*'s tremendous success is the fact that the show is performed live. There are no rehearsals but somehow each show seems to miraculously fall together at the last minute. While entertainers take center stage, family members and other people with backstage passes watch from the sidelines or sit in the big wooden benches on the back of the stage. Band members and backup singers casually wander back and forth and chat on the stage—while the show is going on.

After a devastating flood in May 2010, the *Grand Ole Opry* came back stronger than ever. Although the *Opry* House was closed for five months, the show was broadcast throughout the summer from other Nashville venues—such as the Ryman Auditorium and War Memorial Auditorium—without missing a single broadcast. Following a $20 million renovation, the *Opry* House welcomed the *Grand Ole Opry* back to its permanent home on September 28, 2010.

The *Opry* stage was under about 4 feet of water in some area. Painstakingly refurbished after being covered by 46 inches of floodwater, the 6-foot circle of oak wood was returned to its place of honor. "It is as it should be," *Opry* member Brad Paisley said at the time. "That circle means the world to all of us who love country music."

Highlights of the post-flood project include 18 new dressing rooms, each themed to celebrate some of the people and styles of country music that have made the *Opry* an American icon. Themed rooms include the No. 1 dressing room, "Mr. Roy" (in honor of Roy Acuff), with a placard containing a line from the *Opry* patriarch: "Ain't nothing gonna come up today that me and the Lord can't handle."

i Did you know that airmail originated in Nashville? In 1877 John Lillard had the first airmail stamp issued—for balloon service. Although that idea never got off the ground, Lillard was vindicated when the first practical airmail service—on an airplane—departed from Nashville on July 29, 1924.

***GRAND OLD OPRY* HOUSE,** 2804 Opryland Dr., Nashville, TN 37214; (615) 871-6779; opry.com. The *Grand Ole Opry* is the show that started it all, and this is where it has happened since the *Grand Ole Opry* moved from the Ryman Auditorium in 1974. A typical *Opry* performance features a mix of country music legends, today's top stars, and up-and-coming new artists. More than just traditional country, the *Opry* features bluegrass, gospel, Cajun, western swing, country-rock, and comedy. The lineup is released a couple of days before showtime. It's not unusual, however, for a special guest to drop by for a duet or surprise appearance during these unrehearsed performances. The schedule of showtimes varies and is subject to change, so it's a good idea to call ahead before planning a visit. Tickets range from $40 to $70. Tickets are sometimes still available just before showtime, but since shows often sell out, you might want to order them in advance if you're planning to visit on a specific day.

MARTHA RIVERS INGRAM CENTER FOR THE PERFORMING ARTS, Blair School of Music, 2400 Blakemore Ave., Nashville, TN 37212; (615) 322-7651; blair.vanderbilt.edu. Inaugurated in January 2002, the stunning Martha Rivers Ingram Center for the Performing Arts is a dramatic addition to the Blair School of Music. Its superb acoustics and state-of-the-art stage equipment make it an ideal setting for symphonic, operatic, or chamber orchestra events. The Ingram Center seats around 600; parking is across the street at the Capers Garage.

NASHVILLE MUNICIPAL AUDITORIUM, 417 Fourth Ave. N., Nashville, TN 37201; (615) 862-6390; nashvilleauditorium.com. Once Nashville's premier entertainment venue, 9,600-seat Municipal Auditorium, which opened in 1962, has taken a backseat to some of the newer and larger venues around town. But it still plays host to a wide range of performers. Municipal Auditorium occasionally holds trade shows and family shows, religious crusades, rodeos, circuses, and truck pulls.

Ascend Amphitheater hosts a concert. Courtesy of Nashville Convention & Visitors Corporation

NISSAN STADIUM, 1 Titans Way, Nashville, TN 37213; (615) 565-4300; titansonline.com. The 67,000-seat home of the National Football League's Tennessee Titans also plays host to occasional outdoor concerts. Formerly known as the Coliseum and LP Field, Nissan Stadium is the site of the nightly big-name concerts held during the CMA Music Festival/Fan Fair (see the **Annual Events** section of this chapter for more on that). Tickets to concert events are generally sold through Ticketmaster.

RIVERFRONT PARK, 100 First Ave. N., Nashville, TN 37201; (615) 862-8750 (Metro Parks office); nashville.gov/parks-and-recreation. Riverfront Park is the site of various seasonal concerts and events, some free and some with an admission charge. The 5-acre park, across the Cumberland River from the stadium, includes a tiered grassy hill that approximates an amphitheater. General capacity for concerts is 10,000.

RYMAN AUDITORIUM, 116 Fifth Ave. N., Nashville, TN 37219; (615) 889-3060; ryman.com. If any venue qualifies as Nashville's music mecca, it is the Ryman, former home to the *Grand Ole Opry.* Construction began on the historic, 2,362-seat former tabernacle in 1889, with significant financial support from steamboat captain Thomas G. Ryman, who had recently "found" religion and banned drinking and gambling on his boats. It opened in 1892 as the Union Gospel Tabernacle. The auditorium, though built for religious services, soon became known for hosting lectures and theatrical performances.

Through its early history, in addition to legendary preachers, the stage was graced by speakers and by performers. After Thomas Ryman's death in 1904, the building was renamed in his honor. From 1943 to 1974 it was the home of the *Grand Ole Opry.* After the *Opry* moved to Opryland in 1974, the Ryman was neglected for years, but it reopened in June 1994 after a full restoration. Now it is noted for its excellent acoustics.

A statue of Bill Monroe honors "The Father of Bluegrass" outside Ryman Auditorium. Jackie Sheckler Finch

Today's Ryman is a fully functioning performing arts center that features concert-quality sound and lighting and has radio and TV broadcast capabilities. The main floor and balcony seat about 1,000 people each. The *Grand Ole Opry* returns to the Ryman for special engagements. See the **Attractions** section of this chapter for information about Ryman exhibits and tours.

TENNESSEE PERFORMING ARTS CENTER (TPAC), 505 Deaderick St., Nashville, TN 37219; (615) 782-4040; tpac.org. TPAC (pronounced tee-pack) is mainly devoted to productions like its Broadway series and those of its resident groups. TPAC is occasionally the site of a pop or rock concert as well as private shows. TPAC consists of 4 venues: 2,408-seat Jackson Hall, 1,003-seat Polk Theater, 1,668-seat War Memorial Auditorium, and 288-seat Johnson Theater.

WAR MEMORIAL AUDITORIUM, 301 Sixth Ave. N., Nashville, TN 37243; (615) 782-4030; wmarocks.com. Located in the heart of downtown Nashville, the historic War Memorial Auditorium was dedicated in 1925 to honor the state's role in World War I and commemorate the Tennesseans who fought and died in the war. From 1925 to 1980, the auditorium was home to the Nashville Symphony. The *Grand Ole Opry* also called it home from 1939 to 1943. Minnie Pearl, Bill Monroe, and Ernest Tubb were all inducted into the *Grand Ole Opry* here. Today, the 2,000-seat auditorium is a popular performance venue. Artists who have performed here include Ray Charles, David Bowie, the Eagles, Elton John, Aretha Franklin, Lady Gaga, Mumford and Sons, Dolly Parton, Jack White, and many more. In the upper level of the

> *Grand Ole Opry* star Billy Grammer developed the Grammer guitar, one of the finest flat-top guitars on the market.

auditorium is an eclectic private room called the Attic Lounge where a series of short films feature discussions with emerging artists and touring musicians.

Smaller Venues

AJ'S GOOD TIME BAR, 421 Broadway, Nashville, TN 37203; (615) 678-4808; ajsgoodtimebr.com. Opened in 2017 on Lower Broadway, AJ's Good Time Bar is owned by country superstar Alan Jackson who is "Keepin' it Country" in his new establishment. Housed in the oldest building on Broadway, the venue was once a Civil War hospital, Nashville's first secondhand record store, and home of famous Bullet Records. The three-story building has a rooftop bar to admire the bright lights of Honky Tonk Highway. Each floor features stories and memorabilia about Jackson's life and career. Check out the man cave on the second floor and the fishing-themed third floor with a replica of Jackson's boat from his "5 O'Clock Somewhere."

ARRINGTON VINEYARDS, 6211 Patton Rd., Arrington, TN 37014; (615) 395-0102; arringtonvineyards.com. Owned by country music artist Kix Brooks (of longtime duo Brooks & Dunn), winemaker Kip Summers, and entrepreneur John Russell, Arrington Vineyards is located about 30 miles south of Nashville. The wine is now shipped in 35 states and is also served in restaurants in New York City, New Orleans, and Nashville. Opened July 1, 2007, Arrington Vineyards offers award-winning wines, beautiful rolling hills, wonderful sunsets, and free live Music in the Vines concerts. Bring a picnic dinner, buy a bottle of wine, get comfy on a blanket, and listen to some wonderful music. Music in the Vines is hosted every Sat and Sun from Apr through Oct. Check the website to verify dates and times.

B.B KING'S BLUES CLUB, 152 Second Ave. N., Nashville, TN 37201; (615) 256-2727; bbkings.com/nashville. B. B. King's presents nightly live blues, R&B, jazz, and, occasionally, rock acts. Most of the entertainment is local or regional, but the club features a nationally known performer about twice a month. The cover is $5 to $10. Expect to pay about $20 to $25 for special ticketed events. B. B. King's serves dinner daily. Barbecue, ribs, catfish, fried chicken, and burgers are on the menu.

THE BELCOURT THEATRE, 2102 Belcourt Ave., Nashville, TN 37212; (615) 846-3150; belcourt.org. The historic Belcourt Theatre is a nonprofit venue that features concerts, films, and events. The 340-seat Hillsboro Village venue hosts a variety of music, including jazz, blues, and symphony concerts. The theater sells alcoholic beverages and snacks. Purchase tickets at the theater's website, by phone, or at the theater's box office. Shows often sell out quickly.

THE BLUEBIRD CAFE, 4104 Hillsboro Pike, Nashville, TN 37215; (615) 383-1461; bluebirdcafe.com. You can't talk about songwriter venues in Nashville without mentioning the Bluebird. And you can't talk at the Bluebird without someone hushing you. That may be an exaggeration, but only a slight one, because here the song is meant to be the focus, not background music for conversations. Insiders know that "Shhh!" has become a motto of the famous listening room. A casual look around the 8-by-10-inch photographs covering the walls will tell you why: Practically anybody who's anybody in new country and acoustic music has played here. Some, like Garth Brooks, played here as unknowns and went on to become superstar recording artists, while some have made their names as songwriters who pen hits for other people.

The songwriters in-the-round format, in which four songwriters sit in a circle and take turns playing their own songs, was pioneered here by Fred Knobloch and Don Schlitz, and it's a tradition that continues most nights. Reservations can be made for shows Tues through Sat. Shows on Sun and Mon are first-come, first-served. The evening show begins at 9 p.m. Tues through Thurs and 9:30 p.m. Fri and Sat. The early show each Mon is open-microphone (for more info on that, see the Open Microphones section later in this chapter).

BOURBON STREET BLUES AND BOOGIE BAR, 220 Printers Alley, Nashville, TN 37219; (615) 242-5837; bourbonstreetbluesandboogiebar.com. Bourbon Street features live blues music 7 nights a week in an appropriately dark New Orleans–style atmosphere. The club frequently brings in national acts. The cover is usually $10 to $20 with an occasional exception for special engagements. The kitchen serves Cajun American cuisine.

CRAZY TOWN, 308 Broadway, Nashville, TN 37201; (615) 254-5460; crazytownnashville.com. Crazy Town is massive. The 3-story venue features 6 bars, 3 stages, 2 outdoor patios, and a panoramic view of downtown Broadway. The decor is a funky mix of reclaimed barn walls, gigantic hanging guitars, handmade chandeliers, antique signs, and a barber's chair where guests can take selfies. Check the website for a lineup of live music. The menu features bar food like burgers, hot chicken, nachos, and more. Desserts are pure sugar shots—fried Oreos and fried Twinkies. Crazy Town is open daily from 11 a.m. to 3 p.m.

DIERKS BENTLEY'S WHISKEY ROW NASHVILLE, 400 Broadway, Nashville, TN 37203; (629) 203-7822; dierkswhiskeyrow.com/Nashville.tn. Opened in 2018 by country music star Dierks Bentley, Whiskey Row has 3 stories with a rooftop patio. The menu, described as "American gastropub cuisine," offers lunch, brunch, and dinner. Entrees include chicken and waffles, fish-and-chips, catfish and grits, and a roasted mushroom burger—no hamburger just mushrooms. If whiskey is not to your taste, Whiskey Row offers craft beer, wine, and craft cocktails like the '94 Chevy, a mix of Deep Eddy Ruby Red Vodka, Bruto Americano, and fresh lime, topped with Leinenkugel's Grapefruit Shandy.

DOUGLAS CORNER CAFE, 2106-A Eighth Ave. S., Nashville, TN 37204; (615) 298-1688; douglascorner.com. A favorite with Nashville's top songwriters, Douglas Corner is a cozy, laid-back little club that features songwriters, artists, and bands 6 nights a week. In-the-round performances, featuring a selection of songwriters who take turns performing their tunes, are a highlight. The cover charge varies; on weekends, it's typically around $10. On various nights, there will be a 6 p.m. show, when admission is free. Douglas Corner has open microphone on Tues nights (see the subsequent Open Microphones section for details).

Dierks Bentley's Whiskey Row opened in 2018. Jackie Sheckler Finch

THE END, 2219 Elliston Place, Nashville, TN 37203; (615) 321-4457; endnashville.com. A longtime fixture on Elliston Place, this hole-in-the-wall club is known for booking independent rock acts. We used to visit back in our '80s big-hair days, when the club was known as Elliston Square and the whole area was called the "Rock Block." The vibe hasn't changed much since then. The club is still cramped, the music is still loud, and the sound sometimes isn't so good, but if cutting-edge, indie rock is your scene, this is the place. The End has bands 6 to 7 nights a week. The cover charge is usually $5 to $20. The club sells beer and wine.

> i Before stardom, *Grand Ole Opry* star Alan Jackson delivered mail to the *Opry* House.

EXIT/IN, 2208 Elliston Place, Nashville, TN 37203; (615) 321-3340; exitin.com. After more than 40 years, the legendary Exit/In is still alive and kickin'. The club is one of Nashville's oldest music venues, having first opened in 1971. Longtime patrons have fond memories of many fine performances at the Exit/In. The club is essentially just a big room with a capacity of 500 people, a stage in the front, and a bar in the back. Who needs anything more? The show schedule is inclined toward rock and alternative country with a lot of artist-showcase concerts. The cover varies; it's generally $10 to $20 but sometimes can be as much as $75 or more for prime shows.

FGL House was opened in 2017 by the superstar duo Florida Georgia Line.
Jackie Sheckler Finch

FGL HOUSE, 120 Third St. S., Nashville, TN 37201; (615) 961-5460; fglhouse.com. The FGL House was established by musical duo Florida Georgia Line. Offering the largest "Cruise" rooftop bar in Nashville, FGL House hosts parties with stunning views of the Music City skyline. For a quieter spot, head to the "Little

Red Corvette" basement-level lounge where specialty cocktails inspired by the '90s are all the rage. The 4-story, 22,000-square-foot attraction also features Florida Georgia Line's own Old Camp Whiskey. A massive video wall spotlights performances from the duo along with other country music stars. The menu describes the culinary choices as "Southern-style food with a California flair." Popular choices include the Horseradish Salmon—horseradish crusted salmon, smoked cheddar grits, and green beans, and No Joke Mac 'N Cheese—thick bacon, beer pulled chicken, smoked white and yellow cheddar cheese, and cavatappi pasta.

JASON ALDEAN'S KITCHEN + ROOFTOP BAR, 307 Broadway, Nashville, TN 37201; jasonaldeansnashville.com. Opened in 2018 by country star Jason Aldean, the 4-level live entertainment venue features a rooftop bar, restaurant, outside patio, 6 bars, and live music. For decor, the main restaurant level has a 1961 4020 John Deere tractor as a tribute to Aldean's hit song, "Big Green Tractor." Said to be the largest rooftop patio on Broadway, the rooftop bar and outside patio has an old classic Chevy truck suspended above the eating area. The menu features "Southern cooking with a flair," including Grandma's Pot Roast (braised Angus beef, carrots, parsnips, mashed potatoes, and country gravy) and Southern meat loaf (beef and pork, wild mushrooms, barbecue demi glazes, mashed potatoes, and onion straws.)

Jason Aldean opened a bar and restaurant in 2018. Jackie Sheckler Finch

LAYLA'S HONKY TONK, 418 Broadway, Nashville, TN 37203; (615) 726-2799; laylasnashville.com. Sandwiched between Second Fiddle and Robert's in downtown Nashville is Layla's Honky Tonk, a cozy club that offers traditional bluegrass and much more. Sure, bluegrass legend Ralph Stanley has graced Layla's stage, but so have other musical styles such as Hank Williams III and the Drive-By Truckers. Check out Layla's music schedule and you'll see a wide range of music and performers. Layla's has plenty of seating and bunches of dancing room. When folks get hungry, they can get snacks like corn nuggets, cheese planks, and pickle chips, or choose a burger or chicken sandwich. As for those license plates decorating Layla's, if you've got one handy, take it in and swap it for a cold brew. Then your license will become part of the growing decor.

A doorman stands in front of Layla's on Honky Tonk Highway.
Jackie Sheckler Finch

LEGENDS CORNER, 428 Broadway, Nashville, TN 37203; (615) 248-6334; legendscorner.com. Album covers of country greats plaster the walls at Legends, a popular honky-tonk at the corner of Fifth and Broadway. The bar features a variety of local talent and no cover charge. It's popular with tourists as well as locals who want to kick up their heels on the dance floor or just sit at the bar and drink a beer. Take a gander at the huge mural on the side of Legends and see how many of the greats you can identify.

LONG HOLLOW JAMBOREE, 3600 Long Hollow Pike, Goodlettsville, TN 37072; (615) 824-4445; long-hollow-jamboree-and-restaurant.business.site; $. Long Hollow Jamboree is a drive out in the country to hear some old-timey music and eat old-fashioned home cooking featuring "meat-and-three"—usually fried chicken, fish, or roast beef with choice of three veggies, plus bread. What started as a jam session at a neighborhood grocery store in the 1970s is still going strong with loyal fans. The place is rustic and weather-beaten with well-worn booths and long cafeteria-style tables and chairs. It is sure not slick or modern but it does offer live music and dancing with a packed dance floor. A smoke- and alcohol-free venue, Long Hollow welcomes all ages. Open for lunch Mon through Fri, country music on Fri and Sat nights but call to be sure.

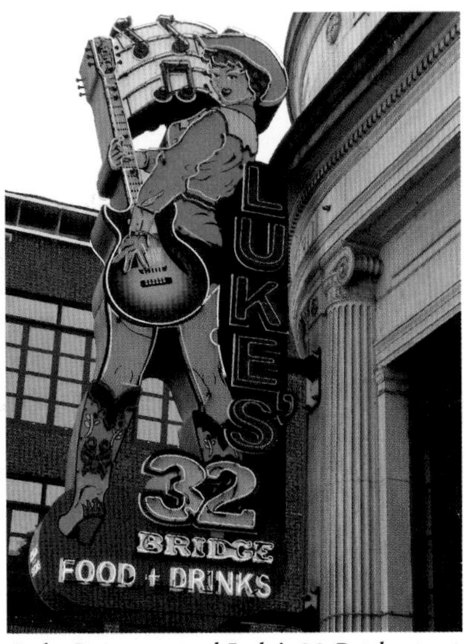

Luke Bryan opened Luke's 32 Bridge in downtown Nashville in 2018.
Jackie Sheckler Finch

LUKE'S 32 BRIDGE, 301 Broadway, Nashville, TN 37201; (504) 355-6565; lukes32bridge.com. Opened in 2018 by country music star Luke Bryan, the new music venue offers 6 floors of entertainment complete with 4 music stages, 8 bars, 2 restaurants, and a rooftop bar. The name is a nod to Bryan's childhood and hometown in Georgia. The 32 Bridge in Georgia crosses over the Flint River and marks the line between Worth and Lee counties. It was here that Bryan said he learned to fish, hunt, and enjoy the outdoors with his family. The restaurant features some of Bryan's favorites like Beer Can Chicken (Nashville house beer, Yukon gold potatoes, and green beans) and Luke's Elk Burger (ground elk, Red Dragon Cheese, garlic aioli, tomato, and pickle). The Sushi Bar offers squid, calamari, pork, shrimp, salmon, tuna, and much more.

NASHVILLE PALACE, 2611 McGavock Pike, Nashville, TN 37214; (615) 885-1541; nashville-palace.com. It's become a part of modern country music lore that Randy Travis had a gig frying fish here and singing on the side when he was "discovered." The Nashville Palace features live country music and a full menu with sandwiches, salads, steaks, chicken, catfish, ribs, and more. Check the website to see who is playing and when.

NUDIE'S HONKY TONK, 409 Broadway, Nashville, TN 37203; nudieshonkytonk.com. To trace the colorful history of "The Rhinestone Cowboy," visit Nudie's and see the iconic pop culture clothing made by Ukrainian-born Nuta "Nudie" Kotlyarenko and his wife Bobbie. The couple started their world-renowned fashion brand in the 1940s in their garage. Nudie created custom fashions for such legends as Johnny Cash, John Lennon, John Wayne, Bob Dylan, Elton John, and many more. On display is one of Nudie's most famous pieces—the $10,000 gold lame suit that Elvis Presley wore on the cover of his *50,000,000 Elvis Fans Can't be Wrong* album. Nudie's Honky Tonk also has 3 live performance stages and Nashville's longest bar at more than 100 feet. The menu features bar food such as fried pickles, hot dogs, hot chicken, tacos, sweet potato fries, and burgers. Open Sun through Thurs 11 a.m. to 3 a.m., Fri and Sat, 10 a.m. to 3 a.m.

OLE RED, 300 Broadway, Nashville, TN 37201; (615) 780-0900; olered.com. Opened in 2018, Ole Red is Blake Shelton's establishment and it's named, of course, after Shelton's hit song, "Ol' Red". The entertainment venue features a 2-story bar and restaurant, dance floor, rooftop with indoor/outdoor bar, shop, and stage. Drink choices include Ole Red Ale by Fat Bottom served in

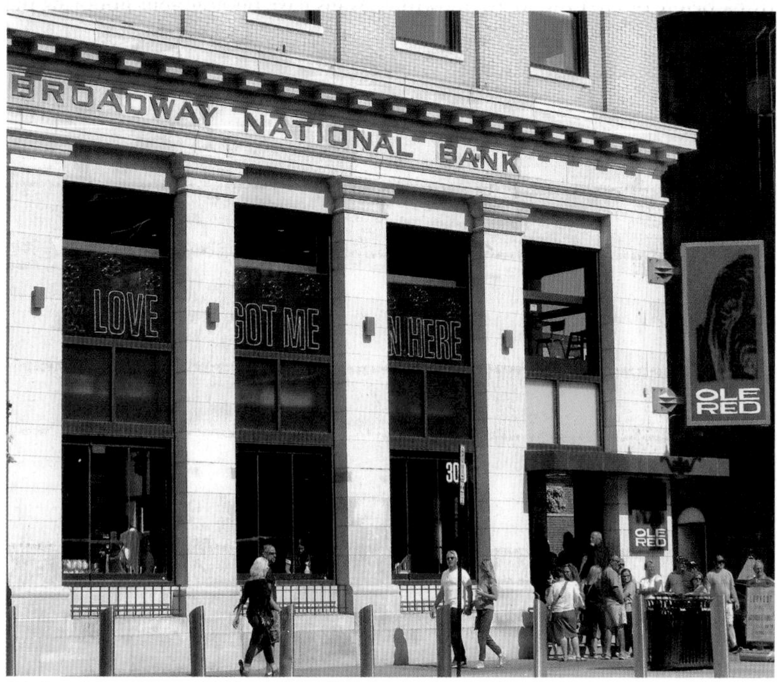

Blake Shelton opened Ole Red in downtown Nashville in 2018.
Jackie Sheckler Finch

an Ole Red mason jar and the Drunk'n Mule cocktail with Smithworks Vodka, ginger beer, fresh lime juice served in an Ole Red mason jar. The menu offers bar food plus entrees such as fried chicken, grilled rib eye, and salmon. Creative side dishes include cheddar smashed potatoes, street corn, hammered beans, and chili-fried cauliflower. Ole Red also has a kids menu and an "Absolutely Obnoxious Lucky Charms Sundae" with cereal milk ice cream, marshmallow sauce, Lucky Charms cookie, doughnut, and cotton candy pop rocks.

RAY STEVENS CABARAY SHOWROOM, 5724 River Rd., Nashville, TN 37209; (615) 327-4630; raystevenscabaray.com. The man who brought us "The Streak" and "Everything is Beautiful" now has his own dinner club and piano bar. Opened in 2018, Ray Stevens CabaRay features performances by the singer and comedian, as well as by other performers. Guests can enjoy a multicourse meal before the show. Or they can choose to arrive just for the theater performance. The theater offers seating for more than 700 guests, plus free parking for 300 cars and 6 buses. A piano bar invites guests to relax and have a drink before or after the show. Showroom walls have photographs honoring the producers and musicians who turned Nashville into Music City. Trophy cases display memorabilia from Ray Stevens's career.

CabaRay Courtesy of Tennessee Department of Tourist Development

John Rich of Big and Rich opened Redneck Riviera in downtown Nashville in 2018. Jackie Sheckler Finch

REDNECK RIVIERA BAR & BBQ, 208 Broadway, Nashville, TN 37201; (615) 436-4070; redneckrivieranashville.com. Opened in 2018 by singer-songwriter John Rich, Redneck Riviera celebrates America and its heroes. With a red, white, and blue color scheme, the three-floor bar offers two stages, rooftop patio, and live music at all hours. The Heroes Bar salutes military veterans, active duty, and first responders who receive special deals on drinks and house-made jerky. The menu offers barbecue pulled pork, chili, pork rinds, nachos, salad, mac and cheese, and John Rich's Redneck Jerky. The bar also features Redneck Riviera American Blended Whiskey.

ROCKETOWN, 601 Fourth Ave. S., Nashville, TN 37210; (615) 843-4001; rocketown.com. This youth-oriented nonprofit entertainment venue is the culmination of a longtime dream for Christian music superstar Michael W. Smith, who wanted to create a safe place for teens to congregate and have fun. Rocketown provides a skate park, classrooms, 3 stages for live entertainment, snack bar, recording studio, and photography, art, and dance studios. Rocketown serves about 800 kids each week. The club presents a mixture of

Broadway is known as Honky Tonk Highway because of all its music clubs and bars. Jackie Sheckler Finch

music styles, including rock, pop, hip-hop, punk, and Top 40. About half of the bands featured are Christian-oriented. The staff keeps an eye on the goings-on, keeping age-appropriateness in mind. Parents or guardians often hang out at the coffee club while the younger set attends a concert or burns off energy in the skate park.

ROBERT'S WESTERN WORLD, 416 Broadway, Nashville, TN 37203; (615) 244-9552; robertswesternworld.com. You can buy a pair of cowboy boots while you listen to bluegrass and honky-tonk music at Robert's. There's live entertainment day and night—from 11 a.m. to 3 a.m. Stars occasionally show up to hang out and often end up taking the stage for a song or two. Famous faces who've visited Robert's include Merle Haggard, Kid Rock, Brooks & Dunn, Dolly Parton, and Tracy Byrd. There's no cover charge. Everyone is welcome to attend the Sunday Morning Gospel Fellowship at 10:30 a.m. on Sun. The service features traditional gospel music with prayer and nondenominational spiritual messages.

SECOND FIDDLE, 420 Broadway, Nashville, TN 37203; (615) 251-6812; thesecondfiddle.com. Step into the Second Fiddle between Tootsie's and Layla's and step back in time. Dozens of old radios and musical instruments line the walls of this large bar. Look for a guitar signed by Mother Maybelle Carter, the Carter family, and Johnny Cash. Bunches of *Grand Ole Opry* memorabilia help provide the country decor. Celebrity performers have been known to walk through these doors, including Tim McGraw, Kix Brooks, David Frizzell, Tracy Byrd, and Trick Pony. If the place looks familiar, it has shown up in music videos and album shots. McBride and the Ride filmed a video here. Second Fiddle was the setting of "40 Greatest Drinking Songs" with Wynonna Judd. Pam Tillis used shots of the honky-tonk for an album.

Second Fiddle is part of Honky Tonk Highway. Jackie Sheckler Finch

STATION INN, 402 12th Ave. S., Nashville, TN 37203; (615) 255-3307; stationinn.com. The Station Inn is one of our favorite places to hear live music. A "Who's Who" of bluegrass have played at the homey (and homely) little club that's almost hidden away down on 12th Avenue S. The club occasionally features country, Americana, and folk performers. Vince Gill has been known to drop in, too. We like to get there early so we can claim a couple of the old worn-out vinyl seats that line the back wall (they're said to have come straight from Lester Flatt's original tour bus), then settle in for an evening of good music. The Station Inn features live bluegrass nightly. The cover charge generally varies from $15 to $25, depending on the band. There is no cover on Sunday, when an open jam session takes place. Snacks include pizza, hot dogs, nachos, Daddy Bob's pimento, Goo Goo Clusters, Moon Pies, and more.

TEQUILA COWBOY, 305 Broadway, Nashville, TN 37201; (615) 742-9078; tequilacowboy.com/Nashville. Five venues under one rooftop means that you are sure to find music at Tequila Cowboy. Rock Bar has a live stage with a full band every night. Karma Lounge hosts a top 40 dance club. The Game Room is the place to shoot pool and watch the big game on TV. The VIP Room is party headquarters. Wanna B's Karaoke Bar gives would-be singers a chance at stardom. If you can't sing—or even if you can—Tequila Cowboy also has the only mechanical bull on Broadway for those who want to test their bull-riding skills. The menu features bar food like nachos, egg rolls, chicken wings, burgers, and pulled pork, plus more serious food like steak and blackened fish. Closed Mon. Open Tues and Wed from 4 p.m. to midnight; Thurs 4 p.m. to 3 a.m.; Fri through Sun from 11 a.m. to 3 a.m.

> i Once a nightclub bouncer, Garth Brooks calls his *Grand Ole Opry* membership the pinnacle of his career.

TEXAS TROUBADOUR THEATRE, 2416 Music Valley Dr., #108, Nashville, TN 37214; (615) 585-9301; texastroubadourtheatre.com. The 500-capacity Texas Troubadour Theatre takes evident pride in the fact that it is an extension of the Ernest Tubb Record Shop—the legendary Tubb was known as "the Texas Troubadour." A popular event is the continuation of the weekly *Midnight Jamboree* radio show, which Tubb started the night of May 3, 1947, the same date he opened his first record shop in downtown Nashville. The *Midnight Jamboree,* which airs on WSM-AM 650 each Saturday after the *Grand Ole Opry,* is the second-longest-running radio show in history, taking a backseat only to the *Opry* itself. After more than 50 years of the show, it continues its tradition of free admission, even when a star such as Alan Jackson, Travis Tritt, or Marty Stuart is in the lineup. That's the way Ernest Tubb, who started the show as a way for new artists to get on the radio, always wanted it. The other regular program at the Troubadour is *Cowboy Church,* a free, nondenominational, come-as-you-are service every Sun at 10 a.m. The Troubadour, which is across from Opryland in the Music Valley area, also features theatrical productions such as *A Tribute to the King* (Elvis).

3RD AND LINDSLEY BAR AND GRILL, 818 Third Ave. S., Nashville, TN 37210; (615) 259-9891; 3rdandlindsley.com. This club, a half mile south of Broadway, boasts live blues, R&B, rock, and alternative music 7 nights a week. It's popular with Nashville's session musicians and singers and is a good spot to catch some local favorites. The cover charge varies according to the band but is usually about $10 to $20. The grill serves lunch and dinner, including prime rib, fish-and-chips, and red beans and rice. Rhythm City Church is held every Sunday at 11 a.m.

TOOTSIE'S ORCHID LOUNGE, 422 Broadway, Nashville, TN 37203; (615) 726-0463; tootsies.net. You can't miss Tootsie's—it's the pale purple

Tootsie's Orchid Lounge was a popular hangout for Grand Ole Opry stars.
Jackie Sheckler Finch

club on Broadway. In the old days this was where legendary songwriters like Kris Kristofferson and Willie Nelson gathered to drink and write. Much of the lounge's history is reflected in the photos on the walls. There's a stage downstairs and another upstairs, where you can walk out into an alley to the side door to the Ryman Auditorium (you can't get in that way, but many legendary stars have been known to come out that door and into Tootsie's). Both stages feature live entertainment day and night; there isn't a cover charge. Tootsie's is worth a visit for anyone who wants to soak up a little of Music City's music history.

THE WILDHORSE SALOON, 120 Second Ave. N., Nashville, TN 37201; (615) 902-8200; wildhorsesaloon.com. The Wildhorse is one of the top tourist attractions downtown in the District. This state-of-the-art music club, which opened in June 1994, is host to a continuing parade of country events. The Wildhorse presents house bands, booked from all over the United States, every night except during tapings. Free line dancing lessons are offered on the largest dance floor in Tennessee. Concert tickets cost about $25.

> **i** Ex-Marine and country music superstar George Jones once experimented with rockabilly music under the name "Thumper Jones."

Garth Brooks played Douglas Corner as a songwriter and held his first fan club party at the venue performing with his band to a jam-packed crowd. He presented the owner with the printing plate used to make the Fan Fair posters for the event. That plate still hangs in Douglas Corner today.

Open Microphones

Several area clubs have open mic nights. Here are some of the more highly regarded open-microphone venues in Nashville.

THE BLUEBIRD CAFE, 4104 Hillsboro Rd., Nashville, TN 37215; (615) 383-1461; bluebirdcafe.com. Open mic night at the legendary Bluebird is Mon from 6 p.m. to 9 p.m. If you're interested in playing, call (615) 943-8168 between the hours of 11 a.m. and noon on Mon morning for the Mon night you want to perform. No advanced sign-ups are accepted. You can only sign up for open mic on the day you are calling. The first 25 sign-ups are accepted and can bring one guest. Each performer must be at the club by 5:15 p.m. on that Mon to perform. The Bluebird has a house Kawai digital piano with 88 weighted keys that is available for use. If you do get on stage, you can play a maximum of 2 songs or 8 minutes, and your songs should be originals. Now relax and play, keeping in mind that if you do screw up, nobody will boo you. Just about everybody else in the audience is a songwriter, and they know what it's like. And while you should enjoy yourself, forget those dreams of being "discovered" at an open mic. It just doesn't happen that way anymore, but it's a great way to work on your musical- and vocal-presentation skills. For more information about the Bluebird, see the listing earlier in the Smaller Venues section of this chapter.

DOUGLAS CORNER CAFE, 2106-A Eighth Ave. S., Nashville, TN 37204; (615) 292-2530 (recording to sign up); douglascorner.com. Douglas Corner's open mic starts at 8 p.m. Tues. You can reserve your spot in line by calling the listed number between 2 and 6 p.m. the same day you wish to attend. Calling Douglas Corner's main number won't do you any good. Performers must arrive by 8 p.m. and will get to perform 2 songs.

ANNUAL EVENTS

March/April

TIN PAN SOUTH, Ryman Auditorium and various Nashville venues; (615) 256-3354, (800) 321-6008; tinpansouth.com. One of Nashville's treasures is its talented songwriting community. Nashville songwriters pen hits that are heard and loved by millions around the world. In addition to countless country songs, numerous pop hits—such as Eric Clapton's Grammy-winning song "Change the World," written by Music City's Gordon Kennedy, Wayne Kirkpatrick, and Tommy Sims—came from the pens of Nashville tunesmiths. We are fortunate that, on just about any night of the week, we can head out to a club like the Bluebird Cafe or Douglas Corner and hear great songs performed by the talented individuals who wrote them.

For about five days and nights at the end of March, Tin Pan South offers the chance to catch a bunch of top songwriters performing their hits acoustically in an intimate club setting. The Nashville Songwriters Association International sponsors this event, the nation's only festival celebrating the songwriter and the song, and writers from around the country join in. Tin Pan South takes its name from Nashville's songwriting predecessor, the famous Tin Pan Alley in New York. Tickets are available through Ticketmaster (615-255-9600, ticketmaster.com) and at the door if tickets aren't sold out. Ticket prices vary. Shows usually begin at 6:30 and 9 p.m.

May

MUSICIANS CORNER, Centennial Park, 2500 West End Ave., Nashville, TN 37203; (615) 862-8400; musicianscornernashville.com. Musicians Corner presents free concerts on Fri and Sat in May and June and on Thurs in Sept. Events feature performances by emerging and established artists, a beer garden, food trucks, local artisans, and family-friendly activities. A few rows of stone benches are available on a first-come, first-served basis but it is recommended that visitors bring lawn chairs, blankets, or beach towels. Dogs on leashes are welcome.

> **i** Blind since birth, *Grand Ole Opry* star Ronnie Milsap played the violin by age 7, piano by age 8, and guitar by age 12.

It's a Grand Ole Cast

How many of these names do you recognize? Those of you who are die-hard country music fans probably know them all. As of early 2019, this was the cast of the *Grand Ole Opry.* The names are followed by the year they joined. The cast changes from time to time, as new members are added and others choose to drop out for a while. New members are invited to join on the basis of their contributions to country music and whether they are available to perform from time to time during the live radio broadcast.

Trace Adkins, 2003; Bill Anderson, 1961; Bobby Bare, 1964; Dierks Bentley, 2005; Clint Black, 1991; Garth Brooks, 1990; Jim Ed Brown, 1963; Terri Clark, 2004; John Conlee, 1981; Dailey & Vincent, 2017; Charlie Daniels, 2008; Diamond Rio, 1998; Joe Diffie, 1993; the Gatlin Brothers, 1976; Crystal Gayle, 2017; Vince Gill, 1991; Tom T. Hall, 1971; Emmylou Harris, 1992; Jan Howard, 1971; Alan Jackson, 1991; Stonewall Jackson, 1956; Hal Ketchum, 1994; Alison Krauss, 1993; Little Big Town, 2014; Patty Loveless, 1988; Dustin Lynch, 2018; Loretta Lynn, 1962; Barbara Mandrell, 1972; Martina McBride, 1995; Del McCoury, 2003; Reba McEntire, 1986; Jesse McReynolds, 1964; Ronnie Milsap, 1976; Eddie Montgomery of Montgomery Gentry, 2009; Craig Morgan, 2008; Lorrie Morgan, 1984; Oak Ridge Boys, 2011; Old Crow Medicine Show, 2013; the Osborne Brothers, 1964; Brad Paisley, 2001; Dolly Parton, 1969; Stu Phillips, 1967; Ray Pillow, 1966; Charley Pride, 1993; Jeanne Pruett, 1973; Rascal Flatts, 2011; Riders in the Sky, 1982; Darius Rucker, 2012; Jeannie Seely, 1967; Blake Shelton, 2010; Ricky Skaggs, 1982; Connie Smith, 1965; Mike Snider, 1990; Marty Stuart, 1992; Mel Tillis, 2007; Pam Tillis, 2000; Randy Travis, 1986; Travis Tritt, 1992; Josh Turner, 2007; Keith Urban, 2012; Carrie Underwood, 2008, Ricky Van Shelton, 1988; Steve Wariner, 1996; the Whites, 1984; Trisha Yearwood, 1999; Chris Young, 2017.

i "Nashville Sound" refers to a style of smooth, heavily produced country music in which piano, strings, and backing vocals are more prominent than traditional fiddle and banjo. The style was popularized in the late 1950s and 1960s by producers Chet Atkins and Owen Bradley. Patsy Cline's recordings are among the most popular examples of the famous Nashville Sound.

June

BONNAROO MUSIC & ARTS FESTIVAL, Manchester, TN 37355; (931) 728-7635; bonnaroo.com. Outdoor music festival aficionados may want to know that Bonnaroo—a massive 4-day music and camping festival—takes place just down the road at a 700-acre farm in Manchester, about 60 miles southeast of Music City. Since Bonnaroo was first launched in 2002, it has become one of the nation's premier music events, drawing almost 100,000 avid music fans from around the country. The artist lineup is heavy on "jam bands"—artists known for their improvisation in a variety of roots music styles. Performers have included Bob Dylan, the Dead, Widespread Panic, Trey Anastasio of Phish, Dave Matthews, Willie Nelson, and Alison Krauss. There are multiple stages, as well as a central area featuring around-the-clock entertainment activities and food and beverage concessions. A Comedy Theatre and a Cinema feature brand-new independent films. Tickets, traditionally available only online at the Bonnaroo website, are about $300 for a 4-day pass, which includes camping and parking. Special VIP packages can cost as much as $1,650. An important note: Traffic surrounding the festival can be a nightmare, so do your research and plan a good route—preferably something other than I-24, which has been known to back up for hours during this event.

CMA MUSIC FESTIVAL/FAN FAIR, various downtown Nashville venues; (800) CMA-FEST; cmafest.com. Country music fans have traditionally been a loyal bunch, and country artists bend over backward to show their gratitude during this annual celebration designed to honor music fans. The bond between country fans and their favorite artists is a unique one in the music industry. You wouldn't find many famous rock bands standing in a booth all day to sign autographs for their fans, but country artists do just that. In 1996, for example, Garth Brooks made a surprise visit to the 25th annual Fan Fair and signed autographs for 23 consecutive hours—reportedly without a

The CMA celebrates at Nissan Stadium Courtesy of Nashville Convention & Visitors Corporation

bathroom break! Since its inception in 1972, Fan Fair, organized and produced by the Country Music Association, has become a tradition for country fans and Nashville's music industry. Autograph sessions take place indoors at the Music City Center, morning and afternoon concerts are staged at Riverfront Park, and headline concerts are presented each night at the LP Field. Various other activities, including fan-club parties and other celebrity events, take place at venues all over town. Typically, more than 200 country music artists participate.

Most major artists participate in the event, although not all stars attend each year. Net proceeds from the festival are used to advance the growth and popularity of country music. For more information, or to register, call the number listed.

JEFFERSON STREET JAZZ & BLUES FESTIVAL, 1215 9th Ave. N., Nashville, TN 37208; (615) 726-5867; jumpnashville.com. In the mid-1900s, Jefferson Street was nationally known for its jazz, blues, and R&B music. As part of an effort to revitalize the historic street's culture, the Jefferson Street United Merchants Partnership began presenting this annual music festival in 2000. The event is usually held around Juneteenth, the June 19 celebration of the ending of slavery.

During the festival, nationally known and local jazz and blues acts perform on the stage throughout the day and late into the evening from noon to 10 p.m.

Performers have included DeFord Bailey Jr., Tyrone Smith, and Marion James. It's a family-oriented event, complete with food and merchandise vendors and activities for children. Admission is $20 in advance, $25 day of event.

July

UNCLE DAVE MACON DAYS, Cannonsburgh Village, 312 S. Front St., Murfreesboro, TN 37129; (800) 716-7560; uncledavemacondays.org. Grab your banjos and shine your dancin' shoes for the annual Uncle Dave Macon Days in Cannonsburgh Village in historic Murfreesboro. Considered one of America's premier summer festivals, the family-oriented event was established to honor the memory of Uncle Dave Macon, who lived near Murfreesboro and is considered one of the first *Grand Ole Opry* superstars. A master banjo player and performer, he died in 1952 and was inducted into the Country Music Hall of Fame in 1966. Uncle Dave Macon Days is one of the very few old-time music competitions in the country. Cannonsburgh is an authentic pioneer village with more than 20 restored log structures. Living-history demonstrations take place during the weekend. A Motorless Parade brings horse-drawn buggies and carriages along a route on Saturday morning. Murfreesboro is 30 minutes southeast of Nashville on I-24.

October

***GRAND OLE OPRY* BIRTHDAY CELEBRATION,** *Grand Ole Opry* House, 2802 Opryland Dr., Nashville, TN 37214; (615) 871-6779; opry.com. *Grand Ole Opry* fans gather each October to celebrate the birthday of America's longest-running radio program. The 2-day party is held in mid-October and includes concerts, a *Grand Ole Opry* performance, and autograph and photo sessions with the stars. Various ticket packages and group rates are available. Call the number listed for more information. For more on the Opry, see our **History** chapter as well as other entries in this chapter.

> i Kitty Wells, the first female country singer to become a major star, was also one of the rare country stars actually born in Nashville. She earned the title "Queen of Country Music."

i Experts say the Ryman Auditorium's acoustics are second only to the Mormon Tabernacle, surpassing even Carnegie Hall.

DOVE AWARDS, Allen Arena at Lipscomb University, Nashville, TN 37204; (615) 242-0303; doveawards.com. The Gospel Music Association's annual Gospel Music Week traditionally includes the presentation of the Dove Awards, when trophies in more than 35 categories are bestowed upon the industry's best. The show is televised nationally. Some tickets are available to the public; contact the GMA at the number above, or visit the website for more information.

November

CMA AWARDS, Bridgestone Arena, 501 Broadway, Nashville, TN 37203; (615) 244-2840 (Country Music Association); cmaworld.com. The Country Music Association Awards are the industry's most prestigious honors, and the annual star-studded ceremony is the biggest night of the year for Nashville's country music industry. The ceremony is held in early November in Nashville and is televised live on ABC. Awards are presented in more than a dozen categories, including Entertainer of the Year, Album of the Year, and Song of the Year. Winners are determined by the CMA membership. Some tickets are usually available to the public. For more information call the CMA or visit their website.

Shopping

Shopping. It's a favorite pastime for some, a dreaded inconvenience for others. But whether you view it as a fun activity or a necessary evil, Nashville has the stores that will make your shopping experiences pleasant. From antiques to cowboy boots, and toys to Italian-made suits, Nashville has it all. There are so many shopping districts in and around Nashville that it could take years to discover them all. Major malls are in just about any direction, and you can't go wrong shopping at any of these. Shopping meccas like Rivergate, Cool Springs, and Hickory Hollow are always jam-packed and offer almost any merchandise you want. There are also many neighborhood-type shopping districts, such as Hillsboro Village, Berry Hill, Nolensville Road, and Eighth Avenue S., that make shopping superconvenient. You'll often find some interesting stores and merchandise in these areas. Nashville is a top tourist destination, and naturally we also have tons of country music souvenirs. You'll find most of those in shops and attractions on or near Second Avenue and in the Opryland/Music Valley area. We list some of those shops along with record stores in our **Music City** chapter. For information on even more shopping opportunities, see our **Entertainment**, **Attractions**, and **Annual Events** chapters.

We have arranged this chapter by category of goods and have added a section on unique malls. This is definitely not a comprehensive list of stores and shops in Nashville, just a guide to some of the local hot spots and favorites.

NOTABLE MALLS

THE FACTORY AT FRANKLIN, 230 Franklin Rd., Franklin, TN 37064; (615) 791-1777; factoryatfranklin.com. The Factory at Franklin is one of the area's more creative shopping malls. Housed in a renovated 1929 stove factory 6 blocks from historic downtown Franklin, the mall offers an interesting assortment of antiques stores, art galleries, gift shops, and restaurants. You can

> i Don't go into Robert's Western World on Broadway looking for Western wear. Although they do sell boots, this place is really a bar. It's where the band BR549 got its start.

paint your own piece of pottery at Third Coast Clay, get a handcrafted guitar at Artisan Guitars, or watch an artist at work and buy a work of art. The Factory is also the site of special events and concerts.

THE NASHVILLE ARCADE, between Fourth Avenue N. and Fifth Avenue N., and Union and Church Streets at 65 Arcade Alley, Nashville, TN 37219; (615) 255-1034; thenashvillearcade.com. The Arcade is one of Music City's unique shopping areas. This 2-level, glass-covered mall opened in 1903 and was modeled after a mall in Milan, Italy, and others in northern US cities. It is one of only four such structures left in the United States. Today the narrow, block-long mall stays busy with downtown workers and visitors who stop in for a cup of coffee or a quick bite to eat. A fixture at the Arcade is the Peanut Shop, which has been filling the air with the aroma of its freshly roasted nuts since 1927. Other stores include Percy's Shoe Shine, Aunt Pam's Cookies, Kate's Meat & Three, Urban Juicer, Papas Gourmet Stuffed Potatoes, and other restaurants.

OPRY MILLS, 433 Opry Mills Dr., Nashville, TN 37214; (615) 514-1100; simon.com/mall/opry-mills. Opry Mills opened in May 2000 at the site of the former Opryland theme park. Located between Two Rivers Parkway and McGavock Pike, the center is about 7 miles northeast of downtown. Although many people mourned the loss of Opryland theme park, Opry Mills and its

Opry Mills Courtesy of Nashville Convention & Visitors Corporation

200 or so stores turned out to be a big success. Owned by Indianapolis-based Simon Property Group, Opry Mills offers anchor tenants Bass Pro Shops Outdoor World, Banana Republic Factory Store, Under Armour, American Eagle Outfitters, Chico's, Brooks Brothers, Coach, Clarks, and Gap Outlet. For entertainment, options include Regal Cinemas multiplex. More than a dozen restaurants and specialty food stores include the Rainforest Cafe and Johnny Rockets.

WESTERN-WEAR STORES

MANUEL, 800 Broadway, Nashville, TN 37203; (615) 321-5444; manuelcouture.com. Manuel is best known for the flashy rhinestone garb worn by some country music performers, but the store also designs high-quality one-of-a-kind pieces for businesspeople worldwide. Originally founded in Los Angeles in 1972, Manuel today is based in Nashville. Most of the store's business is custom costumes for performers, among them Dwight Yoakam, Brooks & Dunn, Bob Dylan, and Aerosmith's Joe Perry. The prices are steep—a custom coat starts at around $1,250, and shirts start at around $450—but browsing is free. The store welcomes the curious to come in and check out the showroom.

TRAIL WEST, 1183 W. Main St., Hendersonville, TN 37075; (615) 264-2955. Hendersonville-based Trail West has three Western-wear stores in the Nashville area selling clothing and accessories for men, women, and children. The spacious stores are stocked with such brands as Resistol, Stetson, Boulet, Charlie 1 Horse, Corral Boot, and Hat 'n Hand. Other Nashville locations are at 2416 Music Valley Dr. (615-883-5933), 126 Second Ave. S. (615-256-7749); and 209 Broadway (615-651-8685).

CLOTHING & ACCESSORIES

ABLE, 5022 Centennial Blvd., Nashville, TN 37209; livefashionable.com. This hip boutique sells bags, shoes, jewelry, and clothing handcrafted locally and globally by disadvantaged women. The goal is to provide an alternative to give these women an opportunity to earn a living, empowering them to end the cycle of poverty that had kept them trapped.

THE FRENCH SHOPPE, 2817 West End Ave., Nashville, TN 37203; (615) 327-8132; frenchshoppe.com. Known for its selection of good-quality career wear, casual weekend clothes at affordable prices, and helpful staff, the

French Shoppe has been outfitting fashion-minded Middle Tennessee women since 1968, when the store first opened in Murfreesboro. The family-owned business moved to Nashville in 1978. Merchandise varies somewhat by store. The Belle Meade store is at 6049 Hwy 100 (615-352-9296).

LEVY'S, 3900 Hillsboro Pike #36, Nashville, TN 37215; (615) 383-2800; levysclothes.com. Levy's has been dressing Nashville men since 1855 and is one of the few remaining individually owned clothing stores in the area. This family-owned store is in the Hillsboro Plaza shopping center in Green Hills. Upscale men's business clothing and sportswear are the specialty, although Levy's added women's business and casual clothing recently. Levy's lines include Hart Schaffner & Marx, Hickey Freeman, Brioni, Canali, and Ermenegildo Zegna. The store also carries some of the finest leather in town, including the Bruno Magli label. Many of Levy's knowledgeable sales employees have been with the store for decades, and they'll help you put together all the right pieces, whether you're looking for dressy casual wear for "casual Fridays" or a high-power suit fit for the corner office.

OFF BROADWAY SHOE WAREHOUSE, 118 16th Ave. S., Nashville, TN 37203; (615) 254-6242; offbroadwayshoes.com. Shoes! With 35,000 to 45,000 pairs of designer shoes in what seems like acres of space, Off Broadway Shoe Warehouse is shoe heaven. This shoe store chain originated in Nashville around 1990. The first location, just off Broadway, near Music Row, was a huge success, which resulted in stores opening nationwide. The Atlanta-based operator now has about 30 stores around the country. Each store has the latest trendy styles as well as the classics—from penny loafers and must-have sandals to hiking boots and towering stiletto heels—at substantial savings. Women's sizes range from 5 to 12; there are lots of narrows and a few wide widths, too. Although these enormous stores devote most of their space to women's shoes, each has a good selection of men's footwear, too. With prices generally 25 to 50 percent less than at most retail stores, it's hard to leave here with only one box. Off Broadway has additional locations in Opry Mills (357 Opry Mills Dr., 615-800-4783); Bellevue Place (8153 Sawyer Brown Rd., 615-902-3919); Merchant Pointe (217 Indian Lake Blvd., Ste. 600, Hendersonville, 615-826-1548); Murfreesboro (2615 Medical Center Pkwy., Ste. 600, 615-494-5048); and Franklin (545 Cool Springs Blvd., 615-778-1331).

THE OXFORD SHOP, 3830 Bedford Ave., Nashville, TN 37213; (615) 383-4442; theoxfordshop.com. The Oxford Shop carries high-end suits and casual wear for men, including such lines as Samuelsohn, Southwick, Corbin,

Robert Talbott, Bills Khakis, and Barbour. The locally owned store, in business since 1961, also offers expert tailoring and alterations.

TWO OLD HIPPIES, 401 12th Ave. S., Nashville, TN 37203; (615) 254-7999; twooldhippies.com. A fun lifestyle boutique, Two Old Hippies offers clothing, jewelry, accessories, unique gifts, and rock-and-roll memorabilia. Live music is hosted five nights a week. Take time to enjoy rock memorabilia lining the walls, all available for sale. Step into "The Vault," which is home to a premium selection of guitars and offers a quiet place for those who would like to play without public eyes.

ANTIQUES

There are numerous antiques malls and shops in and around Nashville. Nashville's Eighth Avenue S., Franklin, Goodlettsville, and Lebanon are some of the best-known antiques hot spots, but you can find shops almost anywhere. Take a drive out in the country and you're bound to come across several charming little stores filled with all sorts of furniture and collectibles from years gone by. We've highlighted a few locations, enough to keep weekend treasure seekers busy. FYI: An antique, in the strictest sense, is something more than 100 years old, while a collectible is usually at least 20 years old but may be older. But keep in mind that the definition of *antique* can vary around Middle Tennessee. For example, this *Insiders' Guide to Nashville* author usually uses the term to refer to the kinds of relics she finds in her grandparents' attic or chicken coop, but some Nashvillians tend to reserve the term for items like those lovely 250-year-old dressers that fetch upward of $10,000 at some of the area's finer antiques stores.

Nashville's Eighth Avenue S. District

ANTIQUE ARCHAEOLOGY NASHVILLE, 1300 Clinton St., #130, Nashville, TN 37203; (615) 810-9906; antiquearchaeology.com. How appropriate. The host of the History Channel's popular *American Pickers*, Mike

i A $2.48 yellowed rolled-up document at Music City Thrift Shop turned out to be a rare bargain. The document was an official copy of the Declaration of Independence, one of 200 commissioned by John Quincy Adams and printed in 1823. It sold at a 2007 auction for $477,650.

> **i** In 1950 Aladdin Industries of Nashville fancied up its plain steel lunch boxes and thermos bottles with Hopalong Cassidy decals. Sales jumped from 50,000 to 600,000 lunch kits the first year. The lunch boxes are now collector's items.

Wolfe, has a store in Music City, home of the original pickers. Of course, this antique-type shop deals with two guys who travel all over the United States finding treasures in other people's trash—not the musical kind of pickers for which Nashville is famous. Opened in 2011 in an old car factory, Antique Archaeology features antiques, folk art, vintage items, and Antique Archaeology merchandise. Wolfe is happy to share the tale of each antique, part of the pleasure he enjoys in finding little gems.

DEALER'S CHOICE ANTIQUES AND AUCTION, 2109 Eighth Ave. S., Nashville, TN 37204; (615) 383-7030; dealerschoiceauction.com. Antiques auctions take place here the first Saturday of every month at 11 a.m. and draw about 150 dealers and individual antiquers. Dealer's Choice also sells off the floor, but you might want to call before visiting because operating hours vary. You'll find everything from decorator items to fine furnishings here, including Victorian, French, country, and mahogany furniture.

DOWNTOWN ANTIQUE MALL, 612 Eighth Ave. S., Nashville, TN 37203; (615) 256-6616. Housed in a creaky old historic warehouse beside the railroad tracks, this 13,000-square-foot antiques mall is a fun place to get lost on a rainy afternoon. You never know what you'll find—or should we say excavate—here. The mall's aisles are piled high with all sorts of neat stuff, including furniture from the 1800s to 1950s, collectibles, and textiles. Best of all, most of the antiques here are of the very affordable variety.

PEMBROKE ANTIQUES, 6610 Hwy. 100, Nashville, TN 37205; (615) 353-0889. The fact that Pembroke Antiques is located near Belle Meade should give you a clue that this isn't your junk-store-variety antiques store. On the other hand, if you're on a budget, don't be put off by the location: Pembroke's prices are actually quite reasonable. The store specializes in quality English and French furniture that has "a sophisticated look but a warm country feel." It's a favorite among local interior designers. This is a good place to find majolica pottery, decorative garden items, and silver. If you're looking for a unique and tasteful item for a wedding or housewarming gift, Pembroke will have it.

POLK PLACE ANTIQUES, 5701 Old Harding Pike, #100, Nashville, TN 37205; (615) 353-1324. Polk Place specializes in items from the American Federal period (1790–1840) and Southern furniture. The store also offers a selection of porcelains, coin silver, copper, pewter, brass, oil paintings, and custom-made lamps.

> i *Grand Ole Opry* star Joe Diffie once worked on an oil rig, in an iron foundry, and in Gibson Guitar's Nashville warehouse.

Franklin

There are two concentrated areas of shops and several others scattered about in Franklin. One concentration is on and near Second Avenue while the other is on Bridge Street, which runs parallel to Main Street.

FRANKLIN ANTIQUE MALL, 251 Second Ave. S., Franklin, TN 37064; (615) 790-8593. If you're planning to go antiquing in Franklin, you'll want to be sure to put the Franklin Antique Mall on your list of stops. In fact, go ahead and put it at the top of your list, and allow plenty of time for browsing here. Housed in the historic handmade brick icehouse building, Franklin Antique Mall has 60 booths. There is a good selection of furniture and glassware, lamp parts, and glass replacement shades, as well as collectible magazines and prints. The furniture selection ranges from rustic to fine quality, and we usually find that the prices are very reasonable.

WINCHESTER ANTIQUE MALL, 121 Second Ave. N., Franklin, TN 37064; (615) 791-5846. There are about 25 booths in this cozy, 2-story cottage located near Franklin's town square. They're filled with reasonably priced American and English furniture, fine porcelain, sterling, linens, and books. This store is a local favorite.

Goodlettsville

Goodlettsville's antiques district stretches along the historic Main Street. To get there, take I-65 North to exit 97 and go west to Dickerson Pike. Note: In Goodlettsville, Dickerson Pike, Main Street, and US 41 are the same road.

GOODLETTSVILLE ANTIQUE MALL—ANOTHER ERA, 213 N. Main St., Goodlettsville, TN 37072; (615) 859-7002; goodlettsvilleantiquemall.com. You can spend hours treasure hunting in this enormous mall. With

20,000 square feet of space and more than 100 booths, the mall is stocked full of furniture, glassware, collectibles, quilts, clocks, and toys.

RARE BIRD ANTIQUE MALL, 212 S. Main St., Goodlettsville, TN 37072; (615) 851-2635; rarebirdantiquemall.com. Scout for furniture, toys, gas station memorabilia, linens, and glassware in more than 50 booths here.

CONSIGNMENT STORES

DESIGNER RENAISSANCE, 2822 Bransford Ave., Nashville, TN 37204; (615) 297-8822; designerrenaissance.com. Jodi Miller opened this women's consignment shop in 1988, operating for years in Green Hills. In 2004 she relocated to nearby Berry Hill, setting up shop in a house in the tiny satellite city's hip shopping district. Some of Music City's best-dressed women consign their clothing here. As its name suggests, Designer Renaissance carries designer clothes as well as high-end secondhand clothing. Miller also stocks accessories. Open Mon through Sat, the store closes on all major (and some minor) holidays. If this store isn't in or near your neighborhood, you might want to call before you come because it sometimes closes on special occasions. If you have items you want to consign, you'll need to make an appointment. Consignors receive 50 percent of the selling price.

TOYS

PHILLIPS TOY MART, 5207 Harding Rd., Nashville, TN 37205; (615) 352-5363; phillipstoymart.com. In business for more than half a century, Phillips Toy Mart has been in the Belle Meade area for more than 40 years. An old-timey kind of toy store, Phillips sells all sorts of toys, including games for kids and adults and a large selection of imported educational toys. The store also sells a variety of collector dolls and has one of the largest model selections in the South, including tools and hobby supplies.

GIFTS

MARKET STREET MERCANTILE, 111 Second Ave. N., Nashville, TN 37201; (615) 251-4092. Market Street Mercantile is the general store for collectors—of Jack Daniel's, John Deere, I Love Lucy, and Elvis paraphernalia. The shop also carries Nashville souvenirs and a multitude of other items. Open daily 10 a.m. to 10 p.m.

PANGAEA, 1721 21st Ave. S., Nashville, TN 37212; (615) 269-9665; pangaeanashville.com. This Hillsboro Village boutique has lots of funky and fun clothing and home decor items. Mexican folk art is the main feel, and there is a lot of primitive- or antique-style, natural fiber clothing from Mexico and India, as well as unique and interesting tabletop items. The store has a good selection of candles and candleholders, as well as Mexican mirrors, jewelry, books, and Day of the Dead objects.

WHITE'S MERCANTILE, 2908 12th Ave. S., Nashville, TN 37204; (615) 750-5379; whitesmercantile.com. "A general store for the modern tastemaker," White's Mercantile is owned by singer/songwriter Holly Williams, daughter of country legend Hank Williams Jr. The place used to be a former gas station. Named after her maternal grandparents, the shop is filled with a diversity of items, from dog food and French antiques to organic popcorn and baby clothes. White's also carries a large line of books and a small but classy collection of men's and women's apparel. White's has become so successful that the store has two other Nashville area locations—at 345 Main St., in Franklin (615-721-8028) and in Leiper's Fork at 4150 Old Hillsboro Rd.

White's Mercantile is owned by Holly Williams, daughter of Hank Williams Jr.
Jackie Sheckler Finch

GARDENING STORES

BATES NURSERY & GARDEN CENTER, 3810 Whites Creek Pike, Nashville, TN 37207; (615) 876-1014; batesnursery.com. Bates is one of Nashville's favorite garden centers. It has been in business since 1932. It began during the Great Depression, when Bessie Bates, grandmother of the current owner, David Bates, started selling flowers and shrubs from her backyard greenhouse on Charlotte Pike. The store offers free landscaping design services (call for an appointment) and, for a fee, will come to your home and design a more detailed plan for you. Bates has a great website. You search for plants by category, see if they're currently in stock, check the prices, and get detailed instructions on how to care for them.

We like the fact that most of Bates's plants come with a 1-year warranty. Combine that with their competitive prices, and it's no wonder that Nashvillians have been shopping here for almost a century.

GRASSLAND AQUATICS, 2164 Hillsboro Rd., Franklin, TN 37069; (615) 790-0776; shop.grasslandaquatics.com. If you're one of the many Nashvillians with garden ponds—or if you're planning to add one to your yard—you'll want to pay a visit to this huge aquatic nursery and garden supply center. They sell all sorts of floating and underwater plants, as well as materials for building and maintaining ponds, water treatment supplies, and more. In addition to plants, they have a variety of decorative fish, including imported Japanese koi and fancy goldfish, which they will ship anywhere in the United States. The store conducts classes on a variety of pond-related topics.

LITTLE MARROWBONE FARM, 1560 Little Marrowbone Rd., Ashland City, TN 37015; (615) 792-7255; littlemarrowbone.com. Bill and Andrea Henry's little off-the-beaten-path growing nursery has developed a loyal clientele since opening back in the mid-'80s. They specialize in unique varieties of plants, including herbs, hostas, perennials, conifers, hellebores, and—our favorite—adorable tabletop topiaries made from pesticide-free herbs and shrubs. The farm—it's nothin' fancy—is about 25 miles northwest of Nashville, off Highway 12 N. Little Marrowbone Farm is generally open daily, but it's a good idea to call before visiting, as hours vary.

> **i** Nashville's many crafts fairs offer a variety of creative items that make wonderful gifts. See our **Annual Events** chapter for more information on these events.

MOORE & MOORE WEST GARDEN CENTER, 8216 Hwy. 100, Nashville, TN 37221; (615) 662-8849; mooreandmoore.com. Moore & Moore has been voted Nashville's best garden center by readers of the *Nashville Scene* on more than one occasion. In business since 1980, this friendly, full-service garden store specializes in native plants from trees and shrubs to woodland wildflowers. If you don't know what to plant or don't know how to plant it, you're in luck because the store offers landscaping and design services. The store also has one of the best selections of bulbs around. The knowledgeable staff is always a good source of free, friendly advice on any gardening topic, from soil science to the latest trends in gardening.

BOOKSTORES

ALKEBU-LAN IMAGES, 2721 Jefferson St., Nashville, TN 37208; (615) 321-4111. The small, bright yellow building at the corner of 28th Avenue N. and Jefferson Street is home to Alkebu-Lan Images, an independently owned bookstore specializing in African-American books, including fiction, nonfiction, and religious titles. The store also sells some apparel, greeting cards, and gift items such as figurines, note cards, body oils, incense, jewelry, and imported African carvings. Many of the store's products are educationally focused. The store is open daily. Incidentally, translated from Moorish-Arabic, the name Alkebu-Lan means "Land of the blacks."

LOGOS CHRISTIAN BOOKSTORE, 4012 Hillsboro Pike, Nashville, TN 37215; (615) 297-5388; logosbookstores.com. This cozy and friendly Christian bookstore in Green Hills, adjacent to the Green Hills Court Shopping Center, is one of about 30 independently owned Logos stores nationwide. The store carries a variety of Bibles and religious books, including an extensive selection of Reformed theology literature. You can also find homeschooling books here. There's a good selection of CDs, greeting cards, and gift items, too. Logos also

White's Mercantile carries a wide assortment of books. Jackie Sheckler Finch

buys and sells used books and CDs. The knowledgeable staff is always happy to place special orders.

ST. MARY'S BOOKSTORE & CHURCH SUPPLIES, 1909 West End Ave., Nashville, TN 37203; (615) 329-1835; stmarysbookstore.com. Located at 19th Avenue and West End, St. Mary's Book Store & Church Supplies has been in business since 1939. It is a full-line Christian bookstore, with Bibles, hymnals, church supplies, gifts, CDs, and cassettes.

Used Books

ELDER'S BOOKSTORE, 101 White Bridge Rd., Nashville, TN 37209; (615) 352-1562; eldersbookstore.com. Elder's Bookstore is one of Nashville's oldest used- and rare-book stores. The store was founded by Charles Elder, but it is now owned and managed by his son Randy. Elder's is known for its tremendous collection of regional, Southern, and Civil War books. Tennessee-history buffs will find plenty to occupy them. Elder's also has a good collection of Native American books, rare and out-of-print books, children's books, cookbooks, art reference books, books on genealogy, late-edition encyclopedias, and more. They have done reissues of important titles through the years.

THE GREAT ESCAPE SUPERSTORE, 5400 Charlotte Ave., Nashville, TN 37209; (615) 385-2116; thegreatescape.com. If you're looking for comic books, the Great Escape is the place to go. The Great Escape has more than 100,000 comics in stock, including a huge selection of back issues, and the shop receives weekly shipments of the latest books. Collectors will find collectible comics here that range in price from 50 cents to $500 or more. The Great Escape also has used paperbacks, mostly fiction, with an emphasis on pop culture. The store has a large selection of used CDs, tapes, and records, as well as videos, used video games, gaming cards, and trading cards. A second Great Escape location is at 105 North Gallatin Rd., Madison (615-865-8052).

i The Public Library of Nashville and Davidson County is online. You can search the card catalog, renew or request books, and view your library record from the convenience of your own computer. You'll find the website at library.nashville.org. For general library information call (615) 862-5800.

SPORTING GOODS/OUTDOOR GEAR

ASPHALT BEACH IN-LINE SKATE SHOP, 961 Woodland St., Nashville, TN 37206; (615) 228-1005; asphaltbeach.com. Asphalt Beach is one of the largest, most complete in-line skate shops in the United States. Skater-owned, Asphalt Beach offers sales, repair, parts, accessories, and instruction for fitness, recreation, speed, aggressive, and roller hockey.

SHOPPING

BASS PRO SHOPS OUTDOOR WORLD, 323 Opry Mills Dr., Nashville, TN 37214; (615) 514-5200; basspro.com. This massive store has 154,000 square feet of fishing, boating, hunting, camping, and golf gear and equipment, plus outdoor apparel. From fishing licenses to boats, you should be able to find everything you need here. Even if you're not into the aforementioned activities, you'll want to check out this spectacular store next time you visit Opry Mills. There's a 25,000-gallon aquarium, waterfalls, an adventure travel agency, and a snack bar inside. Feeding of the fish in the aquarium takes place at 4 p.m. on Mon and Fri.

CUMBERLAND TRANSIT WEST, 2807 West End Ave., Nashville, TN 37203; (615) 321-4069; cumberlandtransit.com. Adventure-minded outdoor types will find all sorts of clothing and equipment at Cumberland Transit. In business since 1972, the store has gear for backpacking, camping, rock climbing and rappelling, canoeing, fly-fishing, and about every other outdoor activity you can think of. In addition to sporting equipment, the store has men's and women's clothing, travel gear, and luggage. If you need to brush up on your outdoor skills, sign up for one of Cumberland Transit's classes in rock climbing, rappelling, fly-fishing, fly tying, or backpacking. The store's large bike shop specializes in all aspects of biking, including custom frame fitting. The store has a large stock of mountain bikes, road bikes, hybrids, and BMX bikes.

PETS & PET SUPPLIES

AQUATIC CRITTER, 5009 Nolensville Rd., Nashville, TN 37211; (615) 832-4541; aquaticcritter.com. Freshwater and marine aquarists alike will want to check out this store. It has an excellent selection of fish, plants, corals, and reptiles and a knowledgeable and helpful staff. The fish are guaranteed to be healthy. The store also sells clean, filtered saltwater and provides a variety of services.

> Shopping for a pet? The Nashville Humane Association is a great place to find a furry friend who needs a home. It's open daily. Hours are 10 a.m. to 5 p.m. Tues through Sat and noon to 5 p.m. Sun. The facility is closed Mon. For more information call (615) 352-1010 or visit nashvillehumane.org.

THE CAT SHOPPE & DOG STORE, 2824 Bransford Ave., Nashville 37204; (615) 297-7877; catshoppedogstore.com. The Cat Shoppe & Dog Store has been catering to dogs and cats and their people since November 1992. It is stocked full of all sorts of kitty- and doggy-themed gift items, including picture frames, T-shirts, coffee mugs, and sweaters, as well as food, litter, and grooming tools for your feline and canine friends. The store has lots of dog and cat toys. The helpful staff can recommend pet-sitters, and they'll loan you a trap for catching the neighborhood stray.

NASHVILLE PET PRODUCTS CENTER, 2621 Cruzen St., Nashville, TN 37211; (615) 242-2223; nashvillepetproducts.com. Nashville Pet Products Center is a locally owned chain of stores that sells pet supplies. The stores stock a variety of premium pet foods, vitamins, shampoos and conditioners, toys, and collars, as well as kennels, carrying cages, doggie sweaters, and books about pets. The stores also have birdcages and bird supplies and fish supplies, mainly for tropical fish. Additional locations are at 7078 Old Harding Pike (615-662-2525); 1010 Murfreesboro Rd., Franklin (615-599-0200); 4825 Main St., Spring Hill (615-595-0778); and 4066 Andrew Jackson Pkwy, Hermitage (615-885-4458).

FRESH PRODUCE

FARMERS' MARKET, 900 Rosa Parks Blvd., Nashville, TN 37208; (615) 880-2001; nashvillefarmersmarket.org. The Farmers' Market is a favorite spot for buying fresh produce. The indoor-outdoor market is packed with farmers and resellers offering fresh vegetables at very good prices. Indoors, there are a few international markets and specialty shops, including an Asian market, a meat shop, and a fresh seafood shop. The market does a brisk lunchtime business. You'll find restaurants serving everything from gyros to barbecue to Jamaican fare. At one end of the market is the seasonally operated Gardens of Babylon, where you can find all sorts of plants and garden supplies. The market has several festivals each year with live music, carnival games, and craft making. The Farmers' Market is open every day except Thanksgiving, Christmas Day, and New Year's Day. Special hours are in effect in winter so check the website before shopping.

MADISON CREEK FARMS, 1228 Willis Branch Rd., Goodlettsville, TN 37072; (615) 448-6207; madisoncreekfarms.com. Madison Creek Farms is a third-generation family organic farm owned by Peggy and Mark Marchetti. Peggy is the daughter of Loretta Lynn, and Mark is a songwriter who co-wrote the number-one country song, "My Baby's Got a Smile on her Face," sung by seventh-season *The Voice* winner Craig Wayne Boyd. The farm's Market Pavilion is open Sat 9 a.m. to 2 p.m. from May through Oct. The market is a wonderful mix of fresh veggies, herbs, and flowers, plus the Farm House Kitchen's freshly baked cakes, muffins, artisan breads, and homemade pies. Each season, Madison Creek Farms plays host to public farm events like "Banjos, Butterflies and Blueberry Pies," "Dinner in the Field," and "Fall Festival."

PRODUCE PLACE, 4000 Murphy Rd., Nashville, TN 37209; (615) 383-2664; produceplace.com. Produce Place is a natural-foods grocery store that caters to customers who want organic produce. The store opened in 1988 in the Sylvan Park neighborhood. In addition to fresh fruits and vegetables, Produce Place carries some gourmet food items and meals-to-go from local caterers. The store also carries health and beauty items and has a reverse-osmosis water-filtering system.

THE TURNIP TRUCK, 970 Woodland St., Nashville, TN 37206; (615) 650-3600; theturniptruck.com. This small, locally owned natural foods market gets much of its produce from 6 or 7 organic farms in the area. In addition to produce, Turnip Truck sells natural, grass-fed Australian beef; organic meat; and free-range chicken. The store also carries grocery items, including frozen foods, and a full line of supplements. Soups and sandwiches to go are served at the front counter. Turnip Truck is located in east Nashville's Five Points area at the corner of Woodland and South 10th Streets. It is open daily.

Attractions

There is a lot more to Nashville than music, as you'll see in this chapter. Whether you are a longtime resident, a frequent visitor, or a first-timer, Nashville has a great mix of attractions to entertain and enlighten. In fact, we have so many great places to visit and so many fun things to do, we can't possibly list them all here. For that reason, we're highlighting some of the Nashville area's most popular attractions—the ones residents and tourists alike visit year after year. In this chapter we arrange attractions by the following categories: Historic Sites, Museums, Amusements & the Zoo, and Fun Transportation & Tours. Also, be sure to look in our **Recreation**, **Music City**, **Annual Events**, **Entertainment**, **Kidstuff**, and **Shopping** chapters for other fun and interesting places to visit in and around Nashville. Since fees and hours of operation are subject to change, it's a good idea to call before visiting the attractions listed in this chapter.

Nashville was founded along the Cumberland River. Jackie Sheckler Finch

Price Code

Use the following as a guide to the cost of admission for 1 adult. Keep in mind that children's admission prices are generally lower (usually about half the cost of adult admission), and very young children are admitted free to most attractions. Discounts for senior citizens, students, and groups are usually available.

$	**Less than $10**
$$	**$10 to $20**
$$$	**$20 to $30**
$$$$	**More than $30**

HISTORIC SITES

BELLE MEADE PLANTATION, 5025 Harding, Rd., Nashville, TN 37205; (615) 356-0501; bellemeadeplantation.com; $$$. The Greek Revival mansion on this property was once the centerpiece of a 5,400-acre plantation known the world over as a thoroughbred farm and nursery. In 1807 John Harding and his wife, Susannah, purchased the property and in the 1920s began construction of the present-day Belle Meade (a French term meaning "beautiful meadow") mansion, originally a 2-story, Federal-style farmhouse.

Belle Meade is a Greek Revival historic landmark.
Nashville Convention & Visitors Corporation

Close-up

Nashville Visitor Information Center

The Nashville Visitor Information Center is located in the glass tower of Bridgestone Arena at 501 Broadway. You can find brochures, coupons, and discounted tickets to area attractions there. The center is open daily and the staff is very friendly and helpful. The center also has a gift shop with locally inspired and music-themed items. For more information call (615) 259-4747 or go to visitmusiccity.com. Another Visitor Information Center is located in the tower level of Regions Bank Building at Fourth Ave. N. and Commerce St., (615) 259-4730.

Nashville Visitor Information Center is easy to locate in downtown Nashville.
Nashville Convention & Visitors Corporation

During the Civil War the federal government took the horses for the army's use and removed the plantation's stone fences. Loyal slaves are said to have hidden the most prized thoroughbreds. The mansion was riddled with bullets during the Battle of Nashville (see our **History** chapter). After the war William Giles Harding and his son-in-law, Gen. William H. Jackson, expanded the farm. The stables housed many great horses, including Iroquois, winner of the English Derby in 1881. In the early 1900s Belle Meade was the oldest and largest thoroughbred farm in America. It enjoyed international prominence until 1904, when the land and horses were auctioned. The financial crisis of 1893, an excessive lifestyle, and the mishandling of family funds led to the downfall of Belle Meade. The mansion and 24 remaining acres were opened

Iroquois, a horse bred at Belle Meade Plantation, was the first American winner of the English Derby in 1881. Such modern thoroughbreds as Secretariat trace their bloodlines to Iroquois.

to the public in 1953, under the management of the Association for the Preservation of Tennessee Antiquities. The beautifully restored mansion is listed on the National Register of Historic Places. It is furnished with 19th-century antiques and art of the period. The site also includes the 1890s carriage house and stable filled with antique carriages; the 1790s log cabin (one of the oldest log structures in the state); and several other original outbuildings, including the smokehouse and mausoleum. Guides in period dress lead tours of the property. A Southern-inspired restaurant, Harding House, is a great place for lunch or weekend brunch, but be aware that Harding House closes on Tues and Wed during winter months. A refurbished ice cream and fudge shop offers sweet choices. Belle Meade Winery also has complimentary wine tastings and features such interesting wines as Big Win Zin, Founder's Red, Gentlemen's Blend, and Iroquois Red. Belle Meade Plantation is open daily year-round except Easter, Thanksgiving, Christmas Eve, Christmas, and New Year's Day.

BELMONT MANSION, 1700 Acklen Ave., Nashville, TN 37212; (615) 460-5459; belmontmansion.com; $$. Belmont Mansion was built in 1850 as the summer home of Joseph and Adelicia Acklen. The beautiful and aristocratic Adelicia was said to have been the wealthiest woman in America during the mid-1800s. She owned more than 50,000 acres of land in Louisiana, Texas, and Tennessee, all of which she inherited after her first husband, wealthy businessman Isaac Franklin, died in 1846. Her wealth placed her in the top half of 1 percent of antebellum society. The Italianate villa is furnished in original and period pieces, including gilded mirrors, marble statues, and art that Adelicia collected as she traveled the world. A 105-foot water tower, which still stands, irrigated the gardens and provided water for the fountains. Also on the property were a greenhouse and conservatory, an art gallery, gazebos, a bowling alley, a bear house, a deer park, and a zoo. Adelicia opened the gardens as a public park.

BICENTENNIAL CAPITOL MALL, 600 James Robertson Parkway, Nashville, TN 37243; (615) 741-5280; tnstateparks.com; free. This 19-acre downtown attraction offers a trip through Tennessee history. It opened in 1996 to

Bicentennial Capitol Mall State Park honors Tennessee's 200th birthday celebration. Jackie Sheckler Finch

commemorate the state's bicentennial. A 200-foot granite map of the state, 31 fountains designating Tennessee's major rivers, and a Pathway of History are among the attractions. The mall also offers a great view of the Tennessee State Capitol. (See our **Recreation** and **Kidstuff** chapters for more information.)

CANNONSBURGH VILLAGE, 312 S. Front St., Murfreesboro, TN 37219; (615) 890-0355; free. Get a glimpse of what life was like in the 1800s at this reconstructed pioneer village. The village features restored original buildings such as a church, general store, guesthouse, and gristmill from Rutherford and

Close-up

County Music Legend George Jones Honored at Namesake Museum

George Glenn Jones almost died before he got a chance to live. The family doctor dropped the baby shortly after delivery. The sturdy newborn survived with only a broken arm. But what a life the country music legend went on to live in that interval between the day he entered this world on September 12, 1930, and the day he left it on April 26, 2013.

"George went to hell and back with many addictions and he beat them all," said his widow, Nancy Jones. "He loved God and loved his fans. He was a great man."

To share the story of the man many consider the greatest voice in country music, his widow opened the George Jones Museum on April 26, 2015, the second anniversary of his death. The museum is a world-class facility with a wealth of artifacts and information about the elusive Jones. The 50,000-square-foot facility also contains a gift shop, restaurant, and rooftop tavern overlooking the Cumberland River.

"I collected all the memorabilia over the 32 years I was with George," she said. "I don't have one favorite item in the museum. I love the whole story in the museum from his childhood to his whole history in country music, his ups and downs and how he came through it all."

Starting with Jones's early poverty-filled childhood in the east Texas town of Saratoga, the museum showcases treasures like his first guitar—a well-worn Gene Autry instrument with a horse and lariat on the front. Jones pawned the Melody Ranch acoustic guitar during hard times and thought it was lost forever. But his sister Loyce found it, bought it, and returned it to a surprised Jones once he was back on his feet. Although he later owned many expensive guitars, Jones always said that first one was his favorite.

A timeline of Jones's music invites visitors to put on headphones and listen to his songs over the years. A small theater with rocking chairs—a nod to his "I don't need no rocking chair" hit—allows guests to rock in comfort while watching Jones's video clips.

A statue of George Jones welcomes visitors to his new museum opened in 2015. Jackie Sheckler Finch

Other relics of the honky-tonk hero include the infamous blue American Tourister overnight case that Jones called his "getaway bag," always kept packed and ready for a quick exit. A green John Deere lawn mower recalls the time family members hid Jones's car keys so he couldn't drive while drunk. Instead, Jones rode his mower to the nearby liquor store. Visitors are now invited to take a photo seated on the mower.

Another exhibit dedicated to Jones's tumultuous marriage to county icon Tammy Wynette showcases her white satin and chiffon dress which she left behind after their divorce. A display sign shares the sad message that Jones held on to the dress with its glittery lace and rhinestones after she was gone.

A hastily scrawled note on a crumbled piece of yellowing paper begs airport officials not to tow his car. In a hurry to catch a 1978 flight and unable to find the airport parking lot, a frustrated and cocaine-fueled Jones parked his car on a sidewalk outside the terminal and left it running. Identifying himself as "George Jones with the *Grand Ole Opry,*" the singer implored airport security not to haul it in. Amazingly, the car was still there and running when Jones returned two days later.

A major turning point in Jones's troubled life occurred when he married Nancy Sepulvada in 1983. Settling down with the woman he called "my rock," Jones recorded more hits and garnered top awards in his final decades. In 2013, he embarked on his farewell tour appropriately named The Grand Tour. However, on April 18 the music was cut short when Jones was hospitalized at Nashville's Vanderbilt University Medical Center with a fever and irregular blood pressure. He was 81 years old.

"I was with George the whole time," Nancy said. Although she continued talking to him, she said that Jones didn't open his eyes or talk for his final five days—until the last minute. "I was standing at the foot of his bed rubbing his feet. Suddenly, he opened his eyes and said, 'Well, hello there. My name is George Jones and I've been looking for you.' I know he was talking to God. And then he was gone."

other Middle Tennessee counties. There is also an art league exhibit, a historical Murfreesboro exhibit, and displays of antique farm equipment and automobiles. The giant cedar bucket situated near the village entrance is the world's largest—it holds 1,566 gallons. Self-guided tours are free. The buildings are open Tues through Sun from May 1 through Dec 1; the grounds are open year-round.

CARNTON PLANTATION, 1345 Eastern Flank Cir., Franklin, TN 37064; (615) 794-0903; boft.org; $$. This 1826 antebellum plantation was built by Randal McGavock, who was Nashville's mayor in 1824 and 1825. The late-neo-classical plantation house is considered architecturally and historically one of the most important buildings in the area. In its early years the mansion was a social and political center. Among the prominent visitors attending the many social events there were Andrew Jackson, Sam Houston, and James K. Polk.

The home was used as a Confederate hospital after the bloody Battle of Franklin on November 30, 1864. The Confederates lost at least 12 generals during the battle. The bodies of four of the generals were laid out on the mansion's back porch. At that time Carnton was the home of McGavock's son, Col. John McGavock, and his wife, Carrie Winder McGavock. In 1866 the McGavock family donated 2 acres adjacent to their family cemetery for the burial of some 1,500 Southern solders. The McGavock Confederate Cemetery is the country's largest private Confederate cemetery. Carnton Plantation is open daily.

FONTANEL MANSION & FARM, 4225 Whites Creek Pike, Nashville, TN 37189; (615) 724-1610; fontanelmansion.com; $$$. Jesse James hid out here. The Confederate cavalry used it for a gathering site. And entertainer Barbara Mandrell chose it for her log cabin home. With a wealth of history behind it, the Fontanel Mansion & Farm started a new chapter in its long life when it was opened to the public in June 2010. Less than 15 minutes from downtown Nashville, the place has grown to be an entertainment center with the Inn at Fontanel offering 6 suites, the Woods at Fontanel featuring concerts, Adventureworks Zipline, Natchez Hills Winery, Prichard's Distillery, Cafe Fontanella, Vintage Creek Boutique, and walking trails.

Formerly owned by County Music Hall of Fame member Barbara Mandrell, the Fontanel Mansion boasts 3 stories, more than 20 rooms, 13 bathrooms, 5 fireplaces, 2 kitchens, an indoor pool, and even an indoor shooting range on 136 acres of pristine land. The mansion also is filled to the brim with photos, memorabilia, and personal items from when the Mandrell family lived here. Guests are invited to touch, see, feel, and relax in this magnificent home.

FORT NASHBOROUGH, 170 First Ave. N., Nashville, TN 37201; (615) 862-8400 (Parks Department); nashville.gov/parks-and-recreation/historic-sites/fort-nashborough; free. On the banks of the Cumberland River at Riverfront Park stands the reconstruction of the original settlement of Nashville. The original log fort was built slightly north of this location by James Robertson when he and his party first settled in the area in 1779 (see our **History** chapter). It occupied about 2 acres of land on a bluff overlooking the river. Named in honor of Gen. Francis Nash, who was killed during the Revolutionary War, the fort is where early Nashvillians met and adopted the Cumberland Compact for government of the new settlement. In 1930 the Daughters of the American Revolution sponsored the construction of a replica of the original structure near the site of Fort Nashborough. Reopening in the summer of 2015, the fort underwent a $1 million project to make it more visitor-friendly. It now features an open plaza with contemporary elements such as touch screens allowing visitors a glimpse at the lifestyle of Nashville's first settlers. The fort is open to the public for self-guided tours daily from 9 a.m. to 4 p.m.

HATCH SHOW PRINT, 224 Fifth Ave. S., Nashville, TN 37203; (615) 577-7710; hatchshowprint.com; $$. Founded in 1879 in downtown Nashville, Hatch Show Print is the oldest working letterpress print shop in America.

Hatch Show Print is still printing posters the old-fashioned way.
Jackie Sheckler Finch

ATTRACTIONS

Southern Belle Lived at Belmont

The dark-eyed beauty seemed a real-life Scarlett O'Hara. And, like the Southern belle in *Gone With the Wind*, nothing could protect this woman from great tragedy and sorrow. At Belmont Mansion, visitors can see reflections of the woman who once lived in this antebellum Tennessee home and hear the tale of her bittersweet life.

"She had everything," said Mark Brown, director of Belmont Mansion. "She became one of America's wealthiest women, but she also had such sadness."

Born on the Ides of March in 1817 to a prominent Nashville family, **Adelicia Hayes** was said to be an accomplished horsewoman who preferred to jump a fence rather than open a gate. She was described as marrying first for money, second for love, and third because she could.

At age 22, Adelicia wed a wealthy businessman and planter 28 years her senior, **Isaac Franklin.** During their seven years of marriage, they had four children—all of whom died by age 11. A son died at birth and three daughters died of simple childhood illnesses.

When her husband died in 1846, Adelicia was left a wealthy widow. "In the 1840s, she was said to have a net worth of almost $1 million," Brown said. "That was a tremendous amount of money in those days."

Three years later, she married the man said to be the love of her life. **Joseph Acklen** was handsome and socially acceptable, but somewhat lacking financially. However, Adelicia didn't let her heart overrule her head. "Her second husband had to sign a prenuptial agreement," Brown said. "But he ended up turning that $1 million estimated wealth into $3 million."

Soon after their marriage, the Acklens began building **Belmont Mansion.** Constructed in the style of an Italian villa, the mansion was set in elaborate gardens with numerous outbuildings. The water tower, still standing, provided irrigation for the gardens and water to run the fountains.

The grounds also contained a 200-foot-long greenhouse and conservatory, an art gallery, gazebos, a bowling alley, bear house, and zoo. "It was built to be a summer home, not a working plantation," Brown said.

Since the city had no public park, Adelicia opened her summer home to the citizens of Nashville every day except Sunday. Then tragedy struck again. Adelicia's only surviving child from her previous marriage died, as did her 2-year-old twins, who passed away from scarlet fever within days of each other in 1855. The remaining four Acklen children survived to maturity—but without their father.

Adelicia's husband died of malaria during the Civil War, leaving 2,800 bales of Acklen cotton threatened by both Union and Confederate troops. Hearing that her cotton was about to be confiscated or burned, Adelicia hurried to Louisiana and outsmarted both the Confederates and the Yankees by smuggling her cotton to England. There it brought nearly $1 million in gold, which she deposited into a British bank account and reclaimed after the war.

During the Battle of Nashville in December 1864, Belmont became the headquarters of a Union general and his troops camped out on the lawn of the estate. Adelicia spent that time as the guest of her old friend, Mrs. James Polk, widow of the former president of the United States.

When she returned to Belmont, Adelicia found much destruction but the interior of her home was still intact. At the age of 50, Adelicia married for a third time to Nashville physician **William Cheatham.** But this marriage proved to be less than a charm. Soon Adelicia began spending most of her time in Washington, DC, with her only surviving daughter, Pauline. By 1887, Adelicia was busy building a home in Washington. While shopping for home furnishings in New York City, the 70-year-old caught pneumonia and died in a Fifth Avenue hotel.

Adelicia's body was returned to Nashville for burial in the family mausoleum. Two ladies from Philadelphia bought Belmont in 1890 and opened a women's school. Later merging with Nashville's old Ward Seminary, it was renamed **Ward-Belmont** and operated as an academy and junior college for women. In 1951, it became **Belmont College,** a coeducational, church-related college.

Today, visitors can tour the 15 restored rooms of Belmont Mansion and see the Victorian opulence with original and period pieces, gilded mirrors, marble statues, and paintings.

Even such decorations as a collection of seashells were of great importance in Adelicia's day, Brown said, pointing to the shell arrangement prominently displayed on a table. "Seashells were very much a status display," Brown said. "They meant that you had wealth to travel to the seashore."

For years the shop produced promotional handbills and posters for vaudeville acts, circuses, sporting events, and minstrel shows throughout the Southeast, but it is best known for its posters of *Grand Ole Opry* stars. From 1925 to 1991 it was on Fourth Avenue N., near the Ryman Auditorium; it relocated a few times before settling at its current site in the Fifth Ave. lobby of the Country Music Hall of Fame & Museum in 2013. Today Hatch finds its letterpress posters and designs in constant demand. The shop continues to create posters and art for such clients as Nike, the Jack Daniel's Distillery, local bands, and national recording artists, including Bob Dylan and Bruce Springsteen. One wall of the tiny space is lined with thousands of wood and metal blocks of type used to produce posters. Tours are offered at 12:30, 2, and 3 p.m. with visitors making their own commemorative posters. Or take home a sample of Hatch's product from the gift shop. Hatch is open daily.

THE HERMITAGE: HOME OF PRESIDENT ANDREW JACKSON, 4580 Rachel's Ln., Nashville, TN 37076; (615) 889-2941; thehermitage.com; $$$. A tour of the Hermitage offers insight into one of America's most interesting presidents, as well as a look at life on a 19th-century plantation. Andrew Jackson, seventh president of the United States and hero of the Battle

Built between 1819 and 1821, the Hermitage was the home of Andrew and Rachel Jackson. Jackie Sheckler Finch

> Legend has it that Andrew Jackson built the driveway at the Hermitage to please his daughter-in-law Emily. The tornadoes that struck Nashville in 1998 destroyed hundreds of trees along the driveway, and more than 1,000 on the property. The trees were more than 2 centuries old.

of New Orleans, lived and died here. The Hermitage was first built in 1821 as a Federal-style brick home. It was enlarged in 1831, then rebuilt in Greek Revival style, as it appears today. A National Historic Landmark, managed since 1889 by the Ladies' Hermitage Association, the mansion has been restored to the period of Jackson's retirement in 1837. It contains a large collection of original furnishings and personal belongings, including furniture, porcelain, silver, and rare French wallpaper. Jackson filled the house with elegant and sophisticated pieces from the same dealers who supplied the White House. At the north border is the original "necessary house." The southeast corner of the garden contains the Jacksons' tomb. Rachel died December 22, 1828, weeks before Jackson was inaugurated as president. Jackson is said to have visited the tomb every evening while he lived at the Hermitage. Jackson died in his bedroom on June 8, 1845. Per his directions, he was buried next to his wife. Other members of his family are buried next to the Jackson Tomb. On the other side of the tomb is the grave of Alfred, a slave who lived at the property all his life and was Jackson's devoted servant. Other historic structures on the grounds include the original cabins where the Jacksons lived from 1804 to 1821, the Old Hermitage Church, an original slave cabin, a smokehouse, a springhouse, and a kitchen.

At the visitor center you can get a quick bite at the Kitchen Cabinet Cafe and browse for gifts at the Hermitage Museum Store. The Hermitage is open daily. It is closed on Thanksgiving and Christmas.

HISTORIC MANSKER'S STATION, 705 Caldwell Dr., Goodlettsville, TN 37072; (615) 859-3678; cityofgoodlettsville.org; $$. Bowen Plantation House and Mansker's Station are at this site. The 2-story, Federal-style house, built in 1787, is the oldest brick home in Middle Tennessee. It was built by Revolutionary War veteran and Indian fighter William Bowen, who brought his family to the area in 1785. He received the land as partial compensation for his military service and later expanded the plantation from 640 acres to more than 4,000. In 1807 William Bowen Campbell was born here. He fought in

Close-up

Carter House . . . The Most Battle-Damaged Building from the Civil War

After almost 3 years serving with Confederate troops in the Civil War, **Capt. Tod Carter** was going home. The young officer had a furlough and was looking forward to seeing his family again. As with many soldiers, Carter had been through hell. An attorney and a Master Mason, Carter had enlisted and participated in most of the Army of Tennessee battles. He had been captured at Chattanooga on November 25, 1863, but had escaped from a prison train in Pennsylvania in February 1864 and quickly rejoined his troop. Now he had furlough papers in hand and was headed home.

Carter had no idea that the battleground for one of the most horrific fights of the Civil War would take place right at his own home. **The Carter House,** built in 1830 by Fountain Branch Carter, was caught in the swirling center of one of the bloodiest battles of the War Between the States.

"They said the ground ran red with blood," our tour guide said. "It was one of the most fiercely contested battles of the war. It was a complete slaughter. . . . We are not here to glorify death but to glorify their lives."

The morning of November 30, 1864, dawned a beautiful Indian summer day. At sunrise the Confederate army marched north from Spring Hill in pursuit of fleeing Union forces. General Hood was determined to destroy the Union army before it reached Nashville.

The two forces collided in the **Battle of Franklin.** Hood sent his Confederates across 2 miles of open fields against the Union front. The Carter House sat directly in the center between the two lines of headlong combat.

Called "The Gettysburg of the West," Franklin was one of the few night battles in the Civil War, beginning about 4 p.m. and ending around 9 p.m. It was also one of the smallest battlefields of the war—only 2 miles long and 1.5 miles wide. "The smoke from the cannons and guns was so thick you could hardly tell friend from foe," the tour guide said.

During the battle the Carter family took refuge in their basement. Their home was commandeered by **Union Maj. Gen. John M. Schofield** for his

Carter House Courtesy of Tennessee Department of Tourist Development

headquarters. The head of the family, 67-year-old widower Fountain Branch Carter, and 22 other men, women, and children (many under age 12), barricaded themselves in the basement while the horrible cries of war rang out above them.

Federal soldiers used the front bedroom and parlor as sniping positions while they fired their muskets at the enemy, who returned fire from the far side of the barn and icehouse. Not one brick in the south wall of the kitchen seems to have escaped a bullet hole.

Sometime after midnight, they realized that the sounds of war had stopped. Since Tod Carter had not come home, the family feared that he was dead or wounded. His commander told the family where the young man had last been seen. Tod Carter had been heard to cry out, "Follow me, boys, I'm almost home." With a 9-year-old niece carrying the lantern, the four family members found Tod Carter.

He and his horse had been shot down in a small locust grove about 170 yards southwest of his birthplace. "He had probably played in that grove of trees as a child," our tour guide said. Carter had sustained eight or nine bullet wounds, and it was a miracle he was still alive. Carter had likely been wounded at about 4:30 p.m. when the battle first started, and he wasn't found until about 4:30 a.m.

After 12 hours of bleeding, he had probably lost too much blood. The family carried him back home and his 9-year-old niece held the lantern while a bullet was removed from the back of his eye.

Two days later, Carter was dead. He was 24 years old. He was buried in the last casket available in Franklin.

The unofficial count was about 7,500 Confederate and about 2,500 Union casualties. "It's hard to have an exact count of the wounded and casualties because so many of the wounded didn't seek medical attention and marched on to fight in Nashville," our tour guide said.

After the battle, the parlor of the Carter House was converted into a Confederate field hospital and witnessed many surgeries and amputations. In fact, soldiers would be dying for decades afterward from wounds they received at the Battle of Franklin. As late as the 1920s, men were dying of complications from wounds they had received in this battle.

The Army of Tennessee died at Franklin on November 30, 1864, our tour guide said. "It was a fight they would never recover from. I think that's why Fountain Branch Carter decided not to repair the bullet holes in his house and buildings. He realized that this was hallowed ground. He wanted people to remember what had happened here and know this was where Americans had shed their blood."

The evidence of over 1,000 bullet holes remains on the site, including the most battle-damaged building from the Civil War. A small 10-by-15-foot building had 167 bullet holes. For more information, contact the Carter House at (615) 791-1861.

the Seminole War and the Mexican War and served as Tennessee's 15th governor from 1851 to 1853 and a member of Congress in 1855. The restored house was listed on the National Register of Historic Places in 1976. About 200 yards from the house is Mansker's Station, a reconstruction of a 1779 frontier fort where Kasper Mansker lived. Mansker is considered Goodlettsville's first citizen. Living-history encampments held here several weekends a year offer demonstrations of frontier skills such as hide tanning, soapmaking, blacksmithing, butter churning, and fireside cookery. Historic interpreters in period clothing provide tours daily from the first week of Mar through the first week of Dec.

HISTORIC ROCK CASTLE, 139 Rock Castle Ln., Hendersonville, TN 37075; (615) 824-0502; historicrockcastle.com; $. The late-18th-century house on the shores of Old Hickory Lake was at one time the center of a

3,140-acre plantation, home of senator and Revolutionary War veteran Daniel Smith and his family. Today the property occupies 18 acres and includes the furnished 7-room limestone house, a smokehouse, and the family cemetery. Other buildings were claimed by the creation of Old Hickory Lake in the 1950s. Smith, a well-known surveyor of the North Carolina (now Tennessee) boundaries and of Davidson County, made the first map of the area. Some say he gave the state its name as well, adopting the Cherokee word *Tanasie,* which may have meant "where the rivers tangle together." (However, accounts of who named the state, and the meaning of the Cherokee word from which the name was taken, vary quite a bit.) Smith and his wife, Sarah, are buried in the family cemetery. You can learn more about the family and the property on a guided tour. Stop first at the visitor center for an orientation. There's a gift shop that sells souvenirs and items representative of the period. The attraction is open daily Tues through Sun from Mar through Dec. Open-air concerts, an annual Summer Harvest Fest, and other events also are offered.

HISTORIC SAM DAVIS HOME & PLANTATION, 1399 Sam Davis Rd., Smyrna, TN 37167; (615) 459-2341; samdavishome.org; $$. This Greek Revival home, built around 1820 and enlarged around 1850, sits on 169 acres of the original 1,000-acre farm that was the home of Sam Davis. Davis, called the "Boy Hero of the Confederacy," enlisted in the Confederate army at the age of 19. He served as a courier, and while transporting secret papers to Gen. Braxton Bragg in Chattanooga, he was captured by Union forces, tried as a spy, and sentenced to hang. The trial officer was so impressed with Davis's honesty and sense of honor that he offered him freedom if he would reveal the source of military information he was caught carrying. Davis is reported to have responded, "If I had a thousand lives I would give them all gladly rather than betray a friend." He was hanged in Pulaski, Tennessee, on November 27, 1863. The home is a typical upper-middle-class farmhouse of the period. A tour of the property also includes outbuildings. The home is open daily. Closed holidays and Jan.

MADAME TUSSAUDS NASHVILLE, 515 Opry Mills Dr., Nashville, TN 37214; madametussauds.com/Nashville; $$$. Got a hankering to have your photo taken with Reba McEntire? Or maybe Kid Rock is more your selfie star? At Madame Tussauds Nashville, you can strike a pose with lifelike figures of your favorites. Opened in 2017 in Opry Mills, Madame Tussauds invites guests to take a journey through different genres and eras in America's musical history. A multisensory experience visits a mid-century recording studio, the original *Grand Ole Opry* stage in the 1970s, a rock-themed dive bar, Nashville's famous Bluebird Cafe, and backstage at a concert. Visitors are encouraged to take photos, touch, and have fun with the figures. About 50 musical superstars are featured, including Johnny Cash, Elvis Presley, Katy Perry, Justin Timberlake, Tim McGraw, Faith Hill, Bruce Springsteen, and many more. Hours vary so check the website.

NASHVILLE CITY CEMETERY, 1001 Fourth Ave. S. at Oak Street, Nashville, TN 37203; (661) 661-6161; thenashvillecitycemetery.org; free. This cemetery was opened January 1, 1822, making it Nashville's oldest remaining public cemetery. It's also one of the few cemeteries in the state listed as an individual property on the National Register of Historic Places. There are some 23,000 graves here, including the graves of many early settlers, whose remains were brought here for permanent burial. Many graves are unmarked. Among the notables buried here are Nashville founder Gen. James Robertson (1742–1814) and Capt. William Driver (1803–1886), who named the American flag "Old Glory." Three Civil War generals are also buried here: Maj. Gen. Bushrod Johnson (1817–1880), hero of the Battle of Chickamauga; and Lt. Gen. Richard S. Ewell (1817–1872), a commander at the Battle of Gettysburg. In 1878 city officials voted to allow only descendants of owners with unfilled plots to be buried here. This policy is still in place. Metal markers containing historical information are located throughout the grounds. The cemetery is open daily from dawn to dusk. Cemetery records are in the Tennessee State Library and Archives at 403 Seventh Ave. N. (615-741-2764). (See our **Annual Events** chapter for more about the cemetery.)

OAKLANDS HISTORIC HOUSE MUSEUM, 900 N. Maney Ave., Murfreesboro, TN 37130; (615) 893-0022; oaklandsmuseum.org; $$. One of the most elegant antebellum homes in Middle Tennessee, this house began around 1815 as a 1-story brick home built by the Maney family. The family enlarged the house with a Federal-style addition in the early 1820s and made further changes in the 1830s. The last addition was the ornate Italianate facade, completed in the 1850s. Oaklands was the center of a 1,500-acre plantation. Union and Confederate armies alternately occupied the house during the Civil War. On July 13, 1862, Confederate general Nathan Bedford Forrest led a raid here, surprising the Union commander at Oaklands. The surrender was negotiated here. In December 1862, Confederate president Jefferson Davis boarded at Oaklands while visiting nearby troops. Stop by the visitor center for a video orientation before beginning your tour. There is a gift shop on the property. The house is open Tues through Sun, except on major holidays.

PRINTERS ALLEY, Between Church and Union and Third and Fourth Avenues, Nashville, TN 37219; theprintersalley.com; free. Once the center of Nashville's nightlife, Printers Alley was originally home to Nashville's publishing and printing industry. Speakeasies sprang up here during Prohibition. During the 1940s, nightclubs opened. You could come here to catch performances by such stars as Boots Randolph, Chet Atkins, Dottie West, and Hank Williams. Today you'll find several nightspots here, including the Bourbon Street Blues & Boogie Bar.

RYMAN AUDITORIUM, 116 Fifth Ave. N., Nashville, TN 37219; (615) 889-3060 (reservations, tickets); ryman.com; $$. The legendary Ryman Auditorium (see also our **History** and **Music City** chapters) was home of the *Grand Ole Opry* from 1943 to 1974. Today the Ryman hosts concerts by country, bluegrass, pop, rock, classical, and gospel artists and special engagements of the *Grand Ole Opry.* The Ryman also has hosted several musical productions in recent years. Its excellent acoustics have made it a popular spot among recording artists such as Bruce Springsteen, Merle Haggard, Bob Dylan, and Sheryl Crow.

The building was originally called the Union Gospel Tabernacle. Riverboat captain Thomas Ryman, inspired by the preaching of evangelist Sam Jones, built the facility in 1892 as a site for Jones's revivals and other religious gatherings. It soon became a popular venue for theatrical and musical performances and political rallies. The building was renamed to honor Ryman after his death in 1904. Though it wasn't the first home of the *Grand Ole Opry,* which began in 1925, the Ryman earned the nickname "the Mother Church of Country Music." For 31 years the live *Opry* radio show originated from this building. Country legends such as Hank Williams, Roy Acuff, and Patsy Cline performed on the stage. While fans packed the wooden pews, others tuned in to their radios to hear the live broadcast.

A statue of Grand Ole Opry star Little Jimmy Dickens stands outside Ryman Auditorium. Jackie Sheckler Finch

Schermerhorn Symphony Center

Comparable to the greatest music halls in the world, the $120-million **Schermerhorn Symphony Center** opened in 2006 as an acoustic masterpiece. Located on a city block between Third and Fourth Avenues S., the center is home to the **Nashville Symphony Orchestra.** It was named in honor of the late Kenneth Schermerhorn, music director and conductor of the orchestra. The center houses the Laura Turner Concert Hall, named in honor of the mother of Nashville symphony supporters Cal Jr. and Steve Turner.

Designed by architect David M. Schwarz, the 197,000-square-foot center has 30 soundproof windows above the hall, making it one of the only major concert halls in North America with natural light. The Schermerhorn design was inspired by some of the world's great concert halls, many of which were built in Europe in the late 19th century. The result is a sophisticated and modern building that is neoclassically inspired, with a classic limestone exterior and columns.

The shoebox-shaped hall seats 1,844 patrons. During symphony performances, the seats are ramped in a theater-style layout. During Pops performances and for receptions or banquets, however, the seats can be transported to a storage area by an elevator. In 1 to 2 hours, the configuration can change

When the *Opry* moved to the new *Grand Ole Opry* House at Opryland USA, the Ryman became a tourist attraction, and the building was used as a backdrop in such films as *Nashville, Coal Miner's Daughter,* and *Sweet Dreams.*

The Ryman remains a top tourist destination. Individuals and groups stop here daily to tour the building. Various exhibits and displays tell about the Ryman and country music history. Audiovisual displays on the main floor feature a variety of memorabilia. A film details the history of the Ryman. Self-guided and guided tours are available 7 days a week. A concession stand and gift shop are on-site.

STONES RIVER NATIONAL BATTLEFIELD, 3501 Old Nashville Hwy., Murfreesboro, TN 37129; (615) 893-9501; nps.gov/stri; free. One of the bloodiest Civil War battles took place at this site between December

Schermerhorn Symphony Center Nashville Convention & Visitors Corporation

from ramped seating to a flat parquet floor, making it the only building in the world with this ability. Behind the orchestra are 140 seats for choral performances. The seats can be sold to the public when there is no chorus.

The Nashville Symphony performs more than 100 classical, Pops, and special-events concerts in the Schermerhorn each season. Recitals, choral concerts, cabaret, jazz, and world music events also will be presented. The center also features the **Mike Curb Family Music Education Hall,** which is home to the symphony's ongoing education initiatives. Another highlight of the building is a garden and cafe, enclosed by a colonnade. The garden is open to the public throughout the day and during concerts. For more information contact the Schermerhorn Symphony Center at (615) 687-6400 or visit nashvillesymphony.org.

31, 1862, and January 2, 1863. More than 83,000 men fought in the battle; nearly 28,000 were killed or wounded. Both the Union army, led by Gen. William S. Rosecrans, and the Confederate army, led by Gen. Braxton Bragg, claimed victory. However, on January 3, 1863, Bragg retreated 40 miles to Tullahoma, Tennessee, and Rosecrans took control of Murfreesboro. The Union constructed a huge supply base within Fortress Rosecrans, the largest enclosed earthen fortification built during the war. The battlefield today appears much as it did during the Battle of Stones River. Most of the points of interest can be reached on the self-guided auto tour. Numbered markers identify the stops, and short trails and exhibits explain the events at each site. Stop first at the visitor center. An audiovisual program and museum will introduce you to the battle. During summer, artillery and infantry demonstrations and talks about the battle take place. The park is administered by the National Park Service and open daily except Thanksgiving and Christmas.

Close-up

Andrew Jackson Said to Still Walk Grounds of His Beloved Hermitage

Andrew Jackson loved his home so much that he chose to be buried there with his beloved wife Rachel. Some say that the man known as "Old Hickory" keeps watch over his Tennessee plantation. "Many people don't think that he has ever truly left," tour guide David said. "General Jackson had such a strong personality that I think he has stayed around to watch over his home."

The Hermitage is preserved today almost as it was during the days of the man who became an American icon. Built between 1819 and 1821, the home has almost all its original furnishings including the wallpaper, which dates to the early 1800s. "If General Jackson were here with us, he would remember the home as it was the day when he left this world," David said. "I see General Jackson as a rather sensitive spiritual person who loved his God, his country, and his family and did what he had to do during very extraordinary times."

Jackson was born March 15, 1767, on the South Carolina border. His father died in a logging accident before Jackson was born, and the family had to move in with relatives to survive. Both of his brothers died in the Revolutionary War and his mother died when Jackson was 14.

The penniless youth tried his hand at the saddlery trade and teaching but was drawn toward the law and became a lawyer in 1787. Then he went to Nashville and found his future. Staying in a boardinghouse, Jackson fell in love with the owner's daughter, 21-year-old Rachel Donelson Robards who was trying to deal with a rocky marriage. Believing that her husband Lewis Robards had obtained a divorce, three years later Rachel and Andrew were married. Then they found out that Robards hadn't gotten a divorce after all. They were legally remarried in 1794, but the scandal plagued them the rest of their lives.

Jackson's political star rose quickly, and the 37-year-old Jackson bought the Hermitage property outside Nashville during this time. Apparently, Andrew and Rachel Jackson couldn't have children of their own, but they were always taking in other children to raise.

In 1806, an incident occurred that had a lifelong effect on Jackson. A dispute arose over payment when a horse sold by the Dickinson family came up lame. It escalated when Dickinson reportedly insulted Rachel. Finally, Charles Dickinson challenged Jackson to a duel. A well-known marksman, Dickinson shot first, seriously wounding Jackson who continued to stand his ground with a bullet lodged near his heart.

Once the home of Andrew and Rachel Jackson, the Hermitage is now a museum.
Jackie Sheckler Finch

Jackson's second demanded that Dickinson remain on his mark in accordance with the rules of dueling. Jackson shot Dickinson dead. Jackson survived his wound, although the bullet in his chest was never removed and it compromised his health later in his life. The fight enraged many in Nashville, and Jackson was ostracized by much of Tennessee society.

The War of 1812 gave Jackson a chance to save his somewhat tarnished reputation. Jackson racked up a string of victories that gained him a reputation as the country's foremost commander in the field. Then came the Battle of New Orleans. In 1814, Jackson and his ragtag army marched into New Orleans against the British. The British suffered more than 2,000 casualties. The Americans reported fewer than 20.

The victory confirmed the Louisiana Purchase, led to the acquisition of Florida, lent respect to the Monroe Doctrine, and created a healthy regard for America's independence. The victory also made General Jackson an instant legend and propelled him toward the White House.

But his past came back to haunt him—and eventually claimed his wife. The 1828 presidential campaign set a record for mud-slinging and name-calling. The worst attacks in the campaign were those on Rachel's reputation, accusations of adultery and bigamy that hurt Jackson and his ailing wife. Andrew Jackson won the election, of course, but Rachel never lived to be in the White House. Rachel died three weeks before the inauguration.

On December 22, 1828, Rachel died, reportedly of a massive heart attack. Jackson blamed his wife's death on the nasty campaign of 1828 and the stress of the imminent move to Washington. On Christmas Eve, Jackson laid Rachel to rest in her white inaugural gown in the garden at the Hermitage, surrounded by weeping willows. Shrouded in grief, Jackson then made his way to Washington. For the next eight years, through two tempestuous terms in office, Jackson made his mark on the presidency and the nation.

In 1837, Jackson at last retired to the Hermitage at the age of 70. While in the White House, Jackson had a permanent temple made of limestone created for his wife's grave and his own. Every day, he visited Rachel's grave. He missed his wife so much that he had a painting of her put in his bedroom so that she would be the last thing he saw at night and the first thing he saw in the morning.

On June 8, 1845, the 78-year-old Jackson finally joined his wife in death. The former president died of kidney failure and was buried beside Rachel in the Hermitage garden. But tales persist that General Jackson (as he liked to be called) often prowls the grounds—or rides them on his magnificent steed.

TENNESSEE STATE CAPITOL, 600 Charlotte Ave., Nashville, TN 37243; (615) 741-1621; tnmuseum.org; free. Free guided tours of the Tennessee State Capitol are provided throughout the day Mon through Fri at designated times by the staff of the Tennessee State Museum. Tours depart from the information desk on the first floor. If you prefer to take a self-guided tour, pick up a brochure at the information desk. When the legislature is in session, the capitol's hours of operation are extended if either the House of Representatives or the Senate is still in session. On legislative meeting days, visitors can view the Senate and House from their galleries, which are accessed by the second-floor stairwells.

The Greek Revival–style building was begun in 1845 and completed in 1859. Its architect, William Strickland of Philadelphia, began his career as an apprentice to Benjamin Latrobe, architect of the US Capitol in Washington, DC. Strickland died before the Tennessee State Capitol was completed and, per his wishes, was buried in the northeast wall of the building near the north entrance. Strickland's son, Francis Strickland, supervised construction until 1857 when Englishman Harvey Akeroyd designed the state library, the final portion of the building.

The capitol stands 170 feet above the highest hill in downtown Nashville. On the eastern slope of the grounds is the tomb of President and Mrs. James K. Polk and a bronze equestrian statue of President Andrew Jackson. The Tennessee State

Legislative Plaza at night Nashville Convention & Visitors Corporation

Capitol is open Mon through Fri but is closed on holidays. Parking is available at metered spaces around the capitol complex or in public parking lots downtown.

TRAVELLERS REST PLANTATION HOUSE AND GROUNDS, 636 Farrell Pkwy., Nashville, TN 37220; (615) 832-8197; travellersrestplantation.org; $$. Travellers Rest was built in 1799 by Judge John Overton, a land speculator, lawyer, cofounder of Memphis, and presidential campaign manager for lifelong friend Andrew Jackson. The Federal-style clapboard farmhouse offers a glimpse of how wealthy Nashvillians lived in the early 19th century. The well-maintained grounds feature magnolia trees, gardens, and outbuildings. The house began as a 2-story, 4-room house, but additions throughout the 1800s increased its size. Changes in architectural styles are evident in the expansions. It has been restored to reflect the period of the original owner and features a large collection of early-19th-century Tennessee furniture. The home served as headquarters for Confederate general John B. Hood just before the 1864 Battle of Nashville. Overton's son John had financed a Confederate regiment during the war. The Overton family owned the house until 1948. Its last owner, the Nashville Railroad Company, gave the home to the Colonial Dames of America in Tennessee, which manages it as a historic site. Today Travellers Rest is listed on the National Register of Historic Places. Travellers Rest is open Tues through Sat; closed holidays.

MUSEUMS

ADVENTURE SCIENCE CENTER & SUDEKUM PLANETARIUM, 800 Fort Negley Blvd., Nashville, TN 37203; (615) 862-5160; adventuresci.org; $$. A fun place to learn and explore, this museum, formerly known as the Cumberland Science Museum, features exhibits on nature, the universe, health, and more. Since the museum opened in 1973, it has been entertaining and educating children and adults with more than 100 hands-on exhibits, live animal shows, science demonstrations, a planetarium, and traveling exhibits. Permanent exhibits include Adventure Tower, Anatomy of an Earthquake, Beekeeping, Blue Max, BodyQuest, Destination Exploration, Fourth State of Matter, Galactic Gardens, Imagination Playground, Innovation Incubator, Nano, Physics of Flight, Physics of Light, Space Chase, Surge of a Tsunami, Vapor Vortex, and Virtual Reality. In the popular Dino Rumble, visitors can crawl through a tunnel for a face-to-face encounter with a massive *Tyrannosaurus rex* that moves, roars, and growls. The Sudekum Planetarium features a wide variety of shows and special programs such as laser shows honoring Michael Jackson, the Beatles, Queen, and Beyoncé. The center is open daily except major holidays. (For more information see the listing in our **Kidstuff** chapter.)

CHEEKWOOD BOTANICAL GARDEN & MUSEUM OF ART, 1200 Forrest Park Dr., Nashville, TN 37205; (615) 356-8000; cheekwood.org; $$. This magnificent 1929 mansion, surrounded by 55 acres of botanical gardens, lawns, and fountains, is one of Nashville's favorite attractions. It was once the private estate of the Leslie Cheek family. Cheek was the cousin and business associate of Joel Cheek, founder of Maxwell House coffee. In 1960 the family gave the estate to the nonprofit Tennessee Botanical Gardens and Fine Arts Center. Today the mansion houses the Museum of Art, a prestigious collection of 19th- and 20th-century American art as well as major traveling art exhibits (see the **Arts** chapter). The 3-story neo-Georgian mansion was built with Tennessee limestone quarried on the property. The house sits atop a hill surrounded by formal gardens designed by Cheekwood architect Bryant Fleming. The gardens feature marble sculptures, water gardens, and bubbling streams. The design includes an award-winning wildflower garden, an herb garden, a perennial garden, a traditional Japanese garden, and a dogwood trail. Along the border of the property is the Woodland Sculpture Trail, a mile-long trail featuring more than a dozen sculptures by artists from around the world.

Cheekwood's Botanic Hall features horticultural exhibits, flower shows, and the annual Season of Celebration holiday show. New Café 29 is operated by French-American bar and restaurant Sea Salt. Located inside the newly restored

Cheekwood is beautiful any time of year. Nashville Convention & Visitors Corporation

Frist Learning Center Courtyard, Café 29 offers a casual menu including soups, sandwiches, salads, baked goods, children's menu, coffee, and alcoholic beverages. Named for the year Cheekwood was built, Café 29 is open during Cheekwood hours. Cheekwood is open Tues through Sun. It is closed Mon and the second Sat in June, as well as major holidays.

COOTER'S PLACE, 2613 McGavock Pike, Nashville, TN 37214; (615) 872-8358; cootersplace.com; free. *Dukes of Hazzard* fans remember him as "Cooter," the good ole boy sidekick of the Duke boys on the beloved TV show. Cooter is actually actor Ben Jones, who operates this combination museum and theme store featuring all things Hazzard. Visitors can get their photos made in the snazzy 1969 Dodge Charger, the General Lee. Also displayed are Cooter's tow truck, Daisy's Jeep, and Rosco's patrol car. The free museum offers pictures, props, and costumes from the show. The gift shop carries T-shirts, hats, toys, DVDs, Dixie air horns, and other items. Check the schedule for upcoming events to see when Cooter and other cast members might be in the shop for autographs.

COUNTRY MUSIC HALL OF FAME & MUSEUM, 222 Fifth Ave. S. Nashville, TN 37203; (615) 416-2001 or (800) 852-6437; countrymusic halloffame.org; $$$. The Country Music Hall of Fame & Museum is one of Nashville's premier attractions. Originally housed in a barn-shaped building

Close-up

Johnny Cash Museum Honors "The Man in Black"

When Bill Miller was 13 years old, he went to a Johnny Cash concert that changed the course of his life. "Johnny Cash played a harmonica and tossed it into the audience when he was done," Miller said. "I caught it."

That was just the beginning. Over the years, Miller collected a treasure trove of Johnny Cash memorabilia and became friends with the legendary entertainer. "I honestly can't tell you how many pieces I have. It's in the thousands."

After Cash's death, Miller decided to share his collection with the public as a tribute to "The Man in Black." The Johnny Cash Museum opened in downtown Nashville in 2013 and has been drawing visitors ever since.

Walking in his footsteps, visitors traverse exhibits from Cash's life, including his hardscrabble childhood days in Dyess, Arkansas, his Air Force years, his famous prison concert tour, his TV and movie career, his marriage to June

The Highwaymen are honored at the Johnny Cash Museum. Jackie Sheckler Finch

Carter, and his final days. The stone wall from Cash's lakeside room in his Hendersonville house that burned was one of Miller's biggest saves. Displayed in the museum, the stone wall commemorates the mind-boggling "guitar pulls" that Cash hosted with famous friends like Bob Dylan and Kris Kristofferson.

Johnny Cash's sister Joanne visits the graves of Johnny and June Carter Cash.
Jackie Sheckler Finch

As Johnny Cash's youngest sister, Joanne Cash Yates remembers that her brother was determined to become a singer, despite the odds against him. To Yates, however, her big brother was always J.R. "That was the name on his birth certificate. That's what we always called him," she said. "Mommy wanted to name him John after her father. Daddy wanted to name him Ray after himself. They couldn't decide so they named him J.R."

When Cash went in the Air Force, the government wasn't going to allow a serviceman to have two initials for his name. "They told him that wouldn't do. So J.R. said his name was John and that's what people started calling him. I guess Mom won after all."

At the museum, visitors can put on headphones and listen to Cash music from various decades, including one of his final hit releases before his death—the heartrending video for "Hurt." In it, the tormented still-powerful voice intones, "Everyone I know goes away in the end." Cash was 71 years old when the video was filmed in February 2003. He died seven months later on September 12. Seen in the video sadly gazing at her husband, June Carter Cash died May 15, three months after filming.

For Miller, the museum was a labor of love, a tribute to the man he called a friend. "I was with Johnny about a week before he passed. I know he would love the museum."

Cash's sister agrees. "Not long before J.R. passed away, he said to me, 'Baby, when I'm gone, I wonder if anybody will really care,'" she said. "So I think he'd be real proud that this museum is here where people can come and remember him."

on Music Row, the museum opened in its $37-million home at Fifth Avenue S. and Demonbreun Street in May 2001. In 2014, the facility unveiled a $100-million expansion, which doubled its size to 350,000 square feet. The expansion included the 800-seat CMA Theater, Taylor Swift Education Center, Fred and Dinah Gretsch Family Gallery, and relocation of the historic Hatch Show Print to the facility, plus the addition of a restaurant, shops, and event spaces. The facility takes up an entire city block and boasts exhibit space devoted to the history of country music. As you walk through the museum, you'll view music memorabilia, hear clips of country recordings past and present, and learn about the music and its performers. The museum is accredited by the American Association of Museums, certifying that it operates according to the highest standards (fewer than 10 percent of the nation's 8,000 museums are accredited by the association). The museum is open daily except Thanksgiving, Christmas Eve, and Christmas Day. (For more about the museum, see our **Music City** chapter.)

FRIST ART MUSEUM, 919 Broadway, Nashville, TN 37203; (615) 244-3340; fristartmuseum.org; $$. The Frist is Nashville's premier art museum. Housed in downtown Nashville's historic former main post office building, the center has approximately 24,000 square feet of gallery space. Its changing lineup of exhibits includes works by renowned artists that are on loan from galleries around the world. The center is dedicated to education, with a goal of making art accessible and interesting to people of all ages and from all backgrounds. Educational outreach efforts include lectures, concerts, films, gallery talks, and youth and family programs on the center's exhibits and related topics. The Frist Art

Frist Art Museum Nashville Convention & Visitors Corporation

A timeline allows visitors to listen to George Jones hits over the years.
Jackie Sheckler Finch

Museum is open daily except Thanksgiving, Christmas, and New Year's Day. (See our **Entertainment** chapter for more details.)

GEORGE JONES MUSEUM, 128 Second Ave. N., Nashville, TN 37201; (615) 818-0128; georgejones.com; $$$. The legendary "Possum" now has a museum in downtown Nashville. Opened in 2015, the George Jones Museum offers a wealth of memorabilia and personal information about the beloved star. From his birth on September 12, 1931, in Saratoga, Texas, to his death from respiratory failure on April 26, 2013, the museum traces Jones's life with artifacts big and small. Nancy Jones, who married the singer in 1983, said she saved everything she could and promised her husband that she would carry on his legacy. The facility also has a gift shop, George Jones Smokehouse, and Rooftop Bar which offers great views of Nashville.

LANE MOTOR MUSEUM, 702 Murfreesboro Pike, Nashville, TN 37210; (615) 742-7445; lanemotormuseum.org; $$. Opened in 2003, this museum has vehicles that probably wouldn't be seen anywhere else—and most of them are in working condition. Cars that fold in half, drive in the water, lift themselves for a tire change, or open at the top with an airplane-style hatch are just a few of the more than 150 vehicles collected by automobile enthusiast Jeff Lane. Also on display are motorcycles and bicycles. The collection is regularly rotated

Lane Motor Museum features a collection of mostly European vehicles.
Nashville Convention & Visitors Corporation

to keep the exhibit fresh for returning guests. Check the website for hours. Closed on Thanksgiving, Christmas, and New Year's Day.

MUSICIANS HALL OF FAME & MUSEUM, 401 Gay St., Nashville, TN 37201; (615) 244-3263; musicianshalloffame.com; $$. Reopened in 2013 at its new location, the Musicians Hall of Fame & Museum reflects the diversity of what Nashville has accomplished as a music center. With a slogan of "Come see what you've heard," the museum honors the people who provide the sounds behind the music.

A performance stage with a backdrop of real guitars welcome visitors to the Musicians Hall of Fame & Museum.
Jackie Sheckler Finch

THE PARTHENON, 2500 West End Ave., Nashville, TN 37203; (615) 862-8431; nashville.gov/parks-and-recreation/parthenon.aspx; $$. One of Nashville's most dramatic and most recognized attractions, this is the world's only full-size reproduction of the ancient Greek temple. Nashville's magnificent Parthenon, listed on the National Register of Historic Places, mirrors the dimensions of the original to an eighth of an inch. The first Parthenon was built between 1895 and 1897 as the centerpiece for the state's Centennial Exposition. It was a symbol of the city's reputation as the Athens of the South. Like the other exposition buildings, the Parthenon was created of plaster and wood. While the other buildings were demolished after the expo, the Parthenon was so popular that Nashville kept it, and Centennial Park was created around it in the early 1900s. After it had begun to deteriorate, it was rebuilt with concrete from 1920 to 1931. Just as it was in ancient Greece, the focus of this Parthenon is a 42-foot statue of the goddess Athena, created by Nashville sculptor Alan LeQuire. It is the tallest indoor sculpture in the Western world. A 6-foot statue of Nike, the Greek goddess of victory, rests in Athena's right hand.

The Parthenon is also the city's art museum and boasts an impressive collection. Other gallery spaces showcase temporary art shows and exhibits. Docents provide information about the art collection and about mythology and Nashville history. A gift shop is located in the main lobby of the gallery-level entrance. It is open Tues through Sun.

Parthenon Nashville Convention & Visitors Corporation

Close-up

New Patsy Cline Museum Showcases Her Personal Possessions

Patsy Cline saved the memories of her life. After being locked away for more than half a century, that memorabilia is now being seen at the new Patsy Cline Museum in Nashville. "Patsy Cline was very sentimental," said museum founder Bill Miller. "I think people will be really surprised at what we have in the museum."

A 25-cent writing tablet filled with handwritten "biography" entries in red ink notes that the youngster "started tap dancing and won a contest at age 5." Sketches the budding singer created of fringed cowgirl outfits were sewn by her mother on an old-fashioned Singer machine. A carefully arranged photo album commemorates her wedding to Charlie Dick. And the front door key to her "dream home" still dangles from a tattered string.

"The family didn't even know some of these things existed," Miller said. "Charlie Dick had saved them all those years."

After successfully opening the Johnny Cash Museum in downtown Nashville in 2013, Miller thought it was long past time that the legendary Patsy Cline was also honored with a well-organized museum. But where would he find Cline's personal possessions for such a facility?

"I didn't want it to be just a bunch of old pictures and newspaper clippings. I wanted people to see what she was really like. But Patsy Cline's career was only

Patsy Cline's husband Charlie Dick saved his wife's memorabilia for more than half a century. Jackie Sheckler Finch

about six years in its entirety. Finding things to put in her museum could turn out to be an impossible task," said Miller.

Then the "impossible" happened.

After the death of Patsy Cline's husband in 2015, the family was surprised to find a treasure trove of Cline's possessions that her husband had lovingly preserved. "It's really a miracle," Miller said. "When Patsy's daughter Julie called me, she said, 'You have to get over here. You won't believe what we found.'"

Located above the Johnny Cash Museum, the Patsy Cline Museum opened April 7, 2017. Arranged in chronological order, exhibits trace her life from her birth on September 8, 1932, in Winchester, Virginia, until her death in a plane crash near Camden, Tennessee, on March 5, 1963. She was 30 years old. Artifacts are displayed from every stage of Cline's life, including a booth from Gaunt's Drug Store where she used to work. After her father deserted them, Cline dropped out of school at 15 to help support the family.

She sang in juke joints, amateur musicals, and talent shows. It was at a local club where Cline met Charlie Dick. The two married in 1957 and had two children, Julie, born in 1958, and Randy, born in 1961. Dick died November 8, 2015, at age 81 and was buried next to Cline in Winchester, Virginia.

The designs that Patsy Cline created for tailor Nudie Cohn to make were finally done—54 years after her death. Jackie Sheckler Finch

Some of the surprising exhibits are the furniture, ashtrays, and still-running Norge refrigerator that Cline and Dick had in their Nashville home. The recreated rec room includes a floor model black-and-white television showing classic Cline videos. Among the most poignant items are those recovered at the site of the plane crash that took Cline's life, as well as the lives of singers Hawkshaw Hawkins and Cowboy Copas and Cline's manager Randy Hughes who was piloting the plane. The group was returning from a benefit show in Kansas City. Displayed is the silver Elgin wristwatch that Cline was wearing when she died.

The final exhibit showcases outfits that Cline had designed and wanted famed tailor Nudie Cohn to create for her. Cline wrote to Cohn on February 28, 1963, including her instructions and measurements. Nudie responded to Cline that he would take on the work. But his letter arrived too late. Cline was dead.

"We didn't want to leave people with the somber exhibit of Patsy's death so we had Nudie's granddaughter make the outfits from Patsy's designs," Miller said. "When the family found all of Patsy's things that Charlie Dick had saved, it makes me believe that this museum was meant to be. Patsy Cline was an icon, the best loved female singer of all time."

STORYTELLERS MUSEUM & HIDEAWAY FARM, 9676 Old Hwy. 46, Bon Aqua; TN 37025; (931) 996-4336; storytellersmuseum.com; $$$. The museum is the restoration of a building that Johnny Cash once owned, where he supported small concerts for the community including the legendary "Saturday Night in Hickman County" guitar pulls. Visitors can experience a live musical performance on the restored stage and view video footage about Cash. The museum also features Cash photos and memorabilia as well as the iconic "One Piece at a Time" car. The novelty song recorded by Cash tells the story of a poor autoworker who took Cadillac parts home over the years and built a hodgepodge Caddy of his own. Cash became owner of the Cash Hideaway Farm in the early 1970s after discovering that his accountant had been embezzling his money to buy properties, including the farm. Cash fell in love with the 107-acre farm and spent more than 30 years in the house and on the land that he called "the center of my universe."

TENNESSEE AGRICULTURAL MUSEUM, Ellington Agricultural Center, 404 Hogan Rd., Nashville, TN 37220; (615) 837-5197; tnagmuseum.org; free. This attraction, a short drive south from downtown Nashville, is at the beautiful 207-acre Ellington Agricultural Center. It operates under the umbrella of the Tennessee Department of Agriculture and is the department's headquarters. The museum, a 14,000-square-foot, 2-story horse barn built in 1920, houses an extensive collection of home and farm artifacts from the 1800s and early 1900s, a blacksmith shop, and the Tennessee Agriculture Hall of Fame exhibit. A log cabin area, near the main barn, features 5 cabins with exhibits relating to early farm life in Tennessee. An interpretive herb garden is next to the cabins, and a nature trail from the cabin area leads to an iris garden, pond, and gazebo. The property is also designated as an arboretum, featuring 80 tree species. On Saturday in the summer, the museum hosts a variety of fun family-oriented events that spotlight farm life. Past summer Saturday themes have included sheepshearing and wool spinning, heirloom gardening, and miniature mules and donkeys. The museum is open year-round Mon through Fri.

TENNESSEE SPORTS HALL OF FAME AND MUSEUM, 501 Broadway, Nashville, TN 37203; (615) 242-4750; tshf.net; $. This attraction, which pays tribute to Tennessee's athletes, is located on the main level of the Bridgestone Arena adjacent to the glass tower. Inductees and honorees include Wilma Rudolph, Peyton Manning, Tracy Caulkins, Pat Head Summitt, and Chandra Cheeseborough. The 7,200-square-foot museum offers interactive games, exhibits on college football and basketball, NASCAR video games, two 30-seat theaters showing sports videos, and more. The attraction is open Tues through Sat.

The Tennessee Sports Hall of Fame & Museum honors state athletes.
Jackie Sheckler Finch

Close-up

Hotel's Indoor Gardens Are a Bona Fide Attraction

A favorite among Nashvillians and visitors, the massive **Gaylord Opryland Resort and Convention Center** is as much an attraction as it is a hotel. There are 9 acres of impressive indoor gardens, 2,712 guest rooms and 176 suites, more than a dozen restaurants and bars, a variety of retail shops, and much more.

The Conservatory, a 2-acre bilevel space filled with tropical plants, was the hotel's first indoor garden; it opened in 1983. Wander along the winding path, then walk upstairs and check out the view of the 10,000 tropical plants from above. The 1988 expansion featured the **Cascades,** another 2-acre indoor area. The Cascades's 3 waterfalls splash down from the top of a 40-foot mountain into a 12,500-square-foot lake. You can linger here at the tropical Cascades Restaurant or enjoy drinks and appetizers at the revolving Cascades Terrace lounge. Each night, visitors crowd around the Cascades's Dancing Waters fountains, which are the focus of a laser show.

The hotel's **Delta** space opened in 1996. When you step into this 4.5-acre area, you'll be transported to a Mississippi Delta town—complete with a river and flatboats that carry guests through the area. The Delta's glass roof peaks at 150 feet (15 stories). There are 2- and 3-story buildings housing a variety of interesting gift shops, meeting rooms, and lounges. The Delta Island Food Court is the place to find drinks and other goodies.

Opened in 2005, **Relache Spa** features treatment rooms dedicated to pampering, peace, and renewal. The 20,000-square-foot European-inspired spa, fitness center, and full-service salon offers popular services. The newest addition is the $90 million *SoundWaves* which opened December 1, 2018. The exciting 111,000-square-foot water experience features 4 acres of combined indoor and outdoor water attractions on three levels. Rides are intertwined with living walls and plant beds which help it blend in with the resort's 9 acres of garden atriums. The unique SoundWaves' roof brings in the sun while the indoor attraction is kept at 84 degrees year-round.

SoundWaves features tube slides, body slides, family raft ride, rapid and lazy rivers, wave pool, mat racer, multilevel play structure, kiddie pool, rock climbing wall, arcade, cabanas, Decibels restaurant, 2 outdoor food trucks, bars, and an adults-only pool and bar named "Status Cymbal" on the top indoor level. Indoor water attractions are open year-round. Outdoor water attractions are open May through Labor Day. SoundWaves is available only to hotel guests.

For more information visit marriott.com/hotels/travel/gnago-gaylord-opryland-resort-and-convention-center. Also, see our **Accommodations** and **Annual Events** chapters for more on lodging options and yearly happenings at this Nashville showplace. Admission to the hotel gardens is free; parking at the hotel costs $29 per day.

TENNESSEE STATE MUSEUM, 1000 Rosa L. Parks Blvd. Nashville, TN 37208; (615) 741-2692; tnmuseum.org; free. Opened on October 4, 2018, by the Bicentennial Capitol Mall State Park, this museum offers a fascinating look at the history of Tennessee from prehistoric times through the 20th century. With a whopping 137,000 feet of administration and gallery space, the $120 million museum offers permanent and temporary exhibits. Displays include collections of prehistoric Indian artifacts, firearms, silver, quilts, paintings, and pottery. There is an extensive collection of Civil War uniforms, battle flags, and weapons. You can learn about the long hunters, such as Daniel Boone, who hunted in the area beginning in the 1760s, as well as interesting political figures like Andrew Jackson and Sam Houston.

ATTRACTIONS

The Tennessee Time Tunnel traces state history at the new Tennessee State Museum.
Jackie Sheckler Finch

> **i** Fort Negley, a Civil War fort in south Nashville that had been closed for nearly 60 years, reopened in 2004. A $2 million renovation at the Union fort added a visitor center and a walking path with interpretive stops. The fort is located just off Eighth Avenue S. on a hill between Greer Stadium and the Adventure Science Center.

Other exhibits relate to African Americans, Prohibition, women's suffrage, and important events that shaped the history of the Volunteer State. Replicas of building facades and period rooms are featured, too. The Tennessee Time Tunnel serves as the backbone for the state's story. Visitors can use different entrances through the Time Tunnel for a more in-depth look at a specific era in Tennessee history. In Tennessee Tranforms, the 360 Interactive Theater features a cross section of people, places, and events in Tennessee from World War II to the present. The theater features more than 100 topics to examine on a touch table as well as 3 large wall screens that feature related images. The State Museum is open Tues through Sun, closed major holidays.

THE UPPER ROOM CHAPEL AND MUSEUM, 1908 Grand Ave., Nashville, TN 37212; (615) 340-7200; chapel.upperroom.org; free. An interesting attraction here is the chapel's 8-by-17-foot wood carving of *The Last Supper,* based on Leonardo da Vinci's famous painting. It was created by Italian sculptor Ernest Pellegrini in 1953 for the Upper Room, an interdenominational ministry of the United Methodist Church. Speakers from different denominations and countries take part in the weekly Wed morning worship service from 10:45 a.m. to 11:30 a.m. The museum contains religious artifacts, paintings of religious subjects made from 1300 through 1990, manuscripts, books, and seasonal displays of 100 nativity scenes and 73 Ukrainian eggs. Between the wings of the building is the Agape Garden, featuring statues, fountains, and symbols relating to the garden of Gethsemane. Admission and parking are free, but a $5 donation is encouraged. The museum is open Mon through Fri.

AMUSEMENTS & THE ZOO

NASHVILLE SHORES, 4001 Bell Rd., Hermitage, TN 37076; (615) 889-7050; nashvilleshores.com; $$$$. At Nashville Shores, every day is a day at the beach. Located on 385 acres along Percy Priest Lake, the water park offers white sandy beaches, swimming pools, 8 large waterslides, and other water amusements. Pontoon boats and personal watercraft are available for rent at the marina. Attractions include a 25,000-square-foot wave pool called Breaker Bay, and a 1,000-foot-long lazy river, the state's widest lazy river. The wave pool is filled with 400,000 gallons of water, creating up to 5 different types of waves that can reach up to 4 feet high. For landlubbers there's an assortment of amusements, including Treetop Adventure Park, volleyball, and minigolf. Check the website for discounts and promotions. If you plan to make 4 or more visits, you'll save money by purchasing a season pass. Rental cabins and RV sites are available. Nashville Shores is open daily from May through early Aug, then weekends only through mid-Sept. (See our **Kidstuff** and **Recreation** chapters for more information.)

NASHVILLE ZOO AT GRASSMERE, 3777 Nolensville Pike, Nashville, TN 37211; (615) 833-1534; nashvillezoo.org; $$. Nolensville Road between Harding and Thompson Lane is a busy area filled with fast-food restaurants, all types of stores, and lots of traffic. It's an unlikely spot for a wildlife sanctuary, yet just off this road is a 200-acre zoo that is home to 2,675 animals and 375 species from around the world. The Nashville Zoo was accredited by the American Zoo and Aquarium Association in 2004; the zoo is among the 10 percent of the nation's more than 2,000 zoos and aquariums that have the accreditation.

Most of the zoo's animals live in naturalistic environments. In some exhibits, moats separate zoo visitors from zoo residents, offering guests unobstructed views of the animals. For hands-on fun, visitors can enjoy Critter Encounters, Lorikeet Landing, Shell Station, and Kangaroo Kick where visitors can brush a goat, feed a lorikeet and tortoise, and pet a kangaroo. For rides, the zoo offers Wilderness Express Train and Wild Animal Carousel. The zoo's Jungle Gym is a popular site with more than 66,000 square feet for running, swinging, and climbing just like the zoo's residents. Listed on the

Nashville Zoo is popular with people of all ages. Nashville Convention & Visitors Corporation

National Register of Historic Homes, the Grassmere Historic Home was built in 1810 and offers interpreters for walking tours. At the home, visitors can learn how the zoo came to be located on the land as well as stories about the 5 generations who lived in the home. Visitors also can explore the farm grounds, the 3-tier heirloom garden, and family cemetery. Except for New Year's Day, Thanksgiving, and Christmas Day, the zoo is open daily, with extended hours from Mar through Oct. (See our **Kidstuff** chapter for more about the zoo.)

WAVE COUNTRY, 2320 Two Rivers Pkwy., Nashville, TN 37214; (615) 885-1052; nashville.gov/parks-and-recreation; $$. The closest seashore is at least a 7-hour drive away, but this water park will do in a pinch. It's a fun place to cool off on one of our hot, humid summer days. Catch a wave, zoom down a slippery slide, or play in the surf. Wave Country has a wave pool, adult slides, kiddie slide, water flumes, playground, and 2 sand volleyball courts. It's at Two Rivers Park, just off Briley Parkway near Opryland. Wave Country is open daily during the summer from the end of May until the beginning of Sept. All children 12 and under must be accompanied by an adult 18 or older. (For more on Wave Country, see our **Kidstuff** chapter.)

FUN TRANSPORTATION & TOURS

DOWNTOWN TROLLEY TOUR, Gray Line Nashville, Riverfront Train Station, 108 First Ave. S., Nashville, TN 37201; (615) 883-5555; graylinetn.com; $$$$. Gray Line Nashville offers a variety of Nashville sightseeing tours.

The County Music Crawler lets riders drink and pedal around downtown.
Jackie Sheckler Finch

The Downtown Trolley Tour is a 1.25-hour trip that includes a drive by some of Nashville's most famous attractions, including the Ryman Auditorium, State Capitol, Country Music Hall of Fame & Museum, the Parthenon, and Music Row. Trolley tours run regularly from around 10 a.m. to 4 p.m. Make a day of it by using the hop-on/hop-off option of the tour. The Taste of Nashville Walking Food Tour offers 3½ hours of discovering some of the city's favorite eateries and sweeteries. Departing from Riverfront Train Station, the food tour showcases some of the restaurants and bars that have helped make Nashville a popular foodie spot. The tour also includes the Ryman Auditorium, Honky Tonk Highway, and much more. For information on other sightseeing tours, see our **Music City** chapter.

THE *GENERAL JACKSON* SHOWBOAT, 2812 Opryland Dr., Nashville, TN 37214; (615) 458-3900; generaljackson.com; $$$$. March 1817 marked the arrival of the first steamboat in Nashville—the $16,000 *General Jackson*. The boat was named after President Andrew Jackson, whose historic home—the Hermitage—is located 15 minutes from where the showboat is docked. By the mid-1800s Nashvillians traveled to such cities as New Orleans, Memphis, and St. Louis aboard steamboats outfitted with entertainment. Today

General Jackson *dinner boat cruising along downtown Nashville.*
Nashville Convention & Visitors Corporation

you can experience a bit of that bygone era aboard the *General Jackson*. The $12-million, 300-foot-long, 4-deck paddlewheel showboat takes guests on sightseeing, dining, and entertainment cruises along the Cumberland River. It carries up to 1,200 passengers. A highlight of the boat is the ornate Victorian Theater, which can accommodate 620 people for banquets and 1,000 for theater presentations. Top-notch music and comedy shows are featured during the trip. The evening dinner cruise includes a 3-course dinner served in the theater. You can step outside to see the nighttime Nashville skyline and enjoy the sounds of the onboard band. A round-trip cruise to downtown Nashville is 14 miles. The *General Jackson* operates year-round.

OLD TOWN TROLLEY TOURS, 201 Broadway, Nashville, TN 37201; (629) 208-0200; trolleytours,com; $$$$. A relaxing way to see Nashville and learn more about the exciting city, Old Town Trolley Tours offers several options to ride and learn. The hop-on, hop-off trolley has 15 stops and more than 100 points of interest on different tours. One of the most popular is the Country Music Hall of Fame Package which includes a narrated tour of Nashville, unlimited hop-on and hop-off, admission to the Country Music Hall of Fame & Museum, and much more. For a different view of the city, choose the Soul of Music City—Nashville's night tour. Led by a performing guide, visitors will enjoy the city's honky-tonks and famous music venues. The tour also shares insider stories and fascinating facts about the people, places, and events that helped created Nashville's iconic music reputation.

TENNESSEE CENTRAL RAILWAY MUSEUM, 220 Willow St., Nashville, TN 37210; (615) 244-9001; tcry.org; $$$$. The Tennessee Central Railway Museum offers round-trip, 1-day excursions aboard comfy, air-conditioned trains to Middle Tennessee locations. The trains depart 1 to 3 Saturdays per month and are tied to such events as the mile-long yard sale and flea markets in Watertown, fall foliage viewing in Cookeville and surrounding areas, and the North Pole Express with Santa in December. Evening "murder mystery" excursions are sometimes available. You can choose from moderately priced seats in the dining car, first-class seats in a private drawing room, or the

i The Francis Craig Orchestra entertained Nashvillians at the Hermitage Hotel from 1929 to 1945, reportedly the longest-running hotel musical act ever.

Old Town Trolley offers tours. Jackie Sheckler Finch

priciest seats in the special glass-domed car, which offers panoramic views of the beautiful Tennessee countryside. Refreshments and souvenirs are available for purchase on board. Reservations are required for anyone over age 2. Tickets sell out in advance, so plan ahead. Boarding is 30 minutes prior to departure at the museum's Willow Street location (off Hermitage Avenue), and trains arrive back in Nashville by mid- or late afternoon.

Kidstuff

No doubt about it, Nashville is a kid-friendly place. Ask new Nashvillians why they chose to live in Music City, and more often than not, the answer is the same: "We thought this would be a good place to raise children."

That's not idle hyperbole, either. Nashville's diverse arts, sports, education, and religious communities offer a wealth of opportunities for kids of all ages. Nashville's abundant creative energy has given rise to some unique youth-oriented activities, as well. The city is proud home to the country's oldest children's theater and the world's largest community-built jungle gym.

Here are some of our favorite kid-friendly activities and fun spots. Keep in mind that in a city growing as rapidly as Nashville, some attractions will have closed or moved, and others will have taken their place. Remember to call first to check hours of operation.

Price Code

Admission prices can change, but use our price code as a guide:

$	**Less than $10**
$$	**$10 to $20**
$$$	**More than $20**

ARTS & MUSIC

ARTQUEST, FRIST CENTER ART MUSEUM, 919 Broadway, Nashville, TN 37203; (615) 244-3340; fristartmuseum.org; free. This museum is a showpiece for everyone, to be sure. But museum officials were particularly concerned about making this a relevant and engaging place for young people, thus education is a key part of the Frist Center's mission. The result is ArtQuest, a hands-on gallery. After a major renovation, the Martin ArtQuest Gallery opened to the public in May 2018, honoring the generosity of Ellen Martin and the Martin Foundation. The gallery offers more than 30 activity stations designed to bring

> i Tennessee has the largest 4-H Club membership in the United States, boasting more than 184,000 members.

Budding artists can try out their talents at the Frist Art Museum.
Jackie Sheckler Finch

the visual arts alive for kids of varying ages. Children can take part in arts-oriented activities like drawing, painting, and paper sculpture making. A 16-foot interactive Everbright wall composed of color-changing dials lets visitors create large-scale designs using the full spectrum of colors. A full-body animated digital painting experience transforms visitors into colors and shapes on a wall mural. Based on the study of acoustics, a sound pattern station invites visitors to manipulate frequencies to create patterns with sand on metal plates. Visitors are invited to contribute to a collaborative textile-weaving installation using a large 6-sided art deco grid. In addition, workshops, and other education offerings are available throughout the year. As if that weren't enough, the Frist Art Museum demonstrates its commitment to kids at the cash register: ages 18 and under are admitted free, always. You can't beat that. The Frist Art Museum is open daily except Thanksgiving, Christmas, and New Year's Day.

CHEEKWOOD BOTANICAL GARDEN & MUSEUM OF ART, 1200 Forrest Park Dr., Nashville, TN 37205; (615) 353-9827; cheekwood.org; $$. Education also plays a key role at Cheekwood, Nashville's other art museum. Weekend art classes, workshops, and summer art camps are offered at the Frist Learning Center (yes, it's the same folks who are behind the downtown Frist

Art Museum), located adjacent to the Cheekwood mansion. Programs are available for ages as young as 4 on up to teens. The Frist Learning Center includes art studios and classrooms, and art classes and workshops are held here. Opened in August 2018, Café 29 was part of a major renovation of the Frist Learning Center and includes restored horse stables, updated art studios, a new gift shop, and the casual eatery. Operated by Nashville-based French-American bar and restaurant Sea Salt, Café 29 pays homage to the year 1929 when the Cheek family broke ground for the estate. The menu includes soups, salads, sandwiches, baked goods, alcoholic beverages, and, of course Maxwell House coffee, the brew that helped create Cheekwood. Indoor and outdoor seating at Café 29 is available as are picnics to go.

NASHVILLE CHILDREN'S THEATRE, 25 Middleton St., Nashville, TN 37210; (615) 254-9103; nashvillechildrenstheatre.org; $$$. The acclaimed Nashville Children's Theatre offers a variety of productions and programs for children ages 3 to 18. It puts on about 6 shows a year. The regular season runs Sept through May. Nashville Children's Theatre offers creative drama classes on Sat during fall, winter, and spring, and holds summer camps during June and July.

WEIRD SCIENCE

Nashville offers several attractions for the budding astronomer, scientist, or archaeologist of the family. Fun is the name of the game at these places, and sparking a child's natural curiosity is the rule. No stuffy classrooms here—it's all about imagination and entertainment. If a little education happens along the way, well then, that's just gravy.

ADVENTURE SCIENCE CENTER & SUDEKUM PLANETARIUM, 800 Fort Negley Blvd., Nashville, TN 37203; (615) 401-5092; adventuresci.org; $$. A world of hands-on activities designed to stimulate young minds awaits at the Adventure Science Center. The first thing visitors notice is the museum's centerpiece, the Adventure Tower. Rising from the ground floor and stretching all the way through the roof, the 75-foot-tall Adventure Tower is packed with hands-on, minds-on experiences that bring science to life. The tower has 6 concept

> i The Nashville Children's Theatre was established in 1931, making it the oldest children's theater company in America.

Adventure Science Center is home to hands-on science exhibits.
Nashville Convention & Visitors Corporation

areas, each an introduction to the rest of the museum. At the tower's top is a giant model of Earth, from which you get a breathtaking view of the Nashville skyline. Adventure Science Center is open daily except Easter, Thanksgiving, Christmas, and New Year's Day. Be sure to check the museum calendar for special events and kids' festivals, which occur periodically.

NASHVILLE ZOO AT GRASSMERE, 3777 Nolensville Rd., Nashville, TN 37211; (615) 833-1534; nashvillezoo.org; $$$. More than 2,675 animals and 375 species of animals from around the world can be found at the Nashville Zoo, an animal park that is rapidly becoming a world-class facility housing such endangered species as white Bengal tigers. The zoo continues to expand and recently opened its Entry Village, where hyacinth macaws and gibbons greet visitors. A trip to the zoo is a fun day for the entire family, but the zoo has made itself especially appealing to little ones by offering several unique attractions and programs. The zoo's Jungle Gym is a favorite with local kids. There's also Critter Encounters, a petting zoo where young ones can get up close and personal with camels, sheep, goats, and other animals. For a more in-depth experience, programs such as Night Owl Programs are designed for all groups, ages 5 and up. Overnight groups can spend the night in Unseen New World, inches away from the zoo's amphibian, reptile, and fish collection, or in a Croft Center classroom. A light evening snack and morning breakfast are provided. Night Owl Programs include educational activities, crafts, and games, plus a night zoo walk and a chance to see animals when they first wake up. Night Owl activities are available all year on Fri and Sat. The Nashville Zoo is open daily except Thanksgiving, Christmas, and New Year's Day.

VANDERBILT DYER OBSERVATORY, 1000 Oman Dr., Brentwood, TN 37027; (615) 373-4897; dyer.vanderbilt.edu; $. Vanderbilt University's observatory is located in the heart of an upscale residential neighborhood, just south of Radnor Lake. Free public observing sessions are held the second Fri of each month from Mar through Nov. The observatory has an impressive 24-inch telescope for viewing the night sky, an extensive astronomy library, a computer center featuring astronomy software, and a mission control center where telescopes around the country are controlled robotically. Vanderbilt professors also lead Q&A sessions. The observatory is open from Mar through Nov. Call for exact program information and times. Visits to the observatory are by appointment only.

PARKS, PLAYGROUNDS & ADVENTURE

BICENTENNIAL CAPITOL MALL STATE PARK, 600 James Robertson Pkwy., Nashville, TN 37243; (615) 741-5289; tnstateparks.com/parks/bicentennial-mall; free. There aren't too many places where you can get soaking wet while absorbing some fascinating lessons in state history, geography, and culture. But Bicentennial Capitol Mall is just such a place. This 19-acre park just north of the Tennessee State Capitol opened in 1996, and its fountains—31 of them, designating major state rivers—quickly became a cool place to play during a sultry summer. Nearby on the plaza, a 200-foot granite map of Tennessee lets you walk from Memphis to Knoxville in record time; smaller maps provide details about various facets of the state. There's much more, including clean restrooms and a visitor center. Visit the adjacent Farmers' Market, along with the State Capitol, and you've got one nice (and cheap) afternoon.

CENTENNIAL PARK, 2500 West End Ave., Nashville, TN 37203; (615) 862-8400; nashville.gov/parks-and-recreation/parks/centennial-park; free. The centerpiece of Centennial Park, built to celebrate Tennessee's 100th birthday in 1897, is a full-size replica of the Greek Parthenon that houses an art gallery. Children, however, are more likely to be interested in the abundant outdoor activities at the park. There's a small lake populated with ducks and (in season) pedal boats, and you'll also find a band shell, picnic tables, a steam engine and fighter plane, and lots of green grass. Centennial Park is the site of the Nashville Shakespeare Festival, concerts by the Nashville Symphony, various arts and crafts fairs, and other annual events.

Athena at the Parthenon Nashville Convention & Visitors Corporation

THE DRAGON PARK, 2400 Blakemore Ave., Nashville, TN 37212; (615) 862-8400; free. Its official name is Fannie Mae Dees Park, but this popular area just off the Vandy campus, at the corner of Blakemore and 24th Avenue S., is usually identified by its dominant feature: a huge sea dragon or serpent covered with brightly colored tile mosaic. The dragon, which seemingly snakes above and below the "surface," is decorated with animals, flowers, rainbows, musical instruments, historical figures, and countless other fanciful scenes. Its tail doubles as a bench where parents can sit while their children play. In addition to the dragon, there's a tunnel through a "mountain" of rocks topped by a sandy "mesa," with a swinging bridge connecting the mountain to a fort with a slide. The park also contains 3 tennis courts, swings and other playground equipment, wooden benches, picnic tables, a shelter, and 2 covered tables inlaid with chess and checkerboards. A fun addition to Dragon Park is Lily's Garden, a playground for all children designed to accommodate those with special physical or learning disabilities.

THE JUNGLE GYM AT NASHVILLE ZOO AT GRASSMERE, 3777 Nolensville Rd., Nashville, TN 37211; (615) 833-1534; nashvillezoo.org; $$. Lions, tigers, and bears? So what! Nashville kids love the zoo's Jungle Gym so much, some parents bring their children here for this attraction alone. And no wonder: The 66,000-square-foot playground is a massive affair that can accommodate up to 1,000 kids at a time. The Jungle Gym was designed by world-renowned playground architect Robert Leathers and built by volunteers from the community. The playground's centerpiece is the 35-foot-tall Tree of Life tree house. Kids can also explore the sculpture garden, where they can crawl through a giant snake tunnel, explore a bat cave, climb aboard concrete hippos, bounce through cargo netting, or tear through the Jungle Village. The Jungle Gym is a popular spot for birthday parties, and it's available after hours for such events. Otherwise it's open during regular zoo operating hours.

> The Jungle Gym at the Nashville Zoo is the largest community-built playground of its kind in the world. More than 40,000 volunteer hours went into building the rambling play facility, which can accommodate more than 1,000 kids at a time.

SEVIER PARK, 3021 Lealand Ln., Nashville, TN 37204; (615) 862-8466; nashville.gov/parks; free. Located on the south end of the up-and-coming 12 South commercial district, Sevier Park is a welcome expanse of green space in an urban-residential area. The park is easily recognized for the pre–Civil War Sunnyside Mansion, which is on the National Register of Historic Places and is the park's dominant feature. The park's playground and picnic pavilions are frequented by local families. A summer concert series and Friday night dances have brought music and good times back to Sevier, and the park's rolling hills and meandering creek make it a favorite spot for local dog owners. The park contains tennis courts, basketball courts, and a community center that offers various programs. The new Sevier Park Community Center has a gymnasium with an upper level walking track, dance/movement room, fitness center, and community meeting space. The center offers after-school programs and a youth summer enrichment program. Community center hours vary depending on the season, so call for availability and a program schedule.

WARNER PARKS, 7311 Hwy. 100; Nashville, TN 37221; (615) 352-6299; nashville.gov/parks-and-recreation/parks/warner-parks; free. On a late-afternoon summer drive through Percy Warner Park, we once saw three deer and two rabbits within minutes, and we weren't even looking for them. Percy Warner Park, the largest municipal park in Tennessee, and its neighbor, Edwin Warner Park, span more than 4,100 acres, much of which is rugged, scenic woodland. There's a nature center, picnic areas, playground equipment, hiking trails, bridle trails, and a steeplechase area, as well as 2 golf courses. The parks are open daily from sunrise until 11 p.m., and the nature center is open 8:30 a.m. to 4:30 p.m. Tues through Sat.

WATER FUN

There's nothing like a good dose of watery fun to bring out the kid in you, as these attractions attest.

METRO AND YMCA POOLS, YMCA corporate office, 1000 Church St., Nashville, TN 37203; (615) 259-9622; ymcamidtn.org.

METRO PARKS AQUATICS OFFICE, 222 25th Ave. N., Nashville, TN 37208; (615) 862-8480; nashville.gov/parks. YMCA of Middle Tennessee operates 37 pools at 23 recreation centers in the area. About half are indoor pools. The Metro Parks department operates more than a dozen pools, including Wave Country (see below). For more information see our **Recreation** chapter.

NASHVILLE SHORES, 4001 Bell Rd., Hermitage, TN 37076; (615) 889-7050; nashvilleshores.com; $$$$. Sandy shores, luscious palms, cool breezes—Nashville's answer to a beach vacation is definitely here. Located on Percy Priest Lake, Nashville Shores offers a wealth of water fun. Eight giant waterslides with thrilling names like the "Tennessee Twister" and "Tsunami Raft Ride" beckon the adventuresome; for sunbathing and pool play there are 3 pools, each targeted to a different age group; and families can thrill to the raft ride Big Kahuna. There's a real beach—white sand is hauled in to the Priest lakeshore—and lake cruises, or even cabins on the shore available for rent. Opened in 2018, Aqua Park is an interactive playground on Percy Priest Lake featuring 40 colorful, interconnected water elements including monkey bars, action towers, wiggle bridges, hurdles, and more. Reservations are required for Aqua Park and children must be at least 48 inches tall and at least 7 years old. Dry fun activities include minigolf, games like Frisbee and horseshoes, volleyball, and live entertainment. Personal watercraft and boats are also available for rent at the marina. Children 2 and under are admitted free. Nashville Shores opens in early May and runs through mid-Sept.

Nashville Shores offers wet fun.
Nashville Convention & Visitors Corporation

SHELBY PARK, Shelby Avenue and South 20th Street, Nashville, TN 37206; (615) 862-8467; nashville.gov/parks; free. This park in east Nashville is known for its 2 golf courses, but its lake is also a popular fishing spot for kids as well as senior citizens. Features include playgrounds, dog park, baseball fields, and community center.

WAVE COUNTRY, 2320 Two Rivers Pkwy., Nashville, TN 37214; (615) 885-1052; nashville.gov/parks; $$$. Wave Country, just off Briley Parkway, lets you visit the ocean without leaving Nashville. Hold on tight as you ride the wave pool's simulated surf. There are also 2 water flumes and 2 speed slides, plus a kiddie pool with water dropping features. Wave Country is open from Memorial Day weekend through Labor Day.

FUN & GAMES

GRAND OLD GOLF & GO KARTS, 2444 Music Valley Dr., Nashville, TN 37214; (615) 871-4701; grandoldgolf.net; $$. This granddaddy of Nashville minigolf attractions is located near Opry Mills and offers much more than just golf: Go-karts, indoor bumper cars, and a video arcade round out the family fun. Four minigolf courses—3 outside and 1 inside—can provide an entire afternoon's worth of putting pleasure. Three separate minigolf courses are designed to mimic the state's lovely landscape. The GoKart track features hairpin turns, long straightaways, and high-performance vehicles. Hours vary by season. Group rates are available for birthday parties and corporate outings.

LASER QUEST, 166 Second Ave. N., Nashville, TN 37201; (615) 256-2560; laserquest.com; $$. You've seen all the *Star Wars* movies. Now it's your turn to be Luke Skywalker. Laser Quest equips you with a laser gun and sensor pack and turns you loose in a dark maze for a game of high-tech shoot 'em up. Points are gained or lost depending on number of foes hit and number of times hit by foes. It's kind of like cowboys and Indians in outer space, and it's a harmless way for the kids to release some energy. Be sure to check out Laser Quest's video arcade after your game. Laser Quest's hours vary according to the season and the day of the week.

i The Aquatics Center at Centennial Sportsplex is named for Nashville native Tracy Caulkins, who won 3 gold medals at the 1984 Olympic Summer Games in Los Angeles. Caulkins, a 1981 graduate of Harpeth Hall School, has won an unprecedented 48 swimming titles in her career. She broke 5 world records and 63 US records—more than any other American athlete in sports history.

TIME MACHINE

History is a funny thing. Depending on your outlook, it can make you feel old or make you feel young. Here's hoping these selected historical sites will bring out the inquisitive little kid in you and other members of your family.

FORT NASHBOROUGH, 170 First Ave. N., Nashville, TN 37201; (615) 862-8400; nashville.gov/parks-and-recreation/historic-sites/Fort-Nashborough; free. This is where it all got started in 1779, when James Robertson and his fellow settlers established a settlement on the banks of the Cumberland River. This reproduction of the original log fort, which withstood attacks from natives, is open daily, except Thanksgiving and Christmas, for a free self-guided tour. After a $1.7 million renovation of the riverfront fort in downtown Nashville, the attraction celebrated with a ribbon cutting in July 2017. The new fort and interpretive center show how settlers lived and worked. The fort's log cabins and blockhouses were built with historically accurate construction. An interpretive plaza area on the south end commemorates the city's Native American history and features an 8-foot-tall feather sculpture plus interpretive signs about the various tribes and their roles in Nashville's history.

THE HERMITAGE: HOME OF PRESIDENT ANDREW JACKSON, 4580 Rachel's Ln., Nashville, TN 37076; (615) 889-2981; thehermitage.com; $$. Andrew Jackson was a brave and adventurous man who was influential in the early expansion of our country. In addition to being seventh president of the United States, he was a military hero, lawyer, planter, statesman, and true romantic (he once shot a man who said bad things about his wife). The Hermitage, 12 miles east of Nashville off Old Hickory Boulevard, is where he made his home. The 1800s mansion, a mixture of Federal and Greek Revival styles, is open daily (closed Thanksgiving, Christmas, and the third week of Jan). A family admission package is available, and students and senior citizens receive a discount.

Mansker's Station
Richard Suter Photography

HISTORIC MANSKER'S STATION FRONTIER LIFE CENTER, Moss-Wright Park at 705 Caldwell Drive, Goodlettsville, TN 37072; (615) 859-3678; cityofgoodlettsville.org/110/historic-manskers-station; $$. The Frontier Life Center at Historic Mansker's

Station offers a look at the lifestyles of the area's early settlers through a reconstructed 1779 forted station. You'll see and hear people in period costumes as they perform activities such as cooking, spinning, and blacksmithing. Special events and festivals are held throughout the operating season. (For more information, see our **Attractions** chapter.)

TENNESSEE STATE MUSEUM, 1000 Rosa L. Parks Blvd. Nashville, TN 37208; (615) 741-2692; tnmuseum.org; free. Opened on October 4, 2018, by the Bicentennial Capitol Mall State Park, this museum offers a fascinating look at the history of Tennessee, from prehistoric times through the 20th century. With a whopping 137,000 feet of administration and gallery space, the $120 million museum offers permanent and temporary exhibits. Displays include collections of prehistoric Indian artifacts, firearms, silver, quilts, paintings, and pottery. There is an extensive collection of Civil War uniforms, battle flags, and weapons. You can learn about the long hunters, such as Daniel Boone, who hunted in the area beginning in the 1760s, as well as interesting political figures like Andrew Jackson and Sam Houston.

Other exhibits relate to African Americans, Prohibition, women's suffrage, and important events that shaped the history of the Volunteer State. Replicas of building facades and period rooms are featured, too. The Tennessee Time Tunnel serves as the backbone for the state's story. Visitors can use different entrances through the Time Tunnel for a more in-depth look at a specific era in Tennessee history. In Tennessee Tranforms, the 360 Interactive Theater features a cross section of people, places, and events in Tennessee from World War II to the present. The theater features more than 100 topics to examine on a touch table as well as 3 large wall screens with related images. The State Museum is open Tues through Sun, closed on major holidays.

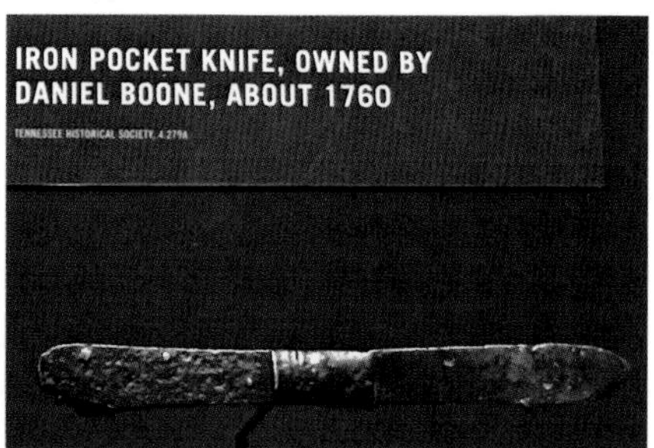

The new Tennessee State Museum traces the history of "The Volunteer State."
Jackie Sheckler Finch

TRAVELLERS REST PLANTATION & MUSEUM, 636 Farrell Pkwy., Nashville, TN 37220; (615) 832-8197; travellersrestplantation.org; $$. Nashville's oldest plantation home was built in 1799 by Judge John Overton, a prominent early citizen and friend of President Andrew Jackson. Over the years the plantation has seen many changes; today it's owned by the National Society of Colonial Dames of America. Visitors can tour the plantation, museum, and grounds and get a glimpse of early Nashville life. The plantation's education department has radically expanded its slate of special events and educational programs; everything from plantation holidays to slavery through the eyes of a child to scavenger hunts to an in-depth look at the Mound Builders is now offered. Music events are also on the calendar. Travellers Rest is open Tues through Sat except Memorial Day, Labor Day, Thanksgiving, Christmas, and New Year's Day. Kids under 6 are admitted free.

STORYTIME

NASHVILLE PUBLIC LIBRARY, Main Library, 615 Church St., Nashville, TN 37219; (615) 862-5800; library.nashville.org; free. Former Nashville mayor Phil Bredesen once declared that a "city with a great library is a great city." With that in mind, the city went out to improve its outdated and dilapidated library system. The result: Several glittering new facilities were built, while many existing ones were renovated or expanded. Nashville now has 21 public libraries located throughout the city, and all of them offer free storytimes for children of different ages several times a week. Nashville's main

The Civil Rights Room at Nashville Public Library commemorates the city's civil rights battles. Jackie Sheckler Finch

library, called the Downtown Library by locals, offers storytime for preschoolers and young children. Group storytime by reservation also is available. Other branches offer services such as homework help and after-school reading programs. Library hours vary by location; call the branch nearest you for information or visit the comprehensive website.

SPORTING LIFE

CENTENNIAL SPORTSPLEX, 222 25th Ave. N., Nashville, TN 37203; (615) 862-8480; nashville.gov/parks-and-recreation/centennial-sportsplex. Located next to Centennial Park, the 17-acre Sportsplex is operated by the Metro Board of Parks and Recreation. The year-round family sports and recreation complex has facilities for aquatics, fitness, and tennis, plus a 2-sheet ice arena where youth hockey and figure-skating clubs practice (as well as Nashville's NHL Predators). Sportsplex facilities are open to the public on a pay-as-you-go basis, or you may purchase season passes at a discount. For kids, the Sportsplex offers a full complement of lessons, clinics, and sports camps. A complete list of classes is available on the website. Sportsplex facilities are open 7 days a week, but hours vary widely because of all the team practices; be sure to call first to ensure the facility you want is open.

GORDON JEWISH COMMUNITY CENTER, 801 Percy Warner Blvd., Nashville, TN 37205; (615) 356-7170; nashvillejcc.org. The Gordon Jewish Community Center's pool and gym are popular with all ages; for kids, the center has a full slate of programs, including drama and ballet. On the recreation side, there are lessons in swimming and kids' yoga. A variety of sports leagues are also available here, such as soccer, T-ball, summer basketball camps, Little League, and the Tiger Sharks swim team. Membership is open to everyone.

YMCA OF MIDDLE TENNESSEE, 1000 Church St., Nashville, TN 37203; (615) 259-9622; ymcamidtn.org. Part of the Nashville community since 1874, today the YMCA has 23 centers in the Nashville area and surrounding counties. All provide a full complement of programs fulfilling the YMCA's mind-body-spirit credo; youth sports programs such as spring/fall soccer leagues, baseball, and basketball leagues for all ages are a Y mainstay. The majority of Nashville Ys have indoor and outdoor pools, separate gyms for kids, even nurseries—after all, the Y is the largest child-care provider in Middle Tennessee. A financial assistance program ensures that all youth can take part in the Y's programs, regardless of financial status. The website is thorough and offers a good overview of what each facility offers. Or call the YMCA's main office in Nashville.

YOUTH INC. ATHLETICS, 4117 Hillsboro Pike, Ste. 103-256, Nashville, TN 37215; (615) 865-0003; youthincorporated.org. Youth Inc. has operated in Middle Tennessee since 1945. Programs and activities include sports leagues such as basketball, bowling, rifle, and in-line hockey. YI also operates the Circle YI Ranch, an ACA-accredited summer camp for boys and girls located on 170 acres at Percy Priest Lake. The ranch houses the organization's football training facility, where high school football camps are held. YI also has state-of-the-art football and hockey facilities in La Vergne, Bellevue, and Spring Hill. Boys' and girls' basketball programs are offered for ages 5 through 14; YI has nonathletic programs as well, including an employment service.

Baseball

LITTLE LEAGUE, littleleague.org. The national pastime is alive and well in Music City; there are dozens of Little League teams operating in the city, providing baseball and softball play for kids 5 to 18 years old. City leagues include Charlotte Park, Paul Lawrence Dunbar (ages 10 to 20), McCabe Park (5 to 13), West Park (10 to 20), and North Nashville (10 to 20); these leagues operate dozens of teams—at last count, McCabe had more than 35 teams in its roster. In addition, the Sounds, Angels, Whitts, Tennessee Patriots, and Nashville Demons operate youth and adult baseball teams. The Triple-A Nashville Sounds, an affiliate of the Texas Rangers, are also very involved with area youth baseball and softball leagues, offering clinics, sports camps, and other special programs. For information call the Nashville Sounds at (615) 690-4487, or visit the team's official website at milb.com

Football

BELLEVUE STEELERS, bellevuesteelers.com. This football and cheerleading program serves youth ages 5 to 12 in the west Nashville area. The Steelers are a charter member of the Mid-State Youth Football league, which operates in Nashville and the surrounding counties and determines regional championships. The program provides instruction in contact football and cheerleading, plus camps and minicamps. The Steelers field Triple and Double A, B, and C teams, plus Pee Wee and a Varsity team. Organizers are volunteers, so contact information may change; visit the group's website for the most current contacts.

TENNESSEE YOUTH FOOTBALL ALLIANCE, tyfa.org. This organization serves boys and girls ages 5 to 14 in football and cheerleading. TYFA has about 15 communities throughout Middle Tennessee, which together sponsor more than 140 teams. Part of the TYFA's mission is teaching kids the values of fair play, teamwork,

Close-up

Goo Goo

If there were a candy hall of fame, Nashville would have a place in it. Music City is where the first combination candy bar was invented, and it's still made right here at the **Standard Candy Company.**

The historic candy—the **Goo Goo**—has been satisfying sweet tooths for more than 8 decades. As they say on the *Grand Ole Opry* radio show, which Standard has sponsored since the early 1960s, "Generations of Southerners have grown up on them." Dozens of people—Southerners as well as non-Southerners—from as far away as California and Canada are gaga over Goo Goos. They write the company each week requesting orders of the chewy, gooey candy. But you don't have to write for it; you can find Goo Goos in just about every part of the country, in stores like Walgreens, Wal-Mart, Kroger, and Safeway. They're most plentiful in Music City, however, and tourist attractions and gift stores here usually keep a good supply on hand for visitors who want to take home a taste of Nashville.

Standard, today operated by Jimmy Spradley, sells about 25 million Goo Goos (approximately $8.5 million worth) each year. The Goo Goo was invented by **Howell Campbell,** who, in 1901 at the age of 19, founded the Standard Candy Company. The company's first products were hard candies and chocolates, but Howell and original plant superintendent **Porter Moore** developed a recipe combining **fresh roasted peanuts, caramel, marshmallow,** and **milk chocolate.** The recipe became a classic. Today the Goo Goo comes in three varieties—the original Goo Goo Cluster, the Peanut Butter Goo Goo, and the Goo Goo Supreme.

The candy bar didn't have a name at first because no one could decide what to call it. Stories of how the candy got its name vary. Campbell's son, Howell Campbell Jr., says his father took the streetcar to work each morning and would discuss the matter with fellow passengers. One passenger, a schoolteacher, suggested Goo Goo. But some people say the candy was given the name because it's the first thing a baby says.

In its early days the candy bar's circular shape made it difficult to wrap, so it was sold unwrapped from glass containers. Later the Goo Goo was hand-wrapped in foil and advertised as a "Nourishing Lunch for a Nickel." While it wouldn't pass for a nourishing lunch today (the Goo Goo Cluster in the silver package has 240 calories, 11 grams of fat, and just a smidgen of calcium, protein, and iron), Nashville's Goo Goo is still a delicious treat. To learn more about Goo Goos, visit googoo.com.

If your hunger can't wait, go to the Goo Goo Shop & Dessert Bar at 116 Third Ave. S. in downtown Nashville. Open daily, the shop is no ordinary retail store. It is also a museum where visitors can walk through Goo Goo history by reading more than a century of timelines complete with Goo Goo memorabilia. Visitors can also watch Goo Goos being made by hand in a glass-enclosed confectionary kitchen. The Dessert Bar serves up all sorts of sweet treats, sundaes, sodas, and milkshakes. Slide into a retro red booth and enjoy. Or for hands-on fun with chocolate, join in a chocolate class. For fans of *The Walking Dead* television show, in an episode's closing scenes, a series character takes a Goo Goo Cluster from his pocket and places it on the altar of a church littered with dead bodies.

Symbolism? Regular viewers can probably figure that out.

The Goo Goo Shop in downtown Nashville is a combination store and museum about the popular candy. Jackie Sheckler Finch

and competitiveness. Visit the website for more information about TYFA and for information about individual communities and teams, including contact numbers.

Hockey

GREATER NASHVILLE AREA SCHOLASTIC HOCKEY (GNASH), gnashhockey.com. While Nashville didn't get its NHL team until 1998, ice hockey has been a presence among the city's youth since 1965, when the nonprofit, all-volunteer NYHL was launched. Today NYHL games are played at the Centennial Sportsplex, with registration beginning in August for the fall/winter season. The NHL Nashville Predators assist the league with fund-raising, organizing youth hockey clinics and camps, and such. NYHL age divisions and teams are Termites (4 through 7), Mites (8 and 9), Squirt (10 and 11), Peewee (11 and 12), Bantam (13 and 14), and Midget (16 and 17). GNASH, Middle Tennessee's high school hockey league, is aptly named for the Predators' lovable saber-toothed mascot, Gnash. Visit the NYHL website for current names and phone numbers.

Soccer

NASHVILLE YOUTH SOCCER ASSOCIATION, 3135 Heartland Dr., Nashville, TN 37214; (615) 268-6349; nysa-soccer.org. Founded in 1972, the nonprofit NYSA has fall and spring soccer programs for boys and girls in 6 different age groups. The group also hosts soccer camps and special events in conjunction with the Nashville Metros, the city's major-league soccer team. The NYSA is affiliated with the US Soccer Foundation (USSF), the Tennessee State Soccer Association (TSSA), and the Federation International Football Association (FIFA). Games are held at Heartland Soccer Park, located just past Opryland. This is an all-volunteer organization, so check the website for current contact and registration information.

Special Needs

SPECIAL OLYMPICS TENNESSEE, 1900 12th Ave. S., Nashville, TN 37203; (615) 329-1375; specialolympics.org. The Special Olympics offers athletic training and competition for children and adults with mental disabilities. There are more than 10,000 participants in Middle Tennessee with more than 100 competitions annually on area, regional, and state levels. Special Olympics Tennessee hosts 8 state games and tournament competitions each year. These events encompass 32 official sports, including softball, aquatics, volleyball, horseshoes, tennis, power lifting, and even bocce (though not all sports are available in all locations). Nashville competitions are held at Vanderbilt and Lipscomb Universities, with aquatic events held at the Centennial Sportsplex.

Entertainment

Ballet. Symphony. Museums. Broadway musicals. Opera. Independent film. Dance clubs. Spectator sports. Nashville has it all . . . and more. These are essential elements of a thriving arts scene befitting a city with the nickname "Athens of the South." Recent years have seen a steady growth in the number of arts groups busily creating new works or new interpretations of old favorites. That's not surprising because Nashville has long been a magnet for creative, energetic people. If there's a downside to all the activity, it may well be that the abundance of artistic and cultural opportunities can lead to difficulty in making a decision. The area's arts scene is rapidly changing, too.

CLASSICAL MUSIC & OPERA

BELMONT UNIVERSITY SCHOOL OF MUSIC, 1900 Belmont Blvd., Nashville, TN 37212; (615) 460-6000; belmont.edu/music. Belmont's comprehensive music program offers studies in diverse music styles, and its free solo and group concerts cover a wide range as well, from classical and jazz to bluegrass and rock. Camerata Musicale, a chamber music ensemble created in 1987, performs several times a year in the Belmont Mansion. Other groups, including the Belmont Concert Band and the University Orchestra, perform at various locations on campus. Student showcases are often an opportunity to catch the stars of tomorrow before they're famous—Trisha Yearwood, Brad Paisley, and Lee Ann Womack are just a few graduates of the Belmont's music business program. Most performances are held in the Massey Performing Arts Center, which includes the 999-seat Massey Concert Hall and 100-seat Harton Recital Hall.

BLAIR SCHOOL OF MUSIC, 2400 Blakemore Ave., Nashville, TN 37212; (615) 322-7651; blair.vanderbilt.edu. The Blair School of Music at Vanderbilt University presents more than 100 free concerts each year by groups including the Vanderbilt Orchestra, Chamber Choir, Symphonic Wind Ensemble, Opera Theatre, and Jazz Band as well as the Nashville Youth Symphony, a precollege orchestra of

> i Martina McBride sold T-shirts for Garth Brooks one year; the next year she was the opening act on his tour.

Nashville & the Bottle: A Continuing Saga

Nashville, a town often associated with cry-in-your-beer songs, has long had a love–hate relationship with "the bottle." Decades before Merle Haggard bemoaned the fact that tonight the bottle let him down, locals had waged battle—literally shedding blood in one infamous landmark case—over alcohol sales.

Travelers during the last quarter of the 19th century knew Nashville as a wild, swinging, "anything-goes" kind of place. Downtown was home to a number of upscale saloons and gambling establishments.

During these years, naturally, many religious leaders and others objected to the drinking, gambling, and carrying on that transpired in the riverfront district. In 1885 steamboat captain **Thomas Ryman** was persuaded to close the bars and gambling dens on his boats after hearing the exhortations of traveling evangelist Sam Jones. Ryman was so moved by the spirit—and away from the spirits—in fact, that he donated money for a tabernacle. (This building, which now bears the captain's name, later became the home of the *Grand Ole Opry* and is now a popular auditorium for a variety of musical performances. During most shows, ironically, alcoholic drinks are sold in the lobby.)

Anti-alcohol sentiment picked up during the early 1900s, and one of the most vocal prohibitionists was **Edward Ward "Ned" Carmack,** editor of the *Tennessean* newspaper. On November 9, 1908, Carmack was shot to death downtown by **Duncan B. Cooper** and his son, Robin, who objected to the editor's often-strident stance. The two were convicted and sentenced to 20 years in prison, but **Governor Malcolm Patterson,** a friend of the Coopers, pardoned them. The resulting furor helped prompt the passage of a statewide **prohibition law** that took effect in July 1909. Despite the law, enforcement was often lax, due in part to corruption by local and state officials who disagreed with the ban.

Prohibition remained a controversial political issue throughout the next decade, and one mayor, Hilary E. Howse, was forced to resign from office in 1916 because of his failure to enforce it. He later was reelected.

One side effect of Prohibition was the birth of the downtown area known as **Printers Alley.** The alley gradually became a hot spot for speakeasies where illegal alcohol was sold. Prohibition in Tennessee, as nationwide, ended with the 1933 passage of the 21st Amendment.

community youth. Performances are held at Steve and Judy Turner Recital Hall, Ingram Hall, and Langford Auditorium campus.

DAVID LIPSCOMB UNIVERSITY DEPARTMENT OF MUSIC, 1 University Park Dr., Nashville, TN 37204; (800) 333-4358; lipscomb.edu/music. Lipscomb's Department of Music presents concerts by soloists and groups, including the A Cappella Singers, who perform sacred music; the Jazz Band, which performs 4 concerts a year; the Lipscomb University String Ensemble; and the Early Music Consort, which combines medieval and Renaissance music with ethnic styles from around the world. Admission is free to student performances. For performances by touring artists or name performers—there are about 3 of those each year—a ticket is required.

NASHVILLE OPERA ASSOCIATION, 3622 Redmon St., Nashville, TN 37209; (615) 832-5242; nashvilleopera.org. Nashville Opera, founded in 1980, merged with Tennessee Opera Theatre in September 1997 to form the Nashville Opera Association. That umbrella group now consists of the Nashville Opera, which produces professional, full-scale operas; Tennessee Opera Theatre, an education division that trains young singers and promotes local talent; and the Nashville Opera Guild, a group of 400 fund-raising and promotional volunteers. The opera season runs Oct through Apr, during which 4 productions are staged. Performances are held at TPAC's Polk Theater and Jackson Hall.

THE NASHVILLE SYMPHONY, Schermerhorn Symphony Center, 1 Symphony Place, Nashville, TN 37201; (615) 687-6400; nashvillesymphony.org. The Nashville Symphony, the largest performing arts organization in Tennessee, puts on more than 200 concerts—ranging from classical and Pops series to children's concerts and special events—during its 37-week season. It also performs with the Nashville Ballet and the Nashville Opera (see previous entries). The Schermerhorn Symphony Center opened in September 2006 at Fourth Avenue S., across from the Country Music Hall of Fame & Museum. The number of performances has increased substantially now that the symphony has moved into its new home.

DANCE

NASHVILLE BALLET, 3630 Redmon St., Nashville, TN 37209; (615) 297-2966; nashvilleballet.com. Nashville Ballet, founded in 1981 as a nonprofit civic dance company, became a professional company in 1986. Nashville

Ballet, which has an affiliated School of Nashville Ballet, serves the community with varied educational and outreach programs. Children's ballet performances entertain and educate youth through artistic presentations in an interactive setting. The Nashville School of Ballet offers youth and adult classes to the community in ballet and modern dance. Beginner to advanced levels are available.

THEATER

You'll find an abundance of theatrical opportunities in Nashville, ranging from professional companies to amateur and dinner theater to children's shows. We've included some of the more visible groups, but independents are always popping up, so keep your eyes open.

ACT I, 4610 Charlotte Ave., Nashville, TN 37209; (615) 726-2282; act1online.com. ACT I, a group of local artists—the acronym stands for "Artists Cooperative Theater"—performs a varied selection of classic and contemporary plays at the Darkhorse Theater at 4610 Charlotte Ave. ACT I presents 3 to 5 productions each year, from Sept to May.

ACTORS BRIDGE ENSEMBLE, 4610 Charlotte Ave., Nashville, TN 37209; (615) 498-4077; actorsbridge.org. What started in 1995 as a theatrical training program has evolved into a progressive professional theater company. Actors Bridge stages original and contemporary theatrical productions on various stages around town. As part of its mission, the nonprofit theater company aims to raise social consciousness and serve the community.

CHAFFIN'S BARN DINNER THEATRE, 8204 Hwy. 100, Nashville, TN 37221; (615) 646-9977; chaffinsbarntheatre.com. Having opened in 1967, Chaffin's Barn is Nashville's oldest professional theater. For a single fee, you can enjoy an all-you-can-eat country buffet followed by a stage production. It could be Shakespeare, a musical, a mystery, or a comedy.

DAVID LIPSCOMB UNIVERSITY THEATER, 1 University Park Dr., Nashville, TN 37204; (615) 966-1000; lipscomb.edu/theater. Lipscomb

The seasons of many concert and theater groups in Nashville run from Sept to Apr or May—roughly in line with school schedules.

Darkhorse Theater

One of Nashville's most popular venues for live theater is the **Darkhorse Theater,** located at 4610 Charlotte Ave., across from Richland Park. The 136-seat alternative theater presents new works, classical theater, dance, film, live music, and multimedia shows. The venue is home to several performing arts groups, including **ACT I** and **Actors Bridge Ensemble,** and also hosts productions from groups such as **Nashville Shakespeare Festival** and **People's Branch Theatre.** For more information on the theater, its resident groups, and season schedule, visit the website darkhorsetheater.weebly.com or call the theater at (615) 297-7113.

University Theater stages several productions a year. They can vary from Shakespeare or other classics to musicals and new works. Productions are presented in the university's intimate 128-seat University Theater.

LAKEWOOD THEATRE COMPANY INC., 2211 Old Hickory Blvd., Old Hickory, TN 37138; (615) 847-0934. Lakewood Theatre Company is a community theater group that maintains its own venue in a historic former bakery just down the street from Andrew Jackson's home, the Hermitage (see our **Attractions** chapter). The building is one of Davidson County's oldest and was renovated by the company in 1983. The company offers drama, comedy, and children's theater.

NASHVILLE CHILDREN'S THEATRE, 25 Middleton St., Nashville, TN 37210; (615) 254-9103; nashvillechildrenstheatre.org. Established in 1931, NCT is the country's longest-running children's theater group. The not-for-profit group has been recognized internationally as a model for excellence in the field of theater for young audiences and has received numerous awards. The theater holds after-school and in-school workshops and a summer drama day camp. The theater has been ranked 1 of the top 5 in the United States by *Time* magazine.

Frist Art Museum

When the **Frist Art Museum** opened its doors in 2001, the fine art museum launched a new era in the city's history and forever changed its cultural landscape.

The Frist Art Museum was born from that perfect marriage of necessity and opportunity. The story begins with a building, Nashville's landmark downtown post office, which was built in 1933–34. On the National Register of Historic Places since 1984, it once served the city as its main post office. But when a new mail-handling facility opened near the airport in 1986, the downtown building was turned into a branch office that required just a small portion of the 125,000-square-foot structure.

Around the same time a group of Nashville's citizens began a long-range community visioning process. Among the needs they identified was for a major art museum, centrally located and large enough to land significant touring shows, something that Nashville's existing museums were not equipped to do. The unused downtown post office was deemed ideal.

Enter the charitable **Frist Foundation.** The Frist family and Dr. Thomas Frist Jr., chairman of HCA, have long supported Nashville's arts community (Cheekwood's Frist Learning Center is one example). They rallied behind the arts center project, and in 1998 the Frist Foundation, Metropolitan Nashville, and the US Postal Service formed a unique public–private partnership. The US Postal Service agreed to sell the building for the purpose of an arts center, provided they could still maintain a customer service window there (today Nashville probably has the only art museum with a working post office on its lower level).

Renovations began in November 1999. In addition to retrofitting the building for its new use, careful attention was paid to repairing the building's unique historic features. The original hardwood floors and art deco ornamental details such as lighting fixtures and decorative metal grillwork were painstakingly preserved. The hard work paid off, however, and today the building is regarded as a work of art in itself.

While work went on inside the building, an advisory council hammered out the nuts and bolts of the museum's mission. From the beginning it was envisioned as a place where the entire community, regardless of age or economic background, could "connect with art." With that in mind, an extensive education and community outreach program was planned, including the decision to allow visitors under age 18 free admission, always.

It was also determined that the Frist Art Museum would have no permanent collection but would accommodate changing exhibitions exclusively, giving visitors a reason to return again and again. The center's **Main Level Gallery** features short-term exhibitions of 2 to 3 months' duration. The main level also includes an **Orientation Gallery,** providing information about present and future exhibits as well as exhibits at Nashville's other art institutions. There's also a 250-seat auditorium, a gift shop, and the Frist Center Cafe.

Exhibitions of up to 3 years' duration are staged in the **Upper Level Gallery.** Adjacent to that is Frist's unique **Martin ArtQuest Gallery,** which fulfills its educational mission by providing various hands-on activities explaining basic art principles. The **Media and Technology Resource Center** offers library resources for those wishing to learn more about the works on exhibit. There are also 3 studio-classrooms and a computer lab used for the educational programs.

The Frist Art Museum opened with an exclusive exhibit, European Masterworks: Paintings from the Collection of the Art Gallery of Ontario. The collection of masterpieces by the likes of Rembrandt, Monet, Degas, and Van Gogh made its only stop at the Frist Art Museum. Exhibits of pieces from Nashville's own private and public collections, a massive sculpture by Nashville artist Michael Aurbach, and an exhibit looking at the building's unique history filled out the center's 4 galleries.

Since then, the Frist Art Museum has brought world-class exhibits to the city, quickly becoming the focal point of a vibrant arts scene.

> Belmont University's Singing Tower was built around 1850 as a water tower; it was transformed into a carillon in 1928 and is now a historic landmark. The carillon is still played for special events and concerts.

THE NASHVILLE SHAKESPEARE FESTIVAL, 161 Rains Ave., Nashville, TN 37203; (615) 255-2273; nashvilleshakes.org. The Nashville Shakespeare Festival is dedicated to producing the plays of the Bard as well as works by other classical, modern, and emerging playwrights. It is best known for its free "Shakespeare in the Park" productions, which since 1988 have drawn thousands of Nashvillians to Centennial Park. In addition to the popular summer Centennial Park productions—which are free—NSF stages winter shows at the Belcourt Theatre.

VANDERBILT UNIVERSITY DEPARTMENT OF THEATRE, Neely Auditorium, West End at 21st Ave. S., Nashville, TN 37212; (615) 322-2404; as.vanderbilt.edu/theater. Vandy's theater department stages 4 major productions a year representing a range of time periods and genres. Shows are held at Neely Auditorium, a flexible black-box theater that seats about 300.

FILM

THE BELCOURT THEATRE, 2102 Belcourt Ave., Nashville, TN 37212; (615) 846-3150; belcourt.org. The historic Belcourt, built in 1925, was barely saved from the wrecking ball by a massive grassroots effort; today it's Nashville's only art-house theater. With a diverse programming of independent, foreign, and art cinema, Belcourt's offerings are always daring, to say the least. Music and performing arts events flesh out the calendar. The theater serves food, wine, and beer along with the traditional popcorn and soft drinks. For a current schedule visit the Belcourt website.

NASHVILLE FILM FESTIVAL, 161 Rains Ave., Nashville, TN 37203; (615) 742-2500; nashvillefilmfestival.org. NIFF is best known for the annual film festival that has brought the likes of maverick director John Waters to town and draws 10,000 or more attendees. The film festival continues to grow in influence and scope. The festival and most screenings are held at the Regal Hollywood 27 Cinema.

WATKINS COLLEGE OF ART, DESIGN & FILM, 2298 Rosa L. Parks Blvd., Nashville, TN 37228; (615) 383-4848; watkins.edu. This highly selective film school program is gaining national recognition for the quality of its diverse programs. Watkins offers a 4-year bachelor of fine arts degree in film, with five areas of specialization: screenwriting, cinematography, producing, directing, and editing. The school also offers a postgraduate certificate in film. The Community Education Program offers noncredit screenwriting courses as well as other classes in filmmaking for those in the community.

SPECTATOR SPORTS

Auto Racing

HIGHLAND RIM SPEEDWAY, 6801 Kelly Willis Rd., Greenbrier, TN 37072; (615) 643-8725; highlandrim.com. Highland Rim Speedway, a 0.25-mile, high-banked "D" shaped asphalt track, features stock car racing every Sat night from Mar through Oct as well as special events throughout the year. Weekly races are held in 7 divisions: Pro 8 Late Models, Super Stocks, Pro 4 Modifieds, Tuner, Pure Stocks, Rim Runners (a beginners division), and Legends. Every other week, there's an Open Wheels division.

Before achieving their current NASCAR stardom, drivers such as Darrell Waltrip, Bobby Hamilton, Donnie and Bobby Allison, and Red Farmer raced at Highland Rim. Seating is about 5,000, including VIP skyboxes, and the atmosphere is family-friendly, with no alcohol. The small track makes for some truly exciting races. Children are always welcome at the Rim with bicycle races for ages 3-12 in the summer as well as a play area in the grandstands. Races are on Sat night; admission is $12 for general admission and $5 for children 6 to 12. Highland Rim Speedway is 20 miles north of Nashville; just take I-65 north to exit 104, then take Highway 257 west for 2 miles. Parking is free.

MUSIC CITY RACEWAY, 3302 Ivy Point Rd., Goodlettsville, TN 37072; (615) 876-0981; musiccityraceway.com. Music City Raceway offers National Hot Rod Association drag racing on Tues and Fri nights from Feb to Nov. Admission is generally $10. Children 12 and under are admitted free with adult. Competition heats up on Sat nights when the programs include Super Pro, Super Gas, Pro, Sportsman, Pro Motorcycles, Street Legal Trophy, Jr. Dragsters, and Heads Up classes. Parking and pit passes are always free. For directions to the track, visit the website.

> *Grand Ole Opry* star Charley Pride pursued a professional baseball career before singing. Born to poor sharecroppers in Sledge, Mississippi, Pride unofficially started his music career in the late 1950s as a ballplayer with the Negro American League's Memphis Red Sox singing and playing guitar on the team bus between ballparks. Self-taught on a guitar bought at the age of 14 from Sears Roebuck, Pride would join various bands onstage as he and the team roved the country.

Baseball

NASHVILLE SOUNDS, First Tennessee Park, 401 Jackson St., Nashville, TN 37219; (615) 690-4487; mild.com/Nashville. The Nashville Sounds, an AAA affiliate of the Texas Rangers, found a new home in 2015 at First Tennessee Park. Located in downtown Nashville, the park can seat up to 10,000 people. The team formerly played at Herschel Greer Stadium from its start in 1978 to 2014. As a nod to its Music City heritage, the new ballpark has an unusual guitar-shaped scoreboard, measuring 142 by 55 feet.

The team, originally an AA affiliate of the Cincinnati Reds when it came to town in 1978, plays about 72 home games from Apr through Labor Day. Check the website for promotional events and giveaways.

Basketball

MIDDLE TENNESSEE STATE UNIVERSITY BLUE RAIDERS, Murphy Athletic Center, Monte Hale Arena, Tennessee Blvd., Murfreesboro, TN 37132; (615) 898-2450; goblueraiders.com. MTSU's Blue Raiders men's and women's teams are members of Conference USA.

> Memorial Gym at Vanderbilt University was dedicated in 1952 to all Vanderbilt men and women who served in World War II. It was built by late master architect Edwin Keeble.

TENNESSEE STATE UNIVERSITY TIGERS, Howard Gentry Complex, 3500 John Merritt, Blvd., Nashville, TN 37209; (615) 963-5841; tsutigers.com. Tennessee State University has a rich athletics history. The TSU Tigers have played in the Ohio Valley Conference since 1988.

VANDERBILT UNIVERSITY COMMODORES, Memorial Gym, 210 25th St. S., Nashville, TN 37240; (615) 322-4653; vucommodores.com. Vanderbilt University's basketball program is the showcase of the school's athletic department. The Commodores are always a formidable opponent at Memorial Gym, the SEC's oldest arena. The gym has an unusual design—benches are behind the goals instead of on the sidelines, and the bleachers start below the level of the floor—which seems to have a disconcerting effect on many visiting teams.

Football

MIDDLE TENNESSEE STATE UNIVERSITY BLUE RAIDERS, Johnny "Red" Floyd Stadium, 1500 Greenland Dr., Murfreesboro, TN 37130; (615) 898-2450; goblueraiders.com. Under head coach Rick Stockstill, the Blue Raiders are members of Conference USA.

TENNESSEE STATE UNIVERSITY TIGERS, LP Field, 1 Titans Way, Nashville, TN 37213; (615) 963-5907; tsutigers.com. Tennessee State University's football team competes as an NCAA Division I team and as a member of the Ohio Valley Conference. TSU football has a proud legacy as one of the nation's great football programs.

TENNESSEE TITANS, LP Field, 1 Titans Way, Nashville, TN 37213; (615) 565-4200; titansonline.com. The team, which relocated to Tennessee from Houston in 1997, spent its first season in a temporary home at Memphis's Liberty Bowl. For the 1998–1999 season, the team, still known as the Oilers,

i In 1957 Tennessee A&I State (now Tennessee State) University in Nashville became the first historically black college to win a national basketball title. In that year the Tigers won the National Association of Intercollegiate Athletics championship.

Tennessee Titans Nashville Convention & Visitors Corporation

played its home games at Vanderbilt Stadium in Nashville. But everything really clicked in fall 1999 with the new name, new look, and $292-million, 67,000-seat, open-air stadium. Titans fans are loyal, and game tickets remain some of the hardest to come by in Nashville.

All season tickets have been sold out for years, and there is already a waiting list of more than 7,500. You can obtain a form to get on the waiting list by visiting the website or calling the ticket office. Parking at the stadium is by permit only. If you don't have a permit, don't even try to park near the stadium—traffic gridlock is a hallmark of Titans games. Shuttles operate from remote lots located around the city; MTA also operates shuttles to and from the stadium on game day.

VANDERBILT UNIVERSITY COMMODORES, Vanderbilt Stadium, Jess Neely Dr., Nashville, TN 37240; (615) 322-4653; vucommodores.com. The early years of VU football featured some of the most powerful teams in the country under College Hall of Fame coach Dan McGugin. McGugin's teams at Vanderbilt dominated Southern football until the 1930s. An NCAA Division I team, the Commodores have played at Vanderbilt Stadium since 1981. Located in the heart of the campus, Vanderbilt Stadium seats 40,550.

Nashville Predators hockey team. Nashville Convention & Visitors Corporation

Hockey

NASHVILLE PREDATORS, Bridgestone Arena, 501 Broadway, Nashville, TN 37203; (615) 770-2000; predators.nhl.com. The Predators first took to the ice on Oct 10, 1998. After 15 years as head coach, Barry Trotz was fired and Peter Laviolette was named new head coach on May 6, 2014. The Predators' season runs from early Oct to early Apr.

Recreation

The typical Nashvillian isn't one to sit around idly and let the world go by. No, there's just way too much to do here for that. Whatever your preferred method of recreation, you'll probably find it in this city. Nashville has earned the nickname "City of Parks," and many of the recreational opportunities available in Middle Tennessee are at parks. We're talking about activities as varied as bicycling, hiking, swimming, tennis, golfing, and skating, to name just a few. And many parks have fields for team sports like baseball, softball, and soccer. But parks don't have a monopoly on the action in Nashville. Tens of thousands of acres of water in area lakes just beg to be swum, fished, boated, and skied. You can put on your boots and cowboy hat and, instead of boot scootin', go for a horseback ride through the country. You can enjoy nature's beauty on an easy-paced walk or a strenuous hike.

Bad weather? That's okay. It doesn't have to ruin your day. As you'll discover in this chapter, we have plenty of indoor recreational opportunities as

John Seigenthaler Pedestrian Bridge in downtown Nashville. Nashville Convention & Visitors Corporation

well, like indoor swimming and tennis, bowling, billiards, and pumping iron. So you don't need to climb the walls—although, if you really want to, that's an option as well.

BICYCLING

Nashville's many parks make it an ideal city for bikers of varying experience. If you're a beginner, you can find relatively flat paths that require little exertion; if you're eager for a challenge, there are plenty of hills that will test your stamina. One excellent guide to biking is "Cycling Tennessee's Highways," a free collection of bicycling touring maps covering various sections of the state, from the Tennessee Department of Transportation by writing to Bicycle & Pedestrian Coordinator, Department of Transportation Planning, 5050 Deaderick St., Suite 900, James K. Polk Building, Nashville, TN 37243. Maps also may be downloaded at tn.gov/idot/multimodal-transportation-resources/bicycle-and-pedestrian-program.

BOATING

Popular Waterways

Nashville's 2 big lakes, **J. Percy Priest** and **Old Hickory,** are both managed by the US Army Corps of Engineers, which also manages some launching ramps on **Cheatham Lake** (Cumberland River). You'll see a variety of watercraft on these lakes, from fishing and skiing boats to houseboats, sailboats, and Jet Skis. Signs to boat ramps are marked at various locations around the lakes.

The Corps of Engineers operates nearly a dozen launching ramps on Old Hickory Lake in such areas as Hendersonville, Old Hickory, Hermitage, and Gallatin. The Corps has about 14 ramps at various sites on Percy Priest Lake.

i J. Percy Priest Lake was named in honor of Representative James Percy Priest, who was a high school teacher and coach and a reporter and editor for the *Tennessean* before being elected to Congress in 1940. He represented Nashville and Davidson County until his death in 1956. Old Hickory Lake was named for President Andrew Jackson, whose nickname was "Old Hickory."

A number of private marina operators lease land from the Corps, and their offerings vary. Most, but not all, have a launching ramp, for example, and while most sell fishing and marine supplies, only a few sell fishing licenses.

Cheatham Lake (Cumberland River)

CHEATHAM LAKE, resource manager's office: 1798 Cheatham Dam Rd., Ashland City, TN 37015; (615) 792-5697; lrn.usace.army.mil/locations/lakes/cheatham-lake/recreation. An impoundment of the Cumberland River, this lake is 67.5 miles long, extending through Nashville to Old Hickory Dam. The lake has 320 miles of shoreline and two commercial marinas.

J. Percy Priest Lake

J. PERCY PRIEST LAKE, visitor center: 3737 Bell Rd., Nashville, TN 37076; (615) 889-1975; percypriestlake.org. About 10 miles east of downtown Nashville, this lake covers 14,400 acres and has 265 miles of shoreline. Launching ramps are available as are campsites and picnic shelters. The visitor center is near the west side of the dam and open on weekdays.

Old Hickory Lake

OLD HICKORY LAKE, resource manager's office: No. 5 Power Plant Rd., Hendersonville, TN; 615-822-4846, (615) 847-2395; lrn.usace.army.mil/locations/lakes/old-hickory-lake. Located northeast of Nashville on the Cumberland River, this lake has more than 22,000 acres of water and 440 miles of shoreline. The visitor center/resource manager's office is located in Rockland Recreation Area in Hendersonville. Old Hickory Lake is named after former president and Tennessee native son Andrew Jackson, who was nicknamed "Old Hickory" because of his toughness.

i For information on lake elevation, water temperature, and fishing conditions at J. Percy Priest Lake or Old Hickory Lake, call the US Army Corps of Engineers fishing information lines Mon through Fri. The number to call for Priest Lake is (615) 889-1975; the number for Old Hickory is (615) 824-7766. The information is updated on weekdays. On weekends, call TVA's Lake Information Line at (800) 238-2264 for information on either lake.

> The Harpeth River, a popular spot for canoeing, is normally rated Class I, which means it's suitable for beginners and children. About 20 percent of the time, the Harpeth is Class I, and suitable only for experienced canoeists. Beginners and children under age 12 are advised not to canoe the river during those times.

CANOEING

The Harpeth River is a blessing to canoeists who don't want to drive far. Several businesses on the river in nearby Kingston Springs rent canoes for trips of varying lengths and times on the Harpeth, which is designated a State Scenic River and nature sanctuary. Because of the Harpeth's 5-mile "hairpin" loop in this area, you can put in and take out at nearly the same spot. Along the quiet, relaxing route—there are no major rapids to negotiate—you'll pass peaceful farmland and green, rolling hills. It's a great way to get away from it all for a few hours.

FISHING

Middle Tennessee has 10 lakes and more than a dozen rivers and streams within a 2-hour drive of Nashville, which is good news for anglers. The 3 closest lakes to Nashville are Cheatham, J. Percy Priest, and Old Hickory.

Game fish species caught in Middle Tennessee include rainbow and brown trout, walleye, sauger, rockfish (also known as stripers), stripe (also known as white bass), bream, black bass (largemouth, smallmouth, and spotted), catfish, and crappie. Not all species will be found in all waters—their presence is often dependent upon habitat and Tennessee Wildlife Resources Agency (TWRA) stocking programs.

Anyone 13 or older who fishes in Tennessee must have a license. You are exempted if you are: (1) a landowner fishing on your own farmland; (2) on military leave and carrying a copy of your leave orders; or (3) a resident born before March 1, 1926. Disabled resident veterans and blind residents are eligible for free licenses. Licenses go on sale Feb 18 of each year. A general fishing license costs $39 and does not include trout. An annual resident fishing and hunting combination license costs $34. An annual trout fishing license costs $22. A one-day fishing license for all species costs $11.50. An annual senior citizen hunting, fishing, and trapping license for 65 years or older costs $5. Nonresident licenses start at $20.50 for a 3-day (no trout) fishing license and

> Tennessee has a Free Fishing Day each June, when everyone can fish without a license, and a Free Fishing Week in June for children ages 15 and younger. Contact Tennessee Wildlife Resources Agency (TWRA) for dates.

$40.50 for a 3-day all-fish license. In addition, special permits are available for TWRA-managed lakes and Reelfoot Preservation (Reelfoot Lake). Fishing licenses are available at sporting goods stores, marinas, hardware stores, and bait-and-tackle shops. You can also order them online or by phone from the TWRA (see subsequent entry).

TENNESSEE WILDLIFE RESOURCES AGENCY, Ellington Agricultural Center, 440 Hogan Rd., Nashville, TN 37220; (615) 781-6500; tennessee .gov/twra. The latest laws governing fishing in Tennessee are available in the booklet *Tennessee Fishing Regulations.* The booklet, as well as other information about fishing, hunting, and other outdoor activities, is available from this office, which is responsible for Middle Tennessee, or Region 2.

You can purchase an instant fishing license from the TWRA online or by phone, using a credit card (there is an extra fee of $3.95 for either service). To order online, visit the TWRA's website.

TENNIS

CENTENNIAL SPORTSPLEX, 222 25th Ave. N., Nashville, TN 37203; (615) 862-8480; nashville.gov/parks-and-recreation/centennial-sportsplex. The Metro Board of Parks and Recreation has more than 160 tennis courts available free at parks around town. Call for information on courts near you. In addition, Metro Parks's Centennial Sportsplex has 13 outdoor courts with 4 hard courts and 8 new 36-foot permanent courts for ages 8 and under play. Outdoor courts are $10 per hour for nonmembers and first hour free for members and $4 per additional hour for members. The indoor court fee is $20 per hour for nonmembers and members. Call or visit the website for details on how and when to sign up for contract time.

YMCAS

YMCA OF MIDDLE TENNESSEE, 1000 Church St., Nashville, TN 37203; (615) 259-9622 (main office); ymcamidtn.org. The YMCA of Middle Tennessee is a not-for-profit health and human-services organization committed to helping persons grow in spirit, mind, and body. The organization operates 24 facilities in 11 counties. The Y offers its members a wide variety of programs and services, including indoor and outdoor pools, aerobics classes, wellness equipment, athletic fields, and gymnasiums. In addition, the YMCA has programs like youth sports, year-round child care, summer camp, personal fitness, family nights, volunteer opportunities, outreach, and activities for teens and older adults. A comprehensive list of local Ys and the facilities each has to offer is available at the website.

PARKS

State Parks

Nashville's first public park was the 8.5-acre Watkins Park at Jo Johnston Avenue and 17th Avenue N. Watkins Park was given to the city by brick manufacturer and construction contractor Samuel Watkins in 1870. The park was ravaged in the early 1860s by the Civil War. Around the turn of the 20th century, residents and the park board stepped in to renovate the area. In 1906 the Centennial Club took over and added the city's first playground. It was such a success that in 1909 the park board opened children's playgrounds on vacant lots throughout Nashville. Watkins Park, by the way, is still there at 616 17th Ave. N. Today it has a community center, tennis courts, basketball court, picnic shelter, and sprayground for cooling off in the summer. In this chapter we've chosen to list only a portion of Nashville's many parks and green spaces—just enough to get you in the mood for getting out and about. To ensure that your park excursions are safe and enjoyable, take note of the rules and hours of operation. Many parks are open from sunrise to sunset.

BICENTENNIAL CAPITOL MALL STATE PARK, 600 James Robertson Pkwy., Nashville, TN 37243; (615) 741-5280; tnstateparks.com/parks/bicentennial-mall. Don't let the word *mall* throw you off: This is not a shopping mall, but rather a mall similar to the National Mall in Washington, DC. This 19-acre downtown attraction, Tennessee's 51st state park, is part park and part outdoor history lesson. It opened in 1996 on the north side of the Tennessee State Capitol to commemorate the state's 200th birthday celebration and preserve the last unobstructed view of the capitol.

In the mall's concrete plaza entrance, a 200-foot granite map will take you on a walking trip through Tennessee. The map highlights major roads, rivers, and other details of the state's 95 counties. At night the county seats light up. A variety of other granite maps detail topics such as the state's geography, musical diversity, and topography. Just past the railroad trestle is the Rivers of Tennessee Fountains, with 31 fountains of varying heights, each representing one of the state's major rivers. The 95-bell carillon has 1 bell for each county in the state. The Pathway of History, starting at the west side of the mall, features marble columns that divide state history into 10-year increments. A World War II memorial, paid for by veterans of the war, takes the shape of an 18,000-pound granite globe supported by a constant stream of water; visitors can rotate the globe to view areas of the world as it was from 1939 to 1945 and see Tennessee's ties to the war's major battlefields. The mall also has a visitor center and 2,000-seat amphitheater. Guided group tours are available. The park offers restrooms and a gift shop. The park closes at dark and is patrolled 24 hours a day.

BLEDSOE CREEK STATE PARK, 400 Zieglers Fort Rd., Gallatin, TN 37066; (615) 452-3706; tnstateparks.com/parks/Bledsoe-creek. The 164-acre Bledsoe Creek offers 57 campsites and more than 6 miles of hiking trails, as well as 2 boat launches, picnic facilities, picnic shelters, and fishing at Old Hickory Lake. Rich in history, the park is named for long hunter and Revolutionary War veteran Isaac Bledsoe who came to the area in the 1770s. Nearby Bledsoe Fort was built in 1783 by Bledsoe to protect settlers from Indian attacks. Bledsoe and his brother Anthony were killed by Indians not far from there and are buried at Bledsoe Monument. An 18th century trade cabin was added in 2018.

CEDARS OF LEBANON STATE PARK, 328 Cedar Forest Rd., Lebanon, TN 37090; (615) 443-2769; tnstateparks.com/parks/cedars-of-lebanon. This park, which is connected to the largest red cedar forest in the United States, is about 31 miles east of Nashville in Wilson County, 6 miles south of I-40 on US 231. Only about 900 of the total acres are used for recreation. The remaining 8,100 acres are operated as a natural area by the Parks Division and as a state forest by the Forestry Division. Numerous wildflowers and other native plants can be found in the open limestone glades, including 19 rare and endangered plants, such as the Tennessee coneflower, which is said to exist only in Middle Tennessee. Accommodations include 117 campsites with electric and water hookups, plus 30 tent campsites and several 2-bedroom cabins with fully furnished kitchens. An 80-person-capacity group lodge offers year-round separate sleeping facilities. Among the other attractions are the Merritt Nature Center, 11 picnic pavilions, an "Olympic-plus-size"

Long Hunter State Park Jed DeKalb

swimming pool, 8 miles of hiking trails through the cedar forests and glades, and 6 miles of horseback-riding trails.

HARPETH RIVER STATE PARK, Off US 70 at 1640 Cedar Hill Rd., Kingston Springs, TN 37082; (615) 952-2099; tnstateparks.com/parks/Harpeth-river. This park, considered a satellite area of Montgomery Bell State Park about 11 miles west, offers recreation on the river, hiking, and a bit of education, too. While you're at the Narrows site, be sure to check out the historic 290-foot-long tunnel hand-cut through solid rock; it is an industrial landmark listed on the National Register of Historic Places and is one of the oldest existing human-made tunnels in the nation. Montgomery Bell, an early iron industrialist, built the tunnel to supply waterpower to his iron forge on the river. Bell is buried on a hillside across the river.

LONG HUNTER STATE PARK, 2910 Hobson Pike, Hermitage, TN 37076; (615) 885-2422; tnstateparks.com/parks/long-hunter. The 2,600-acre Long Hunter State Park, situated on the east shore of J. Percy Priest Lake, is a popular site for boating, swimming, waterskiing, and fishing. If you prefer to stay dry, there are plenty of activities on terra firma too, such as hiking, bird-watching, picnicking, and backcountry camping. The park offers boat rentals, playgrounds, a gift shop, and more. Spanning more than 14,000 acres, the US

Army Corps of Engineers' Percy Priest Reservoir is one of the largest lakes in the state. The 110-acre, landlocked Couchville Lake is part of Priest and is surrounded by a 2-mile paved trail. That barrier-free area also has a fishing pier. Long Hunter State Park was named for the hunters and explorers of the 1700s who stayed in the area for months or years at a time.

MONTGOMERY BELL STATE PARK, 1020 Jackson Hill Rd., Burns, TN 37029; (615) 797-9052; tnstateparks.com/parks/montgomery-bell. This approximately 3,800-acre park is located along US 70, about 2 miles west of White Bluff and 7 miles east of Dickson. The park is named for the state's first capitalist and industrialist, Montgomery Bell, who operated an iron forge on the Harpeth River. Montgomery Bell offers 118 tree-covered campsites, most of which have water and electrical hookups. All sites have a picnic table and grill. A 120-person-capacity group camp—open Apr through Oct—contains individual cabins, a dining hall, bathhouses, and a fishing dock. Montgomery Bell State Park's inn, conference center, and restaurant overlook the park's Lake Acorn. The inn has 120 rooms and 5 suites. The restaurant seats 190 and serves 3 meals a day. Other accommodations include 8 2-bedroom, fully equipped cabins that are available year-round. Privately owned boats are allowed at 17-acre Lake Acorn, 26-acre Creech Hollow Lake, and 50-acre Lake Woodhaven (check with the park for regulations). Lake Woodhaven has a year-round boat launch. Lake Acorn has canoes, paddleboats, and johnboats available for rent. Hikers will find about 20 miles of trails. An 11.7-mile overnight trail has 3 primitive overnight shelters. The park also offers a challenging 18-hole golf course, 2 tennis courts, playground, ball field, basketball courts, and more.

i When visiting area parks, keep your eyes open for the official Tennessee state creatures. The official state insects are the firefly (often referred to as a lightning bug), which glows at night, and the ladybug, a small reddish-orange bug with black spots on its wings. You might also see or hear the state bird, the mockingbird, which not only has its own melodious song but also is skilled at mimicking the songs of other birds. The state animal is the raccoon, which you'll recognize by its bushy ringed tail and bandit-like mask of dark fur around its eyes.

RADNOR LAKE STATE NATURAL AREA, 1160 Otter Creek Rd., Nashville, TN 37220; (615) 373-3467; tnstateparks.com/parks/Radnor-lake. In the late photographer John Netherton's book *Radnor Lake: Nashville's Walden* (Rutledge Hill Press, 1984), Nashville author John Egerton writes, "Words will never suffice to describe it. Radnor must be experienced through the senses. It must be seen, smelled, heard." It's true. Radnor Lake, a natural area spanning more than 1,100 acres just 6 miles south of downtown Nashville, must be experienced—in every season. The park is open during daylight hours.

Radnor is a state natural area and therefore not a recreation-oriented park. Primary activities are hiking, nature observation, photography, and research. Some activities, such as jogging on the wooded trails, boating, swimming, and picnicking, are not permitted. Radnor naturalists conduct a variety of environmental activities, such as birds-of-prey programs, wildflower hikes, canoe floats, and nighttime "owl prowls." You can make reservations for these programs by phone or at the visitor center.

Radnor Lake was created in 1914 by the Louisville & Nashville Railroad Company to provide water for steam engines and livestock at the Radnor Railroad Yards. L&N officials and their guests also used the site for private recreation. In 1962, when the area was purchased by a construction firm that had plans for a housing development, Nashvillians protested and were able to preserve the area. With the financial support of the federal government and thousands of Nashvillians, the Tennessee Department of Conservation purchased the land in 1973, and it became the state's first natural area.

Metro Parks & Greenways

The Metro Parks system consists of regional parks, community parks, neighborhood parks, and miniparks. The regional parks are 50 to 500-plus acres in size and include large, undisturbed tracts of land important for the protection of wildlife habitats. Hiking and picnicking are popular activities at these parks. The 4 largest regional parks are Shelby Bottoms Greenway in the downtown area; Hamilton Creek Park in the eastern part of Davidson County; the Warner Parks, which serve the south and southwestern parts of the county; and Beaman Park in north Nashville. There are at least 9 additional regional parks of 50 to 200 acres, including Centennial Park, one of the parks system's showpieces. Community parks are 20 to 50 acres in size, serve several neighborhoods, and offer numerous recreational facilities, including community centers; there are more than a dozen community parks in Nashville. There are more than 3 dozen neighborhood parks, which are 5 to 20 acres in size and are designed to serve the immediate surrounding neighborhood; these parks may have playgrounds, tennis or basketball courts, ball fields, and picnic areas. Miniparks, which are smaller than 5 acres, include urban plazas, playgrounds, and other small spaces; there are more than 20 of these parks in Nashville.

ALVIN G. BEAMAN PARK, 4111 Little Marrowbone Rd., Nashville, TN 37221; (615) 862-8400; nashville.gov/parks-and-recreation/nature-centers-and-natural-areas/beamon-park. Work on this 1,500-acre woodland greenway in northwest Davidson County, between Joelton and Ashland City, began in 1996, and the park opened in 2005. Beaman Park is Metro's second-largest park, second only to the Warner Parks. The park is named for the late Alvin G. Beaman. His wife Sally originally donated the funds to purchase the property as a tribute to her late husband, who was a parks board member and founder of the Beaman Automotive Group. Nature education and hiking are the focus of Beaman Park. The Beaman Park Nature Center is located at 5911 Old Hickory Blvd, (615) 862-8580. The center is open Tues through Fri noon to 4 p.m., Sat 9 a.m. to 4 p.m. Free admission and free programs are offered at the center year-round. Beaman Park is open daily from dawn to dusk. The park has 3 hiking trails with 5 miles of trail and 3 trailheads. Pick up trail maps at the nature center.

CEDAR HILL PARK, 860 Old Hickory Blvd., Madison, TN 37115; (615) 865-1853; nashville.gov/parks-and-recreation. This 225-acre, hilly park is near Goodlettsville on Dickerson Road at Old Hickory Boulevard. With a 4-diamond baseball and softball complex, it's a top pick for the area's teams. In addition to its baseball and softball diamonds, Cedar Hill Park has 7 tennis courts, a playground, a walking and jogging track, 7 picnic shelters that stay very busy, and restrooms. Many visitors come here just to walk the path around Cedar Hill Lake.

CENTENNIAL PARK, 2500 West End Ave., Nashville, TN 37203; (615) 862-8400; nashville.gov/parks-and-recreation/parks/centennial-park. Home of Nashville's famous replica of the Greek Parthenon, Centennial Park sits on 132.3 acres at West End Avenue and 25th Avenue N., 2 miles west of downtown. In 1897 it was the site of the Tennessee Centennial Exposition, which celebrated (one year late) Tennessee's 100th anniversary of statehood. Construction on the exposition buildings began in October 1895, when the cornerstone for a Parthenon replica was laid. Several elaborate, temporary white stucco

> i More than 1,000 trees have been planted at Centennial Park since the 1998 tornadoes.

buildings were constructed for use during the event, which attracted more than 1.7 million people from around the world. When the celebration was over, the other buildings were removed, but Nashvillians chose to keep the magnificent Parthenon (see our **History** and **Attractions** chapters), the only full-size replica of the Athenian structure. A highlight of the Parthenon is the 42-foot *Athena Parthenos,* the largest piece of indoor sculpture in the Western world.

Centennial Park offers playgrounds, paddleboating on Lake Watauga (a large pond), picnic facilities, swings, a band shell, a sand volleyball court, and plenty of grassy areas just perfect for spreading out a blanket. Various monuments around the park are reminders of Nashville's history. The park is the site of various arts and crafts exhibits, concerts, and other popular events throughout the year.

ELMINGTON PARK, 3531 West End Ave., Nashville, TN 37205; (615) 862-8400; nashville.gov/parks-and-recreation. This popular neighborhood park, on 13.3 acres at West End and Bowling Avenues, was developed by the Works Progress Administration during the 1930s. Today Elmington is a multipurpose park, offering 2 tennis courts, a baseball diamond, various playground pieces, and picnic tables.

FANNIE MAE DEES PARK, 2400 Blakemore Ave., Nashville, TN 37212; (615) 862-8400; nashville.gov/parks-and-recreation. Fannie Mae Dees Park is known to many as Dragon Park because of the mosaic sea-serpent centerpiece sculpture that winds its way through the playground area. But it's the park's recent addition—Lily's Garden, featuring playground equipment that is accessible to children with disabilities—that has given this urban green space a new lease on life. Children of all ages and abilities enjoy playing on the colorful structures. (See the **Kidstuff** chapter for more about Lily's Garden.) As for the dragon, a grant from the Tennessee Arts Commission brought artist Pedro Silva from New York to Nashville to design the sea creature. Nashville children were involved in the work, piecing the tiles together at various community centers and then bringing them to the park. The piece was dedicated April 25, 1981.

If you've never visited this park, it's worth stopping by just to marvel at the sea serpent. Look closely—you'll see many interesting and fanciful designs, including sailboats,

> i The year 1933 saw one of the state's toughest elections. In a race to determine the state bird, the mockingbird beat the robin by a mere 450 votes.

scuba divers, mermaids, and flowers. A portrait of local civic leader Fannie Mae Dees, the park's namesake, can be found on the loop near the serpent's tail. The sculpture is more than art, however; its tail serves as a bench—a great spot to relax while the kids enjoy the playground.

HADLEY PARK, 1037 28th Ave. N., Nashville, TN 37209; (615) 862-8400; nashville.gov/parks-and-recreation. This 34-acre urban community park includes an indoor walking track, pool, community meeting rooms, and a fitness room. The park board purchased the property in 1912 at the request of Fisk University's president and leaders of the north Nashville community. That year Nashville mayor Hilary Howse proclaimed Hadley Park the first public park for African-American citizens that had been established by any government in the nation.

A park board member named the park Hadley Park but did not specify which Hadley he had in mind. The city's African-American newspaper assumed it to be John L. Hadley, whose family had a house on the property. Some say the park might have been named for Dr. W. A. Hadley, a pioneering African-American physician who worked with the park board on the 1897 Centennial Exposition. The entrance gates were built in the late 1930s by the Works Progress Administration. On each side of the main entrance, next to the library, the stone columns contain a listing of the 11 African-American soldiers from Davidson County who were killed during World War I. The Hadley Park Community Center at 1037 28th Ave. N., (615) 862-8451, offers patrons of all ages a modern place to exercise and meet friends. A wide variety of activities and programs are offered. The facility has a fitness center, dance/aerobics studio, indoor swimming pool, indoor and outdoor walking/running tracks, computer lab, game room, and much more.

HAMILTON CREEK PARK, 2901 Bell Rd., Nashville, TN 37217; (615) 862-8400; nashville.gov/parks-and-recreation. Biking and boating are popular activities at Hamilton Creek Park, a 790-acre park on Bell Road along J. Percy Priest Lake. Hamilton Creek Park has a sailboat marina, plus boat slips and boats are available for rent. The park also has a boat-launching ramp, concession stands, restrooms, and hiking and nature trails. The BMX track is the site of national races that attract anywhere from 2,000 to 3,000 people. The park boasts about 9 miles of mountain biking trails that range in difficulty from challenging beginner to advanced.

HARPETH RIVER GREENWAY, Morton Mill Rd., Nashville, TN 37221; (615) 862-8400; nashville.gov/parks-and-recreation. This greenway is along

Parks Information

For additional information on state parks, natural areas, and Metro parks and greenways, contact:

Tennessee State Parks (Tennessee Department of Environment & Conservation), 312 Rosa L. Parks Ave., William R. Snodgrass Tennessee Tower, Nashville, TN 37243; (615) 532-0001 or (888) TN-PARKS; tnstateparks.com.

Metropolitan Board of Parks and Recreation, 511 Oman St. in Centennial Park (administrative office), Nashville TN 37215; (615) 862-8400; nashville.gov/parks-and-recreation.

Greenways for Nashville, Metropolitan Board of Parks and Recreation, 511 Oman St. in Centennial Park, Nashville, TN 37215; (615) 862-8400; greenwaysfornashville.org.

the Harpeth River on Morton Mill Road near Old Harding Pike in Bellevue. A series of 4 disconnected, multiuse trails, Harpeth River Greenway is 5.75 miles with 1 mile of paved path along the river. Along the boardwalk following Morton Mill Road, you'll find an overlook with benches.

MILL CREEK/EZELL PARK GREENWAY, Harding Place at Mill Creek, Antioch, TN 37013; (615) 862-8400; nashville.gov/parks-and-recreation. This greenway offers 3 miles of trails traveling around Antioch Middle School, the community center, and then along Mill Creek. A shallow creek and woods bordering the trail provide good habitat for wildlife-watching.

RIVERFRONT PARK, 100 First Ave. N., Nashville, TN 37201; (615) 862-8750; nashville.gov/parks-and-recreation. Riverfront Park in downtown Nashville is the site of lots of summertime revelry. It's the site of the big Fourth of July celebration and fireworks display, as well as Fan Fair concerts and activities, and other events. Prime viewing spots on the tiered, grass-covered hill fill up fast, so arrive early if you want to sit there. The 7.5-acre park overlooks the Cumberland River. It's just a short walk from bustling Second Avenue and Broadway. Commercial and private boats dock at Riverfront Park. The park was created to commemorate Nashville's bicentennial and pay tribute to the city's river heritage.

SHELBY BOTTOMS GREENWAY AND NATURE PARK, east end of Davidson Street, adjacent to Shelby Park, Nashville, TN 37206; (615) 862-8400; nashville.gov/parks-and-recreation/greenways. Considered one of the jewels of the Metro Parks system, this 810-acre park on the Cumberland River has 5 miles of primitive hiking trails and 5 miles of paved multiuse trails. Along the trails there are boardwalks, interpretive stations, and several rustic bridges. The area also includes an observation deck for birders, lots of bluebird boxes, and a wetlands waterfowl refuge.

SHELBY PARK, Shelby Avenue at South 20th Street, Nashville, TN 37206; (615) 862-8467; nashville.gov/parks-and-recreation. Shelby Park, a historic and scenic park covering 361.5 acres, brings a diverse mix of visitors to the park. Some come to fish in the lake, walk the paved winding roads, or play golf at the 27-hole golf course or the 9-hole course. With a 4-diamond adult softball complex and additional ball fields for kids, Shelby Park is 1 of the 5 large ballparks operated by Metro Parks. Four tennis courts, a playground, hiking/nature trails, 8 picnic shelters, restrooms, and a boat ramp are among the other attractions here. Shelby is also home to Nashville's first dog park, which opened in 2004. At the turn of the 20th century, a real estate development company named the park for John Shelby, an army surgeon who owned much of the original property and built the Fatherland and Boscobel mansions in east Nashville during the 1800s.

TWO RIVERS PARK, 3150 McGavock Pike, Nashville, TN 37203; (615) 862-8400; nashville.gov/parks-and-recreation. This park is a great place to cool off on a hot summer day. This is where you'll find a skate park as well as Wave Country water park. Wave Country has a wave pool, waterslides, a children's playground, and volleyball pits, and it gets packed on summer days. (See our **Attractions** and **Kidstuff** chapters for more information.) Other attractions at the 374-acre Two Rivers Park include 18 holes of golf, baseball and

i Nashville's oldest model-airplane-flying field is located at Edwin Warner Park, at Old Hickory Boulevard and Vaughn Road, across from the steeplechase grounds. The field dates from the 1940s. Members of Edwin Warner Model Aviators show up regularly to fly model planes. The field is also a popular spot for watching meteor showers.

softball diamonds, 6 tennis courts, and a playground. The park also has concession stands, picnic shelters, restrooms, Two Rivers Lake, and more.

WARNER PARKS, 7311 Hwy. 100; Nashville, TN 37221; (615) 352-6299; nashville.gov/parks-and-recreation. The jewel in Metro Parks' crown, Warner Parks encompass at least 2,681 acres in southwest Nashville, making the collective pair one of the largest city parks in the country. Acres of wooded hills, open fields, and miles of scenic paved roads and nature trails provide Nashvillians with excellent recreation and environmental-education opportunities. (See **Kidstuff** for related information.) The parks are named for brothers Edwin and Percy Warner and were acquired between 1927 and 1930. Col. Luke Lea donated the first 868 acres of the land to the city in 1927, with the encouragement of his father-in-law, Percy Warner, a prominent local businessman, park board chairman, and lifelong outdoorsman and nature lover. In 1937 the park board designated all the property west and south of Old Hickory Boulevard as Edwin Warner Park. The stone structures in the park, including the miles of dry-stacked stone retainer walls, were constructed from 1935 to 1941 by the Works Progress Administration, which provided jobs during the Great Depression. The WPA built 7 limestone entrances, 2 stone bridges, a steeplechase course, picnic shelters, stone pillars, scenic drives, overlooks, and trails.

The main entrance to 2,058-acre Percy Warner Park is at the intersection of Belle Meade Boulevard and Page Road. Other entrances are off Chickering Road, Highway 100, and Old Hickory Boulevard. Percy Warner offers miles of hiking and equestrian trails as well as paved roads that wind along forest-shaded hillsides and through open fields. Bicyclists will find the roads make for a challenging workout. In addition to its recreation opportunities, Percy Warner Park is a nice place for a Sunday-afternoon drive or picnic. Percy Warner Park also has a steeplechase course—the site of the annual Iroquois Steeplechase (see **Annual Events**)—as well as 2 golf courses, picnic shelters, restrooms, and equestrian facilities.

Walkin' the Dog

Shelby Dog Park, Nashville's first dog park, opened in 2004 at Shelby Park (Shelby Avenue at South 20th Street). The dog park allows owner-supervised dogs to play and socialize off-leash in a fenced area. There are several rules that owners must follow. Contact Metro Parks for details (615-862-8400), or visit the website nashville.gov/parks-and-recreation/parks/dog-parks. Dogs are welcome at all other Metro parks, but must be leashed at all times.

Edwin Warner Park, divided from Percy Warner by Old Hickory Boulevard, offers paved and nature trails, playgrounds, ball fields, a polo field, model-airplane field, restrooms, and picnic shelters, including several reservable shelters. It's a popular spot for dog walking as well as for company picnics, family reunions, and other group events. The main entrance to Edwin Warner is at Highway 100 near the Warner Parks Nature Center, but you can also enter the park at Vaughn Road off Old Hickory Boulevard. The Warner Parks Nature Center serves both parks and includes the Susanne Warner Bass Learning Center, a natural history museum, office and reference library, organic vegetable and herb garden, pond, bird-feeding area, and wildflower gardens. The park offers environmental programs year-round for adults and children.

GOLF

It should come as no surprise that Nashville is full of golf courses. First of all, there's the terrain, which varies from flat to gently rolling to downright hilly. That means whatever your playing style, you can find a course with a layout to your liking. Second, consider that this is, after all, a city of business. What better way to clinch a plum contract than with a putter in your hand? Add in the fact that a lot of us around here like sports of any kind. And don't forget the music. Country music and golf go together like country ham and biscuits. Just

Nashville offers several challenging golf courses. Nashville Convention & Visitors Corporation

ask Vince Gill, well-known golf tournament host. Gill is renowned for his vocal and guitar skills, but he's equally passionate about his golf. His annual pro-celebrity tournament, the Vinny, attracts country stars, PGA pros, and other celebrities. Since it began in 1993, the Vinny has raised $8 million to benefit the state's high-quality junior golfers' program, becoming one of the nation's top pro-celebrity events in the process.

i It's not unusual to see deer, wild turkeys, and other wildlife at Harpeth Hills Golf Course at Percy Warner Park.

This section covers a selection of area courses that are open to the general public.

Metro Parks Courses

Metro Parks maintains 7 public golf courses in 5 parks. They are open year-round, weather permitting, with the exception of the Vinny Links youth course, which is open May through Oct. From Dec through Feb, each course is closed 1 day a week. During these months, it's a good idea to call first to ensure your course is open. The 6 year-round courses each have a putting green, snack bar, and pro shop; lessons are available at all but Shelby and Vinny Links.

HARPETH HILLS GOLF COURSE, 2424 Old Hickory Blvd., Nashville, TN 37221; (615) 862-8493; nashville.gov/parks-and-recreation/golf-courses/Harpeth-hills-golf-course. Harpeth Hills, 1 of 2 Metro courses in Percy Warner Park, is a busy course, and you'll generally need to reserve your tee times a week in advance. This scenic, slightly hilly 18-hole course is 6,481 yards and par 72, with bent grass greens and no water.

Bear Trace Golf Trail

Serious golfers may want to check out Tennessee's **Bear Trace Golf Trail,** which features 5 spectacular and affordable 18-hole courses throughout the state. Each course was designed by the "Golden Bear" himself, golf great **Jack Nicklaus.** The course closest to Nashville is Tim's Ford, near Winchester, about 90 miles south. Other courses are Cumberland Mountain near Crossville, Harrison Bay near Chattanooga, Chickasaw near Henderson, and Ross Creek Landing near Clifton. For details, call (866) 770-BEAR or visit golftennessee.com.

> Of the seven Metro Parks golf courses, the easiest to walk are McCabe, Percy Warner, and Vinny Links. The most challenging are Harpeth Hills, Ted Rhodes, Shelby, and Two Rivers. Additional details about Metro golf courses are available at nashville.gov/parks-and-recreation/golf-courses.

MCCABE GOLF COURSE, 4601 Murphy Rd., Nashville, TN 37209; (615) 862-8491; nashville.gov/parks-and-recreation/golf-courses/mccabe-golf-course. McCabe is a fairly level, easy-to-walk course with 27 holes—par 70 and par 36. The par 70 covers 5,847 yards. There's no water, but there are some challenges, notably the 162-yard 15th hole, a par 3 with a trap on each side. This is one of Metro's most popular courses.

PERCY WARNER GOLF COURSE, 1221 Forrest Park Dr., Nashville, TN 37205; (615) 352-9958; nashville.gov/parks-and-recreation/golf-courses/percy-warner-golf-course. This scenic 9-hole, 2,474-yard course at the Belle Meade Boulevard entrance to Percy Warner Park features traditional, tree-lined fairways and is par 34. There's no water.

SHELBY GOLF COURSE, 2021 Fatherland St., Nashville, TN 37206; (615) 862-8474; nashville.gov/parks-and-recreation/golf-courses/Shelby-golf-course. Shelby is very hilly—fit for a mountain goat, as one golfer put it. The 18-hole, 5,789-yard, par 72 course has a pond on the 11th hole and creeks running throughout.

TED RHODES GOLF COURSE, 1901 Ed Temple Blvd., Nashville, TN 37208; (615) 862-8463; nashville.gov/parks-and-recreation/golf-courses/ted-rose-golf-course. There's water everywhere at Rhodes, coming into play on about 14 of the 18 holes. The scenic par 72 course is 6,207 yards.

TWO RIVERS GOLF COURSE, 2235 Two Rivers Pkwy., Nashville, TN 37214; (615) 889-2675; nashville.gov/parks-and-recreation/golf-courses/two-rivers-golf-course. Two Rivers is marked by rolling hills, with one water hole on both the front and the back nines. It's 18 holes, 6,230 yards, and par 72.

VINNY LINKS GOLF COURSE, 2009 Sevier St., Nashville, TN 37206; (629) 888-9621; nashville.gov/parks-and-recreation/golf-courses/vinny-links-golf-course. This 9-hole, 1,314-yard, par 29 course along the Cumberland River opened in May 2001 at the site of the former Riverview Golf Course. It is part of the First Tee program, which aims to promote golf and make the sport affordable for young people. The course was based on a Donald Ross design. There is one par 4 hole; the rest are par 3s. While this walking-only course is geared toward youth, adults can play, too.

Other Public Courses

COUNTRY HILLS GOLF COURSE, 1501 Saundersville Rd., Hendersonville, TN 37075; (615) 824-1100; chillsgc.com. Country Hills is a short course, at 5,862 yards, but it's a hilly, wooded, and tough par 70, so it plays long. The biggest challenge is the number 3 hole, a 363-yard par 4 dogleg left with water. Holes 4 and 5 feature water. Country Hills has a pro shop, driving range, putting green, and snack bar.

FORREST CROSSING GOLF CLUB, 750 Riverview Dr., Franklin, TN 37064; (615) 794-9400; thecrossinggc.com. During the Civil War, Confederate general Nathan Bedford Forrest and his men crossed the picturesque Harpeth River at a spot between where holes number 3 and number 4 are today. Designed by Gary Roger Baird, this rolling course commemorates Forrest's event. Water comes into play on 15 of the 18 holes on this 6,968-yard, par 72 course. Forrest Crossing has a putting facility, driving range, and full-service snack bar. The 20-station grass tee practice facility is quite popular.

GAYLORD SPRINGS GOLF LINKS, 18 Springhouse Ln., Nashville, TN 37214; (615) 458-1730; gaylordsprings.com. Gaylord Springs, a links-style course designed by Larry Nelson, lines the Cumberland River. The course, highlighted by large mounds and a bunch of water, has 5 sets of tees. The "everyday" tees at this course are blue instead of white, with a total distance of 6,165 yards. A 19th-century springhouse sits at the back of the green on the signature hole, the 338-yard number 4. The 43,000-square-foot clubhouse is a complete facility with rooms for meetings and banquets, a grill room, and complete locker-room

> i Gaylord Springs is noted for its golf, especially during the Senior Classic. Not as many people seem to realize it also has a great practice putting green.

facilities for men and women. The pro shop offers high-quality rental clubs and golf shoes as well as brand-name balls for the double-sided driving range. The PGA-designed golf course is about 5 minutes from Gaylord Opryland Resort.

GREYSTONE GOLF CLUB, 2555 US 70 E., Dickson, TN 37055; (615) 446-0044; greystonegc.com. Since opening in 1998, this scenic, par 72, 6,002-yard course has become a favorite. It was voted among the 100 best values in the United States by *Maximum Golf* and has hosted several high-profile events. Designed by Mark McCumber, the course is marked by rolling hills and offers several challenging holes. The par 3 16th hole is especially scenic. The kidney-shaped green is guarded by a creek in front and a stone wall. Water comes into play at 7 holes. The club also has a snack bar, pro shop, and driving range.

HERMITAGE GOLF COURSE, 3939 Old Hickory Blvd., Old Hickory, TN 37138; (615) 847-4001; hermitagegolf.com. The Hermitage Golf Course has two 18-hole courses—the General's Retreat and the newer President's Reserve. The General's Retreat is an 18-hole, par 72 course. It measures 6,011 yards. It's mostly a flat, open course with some elevated greens. The bent grass greens are large and undulating. Fairways are Bermuda grass in summer and rye the rest of the year. Six lakes come into play on the course, which lies along the Cumberland River. Hermitage, which is noted for its driving range and putting green, also has a snack bar, pro shop, and PGA instructors. The President's Reserve shares the same pro shop and other facilities. President's Reserve, also a par 72, features 6 sets of tees, with a distance of about 6,000 yards from the white ones. The course is built around a huge natural wetland area with a slough running down its middle. Six holes are on the Cumberland River.

HUNTER'S POINT GOLF COURSE, 1500 Hunters Point Pike, Lebanon, TN 37087; (615) 444-7521; hunterspointgolf.com. Hunter's Point, a 6,212-yard, par 72 course, is flat, with water coming into play on about one-third of the 18 holes. Number 15, a 446-yard par 4, challenges you with water to the left and right of the green and trees to the left of the fairway. Hunter's Point has a pro shop, putting green, driving range, and a snack bar.

i The Hermitage Golf Course has received *Golf Digest* magazine's four-star rating and was named one of the "100 Best Bargain Golf Courses in the United States" by *Maximum Golf* and "One of America's 100 Best Golf Courses for $100 or Less" by *Travel + Leisure Golf*.

THE LEGACY GOLF COURSE, 100 Raymond Floyd, Springfield, TN 37172; (615) 384-4653; golfthelegacy.com. This par 72 course, designed by PGA veteran Raymond Floyd, opened on Memorial Day 1996. But it looks a lot older. That's because Floyd designed the 6,755-yard Legacy—which is marked by undulating greens and water on 4 of the 18 holes—around a collection of mature trees. The Legacy has a driving range, a snack bar, and a pro shop, and lessons are available.

LONG HOLLOW GOLF COURSE, 1080 Long Hollow Pike, Gallatin, TN 37066; (615) 451-3120; gallatintn.gov/485/golf. Long Hollow, a 5,622-yard, par 70 course, is on rolling land, with water a factor on 7 of its 18 holes. Watch out for number 10, a 420-yard par 4—there's water out of bounds to the right on the second shot and trees to the left. Long Hollow has a snack bar, pro shop, and driving range and offers lessons.

MONTGOMERY BELL STATE PARK GOLF COURSE, 800 Hotel Ave., Burns, TN 37029; (615) 797-2578; tnstateparks.com/golf/course/Montgomery-bell. This course, part of Montgomery Bell State Park, is 5,927 yards and par 71. It's hilly and features water on 3 holes. The course has a pro shop, practice green, driving range, and snack bar.

NASHBORO GOLF CLUB, 1101 Nashboro Blvd., Nashville, TN 37217; (615) 367-2311; nashborogolf.com. Nashboro Golf Club, 5 minutes south of the airport off Murfreesboro Road, is set on rolling hills and beautifully lined with trees. Half of the 18-hole course runs through the Nashboro Village housing development, and water comes into play on 6 holes. The course covers 6,384 yards and is par 72. Nashboro has PGA golf pros on staff and offers a driving range, practice putting green, pro shop, and large snack bar.

PINE CREEK GOLF COURSE, 1835 Logue Rd., Mt. Juliet, TN 37122; (615) 449-7272; pinecreekgolf.net. Smaller, undulating greens that can be hard to reach are characteristic of this 6,249-yard, par 72 course, which was built on a farm and has remained largely unaltered. Pine Creek's rolling layout

i Metro's busiest golf courses are Harpeth Hills and McCabe. About 85,000 9-hole rounds are played at Harpeth Hills per year, while McCabe, which has 27 holes, registers about 110,000 9-hole rounds annually.

is marked with water and pine trees, both of which come into play on many of the 18 holes. A lake marks the 136-yard, par 3 number 6 hole.

RIVERSIDE GOLF COURSE, 640 Old Hickory Blvd., Old Hickory, TN 37138; (615) 847-5074. Riverside Golf Course on the Cumberland River features a 9-hole and an 18-hole course. The 1,558-yard, 9-hole executive course is mostly par 3s, with a couple of par 4s. It's a good choice for beginners and good practice for your irons. The 18-hole par 70 course is 5,465 yards. It's flat, and water comes into play on about half the holes. Riverside has a lighted driving range, a 150-yard grass tee, PGA instructors, a snack bar, and pro shop.

SMYRNA MUNICIPAL GOLF COURSE, 101 Sam Ridley Pkwy., Smyrna, TN 37167; (615) 459-2666; smyrnagolfcourse.net. This 6,028-yard, par 72 course is fairly flat with just a few water hazards. Smyrna Municipal has a snack bar and pro shop, plus a 9-hole executive course. The 1,507-yard, par 29 course is part of the nationwide First Tee junior golf program.

Annual Events

Want to have some fun? Learn something new? Mingle with a crowd? Maybe just get out of the house? Then check out some of Nashville's annual events. Music City's calendar is full of festivals, celebrations, sporting events, seminars, shows, and other fun and interesting happenings—enough to keep you busy year-round. Just about any weekend—January through December—you can find at least one special event taking place in or around Nashville. What's your pleasure? From art to antiques, gardening to golf, and mules to Moon Pies, there's something for everyone.

Below are some of Nashville's favorite events, listed by month (roughly in the order they occur). Schedules are subject to change, so before making plans, it's a good idea to check the local newspapers for up-to-date information on events, dates, and admission prices. Most annual events have a gate charge, but you'll find a few that offer free admission. Children's admission is *usually* a few dollars less than adult admission. Most events also offer discounts for senior citizens and groups. Some have special rates during designated days or hours, and some offer discounts if you bring a coupon. Keep your *Insiders' Guide to Nashville* handy all year. The next time you're looking for something to do, check our listing of annual events, then go out and have some fun!

JANUARY

LET FREEDOM SING WITH THE NASHVILLE SYMPHONY, Schermerhorn Symphony Center, 1 Schermerhorn Place, Nashville, TN 37201; (615) 687-6400; nashvillesymphony.org. Each year, the Nashville

> i When the New Year rolls around, the Department of Public Works' Trees to Trails program recycles thousands of Christmas trees. Trees are chipped and spread along area hiking trails. Be sure to recycle your tree. You can find designated tree drop-offs at parks throughout Nashville. For more information visit nashville.gov/public-works/neighborhood-services/recycling or call (615) 880-1000.

Symphony hosts a special concert in honor of the legacy of Dr. Martin Luther King Jr. The concert is free and features the Nashville Symphony accompanied by adult and youth choruses from the local community. The orchestra performs classic pieces while photographs of the triumphs of the civil rights movement are projected on a large screen above the stage. The photographs are provided by the Nashville Public Library. Seats need to be reserved at the box office in advance.

FEBRUARY

ANTIQUES & GARDEN SHOW OF NASHVILLE, Music City Center, 201 Fifth Ave. S., Nashville, TN 37203; (615) 352-1282; antiquesandgardenshow.com. The Antiques & Garden Show, usually held in mid- to late Feb, has been named one of the Top 20 Events in the Southeast by the Southeast Tourism Society. The show features more than 80 antiques dealers from the United States, the United Kingdom, and France, as well as about 70 eastern US horticulturists. It benefits the Cheekwood Botanical Garden & Museum of Art (see our **Attractions** chapter) and the Exchange Club Inc. Charities. The show focuses on high-end items. Surrounding the antiques are beautifully landscaped gardens as well as booths filled with flowers, herbs, and other garden necessities for sale.

MARCH

COUNTRY RADIO SEMINAR, 1009 Sixteenth Ave.; Nashville, TN 37212; (615) 327-4487; countryradioseminar.com. Each Feb or Mar more than 2,000 country radio broadcasters from around the country descend on Nashville for the Country Radio Seminar, a week of educational sessions, meetings, artists' showcases, awards presentations, and parties.

APRIL

CHEEKWOOD SPRING ART HOP, 1200 Forrest Park Dr., Nashville, TN 37205; (615) 356-8000; cheekwood.org. Held the Saturday before Easter, this event features egg hunts for kids, music, storytelling, art activities, a scavenger hunt, and, of course, the Easter Bunny. Admission for nonmembers is $24 for adults and $17 for children 3 to 17; admission for members is $8 for adults and free for children.

MULE DAY, Maury County Park, 1018 Maury County Park Dr., Columbia, TN 38401; (931) 381-9557; muleday.org. Even if you're not particularly interested in mules, you're bound to enjoy this old-time festival, held the first or second weekend (Thurs through Sun) at Maury County Park in Columbia, about 43 miles south of downtown Nashville. The Mule Day tradition began in 1934. Farmers used to bring their mules to town for a livestock show and market once a year, and the festival grew around this annual happening. Today the festival features a mule parade downtown, mule shows, mule pulling, arts and crafts, a flea market, square dancing, a clogging contest, a liars' contest, and more. You can enjoy "pioneer foods" such as roasted corn, fried pies, and apple fritters as well as traditional festival fare like hamburgers, hot dogs, and soft drinks. Admission is $5 on Thurs, $10 on Fri and Sat, and free on Sun. A weekend pass is $18.

TIN PAN SOUTH, various Nashville venues; (615) 256-3354, (800) 321-6008; tinpansouth.com. The Nashville Songwriters Association International (NSAI) sponsors this annual music festival that celebrates songwriters and songwriting. Concerts, awards, and a golf tournament are held during the week. See our **Music City** chapter for information.

GOSPEL MUSIC WEEK, Nashville Convention Center, 601 Commerce St., Nashville, TN 37203; (615) 242-0303; gospelmusic.org. This industry event attracts artists, record company personnel, radio representatives, concert promoters, and others who work in the gospel music industry. Read more about it in our **Music City** chapter.

NASHVILLE EARTH DAY FESTIVAL, Centennial Park, 2500 West End Ave., Nashville, TN 37203; nashvilleearthday.org. Nashville celebrates Earth Day with a free, family-oriented festival on the weekend closest to the April 22 holiday. The event is usually held at Centennial Park and features live

i If you enjoy gardening, you may be interested in Cheekwood's many plant shows held throughout the year. The botanical garden and museum hosts shows devoted to daffodils, wildflowers, bonsai, roses, hostas, daylilies, and more. See our listings in this chapter, or call Cheekwood at (615) 358-8000 for more information.

> In 1897 Nashville candymakers Williams Morrison and John Wharton invented a machine to spin the sugary treat called fairy floss or cotton candy. The confection became a big hit at fairs and festivals.

alternative-country, folk, blues, and bluegrass music; food and drink booths; and speakers from the mayor's office and Tennessee Environmental Council.

MAIN STREET FESTIVAL, Downtown Franklin, TN 37065; (615) 591-8500; downtownfranklintn.com. This 2-day, free-admission event held during the last full weekend in April is definitely worth the short drive to Franklin. The festival takes place on 5 city blocks in the historic downtown area, from First Avenue to Fifth Avenue, and encompasses the town square. Crafts and food booths line the streets. More than 200 artists and craftspeople from across the United States exhibit their works. Food vendors offer tempting festival fare. Park along nearby streets and in downtown lots.

NASHVILLE FILM FESTIVAL, Regal Hollywood Stadium 27, 719 Thompson Ln., Nashville, TN 37204; (615) 742-2500; nashvillefilmfestival.org. This annual event features several days of film and video screenings from renowned and up-and-coming filmmakers from around the world. As many as 200 films are featured, along with 15 to 20 workshops, film analysis, forums, and other events, some of which are led by well-known entertainment-industry figures. Admission ranges from $5 to $15 for a single film; an all-festival pass is available for $250 to $495. Other ticket packages are available. Call for a schedule of daily and evening shows, or watch for a listing in local publications. NIFF members receive discount tickets as well as special benefits throughout the year, such as free admission to monthly screenings and discounts on tickets at Regal Green Hills Cinema.

MAY

TENNESSEE CRAFT FAIR, Centennial Park, West End Ave. and 25th Ave N.; (615) 385-1904; tennesseecraft.org. The craft fairs at Centennial Park are among Nashville's most popular events. This one, a juried crafts festival produced by the Tennessee Association of Craft Artists, is the largest market of Tennessee crafts you'll find anywhere. Some 175 contemporary and traditional artisans, all from the Volunteer State, set up on the lawn of Centennial Park for the 3-day show, held the first weekend in May. Children's crafts activities, live music, demonstrations, and food will keep you in the park for hours. Admission is free. Tennessee Craft (previously TACA) also hosts the Fall Crafts Fair here on the last weekend of Sept (see that month's section for details).

TENNESSEE RENAISSANCE FESTIVAL, 2124 New Castle Rd., Arlington, TN 37014; (615) 395-9950; tnrenfest.com. Weekends in May, ending on Memorial Day, the wooded grounds across from Triune's Castle Gwynn turn into a medieval village where you'll find jousting knights, fair maidens, fortune-tellers, gypsy jugglers, and entertainers, plus medieval-themed arts and crafts and food. Twice daily, knights in full armor mount large Percherons and engage in combat. In addition to jousting exhibitions, you can enjoy drama and comedy (presented in Olde English) at 2 stages on the grounds as well as Renaissance music. Admission is $23.95 for adults, $11.95 for children ages 6 through 12, free for children 5 and under. A season pass is $100. Parking is free.

IROQUIS STEEPLECHASE, Percy Warner Park, Nashville, TN 37221; (800) 619-4802; iroquoissteeplechase.org. The Iroquois Steeplechase, one of Nashville's most popular sporting and social events, takes place the second Saturday in May. First held in 1941, this is the nation's oldest continually run weight-for-age steeplechase. If you come, plan to make a day of it. You can picnic or have a tailgate party. Thousands take blankets, lawn chairs, and their favorite food and drink to a spot on the grassy hillside overlooking the course. Gates open at 8 a.m. and the first race is at 1 p.m. The 7-race card culminates with the featured Iroquois Memorial at 4:30 p.m. Admission is $17 for individual ticket; children ages 12 and under are admitted free with adult ticket holder. Special ticket and party packages are available, too. The event benefits Vanderbilt Children's Hospital.

JUNE

CMA MUSIC FESTIVAL/FAN FAIR, Nissan Stadium and various downtown Nashville venues; (615) 244-2840; cmaworld.com. Tens of thousands of hard-core country-music fans, more than 70 hours of concerts, and long lines of autograph seekers: That's this event in a nutshell. This mid-June festival attracts fans from around the world. (Read more about it in the **Music City** chapter.)

> i Looking for a unique gift for that special someone? Check out one of Nashville's crafts fairs. Centennial Park and the state fairgrounds host several such events each year. You'll find everything from modern art to old-fashioned country crafts.

RC COLA AND MOON PIE FESTIVAL, 4 Railroad Square, Bell Buckle, TN 37020; bellbucklechamber.com/bell-buckle-moonpie-festival-general-info. An RC Cola and a Moon Pie—if you have to ask, you're probably not a Southerner. The RC–Moon Pie combo is a classic. The tiny, charming town of Bell Buckle celebrates the big round chocolate-and-graham-cracker-covered marshmallow treat the third Saturday in June. It all started in 1995, when the town wanted to celebrate the 75th birthday of the Moon Pie, which is made in nearby Chattanooga. As you might guess, this event doesn't take anything too seriously. It's purely for fun. Festival activities might include a Moon Pie toss, Moon Pie hockey, synchronized wading, a Moon Pie dessert recipe contest, a Moon Pie song contest, and the crowning of the Moon Pie King and RC Cola Queen. A 10K run, country and bluegrass music, crafts fair, and clogging demonstrations add to the fun. Admission is free.

JEFFERSON STREET JAZZ & BLUES FESTIVAL, 26th Avenue N. and Jefferson St., Nashville, TN 37208; (615) 726-5867; jumpnashville.com. Historic Jefferson Street, once known for its jazz, blues, and R&B music, is the location of this family-oriented music festival, which usually takes place on the third Saturday in June. (Read more about it in our **Music City** chapter.)

THE VINNY, 400 Franklin Rd., Franklin, TN 37069; (615) 794-9399; tngolf.org. Since its inception in 1993, the Vinny, country star Vince Gill's annual pro-celebrity golf tournament, has raised $8 million for Tennessee Junior golf and youth programs. The 2-day event includes PGA Tour players plus sports and entertainment celebrities. The Pro–Celebrity Am takes place on Mon, while amateurs play with the celebrities on Tues. Pros who have participated in the event include John Daly, Fuzzy Zoeller, and Lanny Wadkins. In addition to Vince Gill and his wife, Amy Grant, celebrity participants have included Alice Cooper, NFL quarterback Brett Favre, Charley Pride, and Kix Brooks of Brooks & Dunn. The event is not open to the public, although many junior golfers are able to participate as volunteers, and the state's top junior golfers have a chance to play in the tournament.

July 4th in downtown Nashville Nashville Convention & Visitors Corporation

JULY

INDEPENDENCE DAY CELEBRATION, 100 Riverfront Park, Nashville, TN 37201; (800) 657-6910; visitmusiccity.com. This is Nashville's largest 1-day event, drawing up to 80,000 to the riverfront to celebrate the Fourth of July. It's a free afternoon and evening of music and fireworks, sponsored by the mayor's office and Metro Parks and Recreation. You'll find food and alcohol-free drinks, too, but you'll have to pay for that. The family-oriented celebration usually kicks off around 4 p.m.; a variety of locally popular bands and the Nashville Symphony perform at the riverfront stage. If you come early, you can find a spot to sit and relax on the tiered hillside facing the Cumberland River; it's a great place to listen to the bands while watching boats travel up and down the river. If you prefer, you can walk along First Avenue while sampling festival food and people-watching. The fireworks display begins around 9 p.m.

UNCLE DAVE MACON DAYS, Cannonsburgh Village, 312 S. Front St., Murfreesboro, TN 37129; (800) 716-7560; uncledavemacondays.org. This nationally recognized old-time music and dance festival is named for Uncle Dave Macon, a pioneer of the *Grand Ole Opry.* The 4-day event, which begins the Thurs following July 4, offers national championship competitions in old-time clogging, old-time buck dancing, and old-time banjo. There's plenty of fiddling, too. Musicians of all ages bring their instruments and get together for impromptu concerts throughout the event. The motorless parade on Sat features mules, horses, and wagons. A gospel celebration is held on Sun. The festival also features a juried crafts show, a variety of food vendors, and historical photo displays, all set against the backdrop of Murfreesboro's Cannonsburgh Village, a re-creation of a pioneer village. Admission is free.

i Nashville's record high temperature of 107 degrees Fahrenheit was set in July 1952. The record low—17 degrees below zero—was set in January 1985.

AUGUST

TENNESSEE WALKING HORSE NATIONAL CELEBRATION, Celebration Grounds, Shelbyville, TN 37162; (931) 684-5915; twhnc.com. This event, the World Grand Championships for the high-stepping Tennessee Walking Horse, has been called "the world's greatest horse show." The 10-day celebration begins in late Aug. When you're not watching the action in the show ring, you can enjoy the trade fairs, dog shows, and elaborately decorated barn area. Shows run 3 to 4 hours, so you'll want to allow plenty of time here. Ticket prices (adults and children) are $7 to $20 for reserved seats. A 10-day package is $100 per person. Groups of 30 or more receive discounts of approximately 30 percent on certain nights. Shows begin at 7 p.m., but the grounds are open all day.

SEPTEMBER

TENNESSEE STATE FAIR, 500 Wedgewood Ave. at Rains Avenue, Nashville, TN 37203; (615) 800-3675; tnstatefair.org. Focusing on livestock and agriculture, the Tennessee State Fair features 4-H Club and Future Farmers and their projects in the Agriculture Hall. Although this isn't one of the better-known state fairs, there's plenty to see and do here. The carnival midway, open until midnight, features all your favorite adult and kiddie rides and games. There are usually crafts, antiques, a petting zoo, and concerts, too, as well as plenty of fair food. The fairgrounds are 4 blocks off I-65. Admission is $8 for adults and teens, $6 for children ages 3 through 17 and free for those ages 2 and under.

AFRICAN STREET FESTIVAL, 1037 Hadley Park, Nashville, TN 37209; (615) 942-0706; aacanashville.org. This 3-day family-oriented ethnic celebration is held the second or third weekend of Sept. It is a major event, drawing tens of thousands to the historic Jefferson Street area. The festival features more than 100 merchants from 25 states, exotic food concessions, and 8 hours of daily entertainment. There is something for everyone. The stage show features art, lots of music—blues, gospel, African drums, jazz, rap, and reggae—as well as poetry and drama. Other attractions are African dance lessons, children's storytelling, a teen tent, art show, fashion show, and lectures. Admission and parking are free.

GREEK FESTIVAL, 4905 Franklin Pike, Nashville, TN 37220; (615) 333-1047; nashvillegreekfestival.com. Celebrated on the church grounds of Holy Trinity Greek Orthodox Church on Fri through Sun, the Greek Festival was first held in 1987. Admission to the 3-day event is $3. Greek music, dancing, food, arts, and handcrafts are featured. Popular menu items are spanakopita (spinach and cheese triangle pastry made with layers of filo dough), dolmades (vegetarian stuffed grape leaves), moussaka (layers of eggplant, grated cheese, and ground beef, topped with creamy béchamel sauce, served with green beans and pita bread), and baklava (filo pastry with walnuts, covered with honey syrup).

i During the summer, Full Moon Pickin' Parties take place at Percy Warner Park's Equestrian Center, 2520 Old Hickory Blvd., roughly at the time of each full moon. The parties feature a variety of small jam sessions. Musicians who bring their instruments get in free. For everyone else, admission is about $20 in advance or $25 at the gate for adults age 18 and up, $10 for youth ages 7 to 17 ($7 in advance), and free for children 6 and under. A season pass for all 6 pickin' parties is $100. For reservations or more information, contact Friends of Warner Park at (615) 370-8053; warnerparks.com.

OCTOBER

CELEBRATION OF CULTURES, Centennial Park, 2500 West End Ave., Nashville, TN 37203; (615) 340-7500; celebratenashville.org. This free international festival began in 1996 to celebrate the cultural diversity of Nashville and Middle Tennessee. Japanese, Korean, African-American, Chinese, Greek, Kurdish, and rural Appalachian are among the more than 40 cultures represented. Dancers, musicians, storytellers, and exhibits provide the entertainment with more than 50 free performances on 7 different stages. Bring your appetite, and sample a variety of ethnic food offerings, including Ethiopian, Indian, Mediterranean, and soul food. A family activity area features storytelling and international games and crafts.

LIVING HISTORY TOUR, Nashville City Cemetery, 1001 Fourth Ave. S. at Oak Street, Nashville, TN 37203; (615) 862-7970; thenashvillecitycemetery.org. For one afternoon only in late Oct, the Nashville City Cemetery is transformed into a theater of sorts, with actors portraying notable Nashvillians who were laid to rest at the historic cemetery. Visitors walk along the paths, taking in mini-skits throughout the graveyard. At dusk, a candlelight tour begins. The whole thing lasts about 90 minutes and is suitable for children. The event, which began in 1999, raises money to support the cemetery. Admission is $5 per person or $10 for families. (See our **Attractions** chapter for more on Nashville City Cemetery.)

NASHVILLE SYMPHONY FREE DAY OF MUSIC, Schermerhorn Symphony Center, 1 Symphony Place, Nashville, TN 37201; (615) 687-6500; nashvillesymphony.org. Free music galore with more than 20 performers on several stages all day long. A favorite is the "Instrument Petting Zoo" where children can get a hands-on introduction to all instrument families in the orchestra, including brass, woodwind, strings, and percussion.

FALL TENNESSEE CRAFT FAIR, Centennial Park, 2500 West End Ave., Nashville, TN 37203; (615) 736-7600; tennesseecraft.org. Nearly 200 crafters from around the country, selected for the quality of their work, exhibit at this juried market of fine crafts. The fair is loaded with pottery, art, jewelry, blown glass, photography, sculpture, and more. Crafts demonstrations and live music round out the activities. A food court with picnic tables is the perfect place to recharge or do some people-watching. Admission is free. The fair is presented by Tennessee Craft (previously the Tennessee Association of Craft Artists).

SOUTHERN FESTIVAL OF BOOKS, War Memorial Plaza, downtown between Charlotte and Union, and Sixth and Seventh Avenues, Nashville, TN 37243; (615) 770-0006; humanitiestennessee.org. More than 30,000 book lovers attend this annual 3-day event sponsored by Humanities Tennessee. Some 200 authors from around the country, with an emphasis on those from the Southeast, gather for readings, panel discussions, and book signings. A children's area features children's authors and activities. Admission is free. The festival is usually held the second weekend of Oct.

***GRAND OLE OPRY* BIRTHDAY CELEBRATION,** *Grand Ole Opry* House, 2804 Opryland Dr., Nashville, TN 37214; (615) 871-6779; opry.com. *Grand Ole Opry* fans gather each Oct to celebrate the birthday of America's longest-running radio program. The 3-day party is held in mid-Oct and includes concerts, a *Grand Ole Opry* performance, and autograph and photo sessions with the stars. (See our **Music City** chapter for more information about the event, and our **History** chapter for more on the *Opry*.)

NAIA POW WOW, Long Hunter State Park, 2910 Hobson Pike, Hermitage, TN 37076; (615) 232-9179; naiatn.org. The Native American Indian Association sponsors this annual event that brings together Native Americans from throughout North America. As many as 25 tribes are represented, and the general public is invited. It's held on the third weekend of Oct. Competitive dancing, arts and crafts, storytelling, demonstrations, and fine art displays are among the festivities. Food booths feature traditional foods from various tribes. Admission is $8 for ages 14 and older, $4 for ages 6 to 12, and free for 5 and under.

NASHVILLE OKTOBERFEST, 998 Fifth Ave. N., Franklin, TN 37219; (615) 686-2867; thenashvilleoktoberfest.com. Spanning 10 city blocks, Oktoberfest has something for everyone. The popular festival offers live German music, arts and crafts vendors, world-class beer from local breweries, German food from local restaurants and vendors, the 2nd largest 5K Race and Run in Tennessee, plus much more. An unusual offering is the free Dachshund Derby. That's right, the beloved "weiner dogs" run down a 50-foot track to see who claims the winning medals. Oktoberfest runs from Thurs through Sun.

NOVEMBER

CHRISTMAS VILLAGE, Tennessee State Fairgrounds, 500 Wedgewood Ave., Nashville, TN 37203; (615) 256-2726; christmasvillage.org. This annual event at the fairgrounds features more than 250 merchants with seasonal and gift items. You'll find Christmas ornaments, hand-painted and personalized items, clothing, pottery, jewelry, toys, and food items. Kids can also visit with Santa. The 3-day mid-Nov event benefits the Vanderbilt Bill Wilkerson Hearing & Speech Center and Pi Beta Phi philanthropies. Admission is $10 for anyone 10 and older; children 9 and younger get in free. Advance tickets are available for $8.

COUNTRY CHRISTMAS, Gaylord Opryland Resort & Convention Center, 2800 Opryland Dr., Nashville, TN 37214; (615) 889-1000; marriott.com/Gaylord-hotels/Gaylord-opryland-nashville. An outing to the Opryland Hotel during the holidays is a tradition for many Nashvillians, and the hotel is a popular place to take visiting friends and relatives this time of year. Wide-eyed visitors marvel at the hotel's outdoor lights display of more than 3 million bulbs. The decorations indoors are spectacular as well. About a million visitors show up for the festivities each year. If you wait until late in the season to visit, you'll probably end up in a major traffic jam (often extending for miles down Briley Parkway), and once inside the hotel, you'll find it jam-packed as well. To avoid the crowds, get in the spirit early and come in November—the earlier the better. If you plan to visit only the hotel, you'll have to pay only for parking, $29. Of course, once inside, you're bound to want to stop in one of the many food and drink spots for a holiday treat. Country Christmas includes a breakfast with Santa for the kids, a room full of life-size ice sculptures, and an art, antiques, and crafts fair. Several events, such as the Yule Log lighting ceremony and nightly Dancing Waters fountain shows, are free.

DECEMBER

YULEFEST, Historic Mansker's Station, 705 Caldwell Ln., Goodlettsville, TN 37072; (615) 859-3678; goodlettsvillechamber.com. "A 1780s Candlelight Christmas" is the theme of Yulefest, held the first weekend in Dec. Guides in period dress reenact colonial Christmas customs at this historic site, which features a reconstruction of a 1779 frontier fort, Mansker's Station. There are refreshments, music, decorations, and horse-drawn wagon rides, too. The historic brick structure on the site is Bowen Plantation House; built in 1787, it was the first brick home in Middle Tennessee and is listed on the National

Register of Historic Places. Admission is free. (For more info about Mansker's Station and Bowen Plantation House, see our **Attractions** chapter.)

DICKENS OF A CHRISTMAS, downtown Franklin, TN 37065; (615) 591-8514; visitfranklin.com. You'll feel like you've stepped back in time to a Charles Dickens Christmas during this event, held the second full weekend in Dec in historic downtown Franklin. For those 2 days, 2 blocks of Main Street are themed to the 1800s. You'll see carolers in Victorian costumes as well as characters such as Scrooge and the ghosts of Christmases past, present, and future. In the store windows, artisans dressed in period clothing demonstrate crafts of the 1800s. Shopkeepers dress in period clothing, too. Take a ride in a horse-drawn carriage, then visit a street vendor for a bag of kettle corn, some sugarplums, plum pudding, tea, or hot cider. Admission is free.

NASHVILLE BALLET'S *NUTCRACKER*, 3630 Redmon St., Nashville, TN 37209; (615) 297-2966; nashvilleballet.com. The Nashville Ballet's version of *The Nutcracker* was an immediate hit when it opened in the late 1980s, and it has become a holiday tradition for many Nashvillians. In addition to the Nashville Ballet, the production features local children and the Nashville Symphony. Tickets range from about $25 to $75.

Itineraries

HONKY TONK HIGHWAY

You might not find it on a map, but Honky Tonk Highway is one of the most popular destinations in Nashville. It's the affectionate nickname for downtown Broadway's row of iconic bars. Live music goes all day, from 10 a.m. to 3 a.m. There's no cover charge. Folks wander in and out as the spirit moves them. Families with children often sit on stools or at tables listening to real musicians play real music. Families are welcome until 6 p.m., then most establishments enforce the over-21 rule.

With its close proximity to the historic Ryman Auditorium—said to be only 26 steps from Tootsie's—you can just imagine the legends who might have stopped on Honky Tonk Highway for a cold one before or after performing at the *Grand Ole Opry*. Even today, you never know who you might spot in these Lower Broadway clubs.

Legend says that Willie Nelson got his first songwriting job after singing at Tootsie's. Kris Kristofferson was known to spend hours at Tootsie's soaking up vibes for the treasured tunes he wrote. Likewise, Roger Miller was said to have been inspired to write "Dang Me" while cooling his toes at Tootsie's. Gretchen Wilson and Dierks Bentley are among the newer entertainers who got their starts on Honky Tonk Highway. That great band or young singer you see performing free in a Honky Tonk Highway bar might be the next big star.

By the way, bring some extra dollar bills. Most of these performers are singing and playing for free. They get paid from the tip jar, so give them a hand and a financial hand up if you can.

Sitting on the corner of Fifth and Broadway, **Legends Corner** (428 Broadway; 615-248-6334; legendscorner.com) guards the entrance to **Honky Tonk Highway.** The walls of Legends Corner are lined with thousands of vintage album covers. Name a favorite star, and his or her album will most likely be there.

Next door to Legends is Nashville's most famous honky-tonk, **Tootsie's Orchid Lounge** (422 Broadway; 615-726-0463; tootsies.net), known far and wide for its orchid-purple exterior. Many famous musicians such as Hank Williams, Willie Nelson, Patsy Cline, Tom T. Hall, Charley Pride, and Kris Kristofferson called Tootsie's "home." The bar's namesake, Hattie "Tootsie" Louis

Broadway is known as Honky Tonk Highway because of all its music clubs and bars. Jackie Sheckler Finch

Tatum Bess, was a singer/comedian who bought the club in 1960. Stories abound that Tootsie would keep a cigar box of food and drink IOUs from *Opry* performers. She was known to slip some cash into the pockets of down-on-their-luck pickers and singers. Tootsie died of cancer on Feb 18, 1978. Loyal customers from minimum-wage earners to country music icons paid their respects at her funeral.

A little farther down the block is **Robert's Western World** (416 Broadway; 615-244-9552; robertswesternworld.com) where you can buy a pair of cowboy boots while you listen to bluegrass and honky-tonk music. Stars sometime show up to hang out and often end up taking the stage for a song or two. Famous faces who've visited Robert's include Merle Haggard, Kid Rock, Brooks & Dunn, Dolly Parton, and Tracy Byrd. Jesse Lee Jones is Robert's proprietor and leader of the house band Brazilbilly. A former house band was BR549, who went on to sign a major-label record deal. If you want to stay up all night or catch a few hours of sleep before coming back, Robert's offers Sunday Morning Gospel Fellowship at 10:30 a.m. every Sunday. Everyone is welcome to the service that features traditional gospel music and nondenominational spiritual messages.

Sandwiched between Second Fiddle and Robert's in downtown Nashville is **Layla's Honky Tonk** (418 Broadway; 615-726-2799; laylasnashville.com), a cozy club that offers traditional bluegrass and much more. Sure, bluegrass legend Ralph Stanley has graced Layla's stage, but so have other music styles such as Hank Williams III and the Drive-By Truckers. Check out Layla's music schedule and you'll see a wide range of music and performers. Layla's has plenty of seating and bunches of dancing room. As for those license plates decorating Layla's, if you've got one handy, take it in and swap it for a cold brew. Then your license will become part of the growing decor.

Blake Shelton at Ole Red Courtesy of Erika Goldring

Step into **The Second Fiddle** (420 Broadway; 615-251-6812; thesecond fiddle.com) between Tootsie's and Layla's and step back in time. Dozens of old radios and musical instruments line the walls of this large bar. Look for a guitar signed by Mother Maybelle Carter, the Carter family, and Johnny Cash. Bunches of *Grand Ole Opry* memorabilia help provide the country decor. Celebrity performers have been known to walk through these doors, including Tim McGraw, Kix Brooks, David Frizzell, Tracy Byrd, and Trick Pony. If the place looks familiar, it has shown up in music videos and album photos. McBride and the Ride filmed a video here. Second Fiddle was the setting of "40 Greatest Drinking Songs" with Wynonna Judd. Pam Tillis used shots of the honky-tonk for an album.

The Stage (412 Broadway; 615-726-0504; thestageonbroadway.com) is exactly that—the biggest stage on Broadway. One of the newer spots on Lower Broadway's famed live music scene, The Stage was home to the Roy Acuff Museum in the 1960s and 1970s. Located just a few doors down from Tootsie's, The Stage has two floors with seating. Upstairs has the best overall views. Wall murals salute legends like Hank Williams, Johnny Cash, Willie Nelson, and the Highwaymen. Famous musicians have dropped in for a drink and a jam session, including Toby Keith and Joe Diffie.

Honky Tonk Central (329 Broadway; 615-742-9095; honkytonkcentral.com) offers live music flowing from all 3 floors of the huge 9,400-square-foot building's balconies. Honky Tonk Central is a popular spot for bachelor and bachelorette parties.

County music stars also are opening new places on Honky Tonk Highway—**Jason Aldean's Kitchen + Rooftop Bar** (307 Broadway; jasonaldeansnashville.com); **John Rich's Redneck Riviera** (208 Broadway, 615-436-4070; redneckrivieranashville.com); **Luke's (Bryan) 32 Bridge** (301 Broadway; lukes32bridge.com); **Dierks Bentley's Whiskey Row** (400 Broadway; 629-203-7822; dierkswhiskeyrow.com); **FGL (Florida Georgia Line) House** (129 Third Ave S.; 615-961-5460; fglhouse.com); Blake Shelton's **Ole Red** (300 Broadway; 615-780-0900; olered.com/nashville); and **AJ's (Alan Jackson) Good Time Bar** (421 Broadway; 615-678-4808; ajsgoodtimebar.com).

WIDOW OF THE SOUTH

The Battle of Franklin is known as "the five bloodiest hours of the Civil War." *National Geographic* described it as "the most unjustly forgotten battle of the entire Civil War." Some 9,500 soldiers were killed, wounded, captured, or counted as missing. Nearly 7,000 of that number were Confederates.

To step back in history, follow a "Widow of the South" itinerary in **Franklin** (695-591-8514; visitfranklin.com), about 17 miles and "100 years south" of Nashville. The name of the tour is a nod to the 2005 *New York Times* bestselling novel *Widow of the South* written by Robert Hicks.

Luminaries at the Carter House Courtesy of Tennessee Department of Tourist Development

A board member at the **Carnton Plantation** (1345 Eastern Flank Cir.; 615-794-0903; boft.org/carnton), Hicks became fascinated with the story of the woman who lived there, Carrie McGavock. "She became famous without ever leaving her farm, renowned for her daily wandering in the cemetery, for her mourning clothes, for her letters to the families of the bereaved, and most of all, for her constancy," Hicks wrote in the book's author note. "From the day the last of the dead was buried in her back yard, she never really left her post in the cemetery, continuously checking her book of the dead."

For extra background, read the book before you start off your day at Carnton Plantation and hear about the role the 1826 antebellum plantation played in the Civil War. Built by Randal McGavock, Nashville's mayor in 1824 and 1825, the elegant estate was on the rear lines of the Confederate forces and witnessed a steady stream of dying and wounded during the battle. The home was used as a Confederate hospital after the bloody Battle of Franklin on Nov 30, 1864. The Confederates lost at least 12 generals during the battle. At one time the bodies of four slain Confederate generals were laid out on the back porch. The floors of the restored house are still stained with the blood of the men who were treated here.

Within view of that historic porch rests the only privately owned Confederate cemetery in the world. In early 1866, John and Carrie McGavock designated 2 acres of land near their family cemetery as a final resting place for nearly 1,500 Confederate soldiers killed during the Battle of Franklin. The McGavocks maintained the cemetery until their deaths.

Guided tours of Carnton Plantation take about an hour with another hour or so spent exploring the grounds and outbuildings and browsing in the gift shop.

About 1.25 miles from Carnton is the **Carter House** (1140 Columbia Ave.; 615-791-1861; boft.org/carter-house), considered to have the most bullet-damaged building from the Civil War still standing anywhere. More than 1,000 bullet holes are evident in the main structure and various outbuildings.

The 1.5-story brick house was built in 1830 by Fountain Branch Carter, a successful farmer. During the battle, Union Brig. Gen. Jacob Cox took possession of the house and made the parlor his headquarters. As the battle raged, the Carter family, the Lotz family from across the street, and several Carter slaves took refuge in the basement.

After the battle, the Carter House parlor was turned into a Confederate field hospital and witnessed many surgeries. In fact, soldiers would be dying for decades afterward from wounds they received at the Battle of Franklin.

Take 110 steps across the street to the **Lotz House** (1111 Columbia Ave.; 615-790-7190; lotzhouse.com) built in 1858 by German immigrant Johan Albert Lotz. When Union soldiers marched into Franklin, they quickly dug protective trenches and created barricades from anything they could find, including the Lotz's white picket fence.

When Lotz saw that the main Union Line was yards from his home, he feared his wooden plank house wouldn't survive the warfare. He and his family sought refuge in the brick basement of the Carter House. When the fighting ended and the families exited the basement the next day, they were horrified to see dead bodies stretching before them almost as far as they could look.

The Army of Tennessee died at the Franklin battle. It was a fight from which they never recovered.

Tours of the Lotz home are available as is a walking tour of the Franklin battlefield. Leaving from the Carter House, the tour helps explain why the battle happened, what took place, and how it ended. The Battlefield Walking Tour lasts about 90 minutes.

While in Franklin, spend some time shopping and eating. The lovely little town was founded Oct 26, 1799, and named after Benjamin Franklin. The historic downtown district is nationally recognized as a Great American Main Street. A gem of Southern hospitality, Franklin has a 16-block National Register district of antiques shops, gift stores, art galleries, brick sidewalks, Victorian buildings, restaurants, and lovingly restored homes.

Before leaving town, stroll around the town square and meet "Chip," the marble Confederate soldier standing permanently on duty. Chip got his nickname from a missing piece in the brim of his hat. On Nov 30, 1899, the 35th anniversary of the Battle of Franklin, several thousand people crowded into Franklin for a commemoration. Part of the festivities included erecting the statue paid for by the Daughters of the Confederacy. However, a rope that workmen had attached to the statue was snagged when a 75-year-old man accidentally drove his horse against it. The statue's hat brim snapped off. Officials decided to leave it that way.

MUSIC VALLEY/OPRYLAND

Some folks come to Nashville to visit the Music Valley/Opryland area and never go elsewhere. Others head straight for Nashville's Broadway and spend all their time there. Oh, what both one-destination travelers are missing.

For me, no visit to Nashville is complete without going to Music Valley and strolling through the grand Gaylord Opryland Resort & Convention Center and attending the *Grand Ole Opry*. Likewise, I can't imagine being in Nashville without hearing music in the downtown honky-tonks.

So this itinerary will feature what to do in the Music Valley/Opryland section of Nashville. Combine it with a trip down Honky Tonk Highway as featured in one of our other itineraries in this chapter and you'll have a heck of a time.

Of course, the real biggie along McGavock Pike is the **Gaylord Opryland Resort & Convention Center** (2800 Opryland Dr.; 615-889-1000; marriott.com/hotels/travel/bnago-gaylord-opryland-resort-and-convention-center). And I do mean big. Like, huge. It is the largest hotel in the world without an attached casino.

Opened on Thanksgiving Day in 1977, the hotel features a stunning Magnolia Lobby with a lovely staircase and Tiffany-style chandelier. The lobby was designed to resemble a grand Southern mansion. Countless wedding photos have been taken on that iconic staircase.

Today, the smoke-free Gaylord Opryland Resort offers 2,712 guest rooms and 171 suites on 6 floors. But that's only part of what this impressive resort has. A river flows through the signature glass atriums, plus there are waterfalls, walking paths, and lush tropical plants in the 9 acres of indoor gardens. There are even flatboats to carry guests through the hotel's Delta.

Hotel amenities include indoor and outdoor swimming pools, health spa, nightclub, 17 restaurants that serve everything from sushi to steak, and shops with everything from bejeweled country and western attire to souvenir T-shirts and local chocolates.

The newest addition is the $90 million SoundWaves which opened Dec 1, 2018. The exciting 111,000-square-foot water experience features 4 acres of combined indoor and outdoor water attractions on 3 levels. Rides are intertwined with living walls and plant beds which help it blend in with the resort's 9 acres of garden atriums. The unique SoundWaves' roof brings in the sun while the indoor attraction is kept at 84 degrees year-round.

SoundWaves features tube slides, body slides, family raft ride, rapid and lazy rivers, wave pool, mat racer, multilevel play structure, kiddie pool, rock climbing wall, arcade, cabanas, Decibels restaurant, 2 outdoor food trucks, bars, and an adults-only pool and bar named "Status Cymbal" on the top indoor level. The indoor water attractions are open year-round. Outdoor water attractions are open May through Labor Day. SoundWaves is available only to hotel guests.

If your budget allows, spend a couple of nights at the Gaylord Opryland Resort. It will take at least a day to explore the resort and another day or two to enjoy other attractions across the street and down the road. Check out the resort website for special package prices and be aware that on-site parking at the resort costs $29 a day. If money is tight, stay across the street at the **Fiddler's Inn** (2410 Music Valley Dr.; 615-885-1440; fiddlersinnopryland.com) where you can park free and walk to the Gaylord Opryland and many local attractions.

At the top of many a visitor's must-do list is attending the ***Grand Ole Opry*** (2804 Opryland Dr.; 615-871-6779; opry.com). Premiering in 1925, the *Grand Ole Opry* had several homes before relocating in 1974 to a new specially built, state-of-the-art facility in the Music Valley area near the Gaylord Opryland Resort. To keep in touch with memories of the *Opry*'s longtime home at the Ryman Auditorium in downtown Nashville, the new *Grand Ole Opry* House has a 6-foot circle of hardwood taken from the Ryman and placed center stage at the *Opry* House. Hard telling what famous folks from Patsy Cline and Hank Williams to Minnie Pearl and Roy Acuff have stood on that circle.

Every *Opry* show includes a dozen performances ranging from the biggest names in country music to up-and-comers making their *Opry* debuts. For a special behind-the-scenes look, take a *Grand Ole Opry* Backstage Tour where you can walk in the footsteps of the great. Guides share stories about past and present *Opry* stars, show photos from the *Opry*'s long history, let you peek in the performers' dressing rooms, and take you to the artist entrance where large photographs of Minnie Pearl and Roy Acuff greet folks—from superstars to new artists and guests—as they enter and exit.

For a pleasant cruise plus a good meal and great music, book a trip on the ***General Jackson* Showboat** (2812 Opryland Dr.; 615-458-3900; generaljackson.com). The 300-foot paddle wheeler has a 2-story Victorian Theater where dinner is served and shows are presented. Cruises include afternoon, evening, and Sunday brunch. The boat landing is near the Opry Mills shopping center. Just look for the signs. If you are staying at the Gaylord Opryland Resort, a shuttle will take you to the landing. The 2- to 3-hour cruise on the Cumberland River provides beautiful views of the Nashville skyline. The boat, of course, is named for native son General Andrew Jackson.

Shoppers love **Opry Mills** (433 Opry Mills Dr.; 615-514-1000; simon.com/mall/opry-mills). The indoor mall boasts more than 200 stores, plus full-service dining options and IMAX and movie theaters.

Across the street from the Gaylord Opryland Resort is a wealth of motels, restaurants, music places, shops, and museums. The **Willie Nelson & Friends General Store & Museum** (2613 McGavock Pike; 615-885-1515; willienelsonmuseum.com) showcases personal items of the old outlaw himself as well as those of his many friends. Some of the items include Willie Nelson's first Martin guitar that he played when he debuted on the *Grand Old Opry* in November of 1963, along with his signed paycheck from that night—take-home pay an amazing $11.71. Also in the museum are famous Nudie rhinestone suits worn by Porter Wagoner and Webb Pierce; handwritten diaries of Patsy Cline; Ronnie Milsap's autographed one-of-a-kind *Playboy* magazine printed completely in Braille; and much more. General Store merchandise includes Willie T-shirts, shot glasses, cowboy hats, souvenir guitars, and other items.

The Texas Troubadour Theatre (2416 Music Valley Dr.; 615-585-9301; texastroubadourtheatre.com) has hosted the *Ernest Tubb Midnite Jamboree* for almost 70 years. The country-music radio show is taped every Saturday night at 10 p.m. following the *Grand Ole Opry* and broadcast at midnight. The free show is hosted by special guests each week. On Sunday mornings at 10 a.m., Cowboy Church is held in the Texas Troubadour Theatre featuring Dr. Harry Yates and Joanne Cash Yates, the sister of Johnny Cash.

Also across from the Gaylord Opryland, the **Nashville Palace** (2611 McGavock Pike; 615-889-1541; nashville-palace.com) is a live traditional country-music venue, bar, restaurant, and souvenir shop. Nearby is **Cooter's Place** (2613 McGavock Pike; 615-872-8358; cootersplace.com), filled with *Dukes of Hazzard* memorabilia. In the beloved TV series, Cooter (actor Ben Jones) was the sidekick of the good old Duke boys. The free museum has Cooter's tow truck, Daisy's Jeep, Rosco's patrol car, and of course, the 1969 Dodge Charger, General Lee.

Save time to experience a celebration of country music from both past and present at the 300-seat **Nashville Nightlife Dinner Theatre** (2416 Music Valley Dr.; 615-885-4747; nashvillenightlife.com). The all-you-can-eat dinner buffet includes country favorites such as fried chicken, ribs, baked potatoes, veggies, and cobblers for dessert.

ARTSY ADVENTURES

Nashville has a well-known reputation as "Music City," but this friendly place along the Cumberland River also has a vibrant arts scene. If you haven't experienced that yet, here are a few of the many artsy places that also have helped Nashville earn the nickname "Athens of the South."

Start off your Artsy Adventures itinerary at the **Parthenon** (2500 West End Ave.; 615-862-8431; nashville.gov/parks-and-recreation/parthenon). Located in Centennial Park, the Parthenon is the world's only full-size reproduction of the Greek Parthenon. The Nashville beauty houses a statue of Athena, a whopping 42 feet high, sculpted by Nashville artist Alan LeQuire. It is the tallest indoor sculpture in the Western world. Unveiled in 1990, the statue was gilded and painted with 23.75-carat gold in 2002. In her right hand, Athena holds the goddess Nike, which stands 6 feet 4 inches tall.

Listed on the National Register of Historic Places, Nashville's Parthenon mirrors the dimensions of the original to an eighth of an inch. The first Nashville Parthenon was built between 1895 and 1897 as the centerpiece for the state's Centennial Exposition. It's a symbol of the city's reputation as the Athens of the South. While the other Centennial buildings were demolished after the expo, the Parthenon was so popular that Nashville kept it and Centennial Park was created around it in the early 1900s. After it had begun to deteriorate, it was rebuilt with concrete from 1920 to 1931. Today, the Parthenon boasts an impressive art collection, including the Cowan Collection, which features more than 60 works by 19th- and 20th-century American painters.

A statue outside Schermerhorn Symphony Center is a thank you from the Nashville Symphony to Nashville citizens for building the beautiful center. Jackie Sheckler Finch

After lunch, head to the **Frist Art Museum** (919 Broadway; 615-244-3340; fristartmuseum.org) and plan to spend the afternoon. It is quite a place, and it is easy to lose track of time here. Housed in a stunning art deco 1934 US Post Office built as a New Deal project, the museum features wonderful exhibits from museums and collections around the world. Browse through the gift shop before leaving. I bought my favorite pair of earrings here. Reasonable prices; beautiful stuff.

Next check out what's playing at the **Schermerhorn Symphony Center** (1 Symphony Place; 615-687-6400; nashvillesymphony.org) for a relaxing musical end to an artsy day. Comparable to some of the greatest music halls in the world, the $120-million Schermerhorn Symphony Center opened in 2006 as an acoustic masterpiece. Located on a city block between Third and Fourth Avenues S., the center is home to the Nashville Symphony Orchestra. It was named in honor of the late Kenneth Schermerhorn, music director and conductor of the orchestra.

The spectacular center boasts 1,872 seats on 3 levels and features 30 soundproof windows, making it one of the few major concert halls in North America with natural light. The 85-member orchestra offers about 150 performances annually in a broad range of classical, popular, jazz, and children's concerts. Guest artists also are featured, so check the Schermerhorn website to see what performance you would like to hear, purchase tickets, and arrange your Artsy Adventures around it.

After the Schermerhorn, it's time for bed or maybe for a nightcap before retiring and getting rested for our exciting second day of Artsy Adventures.

After a leisurely breakfast, it's off to **Cheekwood Botanical Garden & Museum of Art** (1200 Forrest Park Dr., 615-356-8000; cheekwood.org). The 1929 Cheekwood mansion is surrounded by 55 acres of botanical gardens, lawns, and fountains. The private estate was once home to the Leslie Cheek family of the Maxwell House coffee fortune. The Cheeks gave the property to the nonprofit Tennessee Botanical Gardens and Fine Arts Center in 1960.

Today the mansion houses the prestigious Museum of Art with its collection of 19th- and 20th-century American art as well as major traveling art exhibits. Along the border of the property is the Woodland Sculpture Trail, a mile-long trail featuring more than a dozen sculptures by artists from around the world.

Cheekwood has a lovely place for lunch, the new Café 29 operated by French-American bar and restaurant Sea Salt. Located inside the newly restored Frist Learning Center Courtyard, the cafe is open 9 a.m. to 4 p.m. Tues through Sun. The menu features soups, sandwiches, salads, smoothies, baked goods, children's menu, alcoholic beverages, and, of course, famous Maxwell House coffee.

After lunch, spend more time at Cheekwood and be sure to visit the gift shop for neat garden items. Or, if you are ready to leave Cheekwood, you can visit some of the art galleries listed in our **Entertainment** chapter. Nashville's art scene is booming with festivals, art crawls, and galleries. Plan ahead and enjoy one of the art crawls.

The first Saturday of every month 6 to 9 p.m., Nashville art galleries throughout the downtown host receptions and art openings featuring local and world-renowned artists and artwork. Admission is free to the **First Saturday Art Crawl** (nashvilledowntown.com/play/first-saturday-art-crawl; 615-743-3090) and most galleries serve free wine and other refreshments. Some also feature live music. It's a great way to spend a Saturday night and experience downtown Nashville as an art center.

A free shuttle circulates continuously along the art crawl route 6 to 10 p.m. One of the stops on the art crawl is **Hatch Show Print** (224 Fifth Ave. S.; 615-577-7710; hatchshowprint.com). If you haven't already been to this nifty place or if you would like to go again, this is a good chance to catch the shuttle and see some of the artwork at this historic print shop.

Founded in 1879 in downtown Nashville, Hatch Show Print is the oldest working letter-print shop in America. It is best known for its posters of *Grand Ole Opry* stars. Hatch Show Print's Haley Gallery showcases historic restrikes of original posters from the Hatch collection, as well as master printer Jim

Nashville skyline Nashville Convention & Visitors Corporation

Sherraden's monoprints—contemporary interpretations and celebrations of the classic wood blocks of Hatch Show Print.

While you are out and about on Artsy Adventures, look up in the sky to see what many folks feel is an unusual artistic icon on Nashville's skyline. With its two pointy peaks and dark facade, the tallest building in Nashville has a nickname—the Batman Building. Built in 1994, the eye-catching $94-million Commerce Street skyscraper that looks like Batman's visage is actually the AT&T Tower—a terrific 33-story landmark for a terrific artsy city.

APPENDIX: Living Here

In this section we feature specific information for residents or those planning to relocate here. Topics include real estate, education, retirement, and much more.

Relocation

If you're relocating to Nashville, have recently moved here, or are in the market for a new home in the area, this chapter is for you. In the following pages we'll tell you about Nashville-area neighborhoods, give you the scoop on the real estate scene, and provide a list of resources that will come in handy. Nashville has come a long way since the pioneering folks of 1779 established a settlement on the banks of the Cumberland River. The city has continued to grow and expand its boundaries in every direction, and the population has boomed. Today more than 1.9 million people live in the 14-county Nashville-Davidson-Murfreesboro-Franklin Metropolitan Statistical Area. (MSA counties are Davidson, Cannon, Cheatham, Dickson, Hickman, Macon, Maury, Robertson, Rutherford, Smith, Sumner, Trousdale, Wilson, and Williamson.)

GETTING ESTABLISHED

This section offers information on resources related to Metro government, schools, utility connections, vehicle registration and driver's licenses, libraries, hospitals, and more. See our **Education & Child Care**, **Retirement**, and **Media** chapters for other useful newcomer information. Most of the listings in this section apply to the Metropolitan Nashville–Davidson County area only.

METRO GOVERNMENT, (615) 862-5000 (information); nashville.gov. Metro Nashville's website—nashville.gov—is an excellent source of information on all things related to Metro government. You'll find information on business, education, employment, health care services, residential resources, transportation, and much more.

Chambers of Commerce & Visitor Bureaus

The Nashville Chamber of Commerce can provide general information about the area as well as information on businesses. For information on other local chambers of commerce and visitor bureaus in the Nashville area, see the individual write-ups on counties, cities, and neighborhoods in this chapter.

NASHVILLE CHAMBER OF COMMERCE, (615) 743-3000; nashvillechamber.com.

NASHVILLE CONVENTION & VISITORS CORPORATION, (800) 657-6910; visitmusiccity.com.

Libraries

The Nashville Public Library has 20 branches throughout Davidson County in addition to the main location downtown. The library also operates the Nashville Talking Library, an audio reading service that broadcasts around-the-clock readings to those who cannot read normally printed matter because of a visual or physical impairment or because of a reading disability. Visit the library online at library.nashville.org or call (615) 862-5800 for more information about the library system or to search the card catalog and check for availability of materials.

NEIGHBORHOODS

With so many great neighborhoods, choosing one in which to live can be tough. You can use the neighborhood descriptions in this section to aid you in your search or just to learn more about the different communities in and around Nashville. We use the term *neighborhood* pretty loosely. While Green Hills could be considered a neighborhood, the area also has several smaller neighborhoods that each has its own character and style. The same is true for most other areas we call "neighborhoods." If you are relocating or are considering moving to another part of town, we highly recommend making several exploratory visits to different parts of town so you can get a good feel for what these areas are like.

Metropolitan Nashville-Davidson County

This very urbanized county includes those satellite cities mentioned previously as well as other extensive residential areas. Following is an overview, including some history of Metro neighborhoods.

Downtown Area

Second Avenue

Among downtown Nashville's numerous historic neighborhoods, the oldest—Second Avenue, or "the District" as we sometimes call it—offers city living in the truest sense. Serious urbanites who want to feel the pulse of the city—day and night—can live here in the heart of downtown, among the neon lights and hustle and bustle of Music City. The Second Avenue area is rich in history. Second Avenue Historic District is listed on the National Register of Historic Places. Until 1903 Second Avenue was called Market Street. The center of commercial activity in the last half of the 1800s, the street was lined with 2- to 5-story brick Victorian warehouses that were 1 block deep. Their back entrances on Front Street (now First Avenue) received goods unloaded from vessels that had traveled down the Cumberland River. Groceries, hardware, dry goods, and other items were sold out of the buildings' Market Street entrances. Most of the buildings were built between 1870 and 1890. Later, as the railroads became the preferred method of transporting goods, and as shipping on the Cumberland declined, many of the buildings closed their doors; others served as warehouses. In the 1960s, when Nashvillians moved to the suburbs in droves, these historically significant buildings were largely unoccupied.

Burgeoning interest in historic preservation during the 1970s was a boon to this district. Businesses such as restaurants and retail shops opened in the old warehouses, and development boomed during the late 1980s. Today Second Avenue's restored 100-year-old warehouses contain unique shops, galleries, restaurants, nightclubs, and offices. For information about residential options in the downtown Nashville area, call the nonprofit Nashville Downtown Partnership at (615) 743-3090 or visit the website at nashvilledowntown.com.

Germantown

Bordered by Eighth and Third Avenues N. between Jefferson and Hume Streets and spanning about 18 city blocks, historic Germantown is Nashville's oldest residential neighborhood. In the past few years, investment and redevelopment in the area have boomed.

German immigrants established the community in the late 1840s, and it grew into a truly diverse neighborhood, home to both wealthy and working-class families. The diversity is reflected in many of the area's homes. Architectural styles here include Italianate, Eastlake, and Queen Anne Victorian homes as well as modest worker cottages. After World War II, many German residents moved out. That exodus, the rezoning of the area to industrial in the 1950s, and the city's urban renewal projects in the 1960s led to the demolition of many of Germantown's historic homes. Preservationists arrived in following decades, however, and have renovated many of the buildings. Much of the new development, such as the row of frame town houses along Fifth Avenue N., is modeled after the area's older buildings.

Today Germantown boasts an interesting mixture of residential, commercial, office, and retail, as well as a diverse community of professionals, blue-collar workers, and others who enjoy living in the inner city. The area attracts lots of single professionals and older professionals who work from their homes. Germantown has its own neighborhood association, Historic Germantown.

> **i** Nashville's historic Germantown area was designated as an Inner City Arboretum by the Nashville Tree Foundation in 1993. Germantown contains more than 135 varieties of trees and major shrubs. For more information about the Nashville Tree Foundation and its Arboretum designations, visit nashvilletreefoundation.org or call the tree hotline at (615) 292-5175.

Visit the association online at historicgermantown.org, or write to it at PO Box 281074, Nashville, TN 37228.

Fisk-Meharry

Between Charlotte Avenue and Jefferson Street and 12th Avenue N. and 28th Avenue S., Fisk-Meharry is a large historic neighborhood full of renovation potential. It is named for nearby Fisk University and Meharry Medical College. Fisk opened in 1866 as a free school for newly freed slaves and is the home of the world-famous Jubilee Singers. Meharry, founded in 1876, was the first medical college for African Americans and today educates 6 out of every 10 of the country's African-American physicians and surgeons.

Architectural styles here include late-1890s and early-1900s 2-story post-Victorian brick homes and American foursquares and stone-and-brick Tudors and clapboard cottages built from 1910 to 1940.

Edgefield

There are several historic districts on the east side of the Cumberland River. The closest to the downtown business district is historic Edgefield, which extends from South Fifth Street eastward to South 10th Street, between Woodland and Shelby Streets. It includes most blocks on Shelby, Boscobel, Fatherland, Russell, and Woodland Streets. Edgefield is one of Nashville's oldest suburbs and was the city's first residential National Trust Historic District (1977) and first locally zoned Historic District (1978), only the second in the state at the time. Edgefield was also Nashville's first urban neighborhood to begin revitalization. Because of Edgefield's designation as one of only two locally zoned historic preservation districts, all new construction, additions, demolition, alterations, and fences must be approved by the Metro Historical Commission.

Though it has changed over the years, Edgefield retains much of the charm of an early Nashville suburb. Tree-lined streets, Historic Edgefield signs marking neighborhood boundaries, an active neighborhood association, and a mix of professionals, young families, and longtime residents combine to create a definite neighborhood feel.

This area was dubbed "Edgefield" by an early resident, Neil S. Brown (Tennessee's governor from 1846 to 1850), who was inspired by his view of the distant fields enclosed by forests. In 1880 Edgefield was incorporated into Nashville's city limits.

Thanks to the arrival of preservationists in the 1970s, Edgefield today boasts a wonderful assortment of lovingly restored old homes, including 2- and 3-story Victorians, post-Victorian Princess Anne cottages, American foursquares, and bungalows. In addition to restoration of historic properties, Edgefield has seen the construction of new single-family homes, apartments, and condominiums. Residents formed the nonprofit neighborhood association Historic Edgefield Inc. in 1976.

East End

This small, middle-class, urban neighborhood east of downtown Nashville is home to professionals, blue-collar workers, and artists, many of whom were drawn to its historic appeal, quietness, and convenience to downtown. East End is between the neighborhoods of Edgefield and Lockeland Springs, extending from Woodland Street to Shelby Avenue between 10th and 14th Streets.

The neighborhood was named East End because at one time it was at the eastern city limits of Edgefield, which was incorporated in 1868. East End boasts nice examples of a variety of architectural styles, including Victorian, Italianate, Eastlake, and Queen Anne.

Lockeland Springs

The third historic neighborhood in the urban area of downtown/east Nashville is Lockeland Springs, just past East End between Gallatin Road and Shelby Avenue, 2 miles northeast of downtown. It's bordered by 14th Street, Eastland Avenue, and Shelby Park. The area was named for Lockeland Mansion, built in the early 19th century by Col. Robert Weakley, whose wife, Jane Locke, was

> i Nashville was ranked the fourth-best US city to retire to in a study by *Black Enterprise* magazine. The rankings were determined based on the following factors: quality of life, health care, taxes, arts and culture, leisure, and climate.

the daughter of Gen. Matthew Locke of North Carolina. Water from the property's Lockeland spring, which some believed to have curative powers, won a grand prize for its mineral composition and "salubrious quality" at the St. Louis Exposition in 1904. The city of Nashville purchased the mansion in 1939, demolished it, and built Lockeland School on the site.

Like East End, Lockeland Springs benefited from the electric streetcar lines installed in the late 1800s. Streetcars allowed residents to travel easily to Nashville's business district across the Cumberland River and made it practical for the middle class to move away from the crowded city.

The well-preserved and architecturally diverse homes in this neighborhood were built from about 1880 to 1940. In the past 2 decades, the neighborhood has seen quite a bit of renovation. This large area is popular with professional renovators as well as first-timers eager to try their hand at restoring a home.

North & Northeast Nashville

Inglewood

Inglewood is a friendly and pleasant community that, according to some local Realtors, is one of the best investment values in Nashville, appealing to first-time buyers as well as investors looking for good rental properties. The neighborhood is just east of Lockeland Springs, off Gallatin Pike. It is bordered roughly by the railroad track at Gallatin Pike, north of Trinity Lane, and extends to Briley Parkway.

Lovers of historic houses will feel right at home here. Inglewood boasts lots of 1920s and 1930s homes with brick and stone exteriors, marble fireplaces, ceramic tile, and good structural quality. There are some newer ranch-style homes, too. You'll find small lots as well as large, well-shaded lots with houses set back off the road. Tidy, well-maintained yards, colorful window boxes, perennial gardens, and lots of green areas add to Inglewood's cheerful personality.

i If you're in the market for a new home and planning to visit open houses, keep in mind that they are usually held on Sunday. When the Tennessee Titans have a Sunday home game, however, some open houses are held on Saturday instead. The *Tennessean*'s weekend editions list the date, location, and other details about open houses.

Madison

Until recently, it was sort of hard to pinpoint the location of the Madison community—one of Nashville's earliest suburbs. If you weren't familiar with the north and east Nashville areas, you could drive right through Madison without even knowing it. Even some longtime Nashvillians are not quite sure where Madison begins and ends. To help identify itself, the community installed signs at several entry points to the area in 1999. Madison doesn't have an identifiable town square or center, just lots of retail areas lining Gallatin Road and established neighborhoods tucked along the side streets.

This neighborhood sits on the northeast edge of Metro Nashville–Davidson County, 8 miles from downtown Nashville. It's south of Goodlettsville and southwest of Old Hickory. The busiest part of town extends along Gallatin Road between Neeley's Bend Road and Old Hickory Boulevard. The community was established in 1840, although a church known as the Spring Hill Meeting House existed in what is now south Madison in the late 1700s.

Between 1859 and 1865, Madison Stratton was hired as a contractor for the L&N Railroad, which passed through the area. The depot he constructed was named for him, putting Madison on the map. The Nashville-Gallatin interurban streetcar track also ran through this community. The old depot was in an area known as Amqui. As the story goes, trains came to such a quick stop in Madison that if you wanted to load something on the train, you'd better do it "damn quick." Madison residents dropped the *d, n,* and the *ck* and came up with the more polite *Amqui* to name their section of town.

Today Madison is home to more than 32,000, including many longtime residents, and has one of the oldest commercial districts in the state.

Goodlettsville

Goodlettsville is one of those cities that offers the best of both worlds: a quiet, small-town feel with all the conveniences of city life close by. An incorporated city within Metropolitan Nashville–Davidson County, Goodlettsville is north of Nashville and Madison and east of Hendersonville.

It encompasses areas around Dickerson Pike, Long Hollow Pike, and I-65. Goodlettsville incorporated in 1857 and again in 1958, but like Nashville's other satellite cities, it remains part of Metro government. Goodlettsville straddles the Davidson and Sumner County lines, so the property taxes vary depending on the county.

Goodlettsville residents receive Goodlettsville city services, not Metro services. The city has a separate police department, including 30 uniformed officers; a separate fire department with 15 full-time firefighters plus volunteers; and separate public works departments, a planning commission, and city manager/city commission government structure. Goodlettsville's easy access to I-65 and the excellent security provided by its police and fire departments make the area appealing to industries. Many businesses have relocated or moved their distribution operations here.

Goodlettsville was originally known as Manskers Station, established by pioneer Kasper Mansker around 1780. For more on Goodlettsville call the chamber of commerce at (615) 859-7979 or visit goodlettsvillechamber.com.

East Nashville

Donelson

Affordable homes draw lots of young families to this southeast Nashville community, which was developed in the 1950s and '60s. The dominant architectural style here is the 1-story ranch. According to a market value report by local real estate appraisers Manier & Exton, homes in the Donelson area have maintained strong appreciation rates since 1993.

In addition to affordability, good location is another plus here. Situated between the Stones and Cumberland Rivers, Donelson offers easy access to the airport and downtown (via I-40) as well as J. Percy Priest Lake. The Tennessee School for the Blind also is located here.

Donelson, named for John Donelson, one of Nashville's founders, is a conservative community with many longtime residents. It boasts a strong chamber of commerce and lots of civic-minded residents. For more information about this area, contact the Donelson-Hermitage Chamber of Commerce at (615) 883-7896 or visit d-hchamber.com.

Hermitage

This east Davidson County community lies between the Stones and Cumberland Rivers. Hermitage Station, a stop along the Tennessee & Pacific Railroad line, once was here. The Hermitage, home of President Andrew Jackson, is nearby.

Affordable land and fairly easy interstate highway access encouraged a lot of speculative building in the Hermitage–Priest Lake area in the 1980s, and the community experienced one of the largest population gains in the area. Today lots of affordable single- and multifamily residences lure home buyers to this neighborhood. For more information about this area, contact the Donelson-Hermitage Chamber of Commerce at (615) 883-7896 or visit donelsonhermitagechamber.com.

Old Hickory

Located in eastern Davidson County between the Cumberland River and Old Hickory Lake, Old Hickory is an unincorporated community of about 9,800 residents. The village was built in 1918 by the DuPont Co. of Philadelphia. The company constructed hundreds of homes for workers at its gunpowder plant, which produced smokeless gunpowder for use in World War I. Today, the area appears much as it did in 1918. Some of the historic homes are being renovated by new owners. The community, which includes the small, incorporated town of Lakewood, is well established and offers affordable housing.

West End/Vanderbilt/Hillsboro Village

Belmont-Hillsboro

Recently, Belmont-Hillsboro has become the hot residential district. Property values have skyrocketed as the academic crowd, artists, musicians, and young professionals clamor for homes in the historic, middle-class neighborhood. Situated between 21st Avenue S./Hillsboro Road and Belmont Boulevard, the area extends north toward Wedgewood and south toward I-440. It's convenient to downtown, Music Row, Vanderbilt University, Belmont University, Green Hills, West End, hospitals, and bus lines. The neighborhood hot spot is Hillsboro Village, a shopping district of eclectic stores, restaurants, and pubs that scores high on the "hip" meter. In the 19th century the area was part of the estate of Adelicia Acklen (see the Belmont Mansion entry in our **Attractions** chapter). In the early 1900s an electric streetcar line along Belmont Boulevard accelerated the neighborhood's transition to a streetcar suburb. Most homes here were built between 1910 and 1940 and range from 1,200-square-foot cottages to 3,500-square-foot bungalows and foursquares on sidewalked streets.

Hillsboro–West End

One of Nashville's oldest neighborhoods, Hillsboro–West End is a large middle- and upper-middle-class neighborhood extending from around Blakemore Avenue to just past I-440, and from Hillsboro Road to West End.

Many Nashvillians refer to this neighborhood as the "Vanderbilt area." The location is great: It's close to Vanderbilt University, Hillsboro Village, Belmont University, Green Hills, and West End, which means there are plenty of places to shop and dine. In fact, many of Nashville's best restaurants are just minutes away. Homes are situated on small, shaded lots, and there are lots of winding, shaded streets leading to little pocket neighborhoods that have their own unique personalities. As for architectural styles here, you'll find mostly classic Tudors, Cape Cods, and bungalows built between 1920 and 1940. There also are some newer properties, including condos.

For more information on this neighborhood, visit the Hillsboro–West End Neighborhood Association online at hwen.org.

Waverly-Belmont to Melrose

Waverly-Belmont/Sunnyside (12th South)

Since the late 1990s, this urban neighborhood has become one of the hottest areas for renovation. The 12th South area has transformed into a hip, eclectic neighborhood with an interesting assortment of businesses, including trendy restaurants, a popular pizzeria, and clothing boutiques.

Renovators are also doing their part, restoring many of the area's old homes, most of which were built from the 1890s to 1930s. Waverly-Belmont is a large neighborhood extending from Belmont Boulevard to Ninth Avenue S. and from Gale Lane north to Bradford Avenue, near Wedgewood. The area includes Waverly Place, adjacent to Woodland-in-Waverly, which is also sometimes considered part of the Waverly-Belmont district. It is convenient to I-440, Music Row, Green Hills, universities, downtown, and the Melrose shopping district. In the center of the neighborhood is Sevier Park and its antebellum Sunnyside Mansion.

The area's great assortment of historic homes makes it appealing to those with an eye to the future. The neighborhood is filled with large Queen Anne, American foursquare, and 1900–1915 Princess Anne homes as well as smaller 1900s shotgun homes and 1920s and 1930s Tudors and bungalows awaiting a renovator's touch.

Waverly Place

When you turn off Eighth Avenue S. onto Douglas Avenue (at Zanies), you'll be greeted by a Welcome to Waverly Place sign. Waverly Place is a small, historic district tucked between Woodland-in-Waverly and Waverly-Belmont, from Eighth to 10th Avenues S. and Wedgewood to Bradford Avenues. It is often considered part of the larger Waverly-Belmont, also referred to as Sunnyside (see separate listings in this section), a larger district that is ripe for renovation.

Sidewalks line both sides of the street, and the small lots are accented with numerous tall trees, ivy, and colorful flowers. Waverly Place features a wide mix of architectural styles, including frame-and-brick cottages, American foursquares, Tudors, and 1- and 1.5-story bungalows from the 1890s and 1930s.

Woodland-in-Waverly

One of Nashville's first streetcar suburbs, Woodland-in-Waverly, is south of Wedgewood Avenue, between I-65 and Eighth Avenue, convenient to downtown, Music Row, colleges, the Melrose area, and Eighth Avenue antiques shops. This is one of Nashville's three "historic preservation zoning districts" (the others being Edgefield and Second Avenue). This zoning means that all exterior additions, alterations, demolitions, new construction, and fences must meet the approval of the Metro Historical Commission.

According to the Historical Commission, Woodland-in-Waverly could serve as a model for neighborhood design now being emulated by progressive new subdivision developments. Part of Woodland-in-Waverly was listed on the National Register of Historic Places in 1980. The neighborhood features many well-preserved homes built mainly from the 1890s through the 1930s. Queen Anne, English Tudor, and American foursquares and bungalows are among the architectural styles found in this small neighborhood, which offers plenty of choices for renovators.

In the 1830s the area was farmland owned by historian and author A. W. Putnam, who named his house Waverly and his farm Waverly Place for the novel by Sir Walter Scott. The farm was sold in 1858. Development increased in the late 1880s following the installation of an electric streetcar line on Eighth Avenue S. that provided easy access to downtown Nashville. This streetcar suburb was a fashionable address and remained so until around 1940, when automobiles became the preferred method of transportation. The neighborhood eventually evolved into an urban middle-class neighborhood. A few houses built during this period still remain.

Melrose

This neighborhood was named for the Melrose Estate, which was granted to its first owner, John Topp, in 1788. Named for the Scottish ancestry of the then-reigning mistress, the mansion was the site of many notable events in Nashville society. The original 2-story brick building burned in 1950 and was rebuilt as a 1-story structure. The rebuilt home was gutted by fire in 1975.

Melrose is bounded by Wedgewood Avenue and I-440 between Franklin Pike and Granny White Pike. It's convenient to downtown, I-440, and Nolensville Road. You'll find a variety of home styles here, ranging from late Victorian to contemporary.

Berry Hill

This tiny satellite city, developed in the 1940s and early '50s, covers approximately 1 square mile, between Thompson Lane near 100 Oaks Mall and Craighead Avenue, and between Franklin Road and into Woodlawn Cemetery.

The city was incorporated in 1950 and today has its own mayor, city manager, and city commissioners. The city provides police protection and other

> **i** The satellite city of Berry Hill has been dubbed a "little Music Row" thanks to the growing number of recording studios that have discovered the area. Albums by Shania Twain and Barenaked Ladies, to name two, were recorded or mixed in Berry Hill.

services for its citizens. In 2008 there were approximately 700 residents and about 500 businesses.

Berry Hill's residential area is transitioning into a quaint commercial district. Businesses have opened in some of the small 1950s cottages that were once homes. Bohemian types are discovering the Berry Hill District, where you can shop for garden supplies, vintage clothing, used records, and quirky gifts in a tree-lined 3-block area. Music Row has also discovered Berry Hill; more than 40 recording studios, including one owned by John and Martina McBride, have moved into the area.

West & Southwest Nashville

Richland–West End

Historic Richland–West End encompasses a triangular area between Murphy Road, I-440, and West End. Developed in the early 1900s on the outskirts of the city, this was an upscale suburb popular with professionals who wanted to escape the noise, smoke, and crime of the city. After World War II some homes were converted to apartments, but young professionals and upper- and middle-income families have been restoring them since the 1970s.

The neighborhood has lots of longtime residents, and many take an active part in the community. Richland–West End features lots of well-preserved early-1900s homes, including spacious bungalows, built from 1910 to 1930, and American foursquares.

Sidewalks, lots of old trees, and a definite community feel are strong selling points for this neighborhood. Location is another plus: It's a straight shot down West End/Broadway to downtown, I-440 access is right off West End, and it's close to Music Row, Green Hills, Belle Meade, and Hillsboro Village. For more information visit the Richland–West End Neighborhood Association's website at rwena.org.

Sylvan Park

This historic west Nashville neighborhood has enjoyed a wave of popularity in recent years. Young professionals, families, creative types, and retirees in search of affordable homes moved to this former blue-collar area and have carefully restored many of the homes. Interest has now expanded to the adjacent Sylvan Heights area near 37th and Charlotte Avenues.

Sylvan Park also has a trendy commercial district that's home to several popular restaurants. If you're new to the area, note that you can usually recognize Sylvan Park by its street names. When the area was planned back in the 1880s, the streets were named after states in hopes that people from across the country would want to relocate to the neighborhood.

Lots of trees, sidewalks, nice landscaping, cheerful window boxes, and a business district contribute to the personality and close-knit feel of this charming neighborhood. Sylvan Park is between West End Avenue and Charlotte Pike and is convenient to West End, I-40, I-440, and downtown. To learn more about Sylvan Park, visit the Sylvan Park Neighborhood Association online at sylvanpark.org.

Green Hills

Green Hills is considered one of Nashville's most desirable addresses. This Area 2 community is bounded by I-440, Belle Meade, Oak Hill at Harding Road, and Forest Hills. It's minutes from Vanderbilt, West End, Music Row, Hillsboro Village, and downtown. If you're looking for an upscale neighborhood; large, well-landscaped lots; and tree-lined streets, you can't miss with Green Hills. Families will find the good schools a bonus.

The area was developed in the 1930s and '40s, and building continues today, so you'll find everything here from modern and spacious homes loaded with amenities to pockets of cluster housing and smaller older properties. There are also some nice condominiums/town houses.

Forest Hills

This desirable west Nashville satellite city extends from Harding Road to Old Hickory Boulevard and from Belle Meade toward Oak Hill and Franklin Road. Forest Hills is home to about 4,700 residents. There is no commercial area.

First developed in the 1950s and '60s, Forest Hills boasts spacious ranch-style homes as well as some architect-designed custom homes. Newer housing developments can be found along Old Hickory Boulevard and Granny White Pike. Houses sit on large, well-tended lots that offer a good amount of privacy. Some have great views.

Oak Hill

A popular choice for music business executives and "move-up" families, Oak Hill is where you'll find the Governor's Mansion and other stately homes, including former homes of the late Tammy Wynette and Minnie Pearl. Covering an area of 8 square miles, Oak Hill extends from Forest Hills to I-65 and from Woodmont Boulevard to Old Hickory Boulevard. You'll find Oak Hill divided between Area 1 and Area 2 on the Nashville real estate maps.

As its name suggests, this residential community of 5,000 boasts lots of rolling tree-covered hills. It is characterized by low-density development, with most homes situated on at least 1- to 2-acre lots. Many of the ranch-style and 2-story colonial homes here were built during the past 30 to 40 years. There are also some beautiful contemporary homes. Incorporated in 1952, this is a well-established, stable neighborhood, and residents often prefer to renovate rather than move out.

Belle Meade

If living in one of the area's most prestigious neighborhoods is a must, look no farther than Belle Meade. This traditionally old-money west Nashville community is the address of choice for many of Nashville's most prominent citizens. A city of about 1,120 homes and about 3,200 residents, Belle Meade is the fifth richest city in America and the richest in the state.

It is one of Nashville's oldest communities—actually a city in itself, having incorporated in 1938. Today it has its own police force, street signs, and building codes, and the powers-that-be keep a pretty tight rein on the neighborhood. It was originally part of the Belle Meade Plantation, a world-renowned thoroughbred farm. The plantation's Belle Meade mansion is now a tourist attraction (see our **Attractions** chapter).

Belle Meade's unique and architecturally interesting homes are surrounded by large, professionally landscaped lawns. Many homes here were built during the 1920s, but Nashville's elite find this address so de rigueur that many are willing to pay top dollar for an older home, demolish it, and build an enormous, new traditional-style home in its place.

Belle Meade is bounded roughly by US 70 (Harding Road), Lynnwood Boulevard, Chickering Lane, and Page Road, and it is bisected by Harding Place. Belle Meade is a residential-only city.

West Meade/Hillwood

Another Area 2 community, West Meade/Hillwood is just west of Belle Meade, across the railroad tracks that parallel Harding Road/US 70. The area is bounded by White Bridge Road, Davidson Drive, and I-40 and encompasses the Vaughns Gap Road area to the south.

This well-established neighborhood is one of Nashville's oldest planned communities. Most homes were built in the 1950s and '60s, so there are lots of ranch-style dwellings. Houses sit on large, shady lots, and the neighborhood's winding streets take you over hills and along forested areas. The Hillwood area, which developed around the Hillwood Country Club, has some of the largest and most expensive homes.

Bellevue

For those who want a fashionable Area 2 address but find such areas as Belle Meade, West Meade/Hillwood, and Green Hills a little pricey, Bellevue is a good choice, offering lots of newer, upscale homes that are affordable for many first-time buyers. This west Nashville community is about 2.5 miles west of the US 70–Highway 100 split, about 7 miles from Green Hills, and about 13 miles from downtown. Most areas are easily accessible to I-40. Bellevue is bordered on one side by the Warner Parks along Tennessee Highway TN 100 and on the other by Charlotte Pike.

As the Welcome to Bellevue sign on US 70 S. informs you, this community was established in 1795. The rolling green hills and wooded valleys inspired the name (French for "beautiful view"). Bellevue remained a largely rural area until the mid-1900s. Development moved in this direction in the 1940s, but it hasn't completely taken over yet. Despite rapid growth since the 1970s, the area still offers a pleasing mix of urban and rural life. Bellevue has maintained a sort of small-community feel that some Nashville suburbs lack. A few farm areas remain around the perimeter, but the conveniences of "city life" are close by for those in the more rural areas.

South & Southeast Nashville

Crieve Hall

Development of this Area 1 neighborhood centered on Trousdale Drive and Blackmon Road in the 1950s, so you'll find lots of ranch-style homes here. Unlike many of Nashville's new developments, Crieve Hall boasts large lots accented with big shade trees. Homes are well maintained and nicely landscaped. It's a nice, quiet area convenient to downtown, Harding Mall, the 100 Oaks/Berry Hill area, and the Nashville Zoo at Grassmere.

Antioch

Affordable housing and location lure many Nashvillians to this diverse southeast Nashville community, which has experienced an enormous boom in new home construction in the past few years. Antioch is convenient to I-24 and the airport and a short drive from downtown via I-24. The area is bordered to the north by Harding Place and extends west from Percy Priest Lake to just past the I-24/Bell Road intersection.

In the past 2 decades, Antioch has undergone tremendous growth, including lots of commercial development along Bell Road, Nolensville Pike, and Harding Place. Large numbers of new housing developments and apartment complexes have joined the ranch-style homes built here in the 1960s.

Neighboring Counties

Cheatham County

The area's best-kept neighborhood secret may be just west of Davidson County: Cheatham County (Area 13). Some real estate agents expect this 305-square-mile county to be the next boom area, but houses are still affordable here, and most of the new developments feature 1-acre lots, large by Middle Tennessee standards. In recent years it has been one of the state's fastest-growing counties. Cheatham County is convenient to Bellevue in west Nashville, easily accessible to I-24 and I-40, and a 25- to 40-minute drive to downtown Nashville, depending on which side of the county you're on. In addition to location, strong drawing points of this rural area include quality of life and lots of outdoor-recreation opportunities. The 20,000-acre Cheatham Wildlife Management Area is popular for hunting, horseback riding, and hiking, and Harpeth River State Park is a good spot for canoeing, fishing, and hiking. Cheatham Lake is popular with boaters.

The four largest cities in Cheatham County are Ashland City, Kingston Springs, Pegram, and Pleasant View. For more information contact the Cheatham County Chamber of Commerce (615-792-6722; cheathamchamber.org).

Ashland City

In central Cheatham County, Ashland City developed around a shallow area along the Cumberland River where riverboats ran aground and had to unload their cargo. Locks have since solved that problem, and today Ashland City is a rapidly growing area.

Ashland City is about a 40-minute drive from downtown Nashville; from courthouse to courthouse, it's about 20 miles. Ashland City's courthouse, with its croquet lawn, is still the focus of downtown. The city is also known for its antiques shops and catfish restaurants. The 3.7-mile Cumberland River Bicentennial Trail, a former railroad right-of-way, is popular for walking, horseback riding, and bicycling along river bluffs, past waterfalls, and through wetlands.

Kingston Springs

Kingston Springs, on the south side of Cheatham County, appears to be one of the next neighborhood hot spots. The area is a nature lover's paradise. All sorts of songbirds, as well as deer, wild turkey, and other wildlife, make their homes here. Affordable homes, easy access to Nashville via I-40, and a quiet rural setting are also part of the scenic bedroom community's appeal. Those who want to live in a country-style home with a big wraparound porch or in a log cabin or hillside chalet will feel right at home in Kingston Springs.

Pegram

At 3,440 acres, this is the smallest of Cheatham County's four cities. This quaint little rural town (population 2,105) is on the south side of the county, next to Bellevue and about a 25-minute drive from downtown Nashville. If you'd like to get a feel for what Pegram is like, visit on July 4, when the town puts on the big Pegram BBQ.

Pleasant View

Incorporated in 1996, Pleasant View, a growing community of 4,409 residents, is located in northern Cheatham County. There is no property tax; the city operates on state and local sales taxes. Pleasant View is the kind of community where the volunteer fire department hosts an annual parade and barbecue for residents. The city also has its own 5-member police department. There is a lot of new home construction under way.

Dickson County

Dickson County (Area 15), just west of Nashville past Cheatham County, is a largely rural area with the lowest population density of any county surrounding Metro Nashville. Officials with Dickson County Chamber of Commerce (615-446-2349, dicksoncountychamber.com) say that is changing fast. Like most counties surrounding Metro, Dickson County is growing. In 2018 its population was 52,853.

The 600-acre Dickson County Industrial Park, established in 1976, is attracting a steady stream of industry. The county's chamber of commerce actively recruits new businesses. At the same time, many city dwellers and suburbanites are deciding they want to live in the country and are heading to Dickson County areas such as Dickson, White Bluff, Burns, and Charlotte. Lower home and land prices are a big draw.

Dickson

Affordable homes and a quiet, small-town setting are luring more people to Dickson these days. New subdivisions are being developed in this city of almost 15,000. Land sales are strong, too, especially small farm properties of 20 acres or less. Dickson is about 40 minutes from downtown Nashville and easily accessible to I-40, so it's a feasible choice for Nashville workers who don't mind the commute; it's a shorter drive for those who work in west Nashville.

Dickson County was established in 1803, and the city of Dickson dates from 1899. There are a few historic homes here, but most of the area is still rural. A sign of Dickson's progressive growth is the Renaissance Center, an educational technology center on Highway 46. This unique public facility offers traditional art, music, and drama education; instruction in high-performance computing; a 450-seat performing arts theater; computer classrooms; a 136-seat domed interactive theater with graphic- and laser-projection systems; a science theater; and more.

For more information call the Dickson County Chamber of Commerce at (615) 446-2349.

Robertson County

With a strong agricultural base and diverse manufacturing industries, Robertson County (Area 14), about a 35-minute drive north of Nashville, is growing fast. According to the 2017 US Census, Robertson County's population is 70,177. County officials attribute the growth to improved quality of life. The majority of this 476-square-mile county is farmland. Principal crops include tobacco, corn, wheat, and soybeans. There are also dairy and beef cattle farms here. Historic family farms and beautiful country scenery surround Robertson County's incorporated cities and towns, which include Adams, Cedar Hill, Coopertown, Cross Plains, Greenbrier, Orlinda, Ridgetop, Springfield, and White House.

To contact the Robertson County Chamber of Commerce, call (615) 384-3800 or visit robertsonchamber.org.

SPRINGFIELD

Renovations and new construction are increasing in busy Springfield, population 16,659. Buyers have snapped up and begun renovating several historic homes. The highest concentration of older residences, including Victorian homes, is in the district north and west of the historic town square. New-home prices are keeping pace with the increase in new construction. Residents who want a night on the town can drive to Nashville in about 45 minutes.

Rutherford County

In the geographic center of Tennessee, Rutherford County (Areas 21–34), southeast of Nashville, is one of the fastest-growing areas in the nation. Most statistics put it neck-and-neck with adjacent Williamson County in population growth with 317,157 in the 2017 census. The county has a diverse economic base and is enjoying a booming economy.

Despite the growth, Rutherford County maintains a small-town charm. Its 615 square miles still include nearly 234,000 acres of farmland. The area is also rich in history. The Battle of Stones River, one of the major battles of the Civil War, was fought near Murfreesboro. You can take a self-guided tour of the battlefield today (see our **Attractions** chapter).

Affordable homes and easy access to Nashville via I-24 are among the county's other pluses. Rutherford County encompasses Murfreesboro, La Vergne, Smyrna, and tiny Eagleville (population 676).

For more information call the Rutherford County Chamber of Commerce at (615) 893-6565 or visit rutherfordchamber.org.

Murfreesboro

Rutherford County's largest city, Murfreesboro was home to 136,372 as of 2017. And the population is growing every day. This city, established in 1812, still has the feel of a small town. The courthouse, built in 1859, is the focal point of the historic and still-lively town square. (The first courthouse, built in 1813, burned before the Civil War. It served as the state capitol from 1819 until 1826, when Nashville became the capital.) A variety of shops and businesses line the square. On the tree-lined streets surrounding the square, you'll find some wonderfully restored old homes, the grandest of which are on West Main between the courthouse and MTSU's campus. East Main Street has some especially lovely Victorian architecture. There are several neighborhoods of 1950s and 1960s ranch-style brick homes as well as newer developments around the city's perimeter.

Smyrna

This former farming community between La Vergne and Murfreesboro enjoyed a boost when the Nissan plant came to town, bringing 6,000 jobs and hastening the development of farmland into subdivisions. In 2017 Smyrna's population

> **i** Every now and then, when one of Nashville's country stars sells their home, they hold a moving sale and invite the public. Trisha Yearwood, Wynonna Judd, Barbara Mandrell, and Tanya Tucker all have held sales. You can't count on the stars showing up in person at these events, but you never know . . .

was 49,969. While you won't find many tree-lined streets here, you will find plenty of new construction and affordable housing. Nearby I-24 provides easy access for Nashville commuters.

Aviators will want to take note of this city. The Smyrna Airport, formerly Sewart Air Force Base, is still active.

La Vergne

Just across the Davidson County line in northeast Rutherford County, La Vergne has experienced dramatic growth. By 2017, the city's population had grown to a total of 35,717. The city is a top pick for incoming industries. It's about a 30-minute drive from downtown Nashville and is close to the Nashville International Airport. Relatively inexpensive homes make this area a viable choice for first-time home buyers.

Sumner County

Sumner County (Area 9), Nashville's northeastern neighbor, has several diverse communities and recreational opportunities that make it a popular choice for everyone from young families to country music stars. This county's communities have distinct personalities. Some remain largely rural, while others have a definite urban feel. Country general stores, pastures, rolling creeks, and antebellum homes are common sights in the more rural areas, while Old Hickory Lake, with its hundreds of miles of shoreline on the county's southern border, boasts some luxurious, upscale properties. Sumner County is also a historic area, the site of two settlements established by long hunters in the late 1700s (see our **History** chapter for details).

Like many other Middle Tennessee counties, Sumner County is growing. In 2017 the population was 183,545. Lots of major business developments in Gallatin, numerous recreational and upscale residential areas in Hendersonville, abundant retail stores in Goodlettsville, and an extensive industrial base in Portland have contributed to the growth.

Hendersonville

Hendersonville, Tennessee's 10th largest city, offers small-town appeal and resident country music stars. It's about a 30-minute drive from downtown Nashville, with easy access from I-65 and Gallatin Pike/US 31E. Some of the biggest country music stars, including Garth Brooks and Johnny Cash, have lived here, along with lots of retirees, families, and professionals. In 2017 the city's population was 57,517.

Hendersonville's 534 square miles offer plenty of residential choices. There is a rural side, a lake side, and lots of apartments, condominiums, and high-density developments. Houses on Old Hickory Lake are in big demand.

For more information call the Hendersonville Chamber of Commerce at (615) 824-2818 or visit hendersonvillechamber.com.

Gallatin

About 45 minutes from downtown Nashville, 10 to 15 miles northeast of Hendersonville on US 31E, is Gallatin, the Sumner County seat. Gallatin is one of Tennessee's original five "Main Street Communities." Its quaint downtown district features more than 25 historic buildings, some of which were built before the Civil War. There are also several historic attractions nearby, including Cragfont and Wynnewood.

In 2017 Gallatin's population was 37,351. The economic base here is 50 percent industrial and 50 percent agricultural.

Call the Gallatin Chamber of Commerce at (615) 452-4000 for additional information or visit gallatintn.org.

Goodlettsville

Half of this historic area, 20 minutes from downtown Nashville, is in Davidson County and half is in Sumner County. See the listing under Metropolitan Nashville–Davidson County in this section for more information.

Wilson County

As the Nashville area continues to expand on all sides, Wilson County (Area 11), about 20 minutes east, is experiencing a boom in residential, commercial, and industrial development. As of 2017 the population was 136,442.

An abundance of affordable land is luring families in search of a more peaceful lifestyle. With its wide-open spaces, small historic towns, and easy access to Nashville via I-40, Wilson County offers what many are finding to be the right mix of country and city life. Businesses also have chosen to make Wilson County home.

For more information call the Lebanon/Wilson County Chamber of Commerce at (615) 444-5503 or visit lebanonwilsonchamber.com.

Mount Juliet

How this small town got its name is something of a mystery. Some say it was named for Aunt Julie Gleaves, a sort of guardian angel of the area, someone who was always helping others. The problem with that story is that she was only 18 years old in 1835, the year Mount Juliet was formed. Most believe the city was named for a castle in County Kilkenny, Ireland. Whatever its beginnings, Mount Juliet, incorporated in 1972, is reputed to be the only town in the world with that name.

If you like rolling green hills, spacious lots, and a relaxed lifestyle, Mount Juliet may be for you. Just about 25 minutes from downtown Nashville and a short drive from the Nashville International Airport, Mount Juliet is an increasingly popular choice for families. As of 2017, 34,726 people called Mount Juliet home.

Lebanon

Lebanon, named for the biblical land of cedars, may be the largest city in Wilson County, but it's also big on small-town appeal. About a 30-minute drive from Nashville, Lebanon (population 32,226) offers a slower pace.

The city was laid out in 1802 and chartered in 1819. A Civil War battle was fought on the town square in 1862, and after the Confederates' defeat, many homes and businesses were burned. The town was rebuilt, and today the Public Square boasts lots of historic buildings. This area, once the site of mule sales, is known mainly for its great collection of antiques shops. In fact, Lebanon has earned the nickname "Antique City of the South"—for antiques lovers, a visit to this town is a must—and has been featured in *Southern Living* magazine.

Williamson County

Wealthy Williamson County (Area 10), south and southwest of Nashville, is the fastest-growing county in the state. The population in 2017 was 226,257. Williamson County includes the rapidly expanding Cool Springs business community, one of the hottest retail and corporate office locations in the country. Cool Springs straddles Brentwood and Franklin along I-65. Williamson County is a definite relocation hot spot in Middle Tennessee, luring more and more Nashvillians and newcomers with its high quality of life, excellent schools, beautiful rural settings, and upscale shops and restaurants. It's about a 20- to 25-minute commute to Nashville via I-65 (if there are no traffic snarls, that is), so neighborhoods here are popular with Music City workers who prefer the Williamson County lifestyle. Lots of music business executives, country stars, professionals, and families live in Brentwood, Franklin, Leiper's Fork, and other areas of the country.

For more information about the county, visit the Williamson County Convention and Visitors Bureau's website at visitfranklin.com.

Brentwood

Nestled among green rolling hills, about 8 miles south of downtown Nashville, is the popular middle-class suburb of Brentwood. A mix of suburban and rural areas covering 35.4 square miles, Brentwood has seen its population grow dramatically since the city incorporated in 1969. The 2017 population was 42,667. Brentwood's location along I-65 and Franklin Road just across Old Hickory Boulevard offers easy commuter access to Nashville.

The city's well-planned new residential and commercial developments lend a brand-new, fresh look. Planned growth includes green spaces around office buildings and commercial complexes and 1-acre lots in subdivisions.

Home buyers can choose from established neighborhoods of 2-story or ranch-style homes and newer developments in upscale "McMansion" subdivisions offering superspacious floor plans, modern amenities, and security.

Franklin

Although it's only about a 30-minute drive from downtown Nashville, Franklin seems worlds away. Its old-fashioned but revitalized town square remains the hub of this town. The 15-block original downtown area is listed on the National Register of Historic Places. Restored 19th-century buildings downtown that house trendy boutiques, antiques stores, restaurants, art galleries, and other unique shops line the square. Franklin's participation in the National Main Street Program brought brick sidewalks, period lighting, underground wiring, and trees to the downtown area.

Many fine old homes on the streets near the square have been restored. The 2-block Lewisburg Avenue Historic District features numerous late-19th- and early-20th-century homes. Sound appealing? Tens of thousands of new Franklin residents would agree. The 2017 population was 78,321.

For more on Franklin visit the city's website franklintn.gov or call (615) 791-3217.

Fairview

This quiet, rural community about 25 miles southwest of downtown Nashville has little in common with its Williamson County neighbors Brentwood and Franklin. Fairview is about 10 miles from Bellevue on Highway 100; it's also accessible via I-40. As of 2017, Fairview's population was 8,763. Many of its residents work in nearby Franklin, Brentwood, and Dickson. Fairview incorporated in 1959, so many of the homes here are brick ranches, although a few subdivisions and condos have been built recently. For more on Fairview, visit fairviewchamber.org.

REAL ESTATE

There's a lot of buying, selling, and building going on in and around Nashville. In some areas new subdivisions and apartment complexes seem to pop up almost overnight.

Local Realtors report a robust real estate market—in-town and suburban homes as well as condos—in and around Nashville, continuing a trend that's lasted several years. In 2018 the average number of days on the market in Middle Tennessee was 25.

Looking for a Good Home

If you're looking for a home in the Nashville area, or even if you're already settled in, you might want to consider sharing your home with a companion. A furry, four-legged companion. Local animal shelters are filled with dogs and cats in need of good, loving homes. If you would like to add a pet to your household, consider adopting from one of the local shelters. There are several shelters in Middle Tennessee. The two largest such facilities in Nashville are the Metro Animal Care and Control Facility, which is operated by the Metro Public Health Department of Nashville/Davidson County, and the privately funded Nashville Humane Association.

THE METRO ANIMAL CARE AND CONTROL FACILITY, 5125 Harding Place, Nashville, TN 37211; (615) 862-7928; nashville.gov/health-department/animal-care-and-control. The Metro Animal Care and Control Facility is on Harding Place, near Nolensville Road. The state-of-the-art facility can house about 400 animals per month; in any given month, about 100 to 200 pets are adopted. You can adopt a pet there daily from 10 a.m. to 4 p.m. Fees, including rabies vaccination fees, microchip, and spay/neuter fees, are $90 for dogs, $60 for kittens, and $40 for cats.

THE NASHVILLE HUMANE ASSOCIATION, 213 Oceola Ave., Nashville, TN 37209; (615) 352-1010; nashvillehumane.org. The Nashville Humane Association adopts out as many as 2,000 pets each year. The facility, located just off White Bridge Road in west Nashville, has space to house about 145 animals. Adoptions take place daily except Mon, when the shelter is closed. Adoption fees range from $85 to $225 for dogs and puppies, and from $45 to $100 for cats and kittens, and include spaying/neutering and vaccinations. Visit the Humane Association's website to view some of the pets available for adoption or to obtain more information.

New jobs, a diversified economy, and incoming business have contributed to the housing boom. Relatively low interest rates have made it easier for first-time buyers to purchase a home and for families moving up to buy a more upscale property.

As a result of recent accelerated construction, there are many new homes on the market. Counties surrounding Metro Nashville are growing rapidly. Williamson and Rutherford Counties have been growing fastest, Rutherford being particularly popular among first-time buyers. Some local Realtors expect to see more buyers looking to other counties—Cheatham and Dickson, in particular—in search of more value for their dollar.

Real Estate Agencies

If you are considering buying or selling a home, you may want to consider working with a Realtor, who can help ensure your home search, purchase, or sale goes more smoothly. A Realtor's knowledge of the market and the ins and outs of real estate transactions can save buyers and sellers time, headaches, and hassles.

Certainly, there are many good firms in and around Nashville, so don't limit your options. As a great place to start looking for a Realtor, call the Greater Nashville Association of Realtors at (615) 254-7516 (greaternashvillerealtors.org) or the Tennessee Association of Realtors at (615) 321-1477 (tnrealtors.com). The Sunday edition of the *Tennessean* is another source of information on properties for sale or rent. Each week you'll find hundreds of properties, a list of interest rates from area lenders, information on Realtors, plus news on the housing market. Other helpful home-hunting resources include several free real estate and apartment guides, which you can find at grocery stores and other locations around town.

Education & Child Care

Higher education, of course, has long been one of Nashville's bragging points. The most prominent institutions are Vanderbilt University, with its highly ranked schools of education, medicine, business, and law; Meharry Medical College, a leading educator of doctors and dentists, which has an alliance with Vanderbilt; and Fisk University, which is highly acclaimed not only among historically African-American colleges and universities but also among all postsecondary schools. And these are far from the only options you'll find in this area. In fact, the region has some 19 colleges and universities offering baccalaureate, graduate, or professional degrees to more than 85,000 students annually.

EDUCATION

Public Schools

Nashville/Davidson County

METROPOLITAN NASHVILLE PUBLIC SCHOOL SYSTEM, Central Office, 2601 Bransford Ave., Nashville, TN 37204; (615) 259-INFO; mnps.org. In the 2018 report, Metro had more than 82,000 students representing more than 120 different countries. It is the 42nd largest school district in the nation. Metro has 154 schools: 73 elementary schools, 33 middle schools, 25 high schools, 8 specialty schools, and 15 charter schools. All public schools in Nashville–Davidson County are under the direction of the consolidated city-county government. The school board consists of 9 elected members and a director, who is appointed. Each Metro student is assigned to a school depending on where the student lives. This is called their "zone" school. School bus transportation is provided. However, there are different options for each child, including magnet schools, which we will cover later in this chapter. Rezoning is also keeping many students closer to home; much of this is the result of a US District Court's 1998 ruling that ended voluntary desegregation after parents sued over the long bus trips their children endured.

Kindergarten

One year of state-approved kindergarten is required for enrollment in first grade in the Metropolitan Nashville Public School System. Kindergarten programs are available at all elementary schools. Kindergarten enrollment for children who will be 5 years old on or before September 30 requires the child's birth certificate, a record of a recent physical examination, an up-to-date Tennessee state immunization form, and proof of residence (a rent receipt or utility bill will work). The child's Social Security number or card is optional.

Enrichment Programs & Options

Metro Schools offer a variety of unique enrichment programs. Gifted students in pre-K through grade 6, for example, can take part in the Encore program, which supplements regular classes with an extended enrichment curriculum. Students in grades 7 and 8 can take high-school classes such as Algebra I and first-year foreign language, often for high-school credit. High-school students can take part in AP classes and the Scholars Program, which recognizes its graduates with a Distinguished Scholars Diploma.

Special Education

Special education programs consist of individual education plans created by committees of parents, teachers, principals, and school psychologists. One committee meets to assess the student's needs; another creates the plan for meeting those needs, which is devised according to the student's disabilities. Students in special education programs may continue in the Metro system until they are 22 years old, if they desire. Whenever possible, they are mainstreamed.

i Metro's Board of Public Education meets on the second Tuesday of each month. Meetings are open to the public and take place at the Administration Building of Metropolitan Public Schools, 2601 Bransford Ave., beginning at 5 p.m. The board also holds work sessions on the fourth Tuesday of each month. The meetings are televised live on Metro's Government Access Channel 3 (Comcast Cable TV in Davidson County).

Metro Magnet & Other Optional Schools

Magnets offer alternatives to assigned or zoned schools and help offer voluntary desegregation for some students. They also allow students to study a theme related to their areas of interest or expertise. No transportation to magnet schools is provided by Metro schools, but bus routes from Metro Transit Authority are available. For information call the transit authority at (615) 862-5950.

A random lottery is held to select students for Metro's magnet schools. All students who meet the academic requirements may apply for admission to Metro's five academic magnets (Meigs Middle, East Nashville High, Hull Jackson Montessori, Hume-Fogg High, and Jones Paideia Elementary School). Any student may apply through the lottery for admission to the various thematic magnet schools.

Applications for admission must be submitted by deadline (dates vary). Applicants will be assigned random magnet lottery numbers, which they will receive in the mail. If your child is selected for admission, you will receive a letter in the mail; you must sign and return the letter in order for your child to enroll. Students who are not selected will be placed on a waiting list. (Nashville School of the Arts does not have a lottery; the school selects 70 percent of its students by audition and 30 percent by essay or interview.)

For more information on magnets, visit the Metro Schools website (mnps.org) or call (615) 259-8676 or Metro Schools' information line listed at the beginning of this section.

In addition to magnets, the system has nine Enhanced Option Schools and 10 Design Centers. The Enhanced Option Schools are kindergarten and pre-K programs that encourage learning through smaller class size and a longer school year. Enrichment and Encore programs are available to gifted students. Enhanced Option programs are offered at Bordeaux, Buena Vista, Caldwell, Fall-Hamilton, Glenn, Kirkpatrick, Napier, Park Avenue, and Warner zones.

Design centers have specialized programs developed to meet the needs of students in a particular area or "cluster." Most programs are K–4, and there are also two preschools and three 5–8 programs. Each program has a particular theme, such as advanced academics or language/literature. For the majority of the centers, students living within the school zone have first choice to enroll in a design center and do not need to apply. Students living in the "high-school cluster" have second priority and must apply through the lottery. Students living outside the cluster are required to apply through the lottery and go on a waiting list until space becomes available.

CHILD CARE

For newcomers, finding child care in Nashville can be tough, especially if you're looking to get into one of the more popular centers. Some programs, however, set a few positions aside for people relocating to Nashville. They generally don't advertise that information, so be sure to ask.

According to the Nashville Area Association for the Education of Young Children, parents should find an out-of-home child care situation that they are secure with and their child is happy in. Talk to your friends, neighbors, and coworkers, and compare their likes and dislikes. Phone several schools, and ask to arrange a visit for both you and your child. Observe the caregivers interacting with children. Do they, for example, speak to children on their level? Attend a school function and observe. Arrange an appointment with the school's director and have a list of questions ready regarding such issues as staff stability and training, teacher education, programs available, fees, and policies for holidays and lateness. All nurseries and day care centers must meet licensing requirements. For more information on these regulations and child care providers, or for information on providers' quality ratings, contact the Tennessee Department of Human Services Child Care Licensing, 400 Deaderick St., 2nd Floor, Nashville, TN 37243; (615) 313-4700; or visit the website tennessee.gov/humanserv.

Child Care Information

NASHVILLE AREA ASSOCIATION FOR THE EDUCATION OF YOUNG CHILDREN, 2021 21st Ave. S., Suite 440, Nashville, TN 37212; (615) 383-6292; naaeyc.org. NAAEYC was established in 1948 as an affiliate of the National Association for the Education of Young Children with two primary objectives: to promote standards of excellence in child care practices

i Many area churches offer day care programs. Among the most popular are St. George's Episcopal Day Kindergarten (4715 Harding Rd., 615-269-9712; stgeorgeskindergarten.org); Westminster Kindergarten (3900 West End Ave., 615-297-0235; wsycnashville.org); and Woodmont Christian Preschool (3601 Hillsboro Pike, 615-297-9962; woodmontchristianpreschool.com).

and to raise public understanding of and support for high-quality educational programs for young children. It does not certify early-childhood programs but provides information on how to identify and select high-quality child care. For educators and child care providers, the association is a resource for information, training, and support.

Other Child Care Options

FAMILY YMCAS, various Metro locations; (615) 259-9622; ymcamidtn.org. Area YMCAs provide day care for children ages 6 weeks to 6 years. Most schools also have YMCA before- and after-school care for kindergartners through 8th-graders.

YMCA OF MIDDLE TENNESSEE, 1000 Church St., Nashville, TN 37203; (615) 259-9622; ymcamidtn.org. With about 30 centers and more than 200 program locations, the YMCA of Middle Tennessee is the area's largest child-care provider. The Y provides day care for children ages 6 weeks to 6 years; Fun Company, the Y's before- and after-school child care program, is offered at about 140 sites. The program offers a variety of stimulating and educational activities for children, ranging from art to music to science. The Y's preschool programs promote productive play and incorporate fun with learning for more than 300 children.

Retirement

Lots of people apparently have chosen to live their "golden years" in the Nashville area. According to the 2018 US census, 19.07 percent of the population in the Nashville area is 65 and older. The same benefits that make Nashville such an attractive place for all ages—in a nutshell, a high quality of life combined with a relatively low cost of living (and no income tax), convenient location, and pleasant climate—make it an especially desirable place for retired people. Those who have left the rigors of the work world now have even more time to take advantage of Nashville's thousands upon thousands of acres of parks and waterways, its golf courses, swimming pools, country clubs, tennis courts, historical attractions, shopping opportunities, music, and much more.

A number of retirement communities offer a range of lifestyle options, from independent to assisted living. A fine senior citizens' center, with convenient branches throughout the area, provides opportunities for recreation, travel, relaxation, and even volunteerism with friends old and new. For many retired people, the issue of health care becomes increasingly important. With such well-respected institutions as Vanderbilt University Medical Center right in town, health care access is excellent in Nashville. The central location near major interstates, along with an international airport, makes getting in and out of town—whether you're going to see the grandkids or they're coming to see you—a snap. And plenty of public transportation is available as well. Of course, being a senior means you get to enjoy many of the fine attractions detailed in this book at a reduced cost! The Nashville area is a great place to grow old and stay young at the same time.

ACTIVITIES FOR SENIORS

EASTER SEALS TENNESSEE, 750 Old Hickory Blvd., #2-260, Brentwood, TN 37027; (615) 292-6640; easterseals.com/tennessee. While Easter Seals serves people of all ages, the organization's Turner Family Center offers a variety of health and wellness programs for seniors. The Turner Center's state-of-the-art, wheelchair-accessible fitness center offers conditioning and physical therapy for all fitness levels. The center's indoor pool is open year-round. Among the programs offered are stroke support and an Arthritis Pain Center; the latter offers physical and occupational therapy, aquatics in the therapy pool, and educational classes.

JEWISH COMMUNITY CENTER, 801 Percy Warner Blvd., Nashville, TN 37205; (615) 356-7170; nashvillejcc.org. The facilities and programs at this center are first-rate, making it popular with families and people of all ages. The center offers a variety of programs for senior citizens, many of them using the center's pool and gym. Classes targeting seniors include water aerobics, gentle yoga, and "golden age" exercise programs. The center also has a variety of classes. You don't have to be Jewish to join, but you do need to be a member; special discounts are available for seniors.

FIFTY FORWARD, 174 Rains Ave., Nashville, TN 37205; (615) 743-3400; fiftyforward.org. Fifty Forward is a private, nonprofit organization for adults 50 years and older. The organization and its centers offer more than 60 classes, including computers, exercise classes, Spanish and French, social dancing, square dancing, quilting, art, and wood carving. Activities vary from center to center.

Two of Fifty Forward's major programs are its adult day care and Meals on Wheels. The day care (615-463-2266) is available Mon through Fri 8 a.m. to 4:30 p.m., with extended care hours if necessary. The Meals on Wheels program (615-463-2264) is one of 12 such programs in Davidson County; Senior Citizens Inc.'s program covers south and west Nashville. Residents ages 50 and older who are homebound can have a lunchtime meal delivered to their homes Mon through Sat for a nominal fee based on income.

Other services offered include a nonprofit travel agency, case management for homebound seniors that coordinates Meals on Wheels, referrals to various agencies, volunteer assistance, and respite care that helps them remain in their homes as long as possible.

SENIOR SERVICES

The following local and national organizations serve as vital resource outlets and information clearinghouses for seniors.

GREATER NASHVILLE REGIONAL COUNCIL, 220 Athens Way, Ste. 200, Nashville, TN 37228; (615) 862-8828; gnrc.org. Greater Nashville Regional Council, a sort of "one-stop shop" for senior needs, is an information referral and assistance program for seniors and those who love and care for them. Using an extensive, nationally applied software program, workers assess callers' needs and then connect them to community resources that can meet those needs. Sometimes the answer can be provided with one call; in other instances follow-up is necessary. Senior Solutions often does the legwork for social workers, calling multiple agencies to find who can provide the needed assistance. Help covers a wide range: anything from finances and health care to depression, residential facilities, and housecleaning.

MID-CUMBERLAND HUMAN RESOURCE AGENCY, 1101 Kermit Dr., Suite 300, Nashville, TN 37217; (615) 331-6033; mchra.com. The Mid-Cumberland Human Resource Agency is a nonprofit organization whose mission is "to help people help themselves by providing knowledge and resources to improve the quality of life." Founded in 1974, the agency serves the counties of Davidson, Cheatham, Dickson, Houston, Humphreys, Montgomery, Robertson, Rutherford, Stewart, Sumner, Trousdale, Williamson, and Wilson, and has offices in each county. The agency's extensive list of services available include homemaking assistance, nutrition/home-delivered meals, home health care, transportation services, and representative payee services for those who are unable to handle their own finances due to disabilities.

Senior Services Information

These organizations may be able to answer questions or help determine which organization can provide you with the senior services information you need.

Eldercare Locator, (800) 677-1116; eldercare.aci.gov.

Greater Nashville Regional Council, (615) 862-8828; gnrc.org.

Legal Aid Society of Middle Tennessee and the Cumberlands, (615) 244-6610; las.org.

Metro Action Commission, (615) 862-8860; nashville.gov/metro-action-commission/aspx.

Mid-Cumberland Human Resource Agency, (615) 331-6033; mchra.com.

National Council on Aging, (800) 677-1116; ncoa.org.

National Institute on Aging, (800) 222-2225; nia.nih.gov.

Tennessee Commission on Aging & Disability, (615) 741-2056; tn.gov/aging.

United Way Help Line, Nashville, (615) 269-4357; unitedwaynashville.org.

Media

Television, cable programming, radio, newspapers, magazines, hit songs, Bibles, books, music videos—when it comes to media, Nashville has it all. Nashville is a major publishing center, and printing/publishing is one of our biggest industries. Numerous cable television programs originate here and are seen by millions of viewers. Country Music Television (CMT) takes country music into the living rooms of viewers worldwide. Many of the videos you see on CMT are shot right here in Music City. As for radio, well, Nashville owes much of its heritage to that medium.

PUBLISHING

Nashville's history as a publishing center dates from the late 18th century. The city's first newspaper, *Henkle's Tennessee Gazette & Mero Advertiser,* was printed in 1799, 20 years after the first settlers arrived and 7 years before the city was incorporated. In 1800 the *Tennessee Gazette* began publishing. The first book was published in 1810, and 14 years later the hymnbook *Western Harmony* was published, marking the beginnings of music publishing in Nashville.

Nashville became a center for religious publishing in the 1800s. As Tennesseans flocked to religious revivals, Protestant denominations began publishing their books, Bibles, periodicals, and other church materials in Nashville. Nashville's publishing industry isn't limited to religious materials, however. Today there are nearly 500 firms here involved in publishing and printing. Nashville is also a center of music publishing, the backbone of the country music industry.

Daily Newspapers

Nashville

THE *TENNESSEAN,* 1100 Broadway, Nashville, TN 37203; (615) 259-8300, (615) 254-5661 (subscriptions); tennessean.com. The *Tennessean* is Nashville's largest daily newspaper, with a weekday circulation of 71,874. It dates from 1907, but the paper evolved from the *Nashville Whig,* which began publication in 1812. A newspaper with a liberal slant, the *Tennessean* is owned by Gannett Co. Inc., the country's largest newspaper publisher. Gannett bought the paper in 1979 from the family of Silliman Evans, who purchased it in the late 1930s at auction and turned the financially ailing operation into a success.

(Gannett had owned the *Nashville Banner,* which folded in 1998, but opted to sell it in order to be able to purchase the *Tennessean.*)

Surrounding Counties

THE *DAILY NEWS JOURNAL,* 201 E. Main St., Ste. 400, Murfreesboro, TN 37130; (615) 893-5860; dnj.com. This afternoon newspaper is published 7 days a week. Founded in 1849 and now owned by Gannett, it has a circulation of about 9,000.

General Interest

NASHVILLE LIFESTYLES, 1100 Broadway, Nashville, TN 37203; (615) 259-3636; nashvillelifestyles.com. *Nashville Lifestyles* is a glossy magazine featuring all that's fashionable in Nashville. The magazine contains articles on local homes, the art scene, decorating, food, and celebrities, with a positive slant.

NASHVILLE SCENE, 210 12th Ave. S., Suite 100, Nashville, TN 37203; (615) 244-7989; nashvillescene.com. *Nashville Scene* is Music City's leading alternative newspaper. About 48,000 of the free weekly papers are distributed at grocery stores, convenience stores, bookstores, restaurants, record stores, and other places around town. Founded in 1983, the *Scene* covers politics, business, music, and arts in an in-depth fashion and does investigative stories.

THE TENNESSEE MAGAZINE, 2964 Sidco Dr., Nashville, TN 37204; (615) 367-9284; tnmagazine.org. This monthly magazine is published by the Tennessee Electric Cooperative Association. The glossy magazine does human-interest stories and has regular features on food, events, people, places, and businesses in the rural electric co-op.

Business

NASHVILLE BUSINESS JOURNAL, 1800 Church St., Nashville, TN 37203; (615) 248-2222; bizjournals.com/nashville. *Nashville Business Journal,* published since 1985, is a weekly business newspaper covering such issues as employee benefits, education, commercial real estate, travel, and home business.

NASHVILLE POST, 210 12th St. S., Suite 100, Nashville, TN 37203; (615) 244-7989; nashvillepost.com. Delivers breaking business, political, and sports news online and twice daily through E-News alerts. A quarterly magazine provides local business news.

TELEVISION

What's on TV? In Nashville, just about anything: all the major networks, local independent stations, and a community-access station. Cable and satellite viewers can choose from dozens more stations.

Major Local Stations

CATV Channel 19 (community-access television)
WHTN Channel 39 (Christian), ctntv.org
WKRN Channel 2 (ABC), wkrn.com
WNAB Channel 58 (WB), wnab.com
WNPT Channel 8 (PBS), wnpt.net
WNPX Channel 28 (PAX)
WSMV Channel 4 (NBC), wsmv.com
WTVF Channel 5 (CBS), newschannel5.com
WUXP Channel 30 (UPN), wuxp.com
WZTV Channel 17 (FOX), fox17.com
W42CR Channel 42 (Telefutura: Spanish language programming), solonashville .com

RADIO

Radio played a key role in Nashville's history. In the 1920s, as Americans became enamored with the new technology of radio, Nashville became an important broadcasting center. Local merchants and insurance companies established their own stations. Cain-Sloan's John E. Cain Jr., for example, founded WEBX in 1924, and in following years, stations were established by several other merchants. National Life and Accident Insurance Company's WSM, which signed on the air in October 1925, and Life and Casualty's WLAC, which arrived on the dial a year later, were the city's major stations. Both are still on the air today, but it was WSM that put the spotlight on Nashville. WSM began broadcasting the *Grand Ole Opry,* originally known as the *WSM Barn Dance,* less than 2 months after the station went on the air (see our **History** chapter for more details). The station took country music into homes and businesses around the country.

Today WSM 650 AM continues to broadcast the *Grand Ole Opry* every Fri and Sat night. WSM is one of the nation's few clear-channel stations, meaning that no other station in a 750-mile radius has the same frequency for nighttime broadcasts. This and the station's 50,000-watt transmitter ensure that the *Opry* can be heard across a large portion of the United States and parts of Canada.

In 1941 WSM launched WSM-FM, the nation's first commercially operated FM station.

Index